MUSIC AND THE LANGUAGE OF LOVE

MUSIC AND THE EARLY MODERN IMAGINATION
Massimo Ossi, *editor*

MUSICAL MEANING AND INTERPRETATION
Robert S. Hatten, *editor*

Music and the Language of Love

Seventeenth-Century French Airs

CATHERINE GORDON-SEIFERT

Indiana University Press
Bloomington and Indianapolis

This book is a publication of

Indiana University Press
601 North Morton Street
Bloomington, Indiana 47404-3797 USA

iupress.indiana.edu

Telephone orders 800-842-6796
Fax orders   812-855-7931
Orders by e-mail iuporder@indiana.edu

Library of Congress Cataloging-in-Publication Data

Gordon-Seifert, Catherine Elizabeth.
    Music and the language of love : seventeenth-century French airs /
Catherine Gordon-Seifert.
        p. cm. — (Music and the early modern imagination)
(Musical meaning and interpretation)
    Includes bibliographical references and index.
    ISBN 978-0-253-35461-7 (cloth : alk. paper) 1. Music—France—
17th century—History and criticism. 2. Love songs—France—
17th century—History and criticism. 3. Love in music. I. Title.
ML270.2.G67 2011
782.4'3094409032—dc22

                                                    2010022316

        1 2 3 4 5   16 15 14 13 12 11

For Lewis C. Seifert
and my sons,
Andrew and Patrick

Contents

Contents

Acknowledgments

It is with the deepest gratitude that I recognize those who have helped me as I endeavored to write *Music and the Language of Love*. I wish to thank various institutions for providing essential logistical support: funding from the Centre de Musique Baroque de Versailles, a CAFR grant from Providence College, a fellowship from the National Endowment for the Arts, and financial support from the American Musicological Society in the form of the Noah Greenberg Award, which lay the foundation for chapter 6 on performing French airs. I would also like to thank my colleagues and students in the Department of Music at Providence College for creating a congenial and stimulating environment in which to teach and to conduct research. I am especially grateful to Hugh Lena, Provost and Senior Vice President for Academic Affairs at Providence College, for providing the funds necessary to obtain permission to reproduce the book's cover image. As well, I thank the Indiana University Press staff for their guidance and support, and particularly Maureen Epp for her extremely helpful editorial advice, Sarah Wyatt Swanson for her invaluable help with figures and examples, June Silay, Robert Sloan, and Jane Behnken.

This book would never have been completed without the advice, encouragement, and support of many people, including Candace Bailey, Tim Carter, Vincent Corrigan, Georgie Durosoir, Donald Fader, Thierry Favier, Claire Fontijn, Anne-Madeleine Goulet, Robert Hatten, Jeffrey Kurtzman, Thomasin LaMay, Massimo Ossi, Edward Parmentier, Lionel Sawkins, and Louise K. Stein. A special thanks must go to Linda Austern, Georgia Cowart, and John Powell for writing letter after letter of support in my efforts to obtain funding for my research. Their advice, encouragement, and assistance have been invaluable to me. I owe a debt of gratitude as well to Jonathan Gibson for reading my book manuscript and for his wise suggestions.

I am deeply grateful for the support of my loving family. My most profound thanks go to my mother, Virgina Gordon, for her faith in me, and my wonderful sons, Andrew and Patrick, who are accomplished musicians and share my love of music. Above all, I am indebted to my husband, Lewis Seifert, without whose support, knowledge, guidance, patience, and love I could never have completed my work. He has been a colleague to me as well, and through his example he has shown a level of discipline and scholarship that I strive to emulate.

Note on Quotations, Translations, and Musical Examples

All primary sources in French cited in this study retain their original spelling and punctuation. I include English translations within the body of the text and the French original in endnotes. Translations for complete airs and chapter 7 emblems are provided in the Appendix. All translations are my own unless otherwise indicated. Most translations of Bénigne de Bacilly's treatise on singing, *Remarques curieuses sur l'art de bien chanter,* are from the published translation entitled *A Commentary upon the Art of Proper Singing* by Austin Caswell.

I include musical examples that resemble as much as possible the original scores, retaining as well the original spelling and punctuation. I was not able to reproduce some of the signs used in the originals, such as the meter signature "3" or the compound signature "3" followed by the sign for cut time. I was also unable to reproduce one specific sign: the double bar filled in with dots used in the publications of airs by Lambert, La Barre, and Le Camus. The musical examples are meant to be illustrative and are not meant for performance; thus, I have not added a text to any bass lines. This proviso applies especially to all of Lambert's scores, published in *Les Airs de Monsieur Lambert* (1660, 1666, 1669), wherein he included two bass lines, one to be sung and one to be played. For reasons of convenience and clarity, I include only the bass line to be played. All examples of Lambert's airs are taken from his 1666 edition, which is available in facsimile. I have also added bar lines to all examples of La Barre's airs to help identify specific fragments under analysis.

MUSIC AND THE LANGUAGE OF LOVE

Introduction

This book is a study of French serious airs or love songs composed from the late 1640s through the 1660s by four of the most important composers of the seventeenth century: Michel Lambert, Bénigne de Bacilly, Joseph Chabanceau de La Barre, and Sébastien Le Camus. Most airs are solo songs for treble voice and basso continuo accompaniment. The majority are in binary form,[1] and some are dance airs, primarily sarabandes, minuets, and gavottes. This repertory belongs to the tradition of what modern scholars call the "courtly love song," but with a twist. In the vast majority of airs, instead of placing the beloved on a pedestal to be admired and worshiped, the male poetic voice complains of her harsh treatment, at times even insulting her, claiming that she is inhumane, unfaithful, and aloof, all the while lamenting her rejection. In a few airs, he either tries to persuade her to love him in return, or he celebrates their mutual love.

When I began my study of the French air, I had no idea it would lead to a consideration of French aesthetics, Parisian salons,[2] performance practice issues, and controversies surrounding music, rhetoric, eloquence, and pleasure. The first challenge I encountered was to find a means to assess the airs. I soon realized that a traditional approach to musical analysis—that is, an analysis based on tonal harmony—would reveal very little of interest. At first glance, the harmonies are not adventurous; the melodies and rhythms seem to ramble; the interaction between bass and melody is not very interesting—there are no contrapuntal intricacies—and the texts seem downright banal to the modern reader. In addition, singing the airs was unrewarding, even frustrating, and the scores were incomplete. How, then, does one go about analyzing a repertory that *seems* on the surface to be extremely simple and exceedingly conventional?

The first task was to find an appropriate method of analysis. There can be no doubt that as a composer set out to write an air, he would have begun by thinking about the song text. He would have had to take into account the poem's phrase structure and overall form, as well as the meaning of the words, phrases, and the entire lyric. In his consideration of the text, he would have had to perceive principles related to rhetoric and poetics—consciously or not—and apply those very same principles to his musical setting. While it is not possible to know whether composers had an intimate knowledge of rhetorical principles, and if they did, to what extent this knowledge informed their approach to composition, it is clear that the relationship between rhetoric and music was widely acknowledged among scholars of the day. A number of seventeenth-century and early-eighteenth-century writers, including Marin Mersenne, Bénigne de Bacilly, Phérotée de La Croix, Jean-Léonor Le Gallois de Grimarest, and Michel de Saint-Lambert,[3] connect and/or compare the two parallel disciplines in their treatises.

While traditional methods of analysis would not have revealed much that was meaningful about the airs, an analysis based on rhetoric —that is, a consideration of how composers responded to and interpreted the structure and meaning of the texts they were setting to music—shows that airs are fascinating miniature discourses in song. As a type of discourse, airs were composed as a musical reflection of the tones of voice and rates of speech associated with a passionate recitation of the song text. Since the lyrics relate in some way to matters of love, the passions that accompany this complex emotion are represented in the notated compositions to be expressed in performance.[4]

I approach the study of this repertory in two parts. Because my work on the meaning and function of the air is based on what the songs express and how, it was imperative to find a way to analyze airs as agents of expressive communication. To this end, chapters 1 through 5 present a stylistic analysis of the air based on principles of rhetoric. But I also discovered that the air was so important, its influence so pervasive, that the repertory was connected in some way to almost every major aesthetic, cultural, and social movement after 1650. In the remaining chapters of the book, then, I explore the function and meaning of the air in French society. Many airs were composed and performed in Parisian salons, were integral to the art of conversation practiced therein, and were subject to women's participation and judgment. Women not only wrote song texts and sang them, they also assessed through conversation the merits of the lyrics and their settings. Airs reflected many aspects of salon culture, not only through emphasizing the connection between the air and conversation but also through an encoded erotic language that pervaded the song texts and musical settings, which were linked to intrigue, pleasure, games of wit, and most importantly, perceptions of love. Writers, poets, and artists associated with salons were indeed obsessed with love, but they were not alone in their fascination with this complex passion. Medical doctors and authors of what we would now identify as pornography also addressed aspects of love, focusing on the causes, symptoms, and cures of lovesickness in medical treatises or describing the art of lovemaking in erotic novels.[5]

Theologians, as well, were concerned with matters pertaining to both divine and mortal love. When airs began to reach a larger public —particularly through the Ballard family publications, the *Livres d'airs de différents autheurs*, published between 1658 and 1694—love songs became objects of attack for Catholic Church leaders and moralists who perceived the repertory as a dangerous source of pleasure that would cause the young and weak-minded to abandon morality and engage in lascivious activities. What is all the more fascinating is that the condemnation of airs grew out of specific beliefs about rhetoric, founded upon the distrust of eloquence or highly figurative language. It was believed that the persuasive capacity of words, their accessory or passionate meaning, and the music that accompanied the provocative texts were capable of reaching and corrupting vulnerable souls. The sentiment behind the attacks was not so different from that expressed during the 1950s by adults who associated rock and roll with moral decay and social chaos. What is truly amazing is that these little songs could cause such a big fuss. But more importantly, we see that music was viewed as a powerful medium of communication. Even seemingly insignificant airs that speak of love by referring to the beloved's eyes, to spring, birds, woods, and streams could come to represent a breakdown in social mores and thus define an entire generation.

The purpose of this book is two-fold. First, it seeks to unveil what is most significant about the French air as an artistic object; specifically, how composers set the various rhetorical features of the song texts to create a musical language expressive of the passions. An analysis based in rhetoric provides a historically informed approach to defining the style of the French air composed primarily during the 1650s and published during the 1660s. Thus, this book seeks to enhance our understanding of music as an agent of affective communication. For the seventeenth-century musician and connoisseur, music did indeed communicate passion; it had meaning. While the aesthetic necessity to express the passions motivated the craft of musical composition during this period, the means of expression was founded in rhetoric. The various musical devices used by composers during this period to convey the passions constitute the essence of French vocal musical style—a style defined by the interconnections between language and music.

The second purpose of this book grows out of its interdisciplinary nature as a demonstration of the power of song, drawing on principles of rhetoric and poetics, seventeenth-century music theory, theories of the passions, medical science, literary theory, social and cultural historiography, and gender studies. I hope to show that along with other major literary genres of the seventeenth century, this repertory takes on a collective meaning and significance and offers insight into love, relationships, attitudes toward a woman's place in society, and some of the major controversies surrounding artistic endeavors in mid-to-late seventeenth-century France.

The study of this repertory was the focus of my dissertation, "The Language of Music in France: Rhetoric as a Basis for Expression in Michel Lambert's *Les Airs de Monsieur Lambert* (1669) and Bénigne de Bacilly's *Les Trois livres d'airs* (1668)," completed in 1994. Up to that point, neither the serious air nor the relationship between rhetoric and French music had received much attention from scholars.[6] The first book to address the development of the air in France was Théodore Gérold's *L'art du chant en France au XVIIe siècle,* first published in 1921. Gérold's book was the foundation for my dissertation and for other studies of the repertory, including Georgie Durosoir's important book *L'air de cour en France, 1571–1655: Contribution à l'étude de la musique dans le monde français du 17e siècle* (1991), which focuses on the *airs de cour* written during the first half of the century. Prior to 1994, the most significant English-language book to consider French music was James Anthony's *French Baroque Music from Beaujoyeulx to Rameau,* which devotes one short chapter to the solo song and related genres, briefly summarizing their development to the middle of the century and outlining the most apparent stylistic features of works by various composers, including Michel Lambert, Joseph Chabanceau de La Barre, and Jean-Baptiste Lully.[7]

Shorter studies on the French air treat either dance songs or the *brunetes.* Patricia Ranum's articles consider rhythmic and metric features and the expression of the passions in dance airs with texts. Paul-

Marie Masson's essay summarizes the historical development of the *brunetes,* defined as simple pastoral airs, which were especially popular during the first years of the eighteenth century.[8] Elissa Poole also examines the *brunetes* in her article "The *Brunetes* and Their Sources," and demonstrates the "triumph" of tonality over modality at the beginning of the eighteenth century. Poole's article draws from her dissertation on Christophe Ballard's *Brunetes ou petits airs tendres,* published in three volumes during the first decade of the eighteenth century. Poole includes concordances for the pieces found in the collections of anonymous airs published by Ballard throughout the seventeenth century, summarizes the historical development of the genre, and presents a stylistic analysis of the repertory.

Two primary studies undertaken before 1994 address issues pertaining to the serious air at the pinnacle of its development during the 1650s and 1660s. Catherine Massip's thesis considers the life and works of Michel Lambert, whose first collection of airs was published in 1660. Massip's work also includes a thematic catalogue of all Lambert's compositions. Austin Caswell's dissertation is a translation of Bacilly's *Remarques curieuses sur l'art de bien chanter* (1668) and a consideration of the performance practice of airs published by Bacilly and Lambert during the 1660s.[9]

More recently, two important books, both in French, have appeared: Catherine's Massip's invaluable monograph on the life and works of composer Michel Lambert, *L'art de bien chanter: Michel Lambert (1610–1696),* published in 1999, and Anne-Madeleine Goulet's 2004 book, *Poésie, musique et sociabilité au XVIIe siècle: Les Livres d'airs de différents autheurs publiés chez Ballard de 1658–1694,* a comprehensive literary study of song texts from the *Livre[s] d'airs de différents autheurs.* In addition, there is Lisa Perella's 2003 dissertation on drinking songs, "Mythologies of Musical Persuasion: Power and Politics of Song in France, 1653–1673."[10] Several editions of airs with helpful introductions have also been published.[11]

The present study differs significantly from these important works. First, it is the only study to offer a stylistic analysis, derived from principles of rhetoric, of airs published during the 1660s, and the only study in English of the most significant genre of vocal music composed during a crucial moment in the history of French music, the years just before the monumental performance of Lully's first opera, *Cadmus et Hermione,* in 1673. The impact of the *tragédie en musique* as created by Lully and Quinault, as well as the popularization of the air, particularly after 1670, would irrevocably alter the style of French song.[12] Thus the works by Lambert, Bacilly, La Barre, and Le Camus under examination in this study represent French vocal musical style at the height of its development during two pivotal decades in the history of French music, the 1650s and 1660s.

The present study also differs from Patricia Ranum's book *The Harmonic Orator: The Phrasing and Rhetoric of the Melody in French Baroque Airs* (2001). Ranum does not focus on serious airs but rather examines only dance airs, most of which were composed for operas and theater productions from the late seventeenth and early eighteenth centuries by Jean-Baptiste Lully, Marc Charpentier, Henri Desmarest, André Campra, André Cardinal Desmarest, Marin Marais, and others. Ranum also concentrates primarily on the poetic structure of texts, the melodies, and performance issues, particularly the pronunciation of the French texts. She depends to a great extent upon two twentieth-century sources for her analysis of text declamation (Henri Morier's *Dictionnaire de poétique et de rhétorique* and Joseph Pineau's *Le mouvement rythmique en français: Principes et méthode d'analyse*) and draws upon treatises that reach far into the eighteenth century, including works by Denis Diderot from 1776 and by Bernard de La Ville Lacépède from 1785.

By contrast, the present book draws upon sources that are as close to the repertory under study as possible, the earliest being works by René Descartes (*Compendium musicae*, 1618, and *Les passions de l'âme* [*The Passions of the Soul*], 1649) and Marin Mersenne (*Harmonie universelle*, 1636–37), and the latest by Jean-Léonor de Grimarest (*Traité du récitatif dans la lecture, dans l'action publique, dans la declamation, et dans le chant,* 1707). In addition, I have tried to make my analysis of the airs and their performance practice issues as holistic as possible, treating the interaction of all elements of the composition—melody, harmony, harmonic rhythm, bass-line movement, rhythm, and meter—in relation to the text. I have also endeavored to explain concepts in as clear and practical a manner as possible. One of my primary goals is to inspire singers to perform these airs, to arouse interest not only by revealing what makes this repertory tick but also by offering practical advice on performance.

The first chapter of the book identifies and describes the repertory and publications of airs by Lambert, Bacilly, La Barre, and Le Camus, who were the most important composers writing airs between 1645 and 1670. I also present in this chapter an introduction to the important issues related to the mid-century air which form the basis for the remainder of the study: the structure and meaning of the song texts, the crucial influence of the hostesses and participants in the Parisian salons, the significance of the *galant* aesthetic to this repertory, and the connection of French song texts to rhetoric.

Chapter 2 is a review of French theoretical sources that concern rhetoric, poetics, music, and musical expression. As this chapter shows, airs were composed *in theory* as passionate recitations of song texts. In short, music had to be expressive of its text.[13] Lyric poetry was considered a special type of discourse, and poets used devices borrowed from rhetoric to enhance the lyric's expressive capacity. In their musical settings of song texts, composers not only had to consider poetic structure, but also rhetorical devices such as the figures and the passions associated with various verbal units (lines, phrases, portions of phrases, and individual words). As this chapter shows, while this compositional process may seem obvious, it is, in fact, much more complicated in both theory and practice.

In the subsequent four chapters, the relationship between rhetorical principles and an analysis of airs as they were composed *in practice* is demonstrated. These chapters show how Lambert, Bacilly, La Barre, and Le Camus used rhetorical devices in their settings to communicate affect or passion. The analysis of the airs is organized according to four of the five components of rhetoric most relevant to composition and performance: invention (*inventio,* or an identification of the topic and the means of portraying it), disposition (*dipositio,* or the arrangement and organization of expressions), style or elocution (*elocutio,* or syntax, diction, and figures), and pronunciation (*actio,* or performance).[14] Chapters 3 and 4 (invention) consider the representation of affect in the airs. In chapter 3, I identify the primary passions expressed in the song texts and demonstrate the specific musical devices that the composers used in association with these passions. Chapter 4 shows how the composers used these devices to project their interpretation of the affects embodied in an entire lyric. Chapter 5, on disposition and elocution, reveals how the parts of the song text correspond to the divisions of an oration and demonstrates how composers set a poem to correlate with the expressive function of each section, a practice that parallels recommendations given by seventeenth-century rhetoricians. I also address the function of the *double,* or ornamented second verse, which is one of the most distinguishable and important features of airs published during the 1660s. This chapter is also devoted to matters of elocution or style, and here I address poetic syntax and how it determined the musical phrase structure of the air. The composers' setting of the rhetorical figures used in the texts is also considered. Chapter 6 concerns performance practice issues relevant to singing and accompanying airs and is based, for the most part, on Bacilly's treatise on singing, *Remarques curieuses sur l'art de bien chanter*. In order to perform airs properly, the singer must consider pronunciation, syllabic quantity, ornamentation, and vocal quality. How to accompany the airs is equally important.

In chapter 7, the function and meaning of the air in French elite society, specifically in the Parisian *ruelle,* or salon, are examined. I address the creation and performance of airs as a salon activity and an extension of the art of conversation promoted by salon participants, as described by Madeleine de Scudéry and others in novels and conversation treatises. I also investigate how airs embodied layers of textual meaning, creating an ironic juxtaposition of appropriate and inappropriate behaviors in keeping with a *galant* aesthetic typical of salon literature. Particular attention is given to notions of love, proper versus improper courtship rituals, and attitudes toward a woman's place in society. By reference to erotic novels, emblematic treatises, and medical writings on lovesickness, I uncover the meaning of an encoded language used in song texts and reflected in the music and show how salon members, who seemingly cultivated notions of non-physical love and controlled discourse, produced a sensuous music set to a man's eroticized utterances and allowed women, often singing as men, to perform airs when they were otherwise forbidden by propriety to express such base feelings.

My study concludes with a brief assessment of the development of the air during the second half of the century and how it came to reflect a "rhetoric of distraction." Theologians believed that the air's lascivious message would imprint upon the weak-minded a desire for pleasure, causing singers and listeners to be distracted away from God's message and a life of devotion. I then investigate the growth of two diametrically opposed forms of the air: the "tender" air and the "spiritual" or "devotional" air. The production of airs, particularly after 1670, meant that a "public" or broader, more diverse taste, rather than that of salon participants, dictated the nature of the air. In this way, musical settings became less passionate than they had been for the serious air, even as song texts continued to concern the pleasures and pain of love. Tender airs, however, were condemned by many as a repertory particularly unfit for youths and women, who were all too susceptible to immoral influences. Spiritual or devotional airs were thus composed as part of an outcry against the "evils" of love songs, which were thought by some to "place in the heart a disposition for crime, libertinism, and impiety."[15] Devotional airs are parodies of serious airs, while the spiritual airs by Bénigne de Bacilly are newly composed songs in the style of the serious air set to newly written sacred texts in the *galant* style. Both sacred parodies and spiritual airs were meant to usurp the profane air as the only type of music suitable for teaching well-bred women and young girls to sing.

In light of this intense reaction against the profane air at the end of the seventeenth century, I conclude the book with an assessment of the influence and legacy of works by Lambert, Bacilly, La Barre, and Le Camus. To what extent did these composers establish and influence a style of French music that persisted into the eighteenth century? Were their accomplishments forgotten after their deaths, or did their works live on? We will see that indeed their legacy persisted, even though descriptions of their works were somewhat distorted. Writers like Lecerf de la Viéville focus on certain airs over others, particularly those which are more dance-like and lyrical, and use these to defend and promote the French style against the "invasion" of Italian music.

What I have uncovered about the French airs that were composed, performed, and published over a very short period of time is relevant to other musical genres written by composers across Europe throughout the seventeenth century and long into the eighteenth. For even though the serious air seems uniquely connected to French aesthetics and culture during a very brief moment in the history of French music, I believe that it shares many features in common with Baroque music of all kinds, if not in musical style then in the aesthetics that formed the rationale for their composition. As such, a study of this repertory will serve to add to, expand upon, and reinforce what we already know about Baroque music.

CHAPTER ONE

Music and Texts:
An Overview of the Sources

A General Description of the Air

The French air, or solo song, was the most abundantly cultivated musical genre throughout the seventeenth century. There were *airs de cour* (courtly airs), *airs à boire* (drinking songs), *airs à danser* (dance airs), *airs sérieux* (serious airs), *chansonnettes* ("little" songs), and *brunetes* (any air with pastoral references, the actual name *brunete* not appearing in publications until the first decade of the eighteenth century). Airs of all kinds were sung in private settings (such as the *ruelle,* or salon) or were part of public productions (ballets, plays, and eventually French operas). Airs also appeared in various kinds of religious works and in French-language cantatas.

No matter what the performance venue was, by the 1650s one type of air, the serious air, would come to define the essence of French musical style.[1] This new type of air, emerging mid-century, bore little resemblance to its predecessor, the *air de cour.*[2] The change in style, exemplified in serious airs by Michel Lambert, Bénigne de Bacilly, Joseph Chabanceau de La Barre, and Sébastien Le Camus, was evidently prompted by Lambert's teacher, the aristocrat-singer Pierre de Nyert, to whom Lambert dedicated his first published collection of airs in 1660. As the story goes, Nyert traveled to Rome during the 1630s, where he heard Italian monodies. Upon his return to France in 1638, he was determined to combine French and Italian vocal styles. Thus, the application of Italian monody to French songs as demonstrated by Nyert inspired mid-seventeenth-century composers to write airs that reflected the "natural declamation of the text."[3]

Serious airs were considered the finest musical genre for solo voice and accompaniment during the seventeenth century in France, but light airs were also quite popular. Generally speaking, serious airs are characterized by rhythmic patterns and melodic contours mimetic of natural speech, which often warrants meter changes and irregular phrasing.[4] Another type of air, considered by contemporary sources as light (the *air léger*), appears occasionally amid the serious pieces. Typically, light airs are *chansons à danser* (particularly gavottes and minuets), *vaudevilles,* and *airs de mouvement,* and are characterized by measured rhythms, symmetrical phrases, and tuneful melodies.[5] Most, though not all, of the light songs found in collections of serious airs are actually hybrid pieces. Later in the century, Christophe Ballard called these *chansonnettes, petits airs,* or *petits airs sérieux.* Many of these are based on more stately dance types, particularly the sarabande and gavotte, and are usually less measured and tuneful than dance airs and popular songs.

Serious and light airs are best differentiated according to subject matter, for the topic of the text determined to a great extent its poetic and musical features. Pierre Perrin, in the introduction to his *Recueil de paroles de musique* (1667), differentiated between serious and light airs by the subject of the lyrics and their affective connotations: serious airs concern "various accidents or events such as presence, absence, return, pursuit, desire, hope, fear, fury, disdain, or enjoyment, . . . [which] call for tender and grave texts; . . . and the *Chansonnettes* . . . are better suited to playful or rustic words."[6]

The Publications

The number of serious airs published between 1650 and 1700 is astounding. Robert (and later Christophe) Ballard published over one thousand anonymous airs in their *Livre[s] d'airs de différents autheurs* (1658–94),[7] averaging thirty airs per year with each book. After 1694, Christophe Ballard, who had taken over the business upon the death of his father in 1673, began publishing *Recueils d'airs sérieux et à boire* every month well into the eighteenth century.[8] In addition, the *Mercure galant,* which was published monthly beginning in 1672, included one air in each issue. Publications devoted to serious airs for treble voice and bass by a single composer appeared less frequently. In 1660, Lambert published his first book of airs, *Les Airs de Monsieur Lambert* (reprinted in 1666 and revised in 1669).[9] Bacilly's first and second books of serious airs, the *Nouveau livre d'airs* and *Second livre d'airs,* were published in 1661 and 1664, respectively; both collections were revised and combined as *Les Trois livres d'airs* in 1668. La Barre published *Airs à deux parties avec les seconds couplets en diminution* in 1669; Le Camus' son published a collection of his father's airs posthumously in 1678; and Honoré d'Ambruis' *Livre d'airs avec les seconds couplets en diminution* was issued in 1685. Lambert issued a second publication of airs entitled *Airs à une, II, III, et IV parties* in 1689.[10] In addition, many airs by Lambert, Bacilly, and others circulated in manuscripts,[11] some even copied directly from printed sources, particularly from the Ballard collections.

Serious airs published by a single composer during the 1660s constitute the most important repertory during the period. These airs are particularly significant because they were published under the supervision of the composers themselves; thus, these represent the versions they wanted to present to the public. Several composers, in fact, complained that inaccurate renditions of their airs were circulating either in manuscripts or in print (most likely referring to the Ballard collections). Lambert addresses this issue in his first publication of airs:

> Even though my inclination has never been to present any [of my works] to the public, I allowed myself after all to give in to the persuasion and reasoning of my friends, the strongest of which is that there are a considerable number of my airs either printed or circulating among people that are not according to my intention.[12]

Thus, the airs considered in this study are those corrected and approved by the composers themselves (or in the case of Le Camus, by his son, who was also a composer). Unlike the airs that circulated in manuscripts or appeared in the Ballard collections, the airs in printed collections devoted to one composer feature corrected bass lines,[13] figured bass, and score format (Figure 1.1a), rather than with the treble and bass placed on separate folios as practiced by Ballard until 1685 (Figure 1.2).[14] Most single-composer editions also include *doubles,* or ornamented settings of second strophes, also referred to as second couplets (Figure 1.1b).

The Composers

Michel Lambert, Bénigne de Bacilly, Joseph Chabanceau de La Barre, and Sébastien Le Camus were the first and only composers to write *and* publish serious airs in the new style. Even though Le Camus' works were published posthumously by his son in 1678, his airs were nonetheless composed earlier than this date and thus need to be considered alongside the other *airs sérieux* composed by his contemporaries.

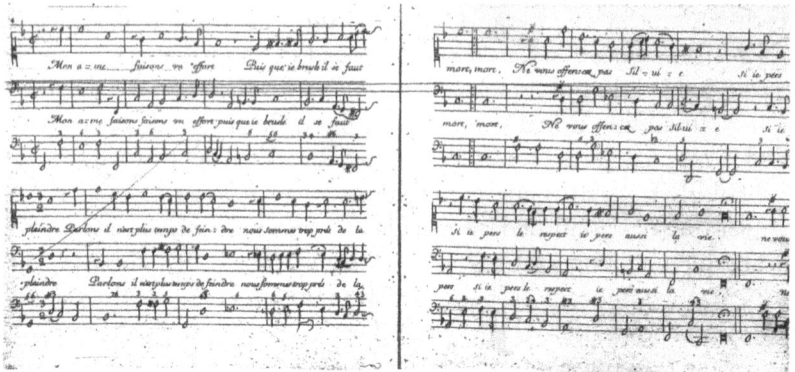

Figure 1.1a. Lambert, "Mon ame faisons un effort," First Strophe, *Les Airs de Monsieur Lambert* (1666), p. 4.

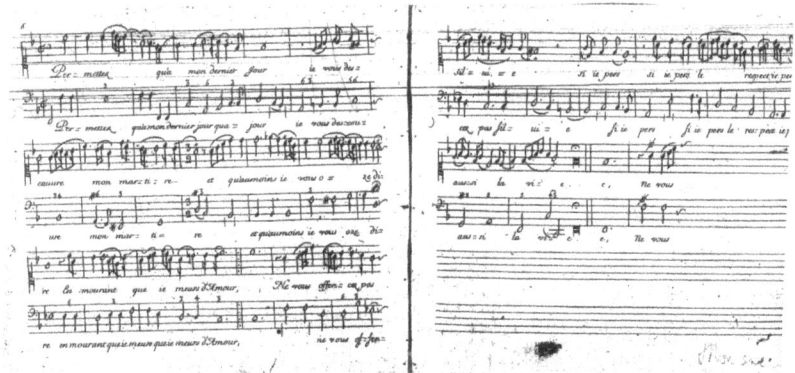

Figure 1.1b. Lambert, "Mon ame faisons un effort," Second Strophe, *Les Airs de Monsieur Lambert* (1666), p. 6.

Furthermore, all but Bacilly held important posts under Louis XIV and other members of the royal family and were thus recognized to be among the most important composers of the day.

Michel Lambert (1610–96) was the most famous and influential composer of airs in his day. Born in Champigny, he moved to Paris as a boy to work for Louis XIII's younger brother, Gaston d'Orléans.[15] Lambert was recognized as a talented singer and singing master as early as 1636 and held several court appointments before becoming *maître de musique de la chambre du roi* in 1661, one year after the publication of

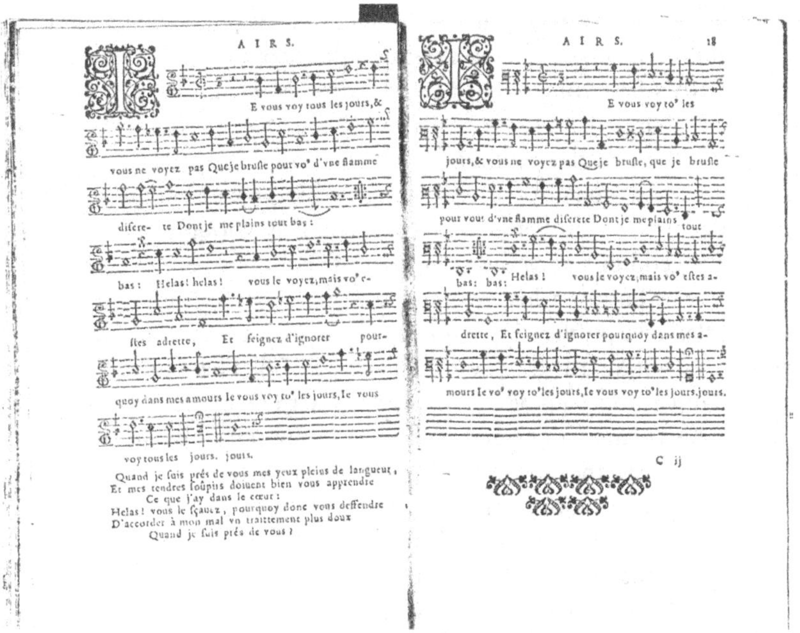

Figure 1.2. [Lambert], "Je vous voy tous les jours," *Livre d'airs de différents autheurs* (Ballard, 1666), 17v.

his first collection of airs, *Les Airs de Monsieur Lambert.* Many of his contemporaries praised his abilities: Pierre Perrin, for example, called him the "Amphion of our days," and Tallemant des Réaux referred to him as the "French Orpheus."[16] Writing several years after Lambert's death, Lecerf de la Viéville judged Lambert to be the greatest master of the composition and performance of airs during the seventeenth century. Lecerf claimed that Lambert's style was to be emulated because it was "natural, clear, graceful, and immediately charming."[17]

Bénigne de Bacilly (ca. 1625–90) was a distinguished composer, singing teacher, and perhaps even a priest.[18] Although he apparently held no official position under Louis XIV, many of his works, both sacred and secular, were printed by the king's official publisher, the Ballard family. All of the dance and drinking airs in Ballard's *Livres de chansons à danser et à boire* (editions of 1663–68) are by Bacilly, and at least one scholar credits Bacilly with having improved the quality of the melody in dance airs during the 1660s.[19] He is known today primarily for his treatise, *Remarques curieuses sur l'art de bien chanter* (1668), a study of seventeenth-century ornamentation, pronunciation, and syllabic quantity as it pertains to singing in French, published seven years after Bacilly's first collection of serious airs, *Nouveau livre d'airs,* was printed (Richer, 1661). He not only published an extraordinary number of airs of all kinds throughout the second half of the seventeenth century, he was also an entrepreneur who sold his works from his own residence on the Rue des Petits-Champs. Strangely enough, Bacilly rarely acknowledged himself as the composer of the songs he published, even attributing to Lambert his own airs used as examples in his treatise on singing. Bacilly's publications, however, can be attributed to him on the basis of his initials (B. D. B. or D. B., or just B.). The works for which he did claim authorship were publications with no contemporary counterparts: his treatise on singing and his two volumes of spiritual airs.

Joseph Chabanceau de La Barre (1633–78) was praised for "his capacity in the composition of music" and "his dexterity in [playing] the organ."[20] At the age of nineteen he accompanied his older sister, Anne, one of the leading singers at the French court, to Sweden, where she had been summoned by Queen Christine. La Barre remained there for two years. After the death of his father, Pierre de La Barre, he was appointed *organiste ordinaire de la chapelle du roi* in 1656. His first and only complete publication of airs, *Airs à deux parties,* appeared in 1669. Other vocal works in French and Italian are scattered throughout various additional publications. He also composed several keyboard works that appear in manuscripts, including the Bauyn and Parville.[21] In 1674, four years before La Barre's death, Louis XIV gave him the benefice of the Benedictine Abbey of Saint-Hilaire in the Diocese of Carcassonne. He was thereafter referred to as L'Abbé de La Barre.[22]

Sébastien Le Camus (ca. 1610–ca. 77) first entered into the service of Louis XIII in 1640 and was appointed as *intendant de la musique* to Gaston d'Orléans in 1648. In 1660, he became *surintendant de la musique* to Louis XIV's bride, Marie-Thérèse, sharing the post with Jean-Baptiste Boësset. Upon the death of Louis Couperin in 1661, Le Camus became *ordinaire de la musique de la chambre* along with Nicolas Hotman. Jean Rousseau claimed that when Le Camus played the treble viol, he "imitated all that a beautiful and accomplished voice can do . . . to the point that even the memory of the beauty and tenderness of his execution erases all that has been heard up to the present on this instrument."[23] Madame de Sévigné described him as "made of the gods,"[24] and fellow composer La Barre claimed that Le Camus was "the first to compose airs which express the words."[25] Evidently this

Music and the Language of Love

opinion was confirmed by Jean-Baptiste Boësset, Honoré D'Ambruis, and Michel Lambert.[26]

Publications by Lambert, Bacilly, La Barre, and Le Camus: A Description

The airs in Lambert's *Airs de Monsieur Lambert* (1660/1666/1669), Bacilly's *Trois livres d'airs* (1668), La Barre's *Airs à deux parties* (1669), and Le Camus' *Airs à deux et trois parties* (1678), which constitute the focus of this study, are presented in score format and include melody and figured bass.[27] Of the sixteen pieces in La Barre's edition, eleven include a bass line with text; only a few of these eleven airs include figures (Figure 1.3). The other five consist of a melody line accompanied by an untexted figured bass.

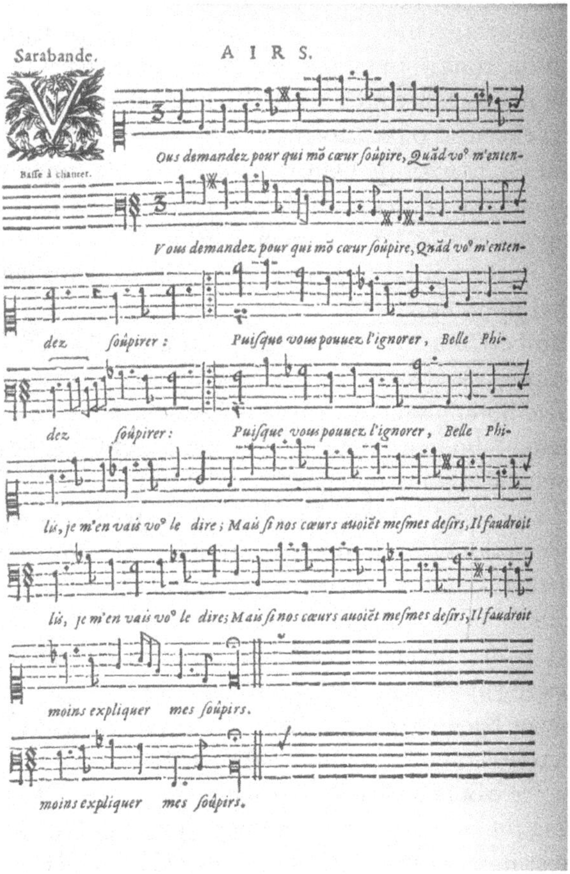

Figure 1.3. La Barre, "Vous demandez," First Strophe, *Airs à deux parties*, 14v.

Like many of La Barre's airs, the first strophe of Bacilly's pieces includes a bass line with text and figures. While none of the bass lines in Le Camus' publication include text, all the airs in Lambert's publication include two separate bass lines, one with a text to be sung and one with the addition of figures to be played (Figures 1.1a and 1.1b).[28] The two bass lines presented in the Lambert pieces are almost identical, except for the addition of notes to the version with text to accommodate syllables. There is also an occasional difference in pitch.

The publication format used for these four editions differs significantly from that used by Robert Ballard in his collections of anonymous airs published between 1658 and 1694. Until 1685, Ballard printed the melody on one folio and the bass line on the other, almost always added a text to the bass line, and did not include figures until 1669 (Figure 1.2). The indication *basse continue* does not appear in the publications until 1674. There is also an absence of bar lines until later in the century. This arrangement not only suggests a former practice carried over from the contrapuntal orientation of the Renaissance but also indicates the manner in which the Ballard family printed music, using movable type instead of engraving.

It was not until the 1670s that Christophe Ballard began omitting texts to bass lines, adding figures to the bass more regularly, and specifying lute accompaniment under the opening measures of the part. As mentioned above, he did not begin printing pieces in score format with the addition of bar lines until 1685.

Pieces by Lambert, Bacilly, La Barre, and Le Camus reflect the transition in compositional style from a contrapuntal orientation to a more progressive homophonic texture.[29] The inclusion of a figured bass accommodated "modern" practice wherein a treble melody was sung with instrumental accompaniment.[30] Yet the addition of the song's text to the bass in airs by Lambert, Bacilly, and La Barre allowed for other performance options besides that of solo singer with instrumental accompaniment: the melody and bass line could have been sung as a duet, with or without accompaniment, or both treble and bass could have been played by instruments. It was also possible that the melody could have been sung alone without any accompaniment, though this is not an option that Bacilly recommends.[31] Performers of pieces from the Ballard collections could have also exercised all three options. The least desirable choice would have been to sing the bass line with a treble instrument playing the melody, for as Bacilly notes, "The bass voice is suitable for almost nothing but the emotion of anger, which appears rarely in French airs. As a result, this voice range must be content with part singing."[32] Even though Robert Cambert was referring to drinking songs in two and three parts in the *l'avis au lecteur* to his *Airs à boire a deux, et a trois parties,* he provides some useful options for performing airs, including playing instruments instead of singing, demonstrating a great flexibility in the approach to performing airs of all kinds:

> You will also observe that most of the Airs in three parts can
> be sung by the Bass and Treble voices without the third Part,
> and played in Ensemble with the Bass, or on the Treble Viol,
> as I have done in several Concerts.[33]

All airs, with the exception of those in the Le Camus publication, differ from pieces in the Ballard publications by the inclusion of *doubles* (second verses or couplets) set to the melody of the first strophe and ornamented with *diminutions,* or *passages* (Figure 1.1b). The *doubles* in publications by Lambert and La Barre are set with a figured bass line, while Bacilly's *doubles* include the ornamented melody alone without bass. When singing Bacilly's *doubles,* one would have to use the bass line of the first verse of the air as accompaniment, presumably as is or with minor adjustments. By contrast, in many of the Ballard pieces, two strophes of the text are given, but only the first appears with music. According to Bacilly, a singer was expected to improvise diminutions in order to accommodate the changes in syllable length and the different character or affect of the second verse. In performing the pieces from the Ballard collections, then, singers were most likely expected to add ornamentation to the melody of the second strophe even though the diminutions were not written out.

There can be little doubt that the publications of airs by Lambert, Bacilly, La Barre, and Le Camus present the versions preferred by the composers themselves, as there are many significant differences between airs that appear in their own publications and those same airs published throughout the Ballard collections. Although it is not clear why there are so many variations between the Ballard airs and other sources, we can surmise that with perhaps a few exceptions, the source of the Ballard version was not the composer himself. Bacilly confirms that often airs were "stolen" from the hands of the composers or from copies by those whose knowledge of the music was second-hand.[34] Thus, we can assume that notated airs not in the composers' hands were copied by those who heard performances of the songs (and wrote the melodies down by ear, the harmonies and bass lines being more challenging to notate) or by those who sang the airs and knew and remembered the melodies rather than the bass lines and harmonies. Because compositions circulated freely in manuscript, versions not sanctioned by composers and full of mistakes could have easily found their way into the hands of Ballard.[35] Bacilly confirms that composers often did not want to publish their airs for a variety of reasons: as a whim; to make revisions; to use them in teaching and so prevent others from doing so (thus retaining control over the versions with proper rhythms and meters); or to withhold them from the public on purpose to maintain "an aura of novelty." This would have made unpublished airs all the more desirable and sought after.[36] And indeed, in the prefaces to his publications, Ballard stresses that his editions include the newest and most popular airs; thus, novelty was of the utmost importance to him and his prospective buyers.[37] This also motivated Ballard to include airs by a variety of composers. In the *texte liminaire* from his *Recueil de chansonnettes* (1675), Ballard admits that he purposefully includes airs by a number of composers to avoid the monotony derived from airs "with the same tone" that present "the same thing."[38]

Twenty-first-century singers and accompanists need to approach the performance of airs using the Ballard publications with great care and whenever possible compare those airs to facsimiles and modern editions of airs by individual composers that are available. Not only do the rhythms, melodies, and bass lines in the Ballard airs differ significantly from the composers' printed versions, but the addition of figures to the bass makes a huge difference because chord sonorities and inversions affect the expressive impact of a song. The bass line accompanying the second phrase of Ballard's version of "Pourquoy vous offencer" (Example 1.2), for example, is quite different from Lambert's original (Example 1.1). The harmonies in Lambert's air on the words "Beauty for whom I die" ("Beauté pour qui je meurs") change from G minor to D major in first inversion to G minor, the harmonies moving in large note values. This same phrase in the Ballard edition is accompanied by more active harmonic movement and different harmonies. The emphasis on minor mode and the harmonic movement I–V–I in the original intensify this cry of despair, while the major mode version in Ballard with its weak cadence lacks the necessary force (without figures, of course, we cannot be sure how to interpret the harmonies).

Lambert's choice of rhythms in the melody is also different than that of the Ballard version. Emphasis is given to "Beauty" in the Lambert version with a larger rhythmic value (the dotted half) on "-té"

"Why are you offended Beautiful one for whom I die"

EXAMPLE 1.1. Lambert, "Pourquoy vous offencer," mm. 1–7, *Les Airs de Monsieur Lambert*, p. 36.

"Why are you offended Beautiful one for whom I die"

EXAMPLE 1.2. Lambert, "Pourquoy vous offencer," mm. 1–7, *Livre d'airs de différents autheurs* (Ballard, 1660), 20v.

of "Beauté," followed by a smaller value (a quarter note) on "pour" (mm. 3–4). In the Ballard version, "-té" of "Beauté" and "pour" are both set with half notes. "Qui je" is set with a dotted quarter followed by an eighth in the original, while these two words appear as equal quarter notes in the Ballard edition. Lambert's version, with its greater rhythmic variety, adds to the agitated affect most likely meant for this phrase and is closer to the intended recitation of stressed and unstressed syllables.

In the Ballard edition, the repetition of the phrase "Beauté pour qui je meurs" appears immediately after its initial presentation, while in the Lambert version, the two phrases are separated by 4½ beats. This rhetorical use of silence in the original prepares the listener for the dramatic change of passion on the phrase's repetition, which is set in a lower tessitura than the first, without any dotted rhythms, and harmonized primarily with major harmonies. In the Ballard edition, the text is accompanied to a great degree by similar harmonies in both appearances of the phrase, though the phrase ends with a G-minor chord in root position. The G-major chord in first inversion at the end of the phrase in the original better represents resignation, appropriate for the repetition of this phrase, than the G-minor harmony in the Ballard version. Again, the affective impact of the phrase, particularly in contrast with its first appearance, is enhanced in the Lambert version.

This brief comparison demonstrates the important relationship between song text and musical setting. A composer's ability to set a song text with a melody line, rhythms, harmonies, and bass line effectively suited to the meaning of the text was paramount. The composer needed to develop the ability to analyze and understand a song text—its structure and especially its meaning. By doing so, a well-composed air could readily be distinguished either from its inferior version, circulating in manuscript or published by Ballard, or from those airs written by lesser composers.

The Song Texts

In his *Recueil de paroles de musique* (1667), Pierre Perrin insists that the nature of the musical setting is determined by the character of the text: serious airs call for tender and grave texts, while "light-hearted" settings "are better suited to playful or rustic words."[39] Despite the crucial connection between the song text and its musical setting, little information from the period about lyric poetry appears in most treatises on music, rhetoric, or poetics.[40] This is most likely due to the negative reactions to mid-century poetry in general, and specifically toward song texts written by men and women associated with the Parisian salons of the day. As Anne-Madeleine Goulet points out in her study of the poetry set by composers of airs published in Ballard's *Livres d'airs de différents autheurs,* writers like Furetière considered lyric poetry to be artificial *(fard)*, deceptive *(tromperie)*, superficially dazzling *(éblouissement)*, gibberish or rubbish *(galimatias)*, and void of reason and finesse *(absence de raison et de finesse)*.[41] With the exception of Goulet's work and Alain Génetiot's *Poétique du loisir mondain,* which considers to some extent song texts, modern scholarship also virtually ignores poetry for music written after mid-century.

According to Génetiot, the poetry that developed after 1640 was influenced by a great number of sources. He writes:

> To study the literary models of fashionable poems [*poèmes mondains*] entails evoking the multiplicity of traditions that informed this poetry of imitation, without, however, losing sight of the fact that their influence can only be diffuse, indirect, and under the constant mediation of a *galant* then classical taste, which keeps adapting them, transforming them, and mixing them in order finally to appropriate them.[42]

Influences included classical sources, such as Ovid's *Metamorphosis,* or pastoral works by Virgil or Theocrates, as well as sixteenth- and early seventeenth-century works by writers like Ronsard, Guarini, Tasso, and, of course, Honoré d'Urfé. François de Malherbe (1555–1628) also influenced poetry, particularly poetry written for musical settings, during the late sixteenth and early seventeenth centuries, but by the 1630s his influence began to wane. The poets Voiture, Scarron, Sarasin, and Vion d'Alibray deliberately rejected Malherbe's example and sought other means of poetic expression and formal arrangement, particularly by avoiding heroic references and using more concise expressions.[43] While mid-seventeenth-century poets writing song texts retained the prosodic structure established by Malberbe (strophic form, end-stops at the end of lines, the emphasis on rhyme, the pause or caesura in the middle of lines, the avoidance of enjambement, the elision of mute "e's," and the alternation of masculine and feminine rhymes), they avoided heroic references and ambiguous symbolism.[44] As Bacilly confirms in his treatise on singing, "It is certain that French lyrics . . . must have clear meaning, without puns or ambiguities. This was not the case in former times, when double meanings were preferred over the most beautiful thoughts."[45]

Although most seventeenth-century scholars did not consider the *chanson* or song text when theorizing about various poetic genres, there are a few exceptions. Perrin provides a description of lyric poetry in the introduction to his *Recueil,* and Phérotée de La Croix, writing later in 1694, also has a great deal to say about this special poetic genre. He defines what he calls *vers à chantez* or *une chanson* as

> a certain small work in verse, rendered in a simple, easy, and natural manner, that one sings under different melodies, following the character of the verse, and each stanza of which is called a "couplet."[46]

La Croix then lists six types of airs, classified according to subject matter: (1) the ordinary or *galant* love song (*ordinaire ou galante*); (2) the drinking song (*bachique ou à boire*); (3) the anti-drinking song (*antibachique*); (4) the anti-love song (*antérotique ou contraire à l'amour*); (5) the opposition song (*par antithèse*); and (6) the pastoral or shepherd song (*des bergers*).[47] According to La Croix, lyric poetry is comprised of four components: (1) subject matter; (2) passionate representation or character in association with various phrases; (3) structure, that is, a work in verse organized into strophes, stanzas, or couplets; and (4) manner, which should be simple, easy, and natural. These aspects correspond to three of the five traditional parts of rhetoric. The first two, subject matter and passionate representation, belong to *inventio* (invention), which is identifying the topic and finding a means of portraying it. Structure refers to *dispositio* (disposition), the organization of the expressions. Manner, then, has to do with *elocutio* (elocution or style), syntax, and diction. A consideration of character influenced every aspect of the text and its musical setting; indeed, La Croix specifically linked passion and text to music in his definition given above. The affective associations of a song text were considered subject to interpretation by composer and performer and need to be examined in conjunction with musical analyses. Accordingly, this topic will receive special treatment in the following chapters and is only generally treated here in the examination of the texts.

The poets and composers who wrote French airs were associated with the most fashionable mid-seventeenth-century salons where airs were performed.[48] Lambert and his famous sister-in-law, singer Hilaire Dupuis, were known to have attended one of the most famous salons at the home of Madeleine de Scudéry. Lambert also frequented the salon of Henriette de Coligny, Comtesse de La Suze.[49] Poets of song texts were also welcomed as participants in salons. Although the poets are not identified in any of the musical collections, Bacilly cites several in his collections of song texts, the *Recueil[s] des plus beaux airs* from 1661, 1667, 1668, 1669, 1670, and 1680.[50] Poets and writers include, among many others, Jean-François Sarasin (1615–54), Pierre Perrin (1620?–75), Madeleine de Scudéry (1601–1701), Paul Pellisson (1624–93), Paul Scarron (1610–60), Charles Vion d'Alibray (1600?–53), François Tristan L'Hermite (1601?–55), Vincent Voiture (1597–1648), and the Comtesse de La Suze (1618–73).[51] Bacilly also wrote many of his own texts, claiming authorship for these in his *Recueils*.

Lambert composed airs on texts by poets such as Isaac de Benserade (1613–91), Pierre Perrin, Philippe Quinault (1635–88), the Comtesse de La Suze, and Bacilly. [52]

One of the greatest influences of the hostesses and participants in salons on the creation of this repertory was the use of a particular range of language or vocabulary.[53] In his *Recueil,* Perrin writes:

> As for lyric vocabulary, I have chosen my words short, such that they never exceed four syllables. . . . I have taken care that they be in current use in *polite society* [emphasis mine], that they be sweet and pleasant-sounding to the ear.[54]

Bacilly summarizes the restriction of language in his statement that "French airs . . . can accept only sweet, flowing terms and familiar expressions."[55]

Salon members also influenced the choice of certain *topoi,* or topics, which concerned all aspects of mortal love. Definitions of love were a common subject of conversation in salons and a favorite topic for literary works of various kinds, especially lyric poetry.[56] In the vast majority of poems from the 1660s, the poetic voice is male.[57] The speaker either narrates or describes his experience with love or directly addresses the beloved. Less often, a narrator recounts the experience of another in affairs of the heart. In addition to the varied means of presentation, there are also distinct types of experience recounted in the texts. Most often, the speaker is rejected by the beloved, which causes him great suffering, but in some texts, the speaker participates in mutual love or attempts to entice his beloved into returning his love.[58] Four different subject types regarding love dominate the pieces in the four publications under examination: (1) painful love; (2) bittersweet love; (3) enticing love; and (4) joyous or pleasurable, usually shared, love. "Painful love" and "enticing love" correspond to La Croix's first type (ordinary or *galant*); "bittersweet" belongs to the fifth category (in opposition).[59] "Joyous love" songs are often pastoral, La Croix's sixth category.

The first type, "painful love," in which the speaker claims that love has caused him only pain and misfortune, is common to all collections.[60] In the following example (which includes the first strophe only), the narrator tells of his hopeless attempt to overcome the loss of his beloved (Bacilly, "Mon sort est digne de Pitié," *Les Trois livres d'airs,* I:12):[61]

LINE NUMBER	SYLLABLE COUNT
1. Mon sort est digne de pitié	8
2. Autant qu'il fut digne d'Envie	8
3. Puisque j'ay perdu l'amitié	8
4. De mon adorable Sylvie	8
5. En vain j'ay crû pour me flatter	8
6. Que je pourrois changer comme elle	8
7. Mon mal ne fait que s'irriter	8
8. Et bien qu'elle soit infidelle	8
9. Mon cœur ne la sçauroit quitter.	8

(My fate is worthy of pity / As much as it was worthy of envy / Since I lost the affection / Of my adorable Sylvie // In vain I believed in order to flatter myself / That I could change like she / My pain only becomes more intense / And although she is unfaithful / My heart could not leave her.)

The second type of song, "bittersweet love," is also represented in all collections. In these songs, the speaker finds that love is simultaneously bitter and sweet (painful and pleasurable), which La Croix called "in opposition" (*par antithèses*), in reference to the antithesis between the two opposite aspects of love (Lambert, "J'aymerois mieux souffrir la mort," *Les Airs*, p. 56):

LINE NUMBER	SYLLABLE COUNT
1. J'aymerois mieux souffrir la mort	8
2. Que de faire le moindre effort	8
3. Pour dégager mon cœur des chaines de Silvie,	12
4. Tout' ingratte qu'elle est J'adore son pouvoir	12
5. Et quand je ne ferois que l'Aymer et la voir	12
6. Je seray trop heureux le reste de ma vie.	12
7. Quand je voudrois pour me vanger	8
8. Porter mon Cœur à la changer	8
9. Au lieu de m'obeir il deviendroit rebelle,	12
10. Et bien qu'il ayt perdu tout espoir d'estre aymé	12
11. Il est à la servir si bien accoustumé	12
12. Qu'il consent d'expirer plustost qu'estre Infidelle.	12

(First Strophe: I would rather suffer death / Than make the least effort / To disengage my heart from Silvie's chains, // Ingrate that she is, I adore her power / Even if I could only love her and see her / I would be exceedingly happy the rest of my life.)

(Second Strophe: Even if I wanted in order to avenge myself / To make my heart change [toward] her / Instead of obeying me it becomes rebellious, // And even though it has lost all hope of being loved / It is so accustomed to serving her / That it consents to die rather than be unfaithful.)

A few pieces belong to a third type of song, "enticing love." In these, the speaker attempts to seduce his object of desire into loving him by various means. He appeals to logic in this air (Lambert, "Puisque chacun doit aymer à son tour," *Les Airs,* p. 52):

LINE NUMBER	SYLLABLE COUNT
1. Puisque chacun doit aymer à son tour	10
2. Philis pourquoy vous en defendre,	8
3. Si vous avez des yeux pour donner de l'amour	12
4. Vous avez un Cœur pour en prendre.	8
5. Si c'est un mal que c'est un mal charmant	10
6. Et qu'il donne un plaisir extreme,	8
7. Pour l'Esprouver Philis vous n'avez seulement	12
8. Qu'a m'aymer comme Je vous ayme.	8

(First Strophe: Since each must have a turn at love / Philis, why defend yourself against it, // If you have eyes for giving love / You have a heart for taking it.)

(Second Strophe: If it is an evil, it is a charming evil / And what an extreme pleasure it gives, // To experience it Philis you have only / To love me as I love you.)

A fourth type of song is one in which the speaker describes the joys of being in love without any complicating circumstances, or as in this example, the loveliness of his beloved. Bacilly's "Petit abeille mesnagere" (*Les Trois livres d'airs,* I:58) is typical in its pastoral references:

LINE NUMBER	SYLLABLE COUNT
1. Petite abeille mesnagere	8
2. Si vous ne cherchez que des fleurs	8

3. Approchez vous de ma bergere   8
4. Vous pourrez bien vous satisfaire   8
5. Sa belle bouche a des douceurs   8
6. Que l'on ne trouve point ailleurs.   8

(Little busy bee / If you are only looking for flowers // Draw near to my shepherdess / You will be able to satisfy yourself / Her beautiful mouth has pleasures / That one does not find elsewhere.)

Airs belonging to the first two categories, painful and bittersweet love, were referred to as serious. The remaining two types, enticing and joyous love, were labeled light because they reveal either flirtatious behavior or pleasurable experiences with love.[62] Génetiot and Pelous discovered the same differentiation in other sources: tender love, corresponding to painful or bittersweet love, and *galant* love, corresponding to enticing or pleasurable love. According to Génetiot, all textual representations of tender love "utilize a finite number of commonplaces, of themes and motifs which always carry with them the same images and the same figured language and which serve precisely to define the 'love genre,' a serious genre *par excellence.*"[63] In these texts, the female is represented as perfect, an ideal woman, but she is also cruel in her treatment of the speaker (the literary *je* or "I" in these texts, referred to as the lover or *l'amant* by Génetiot and Pelous).[64] By contrast, *galant* love is represented as a game without serious consequences.[65] "*Galant* discourse re-establishes the equilibrium between men and women by refusing the tradition that formerly placed the lover at the feet of his woman."[66] Both Génetiot and Pelous note that the *galant* discourse operates as a "parasitism of the serious discourse."[67] It draws upon the traditional "codes" of language and figures found in the serious texts but puts them into a new context, creating a "system void of its contents."[68] Most of Génetiot's examples of *galant* love poetry are wittier, more ironic, and cruder than the texts found in the collections of airs by Lambert, Bacilly, La Barre, and La Camus. Only two aspects of his description pertain to these airs: the equilibrium established between the man and woman, and the "frivolous" representation of love as a game.

Even though the application of the terms *tendre* and *galant* is useful to our understanding of the French air, it is important to keep in mind that a piece can be both *tendre* and *galant*, depending upon whether or not these terms are defined narrowly or broadly. In English, tenderness connotes a mild emotion of fondness, but during the seventeenth century, it was a catchword for every imaginable emotion connected to being in love. Furetière defines *tendresse* as

> a sensitivity of the heart and the soul. The refinement of the century has limited this word to love and friendship. Lovers speak only about the tenderness of the heart, either in prose or in verse; and in fact this word most often signifies love; and when one says, I have tender feelings for you, that is to say, I have much love.[69]

Bacilly also uses *tendre* to refer to love and all the passions associated with this complex emotion: *mouvement,* which Bacilly defines as that quality of music that expresses and evokes passion, "can inspire the hearts of the listeners with whatever passion the singer might wish to evoke and mainly the passion of tenderness."[70] His usage of the word "tenderness" does not imply a moderate feeling of love but rather an expression of intense emotion.

Even though *galant* can refer to a "light" air, we must also keep in mind the broader meaning of this word: a style that was both serious and playful, enabling writers to use a lighthearted tone even though addressing serious and philosophical issues. Bacilly adds, for example, another layer of meaning to the designations "light" or "gallant" and "weighty" or "tender." He writes: "Lightness gives something to singing which is called the '*galant* tone' [or quality], while gravity gives strength to serious pieces which demand much more expression."[71] Bacilly implies here that it is the tone of the voice, not necessarily the depth of meaning, which differentiates the *galant* from the *tendre*. As we shall see in chapter 7, an air, or any other literary work for that matter, written in the so-called *galant* style can offer messages with several levels of meaning such that a seemingly insignificant text (and musical setting) could actually relay an erotic, morally significant, politically charged, or socially subversive message, and perhaps even communicate more than one meaning simultaneously. Thus a serious air may be classified as "tender," therefore passionate, but it can also be "*galant,*" meaning that there may be layers of meaning.

Many song texts, whether labeled *tendre* or *galant,* contain pastoral references. In some serious airs, such references are limited to the use of bucolic names such as Tircis, Silvie, or Philis. These names were taken either from the Italian *pastorales* of the late sixteenth century or French imitations from the early seventeenth century. The most influential French work of this kind was *L'Astrée* by Honoré d'Urfé.[72] In the drinking song "Je suis bien las d'entendre," Bacilly pokes fun at the insipid use in serious airs of pastoral names and their connection to pain and suffering in matters of the heart. He prefers "real" women's names, such as Aminte and Margot, names that rhyme with *pinte* and *pot,* types of containers used for drinking alcohol:[73]

> *Je suis bien las d'entendre*
> *Parler d'Amarilis,*
> *De Cloris, de Silvandre,*
> *D'Amarante et de Philis:*
> *J'ayme le nom d'Aminte,*
> *Et celui de Margot:*
> *C'est que l'un rime à pinte,*
> *Et l'autre rime à pot.*
>
> *Le nom de Celimeine,*
> *Et celuy de Cloris,*
> *Ne produisent que peine,*
> *Que rigueurs, que mespris:*
> *J'ayme le nom d'Amynthe,*
> *Et celuy de Margot:*
> *C'est que l'un rime à pinte,*
> *Et l'autre rime à pot.*

(First Strophe: I am tired of hearing [everyone] / Speak of Amarilis, / Of Cloris, of Silvandre, / Of Amarante and of Philis: / I love the name of Aminte, / And that of Margot: / Because one rhymes with pint, / And the other rhymes with *pot* [a mug].)

(Second Strophe: The name of Celimeine, / And that of Cloris, / Produce only pain, / Only rigors, only contempt: / I love the name Amynthe, / And that of Margot: / Because one rhymes with pint, / And the other rhymes with *pot.*)

More extended pastoral images in serious airs include references to the countryside, particularly dark and gloomy forests, where the lover goes to suffer in solitude when experiencing the pain of unrequited love, a disease called erotic melancholia or lovesickness. In La Barre's air "Forests, solitaires et sombres" (*Airs à deux parties,* 3v), for example, the lover laments his unfaithful beloved and seeks out the shadows and solitude of the forest where he is able to complain openly of his pain:

Music and the Language of Love

LINE NUMBER	SYLLABLE COUNT
1. Forests solitaires et sombres,	8
2. Sejour du silence et des ombres,	8
3. Lieux affreux steriles deserts:	8
4. Aprenez le sujet de ma douleur mortelle,	12
5. Helas! je suis trahy de celle que je sers,	12
6. Mon Iris est une infidelle.	8

(Solitary and somber forests, / Dwelling for silence and shadows, / Terrifying places and barren deserts: // Learn about the cause of my mortal pain, / Alas! I am betrayed by the one I serve, / My Iris is unfaithful.)

According to Doctor Ferrand, author of *A Treatise on Lovesickness,* when suffering from the disease, seeking solitude is the worst thing a lover can do: "Solitude brought no better relief to Phyllis, Echo, Pan, and many others. . . . Indeed I would disapprove it as a cure for this disease,"[74] for those left in solitude and seclusion will be carried away by lust.

By contrast, in light airs, the countryside is portrayed as a place where lovers can find the privacy necessary to express their love. In this air by Le Camus (*Airs à deux et trois parties,* p. 22), the lover wishes his shepherdess were present so that they could enjoy the delights of summer:

LINE NUMBER	SYLLABLE COUNT
1. Delices des Estez,	6
2. Frais et sombres boccages,	6
3. Qui ne sçauriez charmer mon amoureux soucy;	12
4. Que j'aymerois vos doux ombrages	8
5. Si ma Bergere estoit icy.	8

(Summers pleasures, / Cool and dark thicket, / Who would not know how to charm my amorous unease. / How I would love your sweet shadows / If my shepherdess were here.)

Often light airs contain references to sheep, a shepherd's dog, fields, musettes, and so forth. A bucolic ambience may set the scene, or natural elements may be used metaphorically, as in "Petite abeille mesnagere," cited above.

Pastoral images, references to gallant and tender love, the influence of salon culture, as well as the meaning and use of conventional metaphors related to love are complicated and significant concepts related to the air which warrant greater scrutiny than that given in this overview. As such, these issues are addressed at length in the final two chapters of this book.

Poetic Structure

Most song texts, serious or light, are strophic, whether in binary or rondeau form. Each strophe or stanza is called a couplet, defined as a group of free verses or lines that form a system of complete rhymes.[75] The number of strophes varies. Most serious airs consist of two strophes, while light airs could include several.[76] Bacilly's "A l'ombre de ce bocage," from the category of joyous love, for example, comprises four strophes. In serious airs, the second couplet is typically needed to complete the sense of the text,[77] while in light airs, the second or subsequent couplets are often used to expand upon the topic (a rhetorical device known as *amplificatio*).

A strophe must demonstrate a system of complete rhymes.[78] Although patterns of rhymes are varied in this repertory, one of the most common schemes is a rhyme that occurs in every other line, as in "Je voys des amans" (*Les Trois livres d'airs*, I:8) by Bacilly. La Croix called this type of scheme *batalée*;[79] it is also called *croisée*.[80]

First Strophe

LINE NUMBER	SYLLABLE COUNT	RHYME
1. Je voy des amans chaque jour	8	a
2. Sans crainte des rigueurs découvrir leur martire	12	b
3. Mais de tout ce qu'on dit dans l'Empire d'Amour	12	a
4. L'Adieu belle Philis couste de plus à dire.	12	b

Second Strophe

5. Chacun peut donner un beau tour	8	a
6. Au discours qui fait voir que son ame soûpire	12	b

7. Mais pour bien dire adieu dans l'Empire
   d'amour   12   a
8. C'est aimable Philis la mort qui le doit dire. 12   b

(I see lovers each day / Without fear of misfortune discover their martyrdom // But of all that one says in the Empire of love / Farewell, beautiful Philis, costs the most to say.)

(Each can give a beautiful turn / Of phrase which shows that one's soul is sighing // But to really say farewell in the Empire of love / It is, kind Philis, death who must say it.)

Almost any combination of rhyme per strophe is possible.[81] Bacilly's "Le Printemps est de retour" (*Les Trois livres d'airs*, I:56) shows the "abab" scheme extended to six lines (a sixain), while Lambert's "Jugez si ma peine est extreme" (*Les Airs de Monsieur Lambert*, p. 28) demonstrates the scheme "abbaa."[82]

First Strophe

LINE NUMBER	SYLLABLE COUNT	RHYME
1. Le Printemps est de retour	7	a
2. Tout rid dans ce bocage	6	b
3. Et des oiseaux nuit et jours	7	a
4. On entend le ramage	6	b
5. Iris pour faire l'Amour	7	a
6. En faut-il d'avantage.	6	b

(Spring has returned / All is laughing in these woods / And night and day / One hears the songs of the birds // Iris, in order to be in love / Must one do something more.)

First Strophe

LINE NUMBER	SYLLABLE COUNT	RHYME
1. Jugez si ma peine est extreme	8	a
2. Philis je vous sers constamment,	8	b
3. Vous me fuyez incessamment	8	b
4. Et je sçay qu'un autre vous ayme	8	a
5. Jugez si ma peine est extreme.	8	a

Second Strophe

6. Helas ne suis je pas à plaindre	8	c
7. Sans cesse on me void soûpirer,	8	d
8. Je n'ay jamais lieu d'esperer	8	d
9. Et j'ay tousjours sujet de craindre	8	c
10. Helas ne suis je pas à plaindre.	8	c

(Judge if my pain is extreme / Philis, I serve you faithfully, // You incessantly avoid me / And I know that another loves you / Judge if my pain is extreme.)

(Alas am I not to complain / One sees me sighing without end, // I never have grounds for hope / And I still have reason to fear / Alas am I not to complain.)

Most lyric poetry presents a mixture of masculine and feminine rhymes. Feminine rhymes are those that end with a mute "e," as in lines one, four, and five of "Jugez si ma peine est extreme," given above. Lines two and three of this text end with masculine rhymes. Occasionally, a poet will use only one or the other type to produce a particular affect. La Croix, for example, suggested masculine rhymes for expressions of joy and feminine rhymes for sadness.[83]

The number of lines or verses per strophe varies, with a few exceptions. Sarabandes, for example, are made up of four lines (a quatrain), while courantes are comprised of twelve, and passacaglias (*passacailles*) or chaconnes, six (a sixain).[84] The number of lines varies from four to nineteen in the four collections.[85] While light and cheerful songs often favor an equal number of verses or lines (usually four, six, or eight) per strophe, serious airs contain either an odd *or* even number. Bacilly's "Je voys des amans chaque jour" and "Le Printemps est de retour," containing four and six lines per strophe, respectively, are of the former type, and Lambert's "Jugez si ma peine est extreme," with five lines, the latter.

The number of syllables per line also varies. For this reason, lyric poetry is referred to as irregular verse (*vers irréguliers*).[86] La Croix writes: "The *chansons* must be considered as a sort of irregular verse, which is appropriate only for singing, because they have a different number of syllables [per line]."[87] Every syllable is counted as one. The final syllable of a word ending with a vowel (feminine words) is not counted when it is followed by a word beginning with a vowel,[88] as in "peine est" from line one of "Jugez si ma peine est extreme." Here, two syllables are counted instead of three, the second "e" of *peine* being elided with the "e" of *est*. Feminine endings are also not counted if they appear at the end of a line, as in the word *extreme* from "Jugez si ma peine est extreme." Here, two syllables are counted in the word *extreme*. If this word were found within the line of poetry and not followed by a word beginning with a vowel, it would equal three syllables.

In the publications under consideration, serious airs usually contain an even number of syllables, usually eight, ten, or twelve. Twelve-syllable lines, called alexandrines, were also used in the grandest of poetic genres such as tragedies; ten-syllable lines were called commons (*communs*); and eight-syllable lines were said to be the oldest kind of French verse.[89] Light songs, on the other hand, typically contain an odd number of syllables per line, usually five, seven, nine, or eleven. Sometimes verses or lines in either type of air have the same number of syllables, as in the song "Jugez si ma peine est extreme," but most often the syllable count varies from line to line, as in "Le Printemps est de retour" and "Je voys des amans," cited above.

Typically, each verse or line of a strophe divides into smaller units. Longer lines, usually of eight syllables or more, are split into two parts with a break or caesura occurring between each. "The caesura is a certain pause, which divides or separates the verse into two parts of which each is called a hemistich or half-verse."[90] An alexandrine, a twelve-syllable line, divides equally into two parts of six syllables each. The caesura, however, is not always placed in the middle. An eight-syllable line can be divided after four syllables or after five. The significance of the number of syllables and placement of caesura will be discussed at length in chapter 2.

Style or Elocution:
Figurative Language and Poetic Syntax

Literary style refers to diction (choice of words) and syntax (how words are put together to form phrases, sentences, and so forth). Style was determined, in part, by genre, such that the writing of oratory, history, or poetry would each entail a different approach. Poetry required a special type of language directed toward awakening the auditors' senses and captivating their attention.[91] Poets needed to use conventional and understandable expressions in order to "form in the Imagination the picture of the thing that is to be conceived" through the proper images and impressions wrought from a special figurative language.[92] La Croix distinguished between figures of speech used in oratory and those used in poetry. In oratory, figures represent "the agitations of the soul, . . . these figures are . . . violent and appropriate for fighting and winning over minds which are opposed to the truth."[93] Poetic expressions, by contrast, are to be tranquil so as to give pleasure and move the passions of listeners.[94]

Figures, generally speaking, are textual devices in which meaning is changed or enhanced.[95] In this repertory, schemes—figures in which the words retain their literal meaning but are placed in a special arrangement—appear from time to time.[96] Repetition, for example, is a scheme commonly found in the airs in a variety of forms. In "Jugez si ma peine est extreme," cited above, for example, the first line of each strophe is repeated as the last line. Often composers repeated textual phrases for emphasis (even though the phrase is not repeated in the poem); for example, Bacilly repeats the last two lines of each strophe, "Mon cœur ne la sçauroit quitter" and "Qu'un fidelle aime un inconstant" in the air "Mon sort est digne de pitié."[97] Another figure, the exclamation, is frequently used in airs, particularly "Hélas!" (lines six and ten of "Jugez si ma peine est extreme") and "Ah!," as in line four of Lambert's "Que me sert-il": "Ah! c'est trop se flatter" (Ah! I am only deceiving myself).[98] Antithesis (antansgoge) is integral to bittersweet pieces. With this figure, two or more favorable or unfavorable alternatives are juxtaposed. In "J'aymerois mieux," cited above, the poetic voice has two alternatives: to suffer death or to cease loving his beloved. Though he suffers, the speaker chooses to be happy just to see her. In Bacilly's "Mon sort est digne de pitié," present and past events are juxtaposed along with pity and envy. His fate *is* worthy of pity as much as it *was* worthy of envy.

In addition to schemes, poets also used tropes or figures, in which one word is used to mean something other than its usual meaning.[99] Metaphor is the standard trope found throughout the repertory. Death, for example, seemingly refers in airs to the endless torments suffered in love, but it can also mean literal death, the final stage of the disease erotic melancholia, as described by doctors.[100] Death can also stand for orgasm, fantasized or real.[101] Other metaphors include references to "the empire of love" (in which love can be conceived as a specific country or region, as in Madeleine de Scudéry's *Carte de Tendre* from her novel *Clélie, histoire romaine,* published in 1654),[102] fire, heat, or burning (referring to sexual arousal), the beloved's eyes (through which one is afflicted with lovesickness), and combat (often used to mean the aroused lover's pursuit of the beloved or the actual act of lovemaking). A speaker may also use pastoral references metaphorically, as in "Petite abeille mesnagere," given above, wherein the speaker compares his love to a flower.[103]

The style of a text was determined to a great extent by the subject of the poem. In classifying works, most seventeenth-century rhetoricians and poets observed Cicero's three stylistic categories appropriate to various subjects: the sublime, or grand; the moderate, or middle; and the plain, or simple.[104] The sublime style is used for heroic subjects, such as combats, sieges, wars, princes, and heroes. According to Lamy, the sublime style was apropos for the following:

> When things are great and cannot be considered without great Emotion, it is necessary that the Style which describes them be sprightly, full of motion, and inriched [sic] with Figures, and Tropes, and Metaphors.[105]

La Croix also asserts that when the subject is dignified, "filling the soul of the poet with . . . esteem and admiration, his discourse cannot be equal; it must be interrupted by different passions, by which his spirit is moved."[106] Conversely, when the subject does not cause such a reaction, the style must be simple or plain.[107] The plain style, then, is appropriate for common and ordinary things and makes use of familiar terms. Lamy and La Croix both assert that common subjects are treated "without passion" and do not call for many figures and tropes.[108] While La Croix did not mention the moderate style at all, Lamy claims, without much more explanation, that the middle style falls somewhere between the two extremes.[109]

Seventeenth-century rhetoricians and theorists offer little help with an assessment of style and amorous lyrical poetry. Lamy and La Croix avoid categorizing song texts altogether, and even Perrin, who refers directly to the lyric, treats it in an ambiguous manner. He distinguishes three styles that seem to correspond to the traditional three cited above, and then further divides these into six by assigning the three traditional categories of style to representations of sorrow *and* of joy:

> As for styles, since the soul touched by feelings of sorrow or joy may be strongly moved [the sublime style?], may languish [the moderate?], or may feel a moderate emotion [the plain?], . . . I have distinguished six kinds of style: the passionate joyous,

languishing joyous, temperate joyous; . . . the overwhelmingly
sorrowful, the languishing, and the restrained.[110]

He notes that he has

endeavoured to make it [his lyric] elevated and poetic, but
in moderation, and without exaggerated hyperboles, allusions to too-unfamiliar myths, or far-fetched or uncommon
metaphors.[111]

The serious songs by Lambert, Bacilly, La Barre, and Le Camus conform to Perrin's "overwhelmingly sorrowful or languishing" categories, which suggests a link to the sublime or moderate styles. Even
though these airs do not describe subjects appropriate to the sublime
style (heroic themes), there is a moderate use of figurative language.
The serious airs are also impassioned. The light songs, by contrast, are
either "restrained, languishing joyous, or temperate joyous," which
suggests two stylistic designations: medium and light. The light airs
concern "ordinary" or non-elevated topics treated in a pastoral manner
(usually love in springtime or the charms of a lover). These aspects of
love as represented in the airs do not elicit a great variety of passions,
nor make use of much figurative language.

While serious and light airs differ in subject matter, use of figures, and level of affective intensity, there is one aspect of style that
is common to both: syntax. Phrases in lyric poetry are so concise that
no line of text can be spared without its absence rendering the poem
incongruous.[112] Each line usually has a subject and verb (which rhetoricians referred to as *hypozeuxis*), yet few lines of the poetry make
sense by themselves. Each verse is called a "member," or incomplete
phrase which expresses a particular sense, yet it cannot stand alone.
The longest members are the ten- and twelve-syllable lines. Each hemistich, which divides the verse in half, is called a measure; thus, each
member is comprised of two measures.[113] Alexandrines, for example,
are twelve-syllable members that divide equally into two measures,
six syllables each. Members are joined to contribute to the sense of
the entire period (or sentence) which, in Bernard Lamy's view, should
be at least two and at most four members long (equalling two to four
lines of poetry).[114] Periods (usually two) are then combined to form
larger units, which in these pieces form a strophe. The total number of
strophes, then, renders the expression of the entire text complete.

Frequently, several members are grouped together, as in "Que me sert-il" from *Les Airs de Monsieur Lambert* (p. 44), which comprises two six-line strophes.

LINE NUMBER	SYLLABLE COUNT

First Strophe

1. Que me sert-il d'estre fidelle	8
2. De languir nuit et jour pour elle	8
3. Si l'Ingratte ne m'ayme pas,	8
4. Ah c'est trop se flatter d'une Esperance vaine	12
5. Il vault mieux par un prompt trespas	8
6. Finir mon Amour et sa hayne.	8

Second Strophe

7. Ce seroit me tromper moy mesme	8
8. De penser que mon mal extreme	8
9. A la pitié peut l'esmouvoir	8
10. En l'estat ou je suis n'ayons plus d'autre envie	12
11 Aprés avoir perdu l'espoir	8
12 Que celle de perdre la vie.	8

(Of what use is it for me to be faithful / To languish night and day for her / If the Ingrate does not love me, // Ah I am only deceiving myself with a vain hope / It is better to die a quick death / To put an end to my love and her hate.)

(I would be fooling myself / To think that my extreme misfortune / Can move her to pity, // In the condition I am in let us have no other desire / After having lost hope / Than that of dying.)

The first three lines, or members, of the piece (all eight syllables long) form a complete thought (a sentence, or period) and serve as an introduction. If the speaker's beloved does not love him, why be faithful and languish night and day? The pattern of eight-syllable lines is broken by the twelve-syllable verse, line four, which underscores the primary topic of the poem. He is deceiving himself; he hopes in vain for her love. It follows, then, that the only alternative is to die a quick death and put an end to his love and her hate, lines (members) five and six. The first strophe, then, is divided into two sections or periods of three members each. The first sets up the situation; the second proposes a solution.

The second strophe is divided in the same manner. The first three lines parallel the ideas presented in the introduction, lines one to three, and expand upon the theme of self-deception. The speaker is only fooling himself if he thinks that his beloved is moved by his misfortune, as explained in the introduction (she does not love him, so he languishes night and day). The final three lines parallel the last three of the first strophe and serve as the conclusion. Here, the solution to the problem, as presented in the first strophe, is reinforced. After losing hope, there is no other solution than death.

Poetry and Rhetoric

Although the relationship of song text and musical setting to principles of rhetoric is addressed at length in the following chapters, many references to rhetoric were made in this chapter. Indeed, lyric poetry, and by extension the air, was considered a type of rhetorical discourse. As Alain Génetiot confirms in his book *Poétique du loisir mondain:*

> Poetry is also above all a second rhetoric, which suitably unites the ornaments of style and the story whose first goal is, as all works of eloquence, to have an effect on the listener, even if it is only a question of pleasing him.[115]

He goes on to say that during the seventeenth century, the poet continues to share the same goals as the orator: to instruct, to move, and to please.[116] In the following chapters, we will see just how close the relationship between rhetoric, poetry, and music is—how orators, poets, and composers shared similar strategies in their quest to communicate with, move, and please the auditor.

CHAPTER TWO

Rhetoric and Meaning in the Seventeenth-Century French Air

Seventeenth-Century French Sources on Rhetoric and Music

In France, the connection between rhetoric and music was first made explicit by members of the Neoplatonic academies of the sixteenth century.[1] For the academicians, all intellectual and artistic activity was part of a graded hierarchy of knowledge leading to the ultimate cognizance of God. Divine truth was pictured at the summit of a mountain; thus, "raising the intellect" meant that one ascended the mountain, step by step, reaching an even higher level of understanding until ultimate truth, or God, was revealed at the top. All disciplines, such as the arts of rhetoric and poetry and the science of music, were symbolically placed at the base of the mountain; yet four steps from its summit (God), the union of poetry and music, referred to as the first of the four "divine enthusiasms," held a crucial position. After mastering all disciplines, thereby achieving an encyclopedic grasp of knowledge, one ascended to this level. It was here that rhetoric became relevant to poetry and music. Through universal understanding, disorder was transformed into order and discord into harmony by the measured tones of music.[2] Music and poetry purified the minds of the listeners and made them ready to be initiated into the higher levels of knowledge, where all truths are united.[3]

The academicians sought to restore "both the kind of poetry and the measure and rule of music anciently used by the Greeks and Romans."[4] As expressed in Plato's *Republic,* the function of music, in union with poetry, was to bring order and moral discipline to society. Composers who belonged to the Neoplatonic academies, in their attempt to imitate the music of Plato's time, created *musique mesurée,* relying heavily upon quantitative rhythms (the ancient rhythmic modes, or patterns of short and long rhythmic values) over melodic or harmonic means.[5] Music was meant to soothe the soul of the listener rather than move the more agitated passions; thus, the academicians maintained that through this special music, peace and order could be sustained in a society where all religions and philosophies would be reconciled.[6]

The sixteenth-century academicians' view of the encyclopedic relation of rhetoric, poetry, and music, with its religious overtones, continued to some degree into the seventeenth century.[7] But the importance given to vocal music by the Neoplatonic academicians as a valid subject in the company of philosophy, poetics, and rhetoric did not continue, which perhaps explains why most seventeenth-century scholars did not consider music in their treatises on these subjects.[8] Whereas in the previous century, the purpose of vocal music, in theory, was to restore spiritual equilibrium and prepare the listener for spiritual and intellectual enlightenment, during the seventeenth century it was thought suitable primarily for providing pleasure and expressing passions.[9] During the sixteenth century, the most important poets wrote lyric poetry and the primary poetic forms were also musical forms; yet during the following century, poets generally felt limited and constrained by musical considerations.[10] As the most prominent poetic genres, such as tragedy, were not musical, they were less restrictive than lyric genres. Seventeenth-century scholars, especially those later in the century, generally considered prose to be the natural language for conveying subjects such as philosophy or the natural sciences.[11] Rhetoric was considered a most significant discipline, particularly when applied to prose.[12] Indeed, Bernard Crampé, in his article "De Arte Rhetorica," argues that of all the ideals espoused by sixteenth-century humanists, rhetoric was the only one that "gained momentum" during the seventeenth century.[13] And in *Descartes and the Resilience of Rhetoric: Varieties of Cartesian Rhetorical Theory*, Thomas Carr shows that even though René Descartes, Nicolas Malebranche, and Jansenists Antoine Arnauld and Pierre Nicole criticized empty rhetoric that only disguised truth through false eloquence, they all, with the exception of Descartes, recognized that the art of rhetoric was useful if used in a way that led people to truth in God.[14]

If mentioned at all in seventeenth-century treatises on rhetoric or poetics, the relationship between these two disciplines to music is specified within the context of Neoplatonic platitudes.[15] Thus, concepts and ideals that once had significance for the sixteenth-century scholar lost their meaning, becoming mere decoration. In "The Worm in the Apple," Philippe Desan describes this phenomenon metaphorically, using the legend of the golden apple from the garden of the Hesperides.[16] The golden apple symbolizes the humanist ideals of the Renaissance. The inside of the apple represents content and the peel, form. Desan explains that by the time the French discovered the Italian Renaissance (the apple) at the end of the fifteenth century, there was already a worm eating away at it from the inside. By the beginning of the seventeenth century in France, all that remained of the apple (the content of humanist thought) was the peel (its form), the worm having eaten all the way through. An example of this phenomenon is "Monsieur Le Grand"'s brief recollection of the ancient alliance of music and poetry (a story often referred to during the seventeenth century) in the "Discours sur la rhétorique" which precedes René Bary's treatise on rhetoric, *La Rhétorique françoise.*[17] In ancient times, poets, whose works were accompanied by music, were considered the interpreters of the gods. They were able to "civilize stupid and savage men" ("Ils [the poets] polirent des hommes stupides et sauvages") with their works.[18]

Only two scholars (one from the late seventeenth century and one from the early eighteenth century) consider music in any detail in their treatises on poetics and rhetoric: Phérotée de La Croix and Jean-Léonor Le Gallois de Grimarest. Part 3 of La Croix's treatise *L'Art de la poësie françoise* (1694) is entitled "Idée de la Musique" and begins with a Neoplatonic account of *musique universelle* and the power of God's music to rid the world of evil demons.[19] The principal function of music should be to praise God, convert the heretics, and heal the sick. La Croix refers as well to the alliance of ancient music and poetry and recalls the stories of Orpheus, Timothy, and Amphion, illustrating his contention that the link between poetry and music is "so essential, that it would be impossible to treat one separately from the other."[20] After these brief remarks on *harmonie universelle,* he addresses several theoretical matters that are not found in most treatises on music, including the classification of musical genres, the nature and properties of sound, and the relationship between numbers and the soul. In the fifth section La Croix makes the link between rhetoric and music, "the marvelous relation between numbers and our soul": to succeed in the arts of music and persuasion, one must be able to move the passions by imitating impassioned speech.[21]

Like La Croix, Grimarest also considers vocal music in the last section of his *Traité du récitatif* (1707) and relates musical expression to impassioned recitation. Grimarest defines vocal music as "a kind of language, which men agree upon in order to communicate their thoughts and sentiments with more pleasure."[22] Because most of the chapter concerns matters of recitation, he stresses that in singing, as in declaiming, proper syllable lengths must be observed. He also points out that musical compositions must conform to the points of punctuation, figures, and passions expressed in the text.[23]

The writings of Marin Mersenne provide the most thorough explanation of the relationship between music and rhetoric; indeed, he was the only seventeenth-century music theorist in France to provide specific information on the connections between rhetoric, poetry, and musical composition and performance (information he included throughout the body of his works). Of all seventeenth-century writers on music, he was the one most heavily influenced by the philosophical views of the late-sixteenth-century academicians.[24] Mersenne, for example, refers to "perfect" music as *musique accentuelle,* which is the "natural and universal" language of the passions. In order to understand precisely this special brand of music, "one must know all the other sciences," including grammar, rhetoric, history, poetry, dialectics, physics, moral philosophy, architecture, and moral philosophy.[25] For Mersenne, music should not only be expressive and captivating, it should also "fill the learned listeners with admiration and lead them to search for the cause [God] of such a remarkable effect."[26]

On a more practical level, Mersenne, referring to the creation of vocal music, equates the various aspects of musical composition and performance with the different parts of rhetoric. In *Harmonie universelle,* he urges composers to "imitate harangues in all their members, divisions, and periods, and to use all kinds of figures and harmonic embellishments, as does the orator, so that the art of composing melodies will concede nothing to rhetoric."[27] Throughout his works, he describes the association between various musical devices and the passions and argues that composers must devise all musical ideas, such as melodic intervals and harmonic and rhythmic devices, according to the ideas set forth in the text and, more importantly, the emotions represented by these ideas.[28] This step is equivalent to what rhetoricians called *inventio,* or invention, which Mersenne deemed most crucial to the compositional process.

Mersenne also discusses the arrangement of music materials (what rhetoricians labeled *dispositio,* or disposition), pointing out that the ordering of material must heighten the expressive impact of the piece.[29] Mersenne compares the style of an oration (*elocutio,* or elocution) to a musical work as well, and stresses that musical phrases have to conform to the phrase construction of the text. He likens different types of cadences to different kinds of punctuation marks that correspond to demarcations of clauses and sentences.[30] Finally, Mersenne devotes an entire chapter of *Harmonie universelle,* "Embellishment des chants," to aspects of the performance of vocal music, particularly matters of rhythm.

While other scholars were disregarding music, Mersenne searched throughout his life for a means of validating it.[31] Neoclassical theories of art empowered "the word" as subject to reasonable judgment, and like his contemporaries, Mersenne began by proposing that art must be founded on reason. He ended up, however, by declaring that art should be founded upon feeling and rejected the view that the word, as representative of reason, could perfectly interpret the human experience. Language was arbitrary, but sounds associated with the expressions of passions were universal; thus, music was closest to natural expression because the rhythms and sounds of music were based upon the natural signs of the passions. While others condemned music for this reason, Mersenne (who was seemingly ahead of his time) elevated music to a special status because of its affinity to nature.[32]

Just as most rhetoricians and philosophers ignored music, most writers on music disregarded its philosophical-aesthetic aspects altogether, including the Neoplatonic view of music's role in the search for universal truth.[33] Most treatises on music written during the seventeenth century were either instruction books about performance issues or rudimentary accounts of composition. Writers of music treatises such as La Voye Mignot or Charles Masson offer only little tidbits of information about aesthetic issues pertaining to music.[34] Indeed, writing in 1704, Lecerf de la Viéville claims that his work was the first treatise to consider musical aesthetics:

> I have often thought that, although we have in our language enough treatises on music, we have none that enters into a discussion of the beauty of our music. There are only treatises concerned with mechanics and craftsmanship, if I may say so; treatises which teach the rules in a dry manner, and of these none teaches us how to feel the esteem we ought to have for compositions in which these rules are observed. None leads *honnêtes gens* to judge as a whole the worth of a symphony or air. I believe there would be some merit and some glory in being the first to write a treatise of this nature.[35]

Only a few writers before Lecerf mention the relationship of rhetoric to music.[36] Michel de Saint-Lambert was the first author after

Mersenne to describe the affinity between musical works and discourse in any detail in *Les principes du clavecin* (1702):[37]

> A piece of music resembles, more or less, an oration, or rather, it is an oration which resembles a piece of music: because the harmony, the rhythm, the meter, and the other similar things that a clever orator observes in composing his works belong more naturally to music than rhetoric.[38]

In the following brief (and frequently quoted) statement, Saint-Lambert relates the form and stylistic features of an oration to the components of a piece of music.

> An oration has its whole, which is most often composed of several parts; each part is composed of sentences, each having a complete meaning; these sentences are composed of phrases, phrases of words, and the words of letters. In the same way, the melody of a piece of music has its whole, which is always composed of several sections. Each section is composed of cadences, each having their own complete meaning, which are the sentences of the melody. The cadences are often composed of phrases, the phrases of measures, and the measures of notes. Thus the notes correspond to the letters, and the measure to the words, the cadences to periods, the sections to the parts, and the whole to the whole.[39]

Bénigne de Bacilly's work might be considered more typical of seventeenth-century treatises on music in its emphasis upon rhetoric and performance issues; however, he does offer the scholar of vocal music and the singer a wealth of information related to aesthetics and other practical matters. In *Remarques curieuses de l'art de bien chanter* (1668), he states that the performance of vocal music is analogous to the declamation of an oration, alluding only to one aspect of rhetoric, *actio* or *pronunciatio*. Bacilly points out that a musician "must know how to sing well and declaim well at the same time."[40] In the second part of his treatise, he claims that vocal music is a kind of declamation and suggests that the rules he gives regarding syllable lengths also apply to the declamation of French poetry and prose. Singing and pronouncing a discourse are related, so that

> when it comes to reciting, singing, or declaiming some verse in proper fashion, it is obvious that differing syllable-lengths must be observed not only in poetry but also in prose.[41]

The emphasis in music treatises upon the fifth part of rhetoric, declamation, underscores the dominance of performance over composition in the seventeenth-century musical experience and reflects a division between the practice and theory of music.[42] Indeed, Étienne Loulié writes in a manuscript dating from around 1700 that "theory and practice are not bound one to the other, and it even seems that they are two totally different sciences."[43] While compositional theory still concentrated on explaining vocal counterpoint (a concern inherited from the sixteenth century which did not apply to most seventeenth-century genres), the connection of rhetoric to music during this period was, in effect, an attempt to set a rational theory of musical composition.[44] In France, the relationship between rhetoric and musical composition was first and foremost a practical matter. Songs had to express their texts, and poetry was a type of discourse made up of rhetorical devices that composers needed to respect in their settings. The components of rhetoric, such as the general content of the poem, the sentence structure, points of punctuation, the quality of the vocabulary, the kinds of rhetorical figures, and so forth, necessarily guided and inspired the composer. Rhetoric, which defined every aspect of a text, ruled the compositional process.

More importantly, rhetoric provided composers with a means of fulfilling vocal music's primary aesthetic function: expressing and moving the passions embodied in the song text, which listeners, in turn, found pleasurable.[45] Seventeenth-century rhetorical theory and practice was "profoundly modified" by the "psychological" aspects of persuasion; "the orator must know the passions."[46] Although rhetoricians continued to emphasize that the pursuit of truth should be the primary purpose of oratory, "moving the passions" became an important goal as well. René Bary maintains that prominent orators are great because they know how to express passion ("pousser un mouvement"). He justifies his own treatise on the grounds that it gives examples of passions and figures, which were all that one needed to portray various emotional states.[47] In his treatise, Abbé de Bretteville devotes many pages to the affections and even claims "moving the passions" as the fourth part of rhetoric in place of *memoria,* or memory.[48] Even though rhetoric as a discipline was the subject of controversy, all those writing on rhetoric and eloquence acknowledged that a listener was more apt to be persuaded and/or moved to action through an appeal to the senses.[49]

In many treatises, rhetoricians devote entire sections to descriptions of the passions (as did Aristotle in his treatise on rhetoric) and provide instructions on how they were to be aroused in auditors.[50] Bretteville, Bary, Grimarest, and Le Faucheur, for example, describe passions such as love, hate, desire, hope, fear, anger, and sadness.[51] All four authors acknowledge that the use of figures of speech is essential in moving the affections and explain how different figures and the parts of an oration were to be pronounced or declaimed for the maximum expressive effect.[52]

Bernard Lamy treats the affections in greater detail than do other rhetoricians and demonstrates an indebtedness to Descartes' theory of the passions.[53] In his *L'art de parler*, Lamy makes a conventional distinction between the art of speaking well and the art of persuasion.[54] These two disciplines (eloquence and persuasion) are not to be considered synonymous; to be an effective orator requires that one master both. According to Lamy, the art of persuasion has as a specific goal "to bring People to our Sentiments, that were of a contrary Sentiment before." Yet this cannot be done without mastering the art of speaking well, "for one serves little without the other."[55] He then provides rules for both aspects of rhetoric and includes as the most important feature of his work their effect on the human spirit.[56] In his consideration of eloquence, or the art of speaking well, he calls the figures the "language of the passions" and describes in great detail what emotional response their use could elicit from auditors. *Exclamations* are fierce extensions of the voice which announce a violent and rapid change from one emotion to another. Another figure, *doubt,* indicates that passions are changing "like the waves of the sea," in a perpetual state of indecision.[57] An *ellipsis*, or sudden interruption in the discourse, is a sign of a passion so violent that it does not permit one to say all that one could. *Repetition* is a sign of frustration. People will repeat themselves or explain their thoughts in another way when eager to make their message understood.

In Lamy's treatment of the art of persuasion, he argues in no uncertain terms that only passions can move auditors from indifference and calls them "the Springs of the Mind; when the Orator knows how to possess himself of these Springs, and how to manage them wisely, nothing is hard to him, there is nothing but he can perswade [*sic*]."[58] Exciting passions in the listener was not just a means to an end for an orator. Lamy's definition of the art of persuasion—"to bring People to our Sentiments"—together with his account, "How we may express the Passions and Motions of our Mind," from part 1 of his treatise, emphasize that auditors must be made to *believe* the opinions of the speaker and *feel* the same way about the issues at hand. Moving the passions, therefore, is an important result of persuasion.

Although Lamy considers only language in his treatise, he is also concerned with the physiological and psychological effects of various qualities of sound. His advice can easily be applied to another sound source: music. One seventeenth-century writer, Pherotée de La Croix, did indeed link Lamy's theories to musical sounds. Those sections of La Croix's treatise that concern the relationship of numbers to the soul, the quality of sounds, and the physiological effects of sounds on the body were copied directly from Lamy's treatise, differing only by adding the word music to Lamy's statements. Lamy took his account of making sounds agreeable from Descartes' consideration of music in his "Praenotanda" at the beginning of *Compendium musicae* (1618).[59] Lamy notes that both variety and equality in the movement of sounds "are necessary to . . . make them agreeable, whether it be to the sounds of the voice, or of instruments."[60] La Croix, too, asserts that "in order to make an agreeable sound and thus give pleasure in discourse and in music, one must observe seven things."[61] His list of conditions for making sounds agreeable (that is, variable and equal) matches those given by Lamy and Descartes. Like Lamy, La Croix stresses the effects on the soul of the numerical proportions of speech called *nombre,* or number, and calls a well-proportioned speech a *numerosa oratio* or a harmonious discourse (*discours harmonieux*).[62]

Nombre, or number, refers to the relationship between poetic rhythm and meter. Typically each verse or line of a song text divides into smaller units, which must be reflected in the musical setting. Lambert's setting of "Jugez si ma peine est extreme," Example 2.1, breaks the first line of eight syllables after the fifth syllable, "pei-" of "peine," while the three-syllable unit given to "-n'est extreme" makes up the last part. Sometimes a weaker caesura is placed within the first and second portions of the line, thus cutting it into four parts. Lambert, for example, further divided the first line into these segments: "Jugez / si ma pei-/ n'est ex-/ treme." These verbal units are differentiated in the music most commonly by rhythmic means. In this example, large note values in both melody and bass are given to the final syllable of the first two units. The separation between the third and fourth unit, though more ambiguous, is indicated by the large note value in the bass line (the whole note, beat two of m. 4) and the strong (stressed) syllable "-tre-" of "extreme" which begins the final unit. When singing or reciting a line that contains multiple verbal units, the final syllable of a verbal unit receives a slight stress in relation to the unaccented syllables, often indicated in the music by a change in pitch and a longer note value. Lamy notes that in reciting poetry, each verbal unit (from one caesura to the next) must be pronounced at equal intervals. As such, a portion of the line comprising fewer than three syllables, as in "Jugez si ma peine est extreme," slows down the recitation or movement of the words within the unit. If there are more than three syllables per unit, the movement must accelerate in order to fit more syllables into the same amount of time.[63]

Changes in movement caused by pronouncing varying numbers of syllables to fit into equal intervals of time produce certain affects or passions. Slow movement (fewer syllables per interval) is associated with sorrow, as in "Jugez si ma peine est extreme." Rapid movement, or larger units of four or more syllables per interval, is affiliated with joy and the more agitated passions such as despair, boldness, or the burning fires of love.[64] To further illustrate, we see that in "Le Printemps est de retour," Example 2.2, Bacilly acknowledged no caesura within the lines. Instead, he placed pauses at the end of each verse, creating six- and seven-syllable units suited to this joyous expression. Indeed, the placement of a caesura within a line of five, seven, nine, or eleven syllables not only varies greatly but may not even occur at all.

La Croix, who borrowed his explanation directly from Bernard Lamy, defines number in the art of speaking and singing as "everything that the ears perceive as proportioned . . . whether following the proportion of the measures of time, or a just distribution of the intervals of breathing."[65] Number results from the equal recitation of verbal units in relation to the number of syllables recited per unit, the quality of pronunciation (the pitch of each syllable), and syllable lengths. *Nombre* and *accens* (or tones of voice), defined by Mersenne as "an inflection or modification of the voice or of the word," were thought to activate the passions.[66] Mersenne notes that *musique accentuelle* incorporates the accents used for raising or lowering the syllables (*l'aigu* and *le grave,* or high and low accents) and must be accompanied by a quickness or slowness of movement (*nombre*).[67] Lamy (and La Croix, quoting him exactly) writes:

> Cicero tells us that numbers are marvelously suited to excite the passions. . . . Saint Augustine observes that our Souls have a sympathy and allyance with these numbers; and that the dif-

EXAMPLE 2.1. Lambert, "Jugez si ma peine est extreme," mm. 1–5, *Les Airs de Monsieur Lambert,* p. 28.

EXAMPLE 2.2. Bacilly, "Le Printemps est de retour," mm. 1–3, *Les Trois livres d'airs,* I:56.

ferent motions of the mind do correspond and follow certain Tones of Voice, to which the Soul has a secret inclination.[68]

Thus the types and placement of the caesuras, the pitch of the voice, and the rhythmic length given to each syllable were regarded by composers as essential in the realization of affect.

> It is a question of making the numbers conform to the things one expresses, in order to excite with success the movements [passions] that one wants, and it is the means of succeeding in all parts of music, in the art of pleasing and persuading.[69]

In this respect, La Croix and other writers considered texted music a persuasive medium in which composers and performers worked to "persuade" listeners to feel the affects represented in text and music. Grimarest, too, stresses the importance of moving the passions in all kinds of discourse, including music. Mersenne suggests that a composer "must himself be struck by the sentiment that he desires to impress on his auditors."[70] He must be like an "orator [who] has more power over his audience when he feels himself moved and entirely persuaded by his arguments."[71] He urges composers to set texts to music carefully, so that a piece "has at least as much power over the listeners as if it were recited by an excellent orator."[72] Poets chose the rhetorical devices, such as the strategic arrangement of ideas, the vocabulary, or various figures of speech, that best served to arouse various emotional states. These devices were the composer's inspiration in endeavoring to "persuade the passions" through their musical settings.

Persuading the Passions

How to stimulate the affects in auditors was a primary concern for both rhetoricians and musicians. Of the rhetoricians, Grimarest, Bary, Bretteville, Le Faucheur, and Lamy offer the most advice, but only Lamy explains in detail the process of affective representation. He writes:

> The common way of affecting the heart of Man, is to give him a lively sense and impression of the object of that passion wherewith we desire he should be mov'd. Love is an affection excited in the Soul by the sight of a present good. To kindle this affection in a heart capable of loving, we must present him with an object of amiable qualities. . . . It is not without reason that the arts of perswading [*sic*] and well-speaking are not separated; for the one serves for little without the other. To stir and affect the Soul of a man, it suffices not to give him a bare representation of the object of that passion wherewith we would animate him; we must display all the riches of our Eloquence to give him an ample and sensible delineation that may strike it home, and leave an impression, not like those phantasms that slide by suddenly before our eyes, and are seen no more . . . We must animate ourselves and (if I may say so) kindle a flame in our hearts, that it may be like a hot Furnace from whence our words may proceed full of that fire which we would kindle in the hearts of other people.[73]

Lamy argues that passions are "the esteem, contempt, love, or hatred we bear things, which should be the objects of our thoughts and our affections."[74] Impressions are formed in our minds by words that carry with them two ideas. The principal idea represents the thing that is signified; the secondary (which Lamy termed the accessory) represents the principal idea "as invested with such and such circumstance."[75] Lamy gives as an example the word "liar." A liar is someone who does not speak the truth, but "it (liar) imports likewise that the person reprehended is esteemed an ill person . . . and therefore deserves our hatred or contempt."[76] Every idea, then, is accompanied by its accessory meaning, that is, an emotional association.

The view that words have both a principal and accessory meaning was an underlying principle, an implicit consideration, in the composition of vocal music in the middle of the seventeenth century. To move their audiences to feel the emotions expressed in their songs, composers did exactly as Lamy suggests in the passage quoted above: they filled their musical settings with lively impressions of the various passions. In vocal music, as in any discourse, the text supplied impressions of objects that included both the denotative meaning of the words and the connotative, or accessory meaning (the passion, or emotional response). In setting poetic texts to music as persuasive musical discourse, composers had to take into account both the text and its passions. Mersenne argues, for example, that "the most captivating airs are those that are well composed with regard to the text and its meaning."[77] Bénigne de Bacilly stresses that the purpose of vocal music (composition and performance) is to provide a musical vehicle for the expressive content of the words.[78] Charles Masson asserts that the extent to which a composer expresses the text and makes the "spirit pass from one passion to another is the natural proof of a work's perfection."[79]

According to Mersenne, Bacilly, Masson, and others, musical devices need to reflect every aspect of a text, from the simplest points of punctuation to a more complex representation of textual meaning, including the various cadence types which correspond to the phrases and periods of the text and their marks of punctuation.[80] Musical devices need to represent textual themes and their underlying passions. Mersenne asserts that "harsh and angry sentiments call for whole tones and leaps of a minor sixth, while sad poetry requires minor thirds in abundance."[81] Bacilly associates fast tempos with expressions of joy and slow tempos with sadness. He also relates particular ornaments to specific passions. *Plaintes, accents, tremblement étouffé,* slow *cadences* (trills), and *demi-ports de voix,* for example, help to express sadness and grief. Gay and joyful expressions require *doublement de gosier* and short, brillant *tremblements.* Pronunciation can also contribute to an effective expression. An extended *m* on *mourir* (to die) or *f* on *infidelle* can be used to great effect in portraying doleful expressions.[82] Masson gives three reasons for the use of dissonances, linking two of them to their expressive function. "The first reason is to depict harshness which yields a sad and gloomy expression to the melody, whether there are words or not. The second reason is to contribute to the beauty of the melody, by adding a note which makes an ornament, and which gives it [the melody] grace."[83]

For the French, the representation of the meaning of an entire phrase and/or line was more important than the representation of isolated words.[84] Bacilly writes:

> There are others who maintain that an air is not well related to its text if it doesn't express the sense of each particular word and who also contend that there are certain notes in music which are precisely effective for the expression of certain ideas, such as sharpened notes and the use of flats for tender and passionate expressions. Naturally, these persons never hesitate to accuse a composer of dreadful ignorance if he should fail to use one of these particular devices on such words as "languor, torment, sadness, pity, suffering, dying, sighing, weeping, moaning, cruel. . . ." Their fury is equally quick to arise when they observe their precious devices being used inappropriately; for instance, critics become irritated if a composer has used a sharp or a flat on words which don't signify passion.[85]

Bacilly describes a gentleman who fiercely reprimanded a composer for sharpening a note on the word "vient" ("comes") in the verse "D'ou vient que de ce Bocage," indicating that "vient" does not signify any passion. Bacilly argues that the critic did not take into consideration that the entire verse was a lament about the absence of a lover, and therefore phrases, not individual words, needed to be treated in a "tender manner" ("une maniere tendre").[86]

As these statements suggest, many composers, musicians, and theorists connected certain musical devices with particular passions. Two approaches to this challenge are revealed in the criticism that accompanied the musical competition between Joan Albert Ban (a Dutch priest) and Antoine Boësset (a renowned French composer), arranged by Mersenne in 1640.[87] Both composers were to set to music the text "Me veux-tu voir mourir." A panel of French judges was to evaluate both settings and choose the song they deemed most successful. Ban lost the competition for several reasons. First, his setting was criticized because he interpreted the affect of the text as that of indignation or anger, and therefore chose the Lydian mode; whereas the judges felt the poem expressed amorous pleading and agreed with Boësset's choice of the Dorian mode. Ban was also criticized because he claimed that all the power of expression in a song relied upon the pronunciation of the words; that is, the tones attached to each word and the rhythms assigned to depict the rhythms of speech. He created a system of composition whereby melodic intervals were assigned specific affective qualities. Smaller intervals strike the ear more gently and were appropriate for gentle and sweet expressions; the larger ones suited more violent expressions. Ban's approach, then, relied upon choice of mode, specific intervallic relationships, and a reproduction of the spoken rhythms of the text to represent individual words that collectively expressed the overall affect of the text.

The French judges viewed his approach to composition as too rigid.[88] Descartes complains to Mersenne in a letter of 1640 that Ban's air was like a schoolboy's exercise in rhetoric, carefully obeying rules.[89] Since, in the view of the judges, he had missed the dominant affect of the piece, every other aspect of his setting seemed wrong. His melody ascended when it should have descended; Ban used, in his words, "vehement" intervals such as fourths, fifths, and major sixths to express indignation and anger when minor seconds and thirds were in order; he also interpreted the rhythms of French speech incorrectly, and thus his choice of musical rhythms was inaccurate.

It is not surprising that the judges viewed Boësset's setting as superior since they agreed with the interpretation of the text's meaning. In another letter, this time to the Dutch scholar, Constantine Huygens, Descartes praises Boësset for his choice of meter (duple), Dorian mode, intervals (primarily major and minor seconds and thirds), and falling melodic cadences at the ends of phrases as being appropriate to the expression of amorous pleading. He notes that in the penultimate line the affect changes from pleading love to revenge. At this point, the text changes from a twelve-syllable line to eight syllables, and Boësset changed the meter from a smooth duple to an aggressive triple, appropriate to the expression of revenge, in Descartes' view.[90]

Even though Ban and the French had different ideas about the meaning of the text and certain compositional procedures, they agreed that the function of music was to enhance the accessory (affective) meaning of the text, and that musical devices communicated affect in association with the lyrics. Thus, the evidence on both sides of the controversy supports Lamy's view (to use his terminology) that the impressions of objects (as given in the text) had accessory meanings (the passions) and that these, according to Mersenne, Descartes, and many other writers, composers, and musicians, had musical equivalents.

Musical devices and their accompanying meanings were indeed highly conventional in mid-seventeenth-century French vocal music.[91] Bacilly not only points out the existence of a customary use of language and musical devices but also proclaims its benefits, after admitting that language acceptable for use in French airs is limited.

> Whether this attitude is completely without reason, or whether it has some good basis is something that hasn't as yet been decided. It would seem that this exclusion of certain words and expressions from vocal music is indeed an overly strict limitation upon the use of our language, especially since the expressions concerned are viewed as being not only worthwhile outside of a musical context, but are often the very expressions which bear the greatest weight and expressive profundity in the art of poetry. . . . It is unfortunately necessary to observe the current custom in this matter until the passage of time ordains a new and different one.[92]

Bacilly notices that a beneficial change in the composition and performance of French airs had taken place over a substantial period of time and notes with some encouragement and approval that more changes were likely in the future.[93] But more importantly, Bacilly comments on the conventional nature of lyric poetry in his time and the presentation of the same topics and poetic devices in text after text and asks, "How then can a musician prevent himself from using the same combinations of notes over again after he has once applied them to similar words with some degree of success? He is almost unable to do otherwise."[94] For Bacilly, the use of "common" or conventional musical devices was far better than resorting to odd and unnatural melodic lines. (He calls an air "natural" if the vocal line is well-suited to the words: "si le chant convien[t] bien aux paroles.")[95] An air need not be criticized as being a

> patchwork, or . . . a collection of borrowings from other airs. Besides the fact that there is no portion of any composition which hasn't at some time previously been done the same way, all music revolves around no more than six or seven different notes. An air is often thought to have been borrowed, but this is never the intent of the composer . . . [but] even if a similar-

ity were intentional, it is certainly more worthwhile to copy something good than to try stubbornly and obtusely to become an Originator and Initiator.[96]

What were the conventional words, expressions, and musical devices that Bacilly so avidly defended? To study French airs composed mid-century is to begin to assess the conventional use of rhetorical and musical devices, which I refer to as "conventions of expression," that permeated the airs of Lambert, Bacilly, Le Camus, La Barre, and others. French writers on music agreed that the works of the best composers of the day were to be emulated because they demonstrated the conventions acceptable in the composition of vocal music and established standards by which other works were to be judged.[97] Mersenne points out, for example, that a theory of composition should be constructed not by deduction, from principles, but by induction from the practice of great composers.[98] Many years later, Masson makes a similar statement: "The examples that one can see in the best authors will reveal the practice of these rules [of composition]."[99] Given that the most "captivating airs" (and most successful) had to be expressive of the text, one may assume that textual meaning was conveyed through appropriate musical devices, that is, those customarily used to excite the passions implied in the text. Likewise, one would expect that the same types of textual expressions found either within the same piece or in several pieces would be expressed by similar musical devices. By uncovering conventions of musical expression in the works of the best composers writing during the middle of the seventeenth century, the following chapters will show that in practice as well as in theory (such as it was), particular combinations of musical devices carried specific meaning. But the association of devices and affect was founded upon rhetorical principles applied to song texts and made applicable to musical compositions by composers. Indeed rhetoric, as a parallel discipline to music, laid the foundation for the expression of affect in French airs by providing composers with the means of communicating the passions.

CHAPTER THREE

Musical Representations
of the Primary Passions

The importance of "moving the passions" was a commonplace in seventeenth-century writings about French music (and about music in general) and was even incorporated into definitions of the French air, as in La Croix's explanation of the *chanson* as "different melodies [that] follow the character [affect or passion] of the verse."[1] Writers on vocal music insisted that the success of a work depended upon the composer's ability to communicate the affective associations of a text through music. In *Nouveau traité . . . pour la composition de la musique,* Charles Masson asserts that

> the expression of the melody in order to respond to that of the words depends upon the invention and accurate judgment of the composer; this expression being sustained and perfected by a judicious diversity of the movement of the measure, has the force and virtue to make the spirit of one passion pass to another; this is a natural proof of a work's perfection.[2]

For composers of the French air who embraced this aesthetic objective, moving the passions meant that melodic and bass-line contours, phrasing, rhythmic movement, harmonies, the rate of harmonic movement, and the organization of phrases all combined to convey the passions revealed in the text. The musical devices that composers associated with specific passions constitute the expressive conventions that pervade the mid-seventeenth-century French air; how the composers identified and represented affects defines the stylistic essence of vocal music during this period.

In his introduction to *Recueil de paroles de musique* (1667), Pierre Perrin provides insight on how textual images suggest affect. First Perrin identifies three "lyric modes" or subjects: "the supernatural, the amorous, and the playful, or comic." Then Perrin claims that certain "objects and actions [must be chosen] that fit naturally and point for point into the modes [or subjects he] . . . wanted to use." Supernatural subjects require beautiful objects of nature that inspire "joy or wonder of a serious sort," such as "the sky, the stars, and flowers." Pleasantly amorous subjects necessitate "acts of pleasure" associated with joy, such as "singing, dancing, making love, [and] . . . running lightly." Painfully amorous subjects require "images of horror or compassion" that inspire sadness, such as "rocks, prisons, caverns, and wildernesses."[3] Although Perrin does not directly reveal how composers identify and represent affect, he implies that certain words in the text evoke images associated with the passions that in turn may inspire the composer.[4] And indeed, several of the most serious airs in the repertory refer to rocks, caverns, and wilderness in association with the painful loss or infidelity of the beloved, as demonstrated in the following text to La Barre's "Forests solitaires et sombres." Here the lover, who suffers from lovesickness, seeks solitude in a secluded wood, one of the most severe symptoms of the disease, which, if left untreated, would result in death.[5]

> Solitary and somber forests
> A silent and dark abode,
> Horrendous place, barren deserts:
> Learn the cause of my mortal pain,
> Alas, I am betrayed by the one I serve,
> My Iris is unfaithful.[6]

One of the best explanations of the relationships among text, affect, and music is found in *Der General-Bass in der Composition* (Dresden, 1728), by the German theorist and composer Johann David Heinichen, who not only explains how composers determine affect in association with a text and gives examples of their musical representation, but also specifically links this step of musical composition to invention. Heinichen suggests that composers "seek the affect of words in the *inventio* or *ars inveniendi,* just as classical books on rhetoric prescribed the *inventio* as the first step in building an oration."[7] Although Heinichen's nationality, as well as the date of his treatise and his application of three categories of topics or *loci topici* (antecedent, concomitant, and consequence) to the da capo aria seem far removed from the mid-seventeenth-century French air, the essence of his ideas are indeed applicable to this repertory. He recommends looking for words in a text that provide opportunity for expressing affect;[8] words such as "cry out," "burning fires of love," or "sighs of love" are highlighted as "ripe" for passionate representation.

The texts used by French composers of airs are rich with words that would have invited affective representation; the passions themselves are frequently indicated by name. One would assume that composers recognized the correspondence between a passion named in a text and its affective meaning, and between the specified passion and musical setting, thereby establishing a link between a passion and the musical devices associated with it. When the connection between ideas is not based upon final or absolute proof, as I am proposing here, "only liaisons among terms and notions can be built."[9] In this chapter, I show that there is indeed a liaison or connection between a passion specified in the text, its meaning, and its musical representation. In addition, it seems likely that even if the passion is not named but only implied in the meaning of a phrase, similar expressions would warrant similar musical treatment. Thus, I propose to establish an additional liaison between those phrases in which the passion is named and those in which the passion is not named but implied. The link between both types of phrases is the musical representation with which the composers have interpreted the affective meaning of a phrase, even if the passion is not named.

The Primary Passions

Of the twenty-two passions named in the songs of the collections under study, seven primary passions dominate the repertory and are given special musical treatment. These are (1) *le désespoir* (despair); (2) *le pouvoir* (power, courage, or boldness); (3) *les feux de l'amour* (the fires of love or burning love); (4) *la douleur* (sorrow, grief, or pain); (5) *la langueur* (languor); (6) *la douceur* (sweetness or tenderness); and (7) *le contentement* (satisfaction or happiness).[10] It must be stressed that an analysis of affect, text, and music involves, with some exceptions, the treatment of the entire phrase containing the specified passion, and rarely just the word itself.[11] Therefore, variations in the meaning of a passion can change according to its use within the passage and its accordance with the type of subject matter revealed in the song.[12] The word "love," for example, is named in many of the songs, yet it can be represented in the music as a burning desire, as painful, tender, or joyous. The primary passions cited above are distinct from others named in the song texts not only because there is a great consistency in their musical treatment but also because their expression is often the manifestation of the meaning of an entire phrase. The first five dominate the songs concerning painful love, yet all seven are named or represented in the bittersweet airs, wherein love is expressed as both painful and pleasurable. Boldness, tenderness, and joy are the passions that appear most often in songs about shared love.

All of the primary passions named in the airs are defined and described in certain seventeenth-century treatises on rhetoric by Bretteville (*L'Éloquence de la chaire et du barreau*, 1689), Bary (*La Rhétorique françoise . . .* 1673), Le Faucheur (*Traité de l'action de l'orateur*, 1657), and Grimarest's work on proper recitation (*Traité du récitatif*, 1707).[13] These authors were concerned with the way orators imitate passions, not only within the discourse itself but also in its recitation. In this respect, the works by these rhetoricians differ from that by Bernard Lamy, who certainly considers affect and text but does not address proper recitation. Passion was associated with the subjects and images of the oration, but the recitation of the discourse also had to be appropriate to the images and affects found therein. It was the combination of textual expressions, arranged in a proper order, written in an eloquent style, and powerfully recited that would move the auditors to action.[14] Every aspect of the discourse required thoughtful recitation, including the different parts of a discourse and the various figures and tropes. Bretteville, Bary, Le Faucheur, and Grimarest all write about the use of gestures and *accens*, describing in detail the tones and strength of voice and rate of speech associated with the various passions.

Descartes devoted an entire treatise, *The Passions of the Soul* (*Les Passions de l'âme*, 1649), to explaining the nature of the most fundamental passions.[15] One of the chief differences between the treatises on rhetoric and Descartes' treatment of the passions has to do with their purpose: that is, the rhetoricians' descriptive *representations* of passions as opposed to Descartes' attempt to provide a scientific explanation of human emotions, which has been called a psychophysiology of the passions by Thomas M. Carr in his book *Descartes and the Resilience of Rhetoric*. Thus, the rhetoricians define the passions and describe how they were to be represented in oratory, while Descartes includes a detailed physiological account of their origin and expression.

Descartes defines passions as "those perceptions, sensations or emotions of the soul which we refer particularly to it, and which are caused, maintained and strengthened by some movement of spirits."[16] The cause of passions of the soul "is simply the agitation by which the spirits move the little gland in the middle of the brain."[17] Every passion felt by a human being involves the movement of fluids, called animal spirits, within the body by way of the circulatory system to the brain. The movement of the animal spirits is caused by the representation of something associated with a particular passion. The sight of a bear, for example, activates certain spirits to move to the brain, which may cause a person to feel fear.

While Bretteville, Bary, Le Faucheur, and Grimarest consider up to fourteen different passions,[18] Descartes reduces the number to six "primitive" passions: (1) wonder; (2) love; (3) hatred; (4) desire; (5) joy; and (6) sadness. The primary passions found in the works of Lambert, Bacilly, La Barre, and Le Camus correlate with Descartes' final three: desire, joy, and sadness.[19] Descartes classifies sorrow and languor, two passions represented in the airs, as species of sadness. He notes that sadness results when suffering discomfort from an evil or deficiency.[20] In the song texts, sorrow and languor often result when, in response to the beloved's rejection, the speaker resigns himself to his fate. By contrast, happiness or joy is a pleasant emotion resulting from the enjoyment or possession of some good.[21] And indeed, in the song texts, happiness usually results from reciprocated or anticipated love.

The passion most commonly represented in the airs is desire. Descartes classifies burning love, tender love, despair, and power or courage as species of this primitive passion. All four of these are revealed in the song texts in association with the speaker's love or desire for the beloved. According to Descartes, desire for another human being is not true love; it is sexual attraction. Burning love and tender love, as represented in the texts and music, are varying degrees of the speaker's desire, one extreme, one mild. Descartes notes that desire always regards future circumstances; that is, the prospect of obtaining what we desire or avoiding what we do not want. If in the song texts the speaker can not obtain the beloved, he feels despair, represented in both text and music. By contrast, Descartes notes that if there is hope for obtaining what we desire, we are motivated to courageous acts. In the song texts, the appearance of courage, or *le pouvoir*, represents a temporary empowerment of the speaker that makes him consider taking whatever action is needed to acquire the desired beloved.

Descartes recognizes that passions are stimulated by works of art as well as by real-life situations but specifies an important difference between the two. He observes that pleasure can be aroused through the sensation of any passion, even sadness and hatred, when resulting from activities that do not harm us in any way.[22] When we see "strange happenings on stage" or read of "strange adventures" in a book, for example,

> this sometimes arouses sadness in us, sometimes joy, or love, or hatred, and generally any of the passions, depending on the diversity of the objects which are presented to the imagination. But we also have pleasure in feeling them aroused in us, and this pleasure is an intellectual joy which may as readily originate in sadness as in any of the other passions.[23]

In his *Compendium musicae,* Descartes makes a similar observation regarding music. He writes:

> The basis of music is sound; its aim is to please and to arouse various emotions in us. Melodies can be at the same time sad and enjoyable; nor is this so unique, for in some way writers of elegies and tragedies please us most the more sorrow they awaken in us.[24]

Thus, the observation that music must be pleasurable does not discount its capacity to express the most intense passions.

In the airs, the process of moving the affections and pleasing auditors occurs on several levels. First, there is the textual imitation. Revealed in the text is the speaker's reaction to the beloved's rejection. With various musical devices, then, the composers imitated the impassioned tones of voice associated with a speaker's recitation of the poem, thus adding another level of affective representation. These *accens,* indicated in the musical score, "recited" by the singer, and supported by the accompaniment, were the stimuli that moved the passions. Mersenne observes that musical vibrations and the movement of the spirits in the body are identical motions. The different vibrations caused by musical sounds imitating the different *accens,* or tones of the passions, are like the motion of the animal spirits in the body caused by the different emotional states. According to Mersenne, "as a vibration in the air, music causes a kindred motion of air in the ear which in turn 'imprints an emotion in the nerve of the ear canal.'" This is why Mersenne considered music to be "the language of the passions."[25]

There is a remarkably close correlation between Descartes' physiological account of the passions, the descriptions of passions given in the treatises on rhetoric, and the musical devices used by composers to imitate the *accens* of the texts. While Descartes describes the real physical signs of the passions, Bretteville, Bary, Le Faucheur, and Grimarest describe the tone and strength of the voice, as well as the rate of speech, as imitations of these real physical signs. Despite Bretteville's claim that an orator need not know what happens to the body when a passion is felt, his instructions for representing the passions, and those given by the other rhetoricians, agree with Descartes' explanations.[26] The musical representations found in the airs of Lambert, Bacilly, La Barre, and Le Camus are imitations of the *accens* of recitation that are themselves imitations of the physical signs of the passions. The vocal music of these composers is thus an imitation of an imitation.[27] Like Descartes, who notes that there are two "means" of arousing the passions having to do with the "attributes of sound, . . . its differences of duration or time, and its differences of tension from high to low,"[28] composers of airs used musical devices to simulate duration and pitch in order to represent the passions. Duration (rates of speech, including a consideration of syllable length, the number of syllables included in verbal units, and attention to punctuation) was represented primarily by rhythmic means, while the pitch and strength of the voice was achieved primarily by melodic and harmonic means.[29]

In the treatises by Bretteville, Bary, Le Faucheur, Grimarest, and Descartes, passions are generally classified as either agitated, modest, or neutral; these categories apply as well to the musical representation of the passions by composers. In the airs, the most "agitated" or "vehement" passions (to use the terms found in the treatises) are despair, power or courage, and burning love.[30] Composers represented these by using strong musical devices, such as a melody in the highest register of the piece and major harmonies in root position. Sorrow, languor, and tenderness are modest passions (to use Bary's term) and are represented by weak musical devices, such as a descending melody in the middle or low register of the piece, or the use of first-inversion minor harmonies. Happiness is neutral and is represented by a combination of strong and weak devices. The differences between strong and weak devices will be clarified in the following descriptions of the primary passions.

The Agitated Passions

Le Désespoir

Descartes describes the movement of the blood and spirits that causes *le désespoir* (despair, or hopelessness) as a violent kind of agitation. The spirits are sent rapidly from the brain to all parts of the body, particularly the heart, which sends more spirits back to the brain to maintain and strengthen the passion. Because despair causes more spirits to rush to the brain than does any other passion, all the senses are more acute and all parts of the body more mobile.[31] Bretteville confirms this description, asserting that despair "is a violent and impetuous movement by which the soul distances itself from something good that it can not possess, after having searched for it with ardor."[32] Specifically, Grimarest associates despair with exclamations and a tone of voice that is high, abrupt, exaggerated or outraged, and violent ("un ton aigu, précipité, outré, violent").[33]

The musical devices used by composers in setting textual phrases associated with despair correlate with the features and *accens* described by Descartes, Bretteville, and Grimarest. Lambert, Bacilly, La Barre, and Le Camus musically imitated a high-pitched and exaggerated tone with a melody that ascends and/or is placed in the highest register of the piece. According to Descartes, high pitches are more tense than low because singing in a high range requires more energy, such that "the higher the note, the more breath is required for its production."[34] In addition, composers divided textual and musical phrases into large verbal units, creating few units per line (usually two) containing more than three syllables each (usually four to six). Large verbal units create a sense of perpetual movement that requires a continuation of effort to sustain the voice so that the sound is maintained and strengthened. Indeed, Mersenne contrasts frequent and perpetual rhythmic movement to the "weighty and slow movements of sad airs, which represent a broken and languishing life."[35] Finally, composers created abruptness by irregular phrasing (that is, a variation in the number of measures that comprise each phrase) and by the placement of several notes, one note per syllable, into a limited number of measures. In sum, agitation, violence, or ardor is represented by a melody that ascends by step to the highest register of the piece, by decisive and accented rhythmic movement organized into large verbal units, and by an emphasis upon strong tonic–dominant harmonic relationships (first and fifth notes of the mode), often in root position.[36]

Le désespoir, being one of the most intense passions represented in the repertory, is found exclusively in the serious airs about painful and bittersweet love. It is named only once in Lambert's edition in the piece "Inutiles pensers," line two, shown in Example 3.1. However, reference is made to "lost hope" in "Mon cœur qui se rend à vos coups" (Example 4.5, mm. 13–17), and to "a vain hope" in "Que me sert-il" (mm. 18–21; not shown). These examples not only share certain semantic features, particularly in reference to despair or hopelessness, but the musical devices mentioned above are common to each musical phrase as well.[37]

In "Inutiles pensers" (Example 3.1), Lambert strongly contrasts the phrase "et de mon desespoir" ("and of my despair"), mm. 7–10, with "Enfans de ma douleur" ("Children of my sorrow"), mm. 6–7. The first hemistich features a melody descending by step and half step, dissonance on beat three of m. 6, dotted rhythms, a predominance of minor harmonies, and a weak cadence from G minor to D minor (mm. 6 and 7). This is followed by a melody that ascends by step to the second-highest pitch in the song (E), the descent of a fourth to B, followed by an ascent of a major second to C♯, an accented rhythmic movement in which "de-" and "-poir" of "desespoir" are emphasized (a dotted half note and a whole note, respectively), a bass line that moves primarily in contrary motion to the melody, root-position harmonies,[38] and major harmonies at the end of the phrase that form a V–I progression (V/V to V in D).[39]

Lambert also divides this twelve-syllable line into four verbal units. The first hemistich, a sorrowful utterance, comprises three units of two syllables each. The second hemistich, in which "despair" is named, is one verbal unit of six syllables (and should be sung as such, maintaining the energy of the voice to the end of the phrase). According to La Croix and Lamy in their consideration of *nombre*, the more syllables per unit, the more agitated the affect.[40] Large verbal units generate forward momentum by a continuation of sound from one syllable to the next. This is enhanced all the more by the ascending melody, which requires increased effort with the recitation of each syllable.[41] Thus, the singer should not diminish the strength of the voice on "-ses-" of "desespoir" even though it is given a small rhythmic value and descends a fourth (considered a "harsh" interval).[42]

Lambert interprets other phrases as desperate utterances in which the words "despair" or "hopelessness" do not appear, as exemplified in "Jugez si ma peine est extreme," Example 3.2. Lambert imitates desperate tones in setting the words "Philis I serve you faithfully" from this air to represent the speaker's frustration. Even though the lover says he faithfully serves Philis, she avoids him and loves another. The ascending melody, the accented rhythms, the single eight-syllable unit, the strong cadence (C major in second inversion to F major, mm. 7–8),

Music and the Language of Love

"Children of my sorrow and of my despair"

EXAMPLE 3.1. Lambert, "Inutiles pensers," mm. 6–10, *Les Airs de Monsieur Lambert,* p. 8.

"Philis I serve you faithfully"

EXAMPLE 3.2. Lambert, "Jugez si ma peine est extreme," mm. 5–8, *Les Airs de Monsieur Lambert,* p. 28.

and a bass line that moves primarily in contrary motion to the melody are typical imitations of agitated *accens.*

Although the word "désespoir" never appears in the first strophe of airs from *Les Trois livres,* Bacilly interprets several phrases as desperate expressions and treats these similarly to Lambert's setting of this affect. "Mon sort est digne de pitié" ("My fate is worthy of pity"), Example 3.3, is an utterance of despair represented by several of the musical devices most commonly associated with this affect: an ascending melody, one large verbal unit of eight syllables, and stressed rhythms. Here, the lover realizes his fate is hopeless and thus to be pitied.

Expressions of despair are rare in the airs by La Barre and Le Camus. In his air "J'avois juré de n'aymer plus," Example 3.4, composed over a ground bass that descends an octave, La Barre begins with a statement of despair even though the primary passion represented in the piece is one of "tender" love. The desperate utterance appears with the statement "I had sworn to love no longer," but all hope of doing so disappeared with the sight of the adorable beloved—thus hopelessness, typical of despair. The musical setting shows many of the same features as do other examples cited so far, namely an ascending melody in the highest register of the piece, a majority of harmonies in root position,

"My fate is worthy of pity"

Mon sort est di - gne de pi - tié

EXAMPLE 3.3. Bacilly, "Mon sort est digne de pitié," mm. 1–4, *Les Trois livres d'airs,* p. 12.

"I had sworn to love no longer"

J'a - vais ju - ré de____ n'ay - mer plus,

EXAMPLE 3.4. La Barre, "J'avois juré de n'aymer plus," mm. 1–4, *Airs à deux parties,* 9v.

"And without understanding too much about my harsh fate"

Et sans trop pé - né - trer dans mon sort ri - gou - reux,

EXAMPLE 3.5. Le Camus, "Vous serez les témoins de mes vives douleurs," mm. 27–31, *Airs à deux et trois parties,* pp. 46–47.

and in this example, the repetition of notes (and harmonies) in both melody and bass line.

The word "despair" does not appear in the airs of Le Camus, but there are a few expressions that suggest this agitated passion, such as the reference to "harsh fate" in "Vous serez les témoins," Example 3.5. In this air, the poetic voice claims that he is miserable in love. All is hopeless.

LE POUVOIR

Le pouvoir (power, courage, or boldness) is used here as a category for any agitated (usually aggressive) utterance that is not one of despair. There are many passages, especially strongly stated opinions, commands, demands, and emphatic statements, that defy any other classification. Sometimes the more intense passages express anger, but this affect does not appear consistently or often enough to qualify as a primary passion. Powerful or bold expressions appear in the collections of all the composers and are given a specific kind of musical treatment that fits the range of expressions listed above.

Descartes refers to boldness or courage as a "certain heat or agitation which disposes the soul to apply itself energetically to accomplish the tasks it wants to perform."[43] Because it is a species of desire, as is despair, the two passions share many of the same traits. The difference is that courage disposes the soul to accomplish the task required to obtain the object of desire and depends upon hope for success in attaining the goal.[44] Despair, by contrast, results when the attainment of the desired object is impossible, leading to hopelessness and the eventual extinction of the desire altogether.[45] Bretteville describes boldness (la hardiesse) as "a passion of the soul, which strengthens it in the face of danger, and makes it attack the evil, in order to fight it and conquer it."[46] Grimarest and Bary call this passion l'audace (audacity, boldness or daring). Like Descartes and Bretteville, Grimarest notes that audacity and despair are two of the most agitated passions, claiming that audacity should be represented by an impetuous or forceful and lofty voice ("une voix impétueuse et hautaine").[47] Le Faucheur maintains that "confidence . . . will be easily discover'd by a Loud and a Strong Voyce, always keeping-up to a Decent Boldness and a daring Constancy."[48]

Lambert, Bacilly, La Barre, and Le Camus created the energy and force of boldness, as described by these writers, through melodies high in register that often move by skips and stress notes outlining the first and fifth notes of the mode, through the repetition of notes for emphasis, accented rhythms, particularly large rhythmic values at ends of phrases, bass line movement primarily by leaps in large note values, an emphasis upon tonic–dominant harmonic relationships, and occasional dissonances. As with despair, the verbal units usually contain more than four syllables.

Le pouvoir is named once in Lambert's Les Airs de Monsieur Lambert, in "Non n'aprehendez point," Example 3.6. This example embodies all of the devices associated with le pouvoir, yet it also demonstrates how Lambert intensifies and diminishes affect in response to the text. He divides line one (mm. 1–5) into two verbal units of six syllables each, typical of bold statements. The air begins with a forceful "No," which is sustained for the value of a whole note and is placed on one of the highest pitches of the piece. The air is in minor mode on G; thus, one might expect the strength of a G-minor sonority to accompany this negative expression. Instead, Lambert starts with a D-minor chord in first inversion under the "No" (m. 1) to weaken the affect. The D-minor sonority then changes to E♭ major on the downbeat of m. 2. The sustained D in the melody forms a dissonant seventh against the bass note and chord.

The kind of dissonance caused by the D in the melody and the E♭ in the bass was known as *la supposition,* or controlled dissonance. *La supposition* (substitution) was the practice of substituting a dissonance for a consonance and of understanding and treating that dissonance as the consonance it represents. There were two kinds of controlled dissonance: the suspension and the passing dissonance.[49] This, of course, is an example of the suspension. Seventeenth-century theorists considered musical composition as a sequence of consonant intervals that embodied different degrees of tension and relaxation. The ear demanded that there be progress from an interval of more complexity (an imperfect consonance) to one of less complexity (a perfect consonance). The D on beat one of m. 2 takes the place of the supposed consonance, the following C on beat two. The resolution of the D (an imperfect consonance) to the C (a perfect consonance) creates a C-minor chord in first inversion. Although dissonance functions as an ornament, adding variety, grace, and charm to the harmony, theorists emphasize that it was especially useful in association with impassioned expressions, as in this example. This example, then, shows an intensification of affect on the word "No" from apprehension (the D-minor sonority, a perfect consonance, and a point of relaxation) to aggression (the imperfect consonance on the suspension and a point of tension).

Lambert resolves the tension at the beginning of the command, "do not fear that I will make you understand," by using a series of weak musical devices. This is achieved by the resolution of the suspension (dissonance by supposition) to the C-minor sonority in first inversion (on "n'a-" of "n'aprehendez"), a melodic line that after the resolution outlines a minor third, C to A, and by the additional descent of a minor third, from C to A, between "-dez" and "point" at the end of the phrase (mm. 2–3). Mersenne observed that minor thirds are often used to "soften" harsh affects, as in this example.[50] Yet with this command "do not fear," Lambert also projects a more aggressive affect with

"No, do not fear that I will make you understand / The absolute power you have over me"

EXAMPLE 3.6. Lambert, "Non n'aprehendez point," mm. 1–9, *Les Airs de Monsieur Lambert,* p. 24.

strong musical devices: the major harmonies F to B♭ in first inversion (m. 2) to F major on "point," the smaller rhythmic values, larger verbal unit and series of strong syllables, the dotted rhythm in the melody before the downbeat of m. 3, and the dotted rhythmic figure in the bass line followed by two half notes (beat three of m. 2, beat one of m. 3). It is as if the speaker wants to reassure his beloved that there is no reason to fear (as set by Lambert with weak musical devices) but at the same time feels an urgency about his attempt to convince her (represented by Lambert with strong devices).

The last phrase of this line, "that I will make you understand" (mm. 3–5), is interpreted as the more forceful of the two phrases. Lambert begins the line with highly agitated rhythms, a descending leap of a fourth, the harshest interval of all, according to Descartes, ornamented by two sixteenth notes that fill in the interval.[51] With the rush of the sixteenths down to "je" ("I"), Lambert emphasizes this word, perhaps symbolizing the empowerment of the speaker at this moment in the song. The bass line moves only by whole and half notes; major sonorities dominate; the melody concludes with an ascending major second (G to A, mm. 4–5); and the passage ends with a Phrygian cadence: C minor in first inversion to D (the C-minor chord is preceded by a dissonant E♭[7] chord).

Lambert treats the word "power" ("pouvoir") with the most forceful musical devices of all: a shift upward in register combined with repeated notes. He also repeats the harmony, B♭ major, and places the word within a large six-syllable verbal unit, the first of two such units that make up line two (mm. 5–9). Lambert contrasts the forceful affect on "le pouvoir" with a momentary musical expression of tenderness on the word "absolu," created by the change to a G-minor triad in first inversion and the melodic movement by step that outlines a descending minor third. This conveys the sense that the "absolute power" of his mistress causes powerful *and* tender feelings of desire. The representation of sexual desire as painful and sweet (or strong and yet tender) is a common theme in lyric poetry.[52] "Strong" musical devices (melodic and bass movement by skips and major harmonies, for example) are juxtaposed with "weak" devices (melodic and bass movement that outlines thirds, especially minor thirds, accompanied by minor harmonies) to underscore the antithesis.

Lambert ends the phrase forcefully in mm. 8 and 9 by employing another large verbal unit, disjunct rather than conjunct melodic movement, and a B♭–F–B♭ cadence. In mm. 7–9, the bass-line movement is dominated by leaps and moves primarily in half notes. Lambert makes the entire statement all the more emphatic by repeating the two half notes in the melody on "sur moy," which are followed by a dotted half and the final dotted whole note at the end of the line.

Bacilly also sets the word "pouvoir" with bold tones. In addition, he, like Lambert, associates powerful, emphatic, and bold tones with commands, as well as with statements of necessity.

The word "pouvoir" appears in Bacilly's air "Vous sçavez donner de l'amour," Example 3.7: "You know how to inspire love / The power of your eyes makes this clear." Bacilly divides the first line of eight syllables into two groups, one of five syllables and other of three. He creates a bold affect at the outset of the piece by emphasizing the tonic and dominant harmonies, introducing a melodic descent of a fourth in m. 1 and an ascent of a fifth at the end of the line in m. 4, and through his choice of duple meter (though the affect is slightly "softened" by the descent of a minor third in both melody and bass in m. 3). Bacilly maintains the strength of the first expression on the words "le pouvoir" with the ascent of the melody to the highest register of the piece and the rush of the two quarter notes to the dotted half note in mm. 3–4. Although the force of "le pouvoir" is strengthened in the melodic ascent to F, Bacilly then alters the affect, again "softening" it, by the movement to the D-minor harmony on the downbeat of m. 4 and by the change in the previous measure to triple meter on the word "l'amour" ("love").

"You know how to inspire love / The power of your eyes makes this clear"

EXAMPLE 3.7. Bacilly, "Vous sçavez donner de l'amour," mm. 1–6, *Les Trois livres d'airs*, I:68.

Let us avoid death my heart / Let us revolt against her

EXAMPLE 3.8. Bacilly, "Puisque Philis est infidelle," mm. 4–9, *Les Trois livres d'airs*, I:4.

"One must first declare [one's love]"

EXAMPLE 3.9. Bacilly, "Il faut parler," mm. 8–10, *Les Trois livres d'airs*, I:72.

Bacilly associates the words "de vos yeux" ("of your eyes") with tender love by grouping items by three (mm. 4–5). This number was associated with Venus, the goddess of love and the third planet, according to astrologers (the moon was first, then Mercury, then Venus).[53] Bacilly places "de vos yeux" into a three-syllable verbal unit, sets the words into one group of three quarter notes which lead to the downbeat of m. 5 (the last two notes, which descend a major second on the single syllable "vos," form a "sighing" figure), and places a descending minor third between "vos" and "yeux."[54]

Bacilly's treatment of this passage is similar to Lambert's treatment of "absolu" (directly after "le pouvoir") in Example 3.6, "Non n'aprehendez point." In both settings, Lambert and Bacilly move to a minor harmony after "le pouvoir" and emphasize minor thirds in the melody, thus juxtaposing strong and tender affects to convey the "powerful" and "tender" properties of desire. In Bacilly's piece, tenderness is associated with the beloved's eyes. The division of the first six syllables of this line into two units of three syllables slows down the movement of the phrase and isolates it from the stronger passages that surround it. The emphatic tone recurs in this example after the brief reference to tenderness on "de vos yeux," as it does in Lambert's piece on "absolu." In m. 6, Bacilly returns to the forceful affect by restoring duple meter, creating a large verbal unit of six syllables ("le fait assez comprendre"), and using a strong melodic ascent. In addition, the quarter notes on "-sez" of "assez" are grouped in pairs (not into groups of three), the harmonic movement in this passage leads decisively to the cadence on B♭ major, and large rhythmic values make up the cadential figure.

In "Puisque Philis est infidelle" (Example 3.8), Bacilly interprets the two commands—"Let us avoid death my heart / Let us revolt against her"—with bold tones. Here, Bacilly places the melody in the upper register of the piece, assigns repeated notes to the command "Evitons," sets "Revoltons" with an ascending melodic flourish, emphasizes tonic and dominant harmonies, and accentuates the cadence with large rhythmic values. A shift of affect is invoked on the words "mon cœur" (mm. 5–6) in much the same manner as with "de vos yeux" in "Vous sçavez donner de l'amour" in Example 3.7. The melody descends a minor third from "mon" to "cœur" and is accompanied by the movement by thirds in the bass line. The composer also isolates "mon cœur" as a two-syllable verbal unit and surrounds it with larger units, the bold utterances.

The last example by Bacilly is a statement of necessity from the song "Il faut parler," in Example 3.9 (another statement of necessity appears in this air in m. 2). Especially of note are the skips in the melody that outline tonic and dominant harmonies, the dotted rhythms of the melody, the brief use of duple meter in m. 9, and the large verbal units. These are features that composers used most frequently in bold, emphatic, or powerful utterances.

Bold and powerful expressions are also found frequently in airs by La Barre and Le Camus. In Example 3.10, for example, La Barre sets the command "escoutez" ("listen") with repetition (first on C and then B) and strong dominant-to-tonic harmonies (one should consider playing an E-major harmony on beat 2 of the first measure, which would contrast nicely with the E-minor sonority on beat 1 and set up the command, even though a major sonority is not indicated).[55]

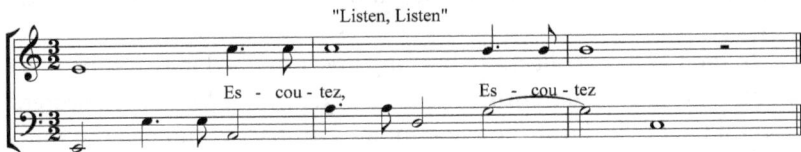

EXAMPLE 3.10. La Barre, "Quand on vous dit que l'on vous ayme," mm. 24–26, *Airs à deux parties*, 15v.

LES FEUX DE L'AMOUR

Les feux de l'amour (fires of love, or burning love) is most often expressed as a verb: "Je brûle nuit et jour" ("I burn night and day"). It is a common metaphor in this repertory and is often used along with "la flamme" (the flame) or "un feu" (fire) or with reference to a disease or illness ("une maladie") to signal intense feelings of love and sexual desire (erotic melancholia). Bretteville, Bary, Le Faucheur, and Grimarest do not describe this passion, but Descartes devotes a short section in his treatise to describing "the desire which arises from attraction." He writes:

> Attraction . . . is specifically ordained by nature to represent the enjoyment of that which attracts us as the greatest of all the goods belonging to mankind, and so to make us have a burning desire for this enjoyment.[56]

He notes that other sorts of attractions are not equally powerful. We are attracted to flowers, for example, but we are only moved to look at them. He points out that the strongest kind of attraction is to a human being of the opposite sex. In other words, Descartes was referring to sexual desire without identifying it specifically. At a certain age, nature represents this desire "as the greatest of all imaginable goods we could possibly possess."[57] Descartes claims that yearning for another human is one of the strongest and most confusing kinds of desire.[58]

Composers represented "burning love" as sexual desire and relief of some sort. References to this affect were set with ascending chromaticism in the melody which suddenly resolves downward at the very end of the phrase, a persistent use of dotted rhythms in the melody, tonic–dominant harmonies, and large verbal units. In contrast to the agitated dotted rhythms in the melody, the bass line often remains relatively inactive until the melodic climax is achieved at the end of the phrase.

In the Lambert collection, burning love is named in two song texts, "Mon ame faisons un effort," Example 3.11, and "D'un feu secret," Example 3.12. In both these examples Lambert combines the musical devices given above to represent sexual anticipation and sudden release, as the melody intensifies in its chromatic ascent to the final word of each line, "complain" and "consumed," respectively, and then resolves downward. In Example 3.11, the act of complaining relieves the anticipation created by the speaker's burning desire or sexual tension. In Example 3.12, the consummation of his desire serves to alleviate such an anticipation.

In neither the La Barre nor the Le Camus publications are there any references to "the burning fires of love." There are, however, a few musical references to sexual desire. Le Camus, for example, sets "I am too much in love not to be jealous" in the air "Que les jaloux transports" as an expression of burning love with a melody that ascends chromatically by sequence, major harmonies, and leaps in the bass. "Relief" is then portrayed by the drop of the octave and subsequent descending minor third on "not to be jealous" (Example 3.13).

In the serious airs, the composers set references to the most agitated passions—despair, power or boldness, and burning love—with the strongest musical devices: (1) a predominately ascending melody in the upper register of the piece (in utterances of despair, the phrase ends with an ascending half step); (2) leaps or ascending chromaticism in the melody and bass line; (3) accented rhythms; (4) large verbal

"Since I burn I must complain"

Puis - que je brus - le^il se faut___ plain - dre

EXAMPLE 3.11. Lambert, "Mon ame faisons un effort," mm. 4–6, *Les Airs de Monsieur Lambert,* p. 4.

"I feel myself consumed by a secret fire"

D'un feu se - cret je me sens je me sens___con-su - mer

EXAMPLE 3.12. Lambert, "D'un feu secret," mm. 1–5, *Les Airs de Monsieur Lambert,* p. 60.

"and I am too much in love not to be jealous"

et moi trop a - mou - reux,

trop a - mou-reux pour n'es - tre point ja - loux.

EXAMPLE 3.13. Le Camus, "Que les jaloux transports," mm. 19–24, *Airs à deux et trois parties,* pp. 48–49.

units; (5) a predominance of masculine rhymes or feminine rhymes treated as masculine (i.e., feminine rhymes at the ends of phrases); (6) frequent major harmonies even if the mode of the piece is minor; (7) melody and bass line moving in contrary motion; and (8) frequent use of tonic and dominant harmonic relationships, often in root position. The combination of these devices to invoke the most agitated passions contrasts sharply with the composers' use of "weak devices" for the modest passions: sorrow, languor, and tenderness.

The Modest Passions:
La Douleur, La Langueur, and *La Douceur*

La Douleur

La douleur (sorrow, grief, or pain) is one of most frequently expressed passions in the collections of airs. Descartes, who has a great deal to say about this passion, associates it with listlessness caused by a severe restriction of the openings of heart. The blood in the veins is not agitated at all, so that very little blood goes to the heart, which causes the limbs to relax and remain motionless. Tears result from a moderate feeling of sadness when accompanied by some feeling of love or joy.[59] Descartes claims that sadness must be combined with these other emotions so that the "quantity of vapors" is sufficient enough to form tears, for extreme sadness causes too great a constriction of blood throughout the body and not enough vapors for weeping. Although Bretteville does not describe the physiological aspects of sadness, he associates this passion with a languishing and fearful voice ("une voix languissante, craintive") which is interrupted by sighs and groans.[60] Grimarest notes that sadness is accompanied by a weak, lingering, and plaintive voice ("une voix foible, trainante, plaintive"), and Le Faucheur describes a sorrowful man as one who will "discover his Grief . . . with a dull, languishing and Sad Moan; not without breaking off abruptly sometimes, with a sob; and fetching-up a sigh or a groan from the heart."[61]

In this repertory, there is little doubt that sadness is represented in association with desire. The combination, according to Descartes, would open up constricted arteries and veins and cause weeping. Indeed, musical devices are used in the airs to simulate sobbing and sighs.[62] Composers imitated weeping with melodies that descend primarily by half steps, and sighing by two-note motives that descend most commonly by half steps, but also by whole steps and major or minor thirds. A weak voice or listlessness was represented with a melody in the middle and low registers of the piece, descending movement, minor harmonies, and phrases that end with weak cadences, often plagal.[63] A lingering and plaintive voice was highlighted by large note values and phrases broken into small verbal units.[64] Lambert, Bacilly,

La Barre, and Le Camus introduced an occasional dissonance, which conforms to Bretteville's observation that sadness can be accompanied by a fearful tone of voice.

La douleur is named once in Lambert's *Airs,* in line two of the air "Inutiles pensers," "Enfans de ma douleur" ("Children of my sorrow"), shown in Example 3.14. The most striking feature of this passage is the descending melodic line, first by a whole step and then by a half, to imitate sobs. Instead of increasing in force, as in the passages of despair, the phrase begins with strength and weakens as it continues. Lambert begins with strong musical devices: the repeated Cs of "Enfans" ("children"), the octave leap F–F in the bass, the repetition of the F-major harmony, and the dissonance (suspension *par supposition*) in the middle of m. 6. But he concludes with weak devices of less intensity: the descending minor second from B♭ to A on "ma douleur," minor harmonies, and the plagal cadence. Lambert also divides the six-syllable phrase into three verbal units of two syllables each, which breaks up and slows down the movement of the phrase to represent a plaintive tone of voice.

EXAMPLE 3.14. Lambert, "Inutiles pensers," mm. 6–7, *Les Airs de Monsieur Lambert,* p. 8.

Although the word "douleur" does not appear in other airs from his collection, Lambert also sets the phrase "of my soul's peace," from "Superbes ennemis" (Example 3.15) with sorrowful tones. He projects sorrow in this example by recourse to a melody that predominantly descends by whole and half steps to imitate sobs, and by a voice that becomes weaker and more listless with each word. Stagnant harmonic movement, a plagal cadence, and small verbal units of three syllables or less invoke lethargy. Sighing is imitated by a melody that resolves downward by a half step at the end of the phrase. The similarity between "du repos de mon ame" and "Enfans de ma douleur" of Example 3.14 is striking. Lambert begins each phrase with repeated Cs; the last C becomes dissonant *par supposition* to the D in the bass and the D-major harmony before resolving to B♭ over a G-minor harmony, and finally to an A supported by the D-minor harmony.

Bacilly's musical representation of sorrow is almost identical to that of Lambert's. In Example 3.16, from the air "Au secours ma raison," the speaker endures the pain of surrendering his heart and soul to one who does not love him in return. This example imitates the sobs and sighs, the plaintive and weak voice, and the listlessness that characterizes sorrow with a melody that descends a minor third by whole and half steps; minor harmonies that dominate the phrase; a melody that descends by a half step at the end of the phrase and is broken up into small verbal units; and a phrase that ends with a plagal cadence from C minor to G minor. There is, however, also a hint of strength accompanying "le perfide" ("treacherous one"), as would be expected, with chromatic movement in the bass that ascends from B♭ to B♮ to C, only to "give in" to the weak melodic descent of a half step on "se rend" ("surrender") and the plagal cadence made up of two minor chords.

Whereas La Barre and Le Camus generally avoid frequent representations of the more agitated passions, both composers include a number of sorrowful expressions, with the words "douleur" and "triste" appearing regularly in the texts they set. In "Tristes enfans de mes desirs," La Barre sets "malheureux et justes soûpirs" ("unhappy and just sighs"), Example 3.17, with musical devices typical of sorrow with a stepwise melodic descent of a fourth, sighing figures, small verbal units, and weak harmonies (the presumed first-inversion chords). However, the setting also suggests tenderness by the parallel movement in tenths between melody and bass line and the alternation of major and minor harmonies.

LA LANGUEUR

La langueur (languor) is a species of sadness and is closely related to *la douleur*, as the representation of fatigue and inertia is common to both passions.[65] But there is a difference in the way the composers set one or the other affect. For languorous expressions, composers emphasize the indecision that often accompanies this passion with a wavering melody that vacillates up and down, ending up where it began, and phrases that begin and end with the same harmony. Composers project the weakness associated with fatigue through melodies, bass lines, and harmonies that stress the interval of a third (usually the minor third), "of my soul's peace"

EXAMPLE 3.15. Lambert, "Superbes ennemis du repos de mon ame," mm. 3–4, *Les Airs de Monsieur Lambert*, p. 20.

"The treacherous one surrenders"

EXAMPLE 3.16. Bacilly, "Au secours ma raison," mm. 5–7, *Les Trois livres d'airs*, I:28.

"Unhappy and just sighs"

EXAMPLE 3.17. La Barre, "Tristes enfans de mes desirs," mm. 8–12, *Les Airs à deux parties*, 19v.

and in particular, by rhythms that simulate gasps for breath within small verbal units. The melody often descends by minor seconds and remains in the middle register of the piece.

Lambert sets the phrase "to languish night and day for her," from "Que me sert-il" (Example 3.18), with a melody that descends a third after each ascent, a wavering bass line, a phrase that begins and ends with the same harmony (G major), an emphasis upon minor harmonies even though the mode is major, and minor thirds in both the melody and the bass line.

The rhythmic movement and small verbal units in this example are also characteristic of languor and add to the effect of fatigue and inertia. Lambert divides the eight-syllable phrase into three units of

"To languish night and day for her"

De lan - guir   nuit et jour   pour el - le

3   5   6   3   5   3   5   6

EXAMPLE 3.18. Lambert, "Que me sert-il," 5–8, *Les Airs de Monsieur Lambert*, p. 44.

"Ah! how difficult it is when love is extreme"

Ah!_____   qu'il est   mal - ai -

6   6   5-4

sé   quand l'a - mour   est ex - tre - me

6   6   #   6   4-#3   #
         5

EXAMPLE 3.19. Bacilly, "Puisque Philis est infidelle," mm. 12–17, *Les Trois livres d'airs*, I:4.

three syllables each (counting the feminine ending at the end of the phrase). The first verbal unit begins energetically by the use of a small rhythmic value (the quarter note), but immediately the motion slows down with the following half and whole notes on "languir." Another burst of energy comes with the dotted quarter to eighth note on "nuit et" (m. 6), which comes to a halt with the dotted half note on "jour" (m. 7). Finally, Lambert repeats the rhythm of the first utterance, "de languir" (m. 5), for "pour elle" at the end of the phrase (m. 7). In this way, Lambert represents a speaker who is only capable of uttering three syllables at a time before he must rest to begin again.[66]

Although *la langueur* is named in Bacilly's air "Auprez des beaux yeux," in which he treats the passion in much the same manner as Lambert does, the best examples of languor by Bacilly are those in which it is not named. The passage from "Puisque Philis est infidelle" (Example 3.19) is just one of several.[67] In this air, Bacilly represents "giving up," or surrendering to the laws of love, with languorous tones, "languor"

EXAMPLE 3.20. La Barre, "Un feu naissant vient d'enflamer," mm. 9–11, *Airs à deux parties*, 17v.

"To languish longer"

EXAMPLE 3.21. Le Camus, "Non, il n'est pas en mon pouvoir," mm. 3–7, *Airs à deux et trois parties*, p. 39.

wherein the speaker pleads with his heart to revolt against Philis, the unfaithful beloved. But the heart refuses; it is too difficult to banish an unfaithful lover from one's heart. Here we see the most common features associated with languor: the melody vacillates up and down; sighing figures imitate expirations of breath; the minor third is emphasized in melody, bass, and harmonies; and the same harmony begins and ends each phrase.

Representations of languor abound in airs by La Barre and Le Camus. In La Barre's air "Un feu naissant vient d'enflamer, " the word "langueur" appears twice. Its second appearance, shown in Example 3.20, is a perfect and extended melodic representation of the passion in the form of the "serpentine" melisma on the first syllable of "langueur," accompanied by the steady movement of the bass in large note values and static F♯ harmonies that lead to the cadence in B minor.

The word "languir" appears once in Le Camus' printed collection in the air "Non, il n'est pas en mon pourvoir" (Example 3.21). Here, Le Camus also sets the passion with a melody that vacillates, only to end up where it began. The bass also "languishes," expressed by a line that descends and ascends a minor third in both directions, large note values, and weak harmonies (several in first inversion), before its chromatic ascent to the end of the phrase.

Extended representations of *la douceur* (sweetness, often refer-ring to facial expressions, tenderness, or pleasantness, particularly with respect to the eyes) are rare in the most serious airs. *La douceur* appears most often in the adjective form "doux." It is most commonly associ-ated with expressions of tender or sweet love (a mild form of sexual desire in contrast to burning love), which are often accompanied by musical representations of sighs.[68] According to Descartes, sweet love presupposes sadness, so we are moved to sigh when "some imagined hope or joy opens the orifice of the venous artery which sadness had constricted."[69] According to Bretteville, this kind of love is expressed by a sweet and agreeable voice ("une voix douce, agréable"). Grimarest uses the words "flattering and tender voice" ("une voix flateuse, ten-dre"), and Le Faucheur notes that a man "will shew his Love best by a soft, a Gay, and charming Voyce."[70]

Lambert, Bacilly, La Barre, and Le Camus associated expressions of sweet love with weak musical devices (such as a melody that appears in the middle register of the piece, repeated rhythmic patterns, and small verbal units) and, as mentioned above, with references to the number three that allude to Venus. The most characteristic device used by composers for tenderness is the alternation of major and minor thirds in the melody, bass, and in harmonic relations. The eighteenth-century German theorist George Andreas Sorge likened the major third to the male and the minor to the female, and asserted that the use of both major and minor thirds side by side symbolized harmony between the sexes and in the universe.[71] Although no French theorist directly connected major and minor thirds to gender, Boësset did refer the major third as "virile" and the minor as "soft."[72] Their alternation in composers' representations of tender love strongly suggests such an interpretation as well.

The word "doux" appears in only one example from Lambert's col-lection, in the air "O Dieux comment se peut il faire" (Example 3.22), on the words "que soubz un visage si doux" (that under a face so sweet). Here, Lambert invokes tenderness with the devices associated with this passion. He places the melody in the middle register of the piece and arranges the pitches to form a melodic arch. He uses other weak musi-cal devices as well, such as first-inversion chords, a bass line that moves by seconds and thirds, repeated rhythmic patterns, and small verbal units, often comprising three syllables each. Lambert also imitates sighs, "that under a face so sweet"

que sous   un vi - sa - - ge si doux

6   6   3   3   5   #6   3

EXAMPLE 3.22. Lambert, "O Dieux comment se peut il faire," mm. 5–7, *Les Airs de Monsieur Lambert*, p. 12.

commonly associated with tenderness in his pieces, with paired quarter notes in the bass (m. 6). The melisma on the syllable "sa-" of "visage" ("face") is also typically associated with tender expressions, particularly on words that refer to the loved one's features.

More importantly, Lambert stresses major and minor thirds in melody, harmony, and bass. The melody is largely conjunct, its pitches outlining major and minor thirds (A to C and C to E in m. 6, and D to B in the final three notes of the phrase, mm. 6–7). The notes at the beginning and end of the melody line are also a third apart. The harmony moves from major to minor almost in regular alternation (C major to D minor, C again to A minor, and D major to G major).

Whereas extended representations of tenderness are rare in Lambert's airs, "doux" or the adverb form "doucement" of *la douceur* appears several times in the airs by Bacilly, La Barre, and Le Camus.[73] Indeed, collections of airs by these three composers contain many songs that are less serious than Lambert's and, therefore, more apt to include this sentiment. One of the best illustrations of "sweet or gentle" musical treatment is found in Bacilly's "Au milieu des plaisirs" ("In the midst of the sweetest pleasures in life"), Example 3.23. Bacilly shapes the melodic line in the form of a graceful arch. It takes five measures to incorporate a twelve-syllable line, giving the line a relaxed feeling (in more agitated expressions a greater number of syllables are often fit into a fewer number of measures to create larger verbal units). As in Lambert's example of sweet love (Example 3.22), Bacilly stresses the relation of major and minor thirds in the melody, bass, and harmonies, divides the phrase into small verbal units, and supports the melody with a bass line that moves predominately by step.

The repetition of two melodic ideas and the two rhythmic patterns associated with each is the most significant feature of this passage. The first musical idea, three notes that ascend by step, appears three times,

"In the midst of the sweetest pleasures in life"

EXAMPLE 3.23. Bacilly, "Au milieu des plaisirs," mm. 2–6, *Les Trois livres d'airs*, I:73.

first in m. 2 (F–G–A), then repeated immediately in m. 3 (A–B♭–C), and again in m. 3 (F–G–A). The second melodic idea, a descending three-note arpeggio, first appears in mm. 3–4 (A–F–D) and then in mm. 4–5 (G–E–C). Thus, tender love is not only established by the movement of the melody (by seconds and thirds), the movement of the bass line (primarily by seconds that often outline thirds), and the emphasis on the closely related harmonies of F major, D minor, and B♭ major, but by repetitions of two melodic ideas that are presented sequentially and by the reiteration of the rhythmic patterns associated with each idea. Bacilly also makes frequent reference to the number three: the first phrase ascends by three notes the interval of a major, a minor, and finally a major third; the second phrase descends by minor and major thirds; the harmonies alternate by major and minor sonorities; and the bass line often parallels the melody at the tenth.

The "modest" passions—sorrow, languor, and tenderness—are related to each other in many respects. Each of these passions invokes sighs. Sorrow and languor, particularly, are kindred affects and share many of the same physiological properties, such as listlessness and physical weakness. Composers employ the following weak musical devices in their representations of these passions: (1) melodies in the middle or low range of the piece; (2) melodies and bass lines that either outline minor and major thirds by conjunct motion or leap by thirds; (3) melodies that descend (sorrow), roam about (languor) or are arched (tenderness); (4) a predominance of minor harmonies (sorrow and languor) or an alternation of major and minor harmonies (tenderness); (5) first-inversion chords; (6) small verbal units; (7) fewer accented rhythms; and (8) weak cadences.

Music and the Language of Love

The Neutral Passion: *Le Contentement*

Descartes describes joy as a pleasant emotion associated with a regular pulse which is faster than usual.[74] He notes as well that

> the nerve located around the orifices of the heart is especially active: by opening and enlarging these orifices it enables the blood which other nerves drive through the veins to enter and leave the heart in larger quantities than usual. And because the blood then entering the heart has come into the veins from the arteries, and so has passed through the heart many times already, it expands very readily and produces spirits whose parts, being very equal and fine, are suited for the formation and strengthening of the impressions in the brain which give to the soul thoughts that are cheerful and peaceful.[75]

Bretteville associates *le contentement* with a full and flowing voice ("une voix pleine, coulante"); Bary assigns it a sweet and flowing voice ("une voix douce, coulanter"); Grimarest suggests a sweet (tender), full and easy tone ("un ton doux, plein, facile"); and Le Faucheur notes that when a man is happy he will "discover his Joy well with a Full, flowing and Brisk Voyce."[76]

Composers imitated these features of joy by balancing strong and weak musical devices. A full tone is achieved in the music by a predominance of major harmonies (usually tonic and dominant), a melody that moves either by skips of fourths or fifths or in conjunct diatonic motion (depending upon the intensity of the passion), a homophonic texture (the bass line and melody moving together in parallel motion), and arched melodic lines. An easy and flowing tone is invoked by regular rhythms that fall into repeated patterns, large verbal units, and phrases with an equal number of syllables set to an equal number of measures.[77]

Le contentement (satisfaction, joy, or happiness) appears in its adjective forms "content" or "heureux." When it is named or represented in Lambert's collection, it occurs in the least impassioned pieces, as in "J'aymerois mieux," a bittersweet air (Example 3.24). Here, the speaker acknowledges that he would rather suffer death than stop loving Silvie. If he could only continue to see her and love her, he would be happy for the rest of his life, but his happiness is tempered by her infidelity. Lambert invokes joy through a melody that leaps by a fourth and ends with an ascending major second. The bass line moves primarily by step and the harmonies are simple, with exclusively major chords

"I will be too happy"

je se - ray trop heu - reux

EXAMPLE 3.24. Lambert, "J'aymerois mieux," mm. 20–22, *Les Airs de Monsieur Lambert,* p. 56.

that move from D major to G major. Though not specified by theorists, these traits—skips of fourths and fifths over simple major harmonies—are typically associated with happiness throughout the repertory.

Bacilly projects happiness on the word "heureux" in several airs. "One is happy to love nothing," from "On est heureux" (Example 3.25), is one of the best examples of an expression of happiness in its imitation of the full, easy, and flowing nature of the passion. The melody leaps by fifths, fourths, and thirds. Bacilly uses dotted rhythms to create a "skipping" effect and repeats the exact rhythmic pattern for the second part of the melody. In addition, the rhythm of the bass follows that of the melody, suggesting a homophonic texture. Typical of representations of this neutral passion, there is a balance between strong and weak musical devices: the bass line moves both by step and by leaps, and there is a combination of root-position and first-inversion chords. One of the most important features of this expression is the way Bacilly groups phrases into a regular number of musical measures. In this example, an eight-syllable line falls into three measures. This line is followed by a four-measure phrase made up of eight syllables (not shown here).

"One is happy to love nothing"

On est heu - reux de n'ai - mer rien

EXAMPLE 3.25. Bacilly, "On est heureux," mm. 2–4, *Les Trois livres d'airs,* I:66.

Summary: A General Description of the Passions and Their Representation in Mid-Seventeenth-Century Airs

Lambert, Bacilly, La Barre, and Le Camus composed their airs in imitation of the tones of voice and rates of speech associated with each of the seven primary passions, as named in or suggested by the poetic texts. The composers' affective representations are remarkably similar and match descriptions of the various passions given in treatises, whether through imitating the tones of voice described by Bretteville, Grimarest, Le Faucheur, or Bary, or reflecting the psychophysiological explanations of Descartes. While composers invoked each of the agitated passions—despair, power or courage, and burning love—with strong musical devices, they also characterized each passion with a specific combination of these musical features. Likewise, composers represented the modest passions—sorrow, languor, and tenderness—with weak devices, yet each is distinctly projected. Happiness, a passion that rarely appears in serious airs, is invoked by combining strong and weak musical devices, thereby neutralizing the passion; it is neither agitated nor modest. I conclude here with a summary of the theorists' descriptions of each primary passion, followed by a list of the most common traits found in the musical representation of that passion. The following chapter will consider how composers altered and combined features of these passions to express the entire lyric.

DESPAIR OR HOPELESSNESS (LE DÉSESPOIR)

DESCARTES: Despair is a violent kind of agitation. The spirits are sent rapidly from the brain to all parts of the body, particularly to the heart, which sends more spirits back to the brain to maintain and strengthen the passion. Because more spirits rush to the brain than for any other passion, all the senses are more acute and all parts of the body more mobile. Despair results when the desired object is hopelessly unattainable.

BRETTEVILLE: Despair is a violent and impetuous movement by which the soul distances itself from something good that it can not possess, after having searched for it with ardor.

GRIMAREST: Its Manifestation in Recitation

Despair is an exclamation and a tone of voice that is high, abrupt, exaggerated or outraged, and violent ("un ton aigu, précipité, outré, violent").

The Musical Representation of Despair

1. The melody is in the highest register of the piece.
2. The melody ascends primarily by step and always ends with an ascent, often by half step.
3. The rhythmic movement is primarily by large values in large verbal units, which gives emphasis to important strong syllables; additionally, dotted rhythms or a whole note followed by two quarter notes are used.
4. The bass line moves by step, skips, or a combination, often in contrary motion with the melody; with the stronger expressions, disjunct bass movement is more likely.
5. Tonic–dominant harmonic relationships are emphasized, especially at the ends of phrases.
6. Chords are most likely to be in root position rather than in first or second inversion.
7. The melodic contour ascends.

POWER, COURAGE, OR BOLDNESS
(LE POUVOIR, USED FOR STRONGLY STATED OPINIONS, COMMANDS, DEMANDS, EMPHATIC STATEMENTS, OR ANGER)

DESCARTES: Courage is a "certain heat or agitation which disposes the soul to apply itself energetically to accomplish the tasks it wants to perform." Because it is a species of desire, as is despair, the two passions share many of the same traits. The difference is that courage disposes the soul to accomplish the task required to obtain the object of desire and depends upon hope for success in attaining the goal. Despair, on the other hand, results when the attainment of the desired object is impossible, leading to hopelessness and the eventual extinction of the desire altogether.

BRETTEVILLE: Courage is "a passion of the soul, which strengthens it in the face of danger, and makes it attack the evil, in order to fight it and conquer it."

GRIMAREST AND BARY (*L'Audace*): Its Manifestation in Recitation

L'Audace and despair are two of the most agitated passions, and audacity should be represented by an impetuous or forceful and lofty voice ("une voix impétueuse et hautaine").

LE FAUCHEUR: Its Manifestion in Recitation

"Confidence . . . will be easily discover'd by a Loud and a Strong Voyce, always keeping-up to a Decent Boldness and a daring Constancy."

The Musical Representation of Power, Courage, or Boldness

1. The melody is in the highest register of the piece, and organized into large verbal units.
2. The melody often stresses chord tones of the tonic and dominant harmonies.
3. The melody either moves in disjunct motion by fourths and fifths or by both disjunct and conjunct motion. Often commands and demands are set with repeated notes.
4. Single pitches are often repeated for emphasis.
5. Dotted rhythms are often used at the end of a phrase, with large rhythmic values at the end of the line.
6. Often two quarter notes ascend to a note of a larger value.
7. The bass line moves primarily by large note values in disjunct motion.
8. Tonic–dominant harmonic relationships are emphasized whether in the key of the piece or not.
9. Although the contour of the melody varies, the phrase most likely ends with a melodic ascent.

THE BURNING FIRES OF LOVE

In song texts, the burning fires of love are referred to in a variety of ways. *Je brûle nuit et jour* ("I burn night and day"), *la flame* or *les feux* ("the fires of love"), *une maladie* (a disease or illness associated with being in love, called erotic melancholia by doctors) are all used to refer to intense feelings of love and sexual desire.

DESCARTES: Burning love is "the desire which arises from attraction. . . . Attraction . . . is specifically ordained by nature to represent the enjoyment of that which attracts us as the greatest of all the goods belonging to mankind, and so to make us have a burning desire for this enjoyment."

No description given by Bretteville, Grimarest, Bary, or Le Faucheur

The Musical Representation of Burning Love

1. The melody ascends chromatically, especially at the beginning of the phrase, and is organized into large verbal units.
2. The melody resolves with a descending motion, often by half step, at the end of phrase.
3. The melody usually appears in the low or middle register of the piece.
4. Dotted rhythms dominate the phrase.
5. The bass line remains relatively inactive at first and then descends by step at the end of the phrase.
6. The harmonies move primarily by fifths.
7. The contour of the melody primarily ascends; it then descends suddenly at the end of the phrase.

SORROW, GRIEF, OR PAIN (*LA DOULEUR*)

DESCARTES: Sorrow is associated with listlessness caused by a severe restriction of the openings of heart. The blood in the veins is not agitated at all, so that very little blood goes to the heart, which causes the limbs to relax and remain motionless. Tears result from a moderate feeling of sadness when accompanied by some feeling of love or joy. Descartes claims that sadness must be combined with these other emotions so that the "quantity of vapors" is sufficient enough to form tears; extreme sadness causes too great a constriction of blood throughout the body and not enough vapors for weeping.

BRETTEVILLE: Although Bretteville does not describe the physiological aspects of sadness, he associates this passion with a languishing and fearful voice ("une voix languissante, craintive"), which is interrupted by sighs and groans.

GRIMAREST: Its Manifestation in Recitation
This passion is accompanied by a weak, lingering, and plaintive voice ("une voix foible, traînante, plaintive").

"He'll discover his Grief . . . with a dull, languishing and Sad Moan; not without breaking off abruptly sometimes, with a sob; and fetching-up a sigh or a groan from the heart."

Musical Representation of Sorrow

1. The melody is characterized by descending conjunct motion, emphasizes the minor second, and is organized into small verbal units.
2. The melody or melodic phrase often encompasses the interval of a minor third.
3. The melody is in the middle or sometimes the low register.
4. Phrases end typically with an interval of a descending minor second.
5. The bass line moves by leap or by half step, depending on the force of the expression.
6. Minor harmonies dominate the phrase.
7. The cadence at the end of the phrase is often subdominant to tonic (or at least forms a relationship of a fourth between the harmonies).
8. The melodic contour descends.

LANGUOR (LA LANGUEUR)

Languor is a species of sadness and is closely related to sorrow, *la douleur,* as the representation of fatigue and inertia is common to both passions.

The Musical Representation of Languor

1. The melody seems to roam about or ramble on. Usually it will ascend a bit and then immediately descend and end up just about where it began, and is organized into small verbal units.
2. The interval of a third (usually minor) is stressed either by a leap of a third or by a conjunct melody that outlines the third.
3. The melody often moves by descending minor seconds.
4. The melody is almost always placed in the middle register of the piece.

5. The rhythms are either two quarter notes followed by a whole note, in a descending passage, or steady half notes leading to a whole note.
6. The bass line either moves in conjunct motion by thirds, or leaps by thirds.
7. The harmonies are often related by thirds (from D minor to F major, for example).
8. Often the phrase begins and ends with the same harmony.
9. The contour of the melody resembles a wave.

Tenderness, Sweetness (*La Douceur*)

Tenderness often pertains to facial expressions or pleasantness, in particular sweet or tender eyes. This sentiment often appears in the adjective form *doux* and is associated with expressions of tender or sweet love. Tenderness is a mild form of sexual desire in contrast to burning love and is often accompanied by the musical representation of sighs.

Descartes: Tender love presupposes sadness, so we are moved to sigh when "some imagined hope or joy opens the orifice of the venous artery which sadness had constricted."

Bretteville: Its Manifestation in Recitation

Tender love is expressed by a sweet and agreeable voice ("une voix douce, agréable").

Grimarest: Its Manifestation in Recitation

Tender love is associated with a flattering and tender voice ("une voix flatteuse, tendre").

Le Faucheur: Its Manifestation in Recitation

"He will shew his Love best by a soft, a Gay, and charming Voyce."

Musical Representation of Tenderness

1. The melody often moves in conjunct motion by minor and major thirds, or outlines triads.
2. The melody appears in the middle register of the piece.
3. The melody and bass often move in parallel motion by sixths or tenths.

4. Major and minor harmonies alternate and are closely related to the tonic.
5. The bass moves by seconds and thirds.
6. First-inversion chords dominate.
7. Rhythmic patterns are repeated throughout the phrase.
8. The melodic contour resembles an arch.

HAPPINESS (*LE CONTENTEMENT*)

DESCARTES: Joy is a pleasant emotion associated with a regular pulse which is faster than usual.

BARY: Its Manifestation in Recitation

Le contentement is associated with a full and flowing voice ("une voix pleine, coulante").

GRIMAREST: Its Manifestation in Recitation

Happiness is associated with a sweet (tender), full and easy tone ("un ton doux, plein, facile").

LE FAUCHEUR: Its Manifestation in Recitation

"He'll discover his Joy well with a Full, flowing and Brisk Voyce."

Musical Representation of Happiness

1. All songs are in major mode.
2. The melody either moves in disjunct motion by fourths and fifths combined with conjunct diatonic motion, or it moves in simple conjunct motion in melody and bass.
3. Often melodic patterns are repeated throughout the phrase.
4. A homophonic texture is suggested by the same rhythmic movement in melody and bass.
5. The harmonies are closely related to the tonic, major, and emphasize the tonic and dominant.
6. Regular rhythms fall into repeated patterns.
7. Duple meter is used in light songs, while triple meter is used for expressions of happiness in bittersweet airs.
8. Phrases contain an equal number of syllables set to an equal number of measures.
9. The contour of the melody resembles an arch.

CHAPTER FOUR

Setting the Texts

In setting each phrase of the song texts, composers had to consider the entire lyric, for as Marin Mersenne asserts, in composing airs "one must . . . see what the entire subject of the discourse aims toward within the air."[1] Insofar as each line of the poem relates to the text as a whole, each musical phrase necessarily relates to and serves to unify the complete piece. Most song texts in their entirety present the speaker's passive and active reactions to a beloved. These two types of response influenced the composer's choice of musical devices used in setting each phrase of the lyric, such that every musical phrase reflected the greater sense of the song text.

In setting most texts, the composers chose the passions to be represented according to the beloved's treatment of the (usually male) speaker and his resulting actions. In the majority of serious airs, composers interpreted the speaker's reaction to the beloved's rejection by invoking the most agitated passions. The more agitated passions were associated with intense actions such as declarations of love or threats of revenge. An act of resignation, however, was linked to weaker passions such as languor, sorrow, or tenderness. In light texts, the speaker responds to his beloved with tenderness and joy, which would appropriately accompany his description of the beloved's charms, inspire him to run joyously through the fields with his beloved, or play his *musette*.

The information revealed in the song texts and the affects represented in the musical settings correspond to several of Descartes' assertions about the passions. Noteworthy is the correlation with his three-step emotive process: (1) the "object" (Descartes' word), or stimulus; (2) the passionate response to the object; and (3) the active response or action taken in response to the movement of the passions.[2] According to Descartes, every passion felt by a human being is caused by the representation of something, the object, associated with particular passions. Once the passions are felt, the soul is disposed to "want the things for which they [the passions] prepare the body."[3] The stimulus or object causes the passions most commonly associated with it to be felt. The passions, then, cause the body to react. The sight of a bear, for example, activates certain spirits to move to the brain which may cause a person to feel fear; fear prepares the body for flight, so we most likely run away. In this example, the bear is the object or stimulus; fear is the passion; and flight is the action. In many of the song texts, the beloved's rejection is the object; despair, sorrow, and boldness may be the affective response; and a declaration of love may be the action taken by the speaker.

Descartes also specifies that the same stimuli may cause different passions and actions in different people:

> The same impression which the presence of a terrifying object forms on the gland [in the brain], and which causes fear in some people, may excite courage and boldness in others. The reason for this is that brains are not all constituted in the same way.[4]

This, too, is reflected in the song texts and the composers' settings: the beloved's rejection may cause despair and boldness, resulting in a declaration of love; but in another poem, she may provoke languor and sorrow, causing the speaker to cower in her presence and suffer in silence.

The composers' settings of the song texts reflect three other assertions made by Descartes: (1) more than one passion is often aroused by the object; (2) passions are felt with greater or lesser intensity; and (3) passions often mix together to form new passions.[5] Except in light airs, composers always represented more than one passion in their settings. They also increased or decreased the intensity of a passion, either by placing a phrase in a high register and adding strong musical devices to weak (to intensify a modest passion) or by placing the phrase in a low register and adding weak musical devices to strong (to decrease the intensity of an agitated passion). The intensity of any passion could be modified in this way. Composers also created new affects by mixing together devices belonging to more than one passion: the combination of sorrow or languor and tenderness, for example, produces regret.[6]

Each subject type (painful love, bittersweet love, enticing love, and joyous love) is identified through the objects, passions, and actions presented in song texts, so each will be considered separately in the following analyses. The greatest difference between airs of different subject types concerns the number of affects represented in the air and how composers altered affective representation to reflect the different passions and actions revealed in the lyric. Each air comprises a common set of musical devices, associated with more than one passion, that are used by the composers in a variety of combinations to unite each poetic and musical expression. In the following analyses, each air will be treated as a case study to demonstrate important features related to the different types of airs.

Painful Love

In the airs belonging to this category, the speaker is represented as greatly impassioned or "full of motion," to use Lamy's words, in response to the beloved's rejection. Composers set these texts to imitate the "diverse movement of passions" that many theorists associated with intensely affective discourse.[7] La Croix describes such discourse as unequal, or devoid of a regular cadence and moderate tones of voice; phrases are interrupted by the "diverse movements" (different passions) that agitate the animal spirits.[8] Mersenne advises composers to alter continually the *accens* that correspond to various passions to "imitate the tidal flow of the spirits of the blood."[9] In these airs, the object (the beloved's rejection) stimulates the most agitated passions in the speaker: despair, boldness or anger, and burning love. Sorrow, languor, and short utterances of tender love also appear, but to a lesser degree. While the texts suggest similar passions, the speakers' active response comprises the greatest difference between the airs in this subject type. Four actions are represented: (1) declarations of love; (2) suffering in silence; (3) complaints of rejection; and (4) threats of revenge. If the more agitated passions dominate in response to the object, the three possible actions are a declaration of love, threats of revenge, or intense complaints. If not, the speaker resigns himself to rejection and chooses either to suffer in silence or protest slightly.

A Declaration of Love

The most important musical manifestation of impassioned texts, particularly those whose subject is a declaration of love, is the mixture and variation of affective representation, not only from phrase to phrase but within the same phrase as well. To demonstrate, I offer the reader a detailed analysis of Lambert's air "Mon ame faisons un effort" (Example 4.1) in order to highlight properties typical of many other airs. (For translations of complete airs, see the Appendix.) In this air, the speaker declares his love to Silvie, knowing that he will be rejected and thus "die." The declaration of one's love is a courageous act and should be accompanied with bold tones, yet rarely are acts of courage accompanied by this passion alone.[10] Soldiers marching into battle, for example, may be courageous, but they are also fearful and/or sorrowful because pain and death are possible consequences. Likewise, in "Mon ame faisons un effort," Lambert varies the *accens* from phrase to phrase and within phrases as well to invoke the variety of passions suggested by the text.

LINE OF POETRY	AFFECT	MEASURES
1. My soul let us make an effort	sorrow and boldness	mm. 1–4
2. Since I burn I must complain	burning love and boldness	mm. 4–6
3. Let us speak it is no longer time to pretend	boldness (sorrow)	mm. 6–8
4. We are too close to death	despair	mm. 8–10
5. Do not be offended Silvie	boldness and tenderness (overall sorrow)	mm. 11–14
6. If I lose [your] respect I also lose my life.	sorrow and boldness (with suggestions of despair, burning love, and tenderness)	mm. 15–20

Passions Juxtaposed and Mixed

Two passions dominate Lambert's setting: boldness, associated with the speaker's declaration of love, and sorrow, associated with his impending death and loss of the beloved. Both passions appear in lines one, three, five and six. Lambert also invokes burning love in line two and despair in line four; not only are the affects in these two lines suggested by the text, but their representation serves as a musical variation of the *accens* represented in the surrounding phrases to better imitate the diverse movement of the passions.[11]

As Example 4.1 shows, Lambert sets the first line (mm. 1–4) as a sorrowful and bold utterance. The musical representation of this line initially seems an expression of sorrow, with its melodic descent through the principal fifth of the triad, and yet closer examination reveals that Lambert mixes both strong and weak musical devices. He uses strong devices to evoke the speaker's bold effort and determination to declare his love despite the consequences (the beloved's rejection and his death) and weak ones to accompany the sorrow associated with the loss of the beloved and the prospect of his death.

The expression of more than one passion in setting this first line of text is achieved in several ways: by the number of syllables that make up each verbal unit, by mixing strong devices with weak, and by altering the register of the melody. Lambert divides the line into two verbal units, three syllables in the first and five in the second. The two units are clearly delineated by the return to an F-major harmony and a large note value on "-me" of "ame" (m. 2), and by the placement of the rest before "fai-" of "faisons" (m. 3). Lambert sets the first unit, the words "mon ame" ("my soul"), with two of the devices most frequently associated with sorrow and tenderness: the repetition of two Cs followed by the descent of a minor third. Frequently Lambert (and other composers) employ the descending minor third for addressing or referring to one's soul, heart, or beloved. Lambert supports the melody at this point with the harmonic progression F–C–F, associated with strong passions, but appropriately softens the utterance by placing the dominant chord (C major) in first inversion. This portion of the phrase is also weakened by the small verbal unit and the use of the two equal whole-note values on "a-" and "-me," which would warrant a slow and equal recitation.

The change of affect occurs on the second verbal unit of five syllables, "Let us make an effort" (mm. 3–4). "Faisons" (m. 3) is a command and is treated as such, yet it is slightly weakened by its placement in a low tessitura and by the use of the first-inversion F chord under "-sons." But the weakening of the command is only secondary, as strong musical devices dominate: the strong syllable "-sons," on a weak portion of the beat, is syncopated (the whole note receives the beat in this portion of the air), and the sustained A in the melody against the B in the bass creates a dissonance. Thus Lambert invokes an agitated affect with rhythmic syncopation and dissonance, in contrast to the previous "gentle" reference to the speaker's soul, and continues the bold affect within this large verbal unit through assigning smaller rhythmic values to "un effort" and repeating the F in mm. 3–4. But he alters the affect again, weakening the expression suddenly at the end of the phrase with a deceptive cadence. We expect a strong cadence, C major to F major, but instead the harmony moves to D minor.

The D-minor harmony prepares the listener for the important allusion to the lament affect in m. 4, the descending minor tetrachord in the bass just before "Puisque."[12] Minor mode, triple meter, ambiguity of phrase length, phrase overlap, and the representation of "spontaneous expressivity" were all common features of the lament.[13] Lambert

EXAMPLE 4.1. Lambert, "Mon ame faisons un effort," *Les Airs de Monsieur Lambert,* p. 4.

displaces the bar line to include three whole notes in m. 4 and not two, suggesting lament at this point through a triple meter with ambiguous metric stress. The lament figure foreshadows the textual references to death, which results from his declaration of love and the beloved's rejection, in lines four and six (mm. 8–10 and 15–20, respectively).

Misplaced Bar Lines, Changing Meters,
and Free Recitation

The musical setting of the second line of text not only introduces a new passion, it also demonstrates how the placement of the bar line affects the vocal "recitation" of a melodic phrase. The line begins with a declaration of burning love, "Since I burn" (mm. 4 and 5) and ends with a statement of necessity, "I must complain" (mm. 5–6). The shift to triple meter in m. 4 not only suggests lament but also serves as an important signal to the performer and a guide to the composer's ideas of proper declamation. In this example, by placing the measure line before "brusle" ("burn," m. 5), Lambert saves the greatest stress for this most important word of the phrase. "Brusle" also appears at the hemistich and should receive a greater stress than "Puisque" in any case. If the bar line had been placed before "Puisque," "brusle" would have begun on the second and weaker beat of the measure. Thus, this important word is stressed structurally and its significance to the meaning of the phrase is emphasized by "misplacing" the bar line. This "misplacement" also articulates the two large verbal units of the line: the first of four syllables and the second, five (counting the feminine ending on "plaindre").

Lambert alters the affect again by setting the third line of the piece with bold tones ("Let us speak it is no longer time to pretend," mm. 6–8). Even though this line is a strong utterance, it resembles the first line of the piece in melodic shape, thereby suggesting sorrow as well as boldness. But Lambert has raised the pitch by a major second so that the melody extends from D to G instead of from C to F (a rhetorical figure known as *gradation*), and has used stronger musical devices: a dissonant seventh chord accompanying the strong syllable "-lons" of "parlons," the command; a chromatically ascending bass at the end of m. 7; and, even though in first inversion, major chords for most sonorities. But Lambert "fools" us again at the end of the phrase to represent the word "feindre" ("pretend"). We expect a movement from D major to G minor, but, instead, the harmony moves to C minor in first inversion. Perhaps the two unexpected cadences, in m. 4 and then again in m. 8, represent the speaker's hesitation to act boldly, as a strong V–I cadence would presume a more decisive action.

Changes from duple to triple meter commonly occur throughout this repertory, but in this example the change causes an ambiguity in the unit of beat, from m. 5 (two whole notes, as the meter indicates at the outset of the piece) to the first part of m. 6 (one whole note or two half notes) to the second part of m. 6 (three half notes) to m. 7 (three whole notes or six half notes).[14] Is the unit of beat the whole note or half note? If in m. 7 the whole note returns as the unit of the beat (3/1), as it was through m. 5, this causes a series of syncopations. Should one consider the half note as the common unit of beat throughout the first half of the piece, or switch to the half-note unit in m. 6? The best solution may be to treat this section as a sort of recitative, that is, as a free representation of speech declamation. Not only does Bacilly point out in his treatise that airs are "a song in free meter," as distinct from dance songs,[15] he also uses anapest rhythms in this example (mm. 7–10) which anticipate Lully's operatic recitative.[16] At this point in Lambert's air, the performer may properly stress important words and syllables as well as enhance the agitated affect of this passage by accelerating the tempo slightly and maintaining a strong tone of voice throughout this large verbal unit. In any case, moving from a whole note beat to the three half notes in the second half of m. 6 effectuates the feeling of a more rapid tempo and more agitated passion which needs to be maintained to the end of the first half of the air.

Lambert's placement of the bar line also guides the performer to stress the word "parlons" ("let us speak"), indicating that "-lons" of "parlons" is the syllable that needs more emphasis than "plus." The word "plus," in fact, should receive less stress than the word "temps" which follows it, a specification that Bacilly addresses in his treatise on singing.[17] This longer measure, then, demonstrates a larger grouping of verbal units than might otherwise be associated with the series of rhythms. To maintain a forceful recitation throughout the measure, the singer needs to stress all three long syllables to some degree: "-lons" of "parlons," "plus," and "temps."

In addition, the placement of the bar line suggests that Lambert wants to emphasize the fifth, third, and first tones of the supporting chord (D, B♭, and G) as in line one (C, A, and F, mm. 1–4). This is accomplished by the placement of the D and B♭ on the downbeat of successive measures. If "plus" (on C, middle of m. 7) had been accented with a downbeat, this pattern could not have been established. Though not given metrical stress, the final G of the triad (m. 8) is emphasized because it forms the cadence, is given a large note value, and is followed by a rest that separates it from the following line.

Lambert interprets line four with yet another affective representation, that of despair ("We are too close to death," mm. 8–10). Yet the reference to death alters his representation of this affect, as despair and death presuppose contradictory musical features. Because this is an expression of despair, one large verbal unit of eight syllables would be a reasonable interpretation of the phrasing. An agitated affect is also evoked by the syncopated bass rhythm and accented weak beat on "de" in the melody (m. 9).[18] The restricted melodic range along with what seems to be a division of the line into small units (in this example, three units), however, are commonly associated with references to death, even in desperate expressions. But here, Lambert creats an ambiguity in the division of the phrase: rhythmic pauses break up the melody, but they occur in the middle of a word ("som-mes"), after a word that normally is not stressed ("de"), and are accompanied by continuous movement in the bass line. It is quite possible that Lambert created an intentional ambiguity in order to represent both despair and impending death. As in the preceding phrase, the singer should also maintain a strong tone of voice and treat this phrase as a large, eight-syllable verbal unit.

Unification through Affective Representation

A command ("Do not be offended Silvie") begins the second half of "Mon ame faisons un effort," mm. 11–14. The repeated As in the melody and Fs in the bass, the ascent of a fourth in the melody, and the return to a measured recitation are typically bold. Because the speaker is addressing his beloved, though, Lambert appropriately turns the command into an utterance of sweet love, associated with the melodic descent by major and minor thirds, the alternation of major and minor harmonies (F major–D minor, m. 11; B♭ major–G minor–E♭ major, m. 12; and D minor–C minor–D major, mm. 13–14) and by the return to a measured recitation in triple meter. Lambert continues the tender affect as the speaker addresses the beloved, "Silvie" (mm. 13 and 14) in the same manner.

Lambert mixes the greatest number of passions in line six, the final line of the strophe: "If I lose [your] respect I also lose my life" (mm. 15–20). His setting of this line also demonstrates how composers treat textual repetitions. The line begins sorrowfully on the words "Si je pers" ("If I lose"), but the sequential treatment given the repetition of the text at a higher pitch level intensifies the affect. All textual repetitions throughout the repertory are treated similarly, a type of the rhetorical device referred to as *polyptoton* or *synonymia*.[19] Even though restatements of text are rarely set to the same music, they are often treated sequentially and express the same passion either with more intensity, as in this example, or with less.

"Le respect" ("respect"), mm. 17–18, continues the stronger affect and resembles the desperate statement regarding death in mm. 8–10. Lambert invokes agitation by a melodic phrase that ascends by a whole step on "-spect" of "respect"; yet he also symbolizes death by the small melodic range and, more significantly, by the return of the descending tetrachord in the bass (D–A, mm. 17–18). Losing respect in this repertory refers to a declaration of love, yet by doing so, the speaker "dies."

It is at this point in the air that Lambert's simulation of dying by the melodic descent of a fifth and its connection to the declaration of love are made explicit, serving to unite almost every phrase of the piece with this idea. Lambert continues to represent death in the last phrase ("I also lose my life," mm. 18–20), but this time in association with bold tones and his declaration of love. Lambert sets the first, third, fifth, and sixth lines of the song text with a descending melody associated with sorrow and death, yet all refer to his declaration of love.

Line one: He asks his soul to make an effort (*to speak out*).

Line three: He must *speak out,* there is no longer time to pretend (because he is too close to death).

Line five: He asks his beloved not to be offended because he must *speak out.* (Here, Lambert extends the melodic range of the fifth by a half-step, to form the interval of a minor six, possibly as a "tender" reference to the beloved, Silvie).

Line six: He is going to *speak out* (lose respect); thus, he will die.

Because the bold act of declaration warrants strong musical devices, this passion is represented throughout each of these phrases along with the implication of death. In the final line of the song (mm. 18–20), Lambert invokes bold tones with predominantly major harmonies, movement by major seconds on the words "la vie," and a strong V–I cadence in F. The combination of the descending melody in reference to death and the strong devices in association with boldness connote facing death with courage.

A final line that summarizes all the passions (and ideas) throughout the piece is a common feature of Lambert's airs. Here are references to all of the passions contained in the entire song: sorrow, tender love, boldness, burning love, and despair. In this last line, Lambert most notably invokes sorrow by a descending melody and boldness by strong musical devices. Tender love appears briefly on the word "also" (the descending minor third and minor harmonies on "aussi," m. 19)—the speaker not only loses his respect and his life, he *also* loses Silvie. Lambert suggests despair by the treatment of "respect" and burning love by the hint of chromaticism on "Je pers aussi" ("I also lose," mm. 18–19). All these passions constitute the reaction of the lover and appropriately accompany his desire to declare his love despite the consequences.

Textual Images and Level of Affective Intensity

Even among song texts that belong to the same category of subject type, the intensity of affect expressed by the text will determine the types of passions represented by the musical setting. In both "Si je vous dis" and "Vous ne pouvez Iris," both songs of painful love set by Bacilly, the speakers declare their love to Philis and Iris, respectively, but only in "Vous ne pouvez Iris" does the speaker refer to death, suffering, the excess of torment, blows, and fears. And indeed, Bacilly's treatment of each text reflects this difference in affective intensity. He sets the less agitated text, "Si je vous dis" (Example 4.2), as a dance (resembling a sarabande), so the meter is regular throughout the piece. Although there is one utterance of despair in line two ("so much severity," mm. 7–9), most of the expressions are sorrowful and tender. Tenderness is particularly suggested by the descending major and minor thirds in the melody and the alternation of major and minor harmonies at the ends of lines and at hemistiches ("ayme," m. 5; "Philis," mm. 6–7; "extreme," mm. 15–16; "tousjours," mm. 17–18; and "la verité," mm. 21–22).

By contrast, Bacilly sets "Vous ne pouvez Iris" (Example 4.3) with predominately bold and desperate utterances, and to a lesser extent, sorrowful tones, to project the defensive action the speaker must take that "commands" him to die. Although there are fewer affects represented in this piece than in "Mon ame faisons un effort" by Lambert, Bacilly invokes agitation by his use of smaller rhythmic values and expressive intervals. Even though Bacilly's setting of the first two lines of "Vous ne pouvez Iris" is almost identical to that of "Si je vous dis" (Example 4.2), the smaller rhythms (quarters and eighths when the half note is the unit) and dotted motion evoke greater agitation.

EXAMPLE 4.2. Bacilly, "Si je vous dis," *Les Trois livres d'airs,* I:52.

BACILLY, LA BARRE, AND LE CAMUS: MINIMIZING AFFECTIVE INTENSITY

Bacilly's airs in general tend to represent fewer passions than many pieces by Lambert do. In his "Vous ne pouvez Iris" (Example 4.3) a number of passions are evoked to imitate impassioned speech, which is "full of motion," yet boldness and sorrow dominate to highlight this most significant aspect of the text. The musical devices associated with boldness and sorrow are juxtaposed and mixed, just as the poetic references to declaration, death, and losing the beloved appear throughout the poem. While devices associated with other passions, such as despair, burning love, or tenderness, add variety to the music, those that invoke boldness and sorrow unify the musical setting.

Like Bacilly, other composers tend to minimize affective intensity in setting the most passionate song texts. Sébastian Le Camus' pieces in his published collection of airs generally express the more moderate passions. There is one example of an intensely impassioned air in La Barre's collection—"Tristes enfans de mes desirs" (Example 4.4)—and yet the text, and thus its musical setting, is constructed in such a way that the representation of extreme suffering is minimized. Here, the speaker does not declare his love directly; instead, his love is revealed "innocently" through "sighs, sobs, weeping, and regret." The musical

EXAMPLE 4.3. Bacilly, "Vous ne pouvez Iris," *Les Trois livres d'airs*, I:60.

setting, then, in major mode on G, is predominantly sorrowful and tender with only a few utterances of despair.

SUFFERING IN SILENCE

In contrast to a courageous declaration of love, a speaker who chooses to maintain "respect" does not tell his beloved he loves her.

EXAMPLE 4.4. La Barre, "Tristes enfans de mes desirs," *Airs à deux parties,* 19v.

Composers represented these texts primarily with sorrowful, languorous, and sweet musical tones. When agitated passions are represented in the text, composers often temper intensity with weak musical devices. Representations of sorrow, languor, and tenderness are frequently combined to create the complex affect of regret, which Descartes describes as a kind of sadness or languor mixed with tender memories of a lost past:

It has a particular bitterness in that it is always joined to some despair and to the memory of a pleasure that gave us joy. For we regret only the good things which we once enjoyed and which are so completely lost that we have no hope of recovering them at the time and in the form in which we regret them.[20]

Resignation and Regret: Combining the Passions

In Lambert's "Mon cœur qui se rend à vos coups," Example 4.5, regret leads to an act of resignation, which is revealed in line one, "My heart which *surrenders* to your blows."[21] The speaker has not been openly rejected by the beloved because he has not declared his love, but her eyes have revealed the bitter truth that she cannot love him in return. Although regret is the dominant affect of the air, created by mixing languorous and tender tones, Lambert also interprets the affective response of the speaker with expressions of boldness and despair (passions indicated in parentheses are not the primary affect of the phrase but are suggested in some way by its musical treatment):

LINE OF POETRY	AFFECT	MEASURES
1. My heart which surrenders to your blows	languor, tenderness	mm. 1–4
2. Will not complain Philis of the heavens nor of you	languor (tenderness)	mm. 5–8
3. I will die a death that I had foreseen	despair (languor) tenderness and sorrow	mm. 8–12
4. I have lost in my misfortunes all hope of being healed	despair (languor)	mm. 13–17
5. And as soon as I saw you	joy	mm. 18–20
6. I had to dream of dying	boldness, languor, tenderness	mm. 21–24

Bary describes a voice filled with regret as broken by sobs and breaths ("coupée de sanglots & d'aspirations").[22] Indeed, the mixture of tenderness (in response to Philis's charms) and languor (at the hopelessness of the situation), full of sighs and aspirations, is evident in almost every line of the piece, even within bold and desperate expressions. The wavering shape of the melody in line one (a line that descends, immediately ascends, and then descends again) is associated with languor, yet the descent of a fourth on "Mon cœur" ("My heart") seems an extended (or exaggerated) sigh of tender love.

EXAMPLE 4.5. Lambert, "Mon cœur qui se rend à vos coups," *Les Airs de Monsieur Lambert*, p. 32.

Although allusions to tender love would usually be accompanied by a mixture of major and minor harmonies, here Lambert accompanies the words "Mon cœur," with two major harmonies, C and G, but the G-major chord is softened by its placement in first inversion and by the bass-line descent of a minor second, also a typical "sighing" figure (the figure 3 under the downbeat of m. 2 does not designate a root-position chord but rather indicates that a D should be played along with the B in the bass and G in the melody).

Again, Lambert mixes musical devices associated with different passions in this first line. Devices associated with boldness or despair are not only found here but in the other languorous utterances throughout the piece. The eight-syllable line is divided into three units (two-plus-three-plus-three syllables), indicative of the frequent aspirations associated with languor and regret, yet the pauses in the melody are made ambiguous by the agitated bass-line movement which propels the declamation of the phrase forward. In m. 3, the E in the melody becomes dissonant as the bass moves to an F on the crucial word "(se) rend" ("surrender"). This not only underscores the word but also adds a sense of pain associated with an act of resignation. Indeed, Descartes refers to the *bitterness* that accompanies the memory of some pleasure now gone.[23]

Lambert's setting of line two (mm. 5–8) demonstrates how a modest passion can be made more intense. The feeling of languor on the words "[my heart] will not complain, Philis, of the heavens nor of you" is suggested by the melody's wavering shape and the predominance of minor sonorities, while at the same time the utterance is intensified by placing the melody in the highest range of the piece (which could also represent the reference to "Ciel," or "heavens"). Within this same phrase, Lambert evokes as well a moment of tenderness on the beloved's name, "Philis," with a sighing figure of a descending minor second. Although "-lis" of "Philis" is given a whole-note value, it receives only a secondary stress due to its placement in the middle of the measure rather than on the downbeat. This reinforces the "gentleness" of the tender reference. But at the same time, Lambert places an A-major-minor-seventh chord in first inversion under "Ne" in m. 5 (where the G of the melody is the seventh of the chord), an A-major chord in first inversion on "se," a D-minor chord on "plain-" in m. 6, a diminished chord under "Phi-," followed by an A-minor chord under "-lis." This series of chords mixes bitterness with tenderness at the mention of the beloved's name and in reference to the pain of remaining silent. After the tender reflection, Lambert returns to a more agitated expression of languor in setting "of the heavens nor of you," the second hemistich of the line (mm. 6–8). The large verbal unit of six syllables, the major harmonies, the syncopated rhythm in melody and bass (m. 7), and the return to triple meter sustain the strength of the expression.

Lambert sets the first half of line three, "I will die a death" (mm. 8–10), in much the same way as he does other desperate references to death, and yet here again, languor is suggested by the mixture of musical devices associated with more than one passion. Typical is the association of death and despair with a small melodic range, the melodic ascent on "d'une mort" ("a death"), the large verbal unit of six syllables, and the predominance of major harmonies in root position (again, the second figure 3 in m. 9 designates that the third above the E is to be played along with the C in the melody).[24]

Lambert concludes line three with tenderness and sorrow as the speaker proclaims that he has foreseen his own death (mm. 8–12). Most importantly, we see here that the change of passion associated with the entire line, from despair to tenderness and sorrow, underscores the contrast between future and past events. Reference to the future evokes despair (mm. 8–10) or fear of the unknown, while reference to past events is a reminder of his sad fate (mm. 10–12). The phrase ends in a low tessitura and there are sighing figures in the melody (a minor second and then minor third), a final descent of a minor third on "preveüe" ("foreseen"), two minor sonorities in m. 10 (A minor to E minor) leading to a first-inversion D-major chord in m. 11. While the first half of the entire phrase concludes with a somewhat strong harmonic progression (D minor through B-diminished to C major, mm. 9–10) to accompany an utterance of despair in the melody, the entire phrase concludes with a strong cadence (G major–D major–G major, all in root position) yet with a sorrowful melodic turn.

Lambert again interprets the fourth line (mm. 13–17), which begins the second half of the song, with a mixture of despair and languor. In the melody, every ascent is met by a descent, yet each descent is by leap, not by step, which is more typical of agitated passions.[25] Lambert seems to imitate gasps of breath associated with languorous utterances by the rhythmic movement of the melody and bass lines, as the quarter notes in the melody and half notes in the bass lead to larger note values on strong syllables that end each small verbal unit (the twelve-syllable verse is divided into four groups of three syllables). Yet the descending leaps, the ascent of the melody at the end of each verbal unit, the predominance of major harmonies, and the dissonance on "mal" ("misfortune") intensify the affect all the more.

Lambert imitates the rapid beating of the speaker's heart in reaction to the sight of the beloved in the next line. As the speaker remembers his beloved, "And as soon as I saw you" (mm. 18–20), more agitation is created by changing to quarter-note rhythms in both melody and bass, accelerating the harmonic movement, and concluding with a Phrygian cadence to E major. Lambert then changes the affect to accompany the speaker's dreams of dying in line six (mm. 21–24), for the image of the beloved evokes sweet love (note especially the descent by thirds on "du songer" ["to dream"] that outlines an A-minor sonority).

In the air "Mon cœur qui se rend à vos coups," the reference to death (mm. 8–10, line three) is represented as it was in "Mon ame faisons un effort" (Example 4.1), by a descending minor tetrachord in the bass (G to D in m. 9). Variations of this figure appear in the second half of the piece in association with this idea (extended to encompass a tritone from C to F♯ in mm. 14–16, then from G to D in mm. 17–18, and A to E in m. 19). Two more appearances of the descending tetrachord, one major and one minor, overlap in the bass: F to C (the end of m. 19 to the downbeat of m. 21) and D to A (beat three of m. 20 to end of m. 21). Each of these tetrachords is illustrated in Example 4.6. The utterances on "à mourir" ("dying") at the end of the piece (mm. 22–23 and m. 24) are separated to represent the speaker's last gasps for breath as he pronounces his dying words. Both are uttered courageously and are symbolic of the ultimate resignation: the acceptance of fate.

EXAMPLE 4.6. Tetrachords in Lambert, "Mon cœur qui se rend à vos coups."

Minor Mode and Greater Affective Intensity

All but one air by Lambert in this category, "suffering in silence," are in major mode on C. And indeed, pieces in major mode tend to be less impassioned than those in minor mode. By contrast, one air in this category, "Superbes ennemis du repos de mon ame," Example 4.7, is in minor mode on D, and the textual differences between it and "Mon cœur qui se rend," in major mode, are immediately dis-

EXAMPLE 4.7. Lambert, "Superbes ennemis du repos de mon ame," *Les Airs de Monsieur Lambert*, p. 20.

cernible.[26] "Superbes ennemis" is rich with words that suggest intense passions, including "enemies," "tremble," "blows," "offended," "suffer," "misfortune," "fear," and "rage." While "Superbes ennemis" is generally more impassioned than "Mon cœur," every utterance begins with despair, anger, or boldness but concludes with a weaker passion, either sorrow or tender love. The musical devices follow suit. Lambert begins line one desperately, for example (see mm. 1–2), but ends the phrase with sorrowful tones (mm. 3–4). Line four begins boldly (mm. 11–13) but ends tenderly (mm. 13–17). Even though Lambert evokes the agitated passions, he combines sorrowful and tender tones at the ends of lines to project regret, the passion most often associated with "suffering in silence."

Meter and Affective Representation

Each half of "Superbes ennemis" is assigned a different meter to distinguish between two affects: cut time in the first half and triple meter in the second. In this song, as in other pieces, the change from duple to triple meter, particularly $\frac{2}{1}$ to $\frac{3}{2}$, initiates a movement to tender love. The strongest language appears in the first half, while the second half includes many tender references, such as the beloved's beautiful eyes and the speaker's sighs and martyrdom. Note the abundance of descending minor thirds on "beaux yeux" (mm. 13–15), "du martire" (mm. 19–20), "soupirer" (mm. 21–22), and "soupirer pour vous" (mm. 24–25). In mm. 16–17, "sighing" is represented by another sighing motive, the descending minor second. All of these words are harmonized with alternating major and minor sonorities. While regret is suggested in the first half of the piece by the tender and sorrowful tones that conclude each phrase, in the second half of the piece, regret is the principal affect because tender and sorrowful tones are mixed in every line.

In both "Mon cœur qui se rend à vos coups," and "Superbes ennemis du repos de mon ame" (Examples 4.5 and 4.7), the speakers resign themselves to their fate and suffer in silence. Even if strong language appears in the text, Lambert associates the act of resignation with the weaker passions. Whereas strong passions cause a violent agitation of the animal spirits within the body and prompt bold and courageous acts, languor, regret, and tenderness slow down the movement of the spirits and render the body immovable and incapable of provocative actions. Particularly in "Mon cœur," Lambert reflects the body's immobility by mixing musical devices associated with more than one passion to a far greater extent than he does in airs belonging to the category "declaration of love." In this way, he creates the complex passion of regret and minimizes the effects of the agitated passions.

COMPLAINTS OF REJECTION

Most songs that concern painful love belong to this category. In these airs, the beloved's rejection of the speaker is the primary subject of the text and the sorrow, anguish, and regret he feels are the passions represented. Condemnation of the beloved and ultimately resignation are the resulting actions. The level of affective intensity varies according to the severity of the speaker's complaints. Composers set texts of lesser affective intensity in major mode on C or B♭, as in Lambert's "Que me sert-il," while texts that connote a greater number of agitated passions are in either minor mode on either D or G, as in Bacilly's "Au secours ma raison."

Bacilly's Propensity for Word Painting, the Juxtaposition of Affect, and Irony

Airs in minor mode, while more impassioned than those in major mode in this category, are not as full of *mouvement* as those in the previous two categories, "declaration of love" and "suffering in silence." "Au secours ma raison" (Example 4.8), in minor mode on G, warrants strong passions given its images of war: the speaker fights against the evil forces of love; the beloved is the enemy who attempts to seduce his heart with a deceitful display of sweetness.

Bacilly's setting of the first line illustrates his propensity for word painting, as he imitates a cry for help in setting "Help my reason rescue my heart" (mm. 1–5). The use of large intervallic leaps that descend and ascend, the dotted rhythms, syncopations in both melody and bass, and the erratic rhythmic movement all create an extremely agitated affect. Bacilly abruptly alters the impassioned utterance with tenderness at the mention of his heart (mm. 4–5). The tender affect associated with the reference to the heart is not only represented by the descending figure in the melody, encompassing a minor third, but also by the use of the three-quarter-note anacrusis. As was pointed out in the previous chapter, an upbeat of two quarter notes in triple meter is almost always reserved for stronger passions, while an upbeat of three quarters in the midst of a forceful expression invokes tenderness.

Bacilly's setting of lines two and three shows how he, like Lambert, mixes and juxtaposes different affective representations. Here, mm. 5–14 are set to languorous and tender tones, in association with regret and resignation: "The treacherous one [reason] *surrenders* without

EXAMPLE 4.8. Bacilly, "Au secours ma raison," *Les Trois livres d'airs*, I:28.

resistance / And *gives in* to the laws of its [his heart's] victor." Yet at the end of line two, Bacilly represents his "reason's" attempt to resist the beloved (failed though it was) in mm. 7–10 with a bold affect, achieved by the stress on three syllables in a row ("-sis-," "-tan,-" and "-ce" of "resistance"), the ascending melody on "resistan-," the duple meter in m. 9, the descent to the third of the D major chord from "-tan-" to "-ce," and the emphasis on major harmonies achieved by the chromatic alteration of the E♭ to an E (mm. 6–7) and the F to an F♯ (mm. 9–10).

Bacilly's preference for juxtaposing passions rather then mixing them is illustrated in his setting of line four. While line three, "gives in to the laws of its victor" (mm. 10–14) is clearly languorous, Bacilly interprets the following line (mm. 14–18), which refers to seduction by deception, as a bold, perhaps even angry, statement.

Bacilly also has a penchant for irony. Before the final cry for help in the last line, "a false sweetness" ("D'une fausse douceur") is mockingly represented (mm. 18–20). This line of the poem stands out because it is a six-syllable line, which rarely occurs in isolation in this repertory, amidst lines of eight and twelve syllables. Bacilly also highlights the line in his musical setting by transposing the melody of the phrase "le perfide se rend" ("the treacherous one surrenders") from mm. 5–7, a rhetorical figure referred to as *paronomasia*. Transpositions of entire phrases are usually associated with textual repetitions, while transpositions on different textual phrases rarely occur. These two phrases constitute the most important idea of the piece: the "treacherous one," his heart, surrenders to the beloved (line two) because it was deceived by her "false sweetness" (line five). In the musical setting, the transposition of line two to line five makes this connection explicit, as Example 4.9 shows.[27] Even though the melodic fragment is usually associated with sorrow, as it was in mm. 5–7, the higher register and the strong harmonic movement from D major to A major to C-sharp diminished to D major in mm. 18–20 make it less sorrowful but certainly not sweet, thus conveying the beloved's deception. Bacilly sets the fourth and fifth lines, then, to summarize the courage and effort of the fight

EXAMPLE 4.9. Bacilly, "Au secours ma raison," mm. 5–7; mm. 17–19.

(line four) and the beloved's victory (the resignation of the speaker to her deceitful powers). These two acts (the fight and the surrender) and their accompanying passions are apparent in every line of the air.

THREATS OF REVENGE

The speakers threaten revenge in only a few song texts. Revenge is an action that results from anger, a passion rarely represented in this repertory.[28] Descartes characterizes anger as a hatred or aversion we feel toward those who have harmed us and notes that although anger is more violent than any other passion, the body responds to anger in much the same way as to courage.[29] Anger generates as much agitation of the blood as boldness does and causes a desire for action, but it motivates acts of vengeance.[30]

Bretteville agrees with Descartes in his description of anger as "a turbulent passion of the soul, by which it raises itself against the cause of the evil and the injury it feels, with a violent desire to avenge itself."[31] It is accompanied by a high, impetuous, violent voice and shortness of breath ("une voix aigue, impeteueuse, violente et frequentes reprises d'haleine").[32] Bary describes the tone associated with anger as bitter or shrill, high, and broken ("un ton aspre, aigüe and coupé"); and Grimarest as a tone that is elevated, loud, and sudden ("une voix elevée, éclatante, subite").[33]

Music theorists considered certain devices more appropriate than others for expressions of anger, such as the use of large intervals, especially fourths, and Lydian mode.[34] Boësset observes, for example, that Lydian mode was considered "suitable to fury, shrieks and despair, because the major third . . . is as virile as the minor third is soft."[35]

The Juxtaposition of Antithetical Passions: Anger and Sorrow/Languor

In Bacilly's "Puisque Philis est infidelle" (Example 4.10), we learn of the desire for revenge in the second strophe, "let us [the speaker and his heart] avenge ourselves of her hate." But the entire text reveals two very different affects and actions: anger and the desire for revenge, and sorrow and languor in association with the refusal of the heart to fight the beloved:[36]

LINE OF POETRY	AFFECT	MEASURES
1. Since Philis is unfaithful	anger/boldness	mm. 1–3
2. Let us avoid death my heart	boldness/anger tender on "my heart"	mm. 4–6
3. Let us revolt against her	boldness/anger	mm. 6–9
4. But you do not agree to it	sorrow and tenderness (Regret)	mm. 10–12
5. Ah how difficult it is when love is extreme	languor (tender)	mm. 12–17
6. To banish from one's heart an ingrate whom one loves.	anger/boldness tender/sorrow	mm. 17–20 m. 21

The air begins with three angry and bold utterances (mm. 1–10), characterized by descending melodic leaps by fourths and rhythmic anapests.[37] In setting line one, Bacilly stresses almost every syllable ("puis-," "Phi-," "-lis-," "del," and even the weak syllable "-le") with large note values and the placement of strong syllables on downbeats. The harmonies in mm. 2–4 are all strong, moving between F, B♭, C, and F. Descartes identified boldness as a passion closely related to anger,[38] and Bacilly accordingly sets the commands in lines two and three with bold and angry tones. Note, however, that he sets the reference to the heart, "mon cœur" (mm. 6–7) as a tender expression amidst the bold utterances.

Bacilly's "Puisque Philis" demonstrates his propensity for juxtaposing extremely different representations of passions, as the agitated affects of the first half of the air contrast with the regret (sorrow and tenderness) expressed at the beginning of the second half, accompanying the speaker's realization that his heart does not agree to fight. At the change of affect, the listener is left in suspense on the word "Mais" ("But," m. 11) for three beats. All movement comes to a complete stop, as if the speaker is listening to his heart's response at that moment. To further underscore this phrase as a turning point in the song, the six-syllable line stands out in contrast to the previous eight-syllable and the following twelve-syllable lines, and Bacilly sets most of this shorter phrase in one measure (m. 12).

In lines five and six, the maxim or "lesson" of the piece as the speaker sees it is revealed, and the two situations and passions represented by

EXAMPLE 4.10. Bacilly, "Puisque Philis est infidelle," *Les Trois livres d'airs,* I:4.

the entire text are summarized: "Ah! how difficult it is when love is extreme / To banish from one's heart an ingrate whom one loves."[39] Bacilly sets line five (mm. 13–18) primarily as languorous; it is useless to fight against the beloved when love is so extreme. But in the second half of the maxim, line six (mm. 18–22), Bacilly recalls the anger and boldness of the first half of the piece. One of the most revealing devices used is the leap up the octave, from G to G, to commence the expression "to banish from one's heart." Many theorists believed that large leaps signaled a radical change in affect, and octaves leaps in particular were indicative of angry expressions, according to Mersenne.[40] Not only is the G on "De" the highest note in the piece, typical of the vehement expression, but there are also frequent skips in the melody; a B♮ against an F appears (mm. 18 and 20), suggesting Lydian mode; and the harmonies are predominantly major and outline strong tonic–subdominant–dominant relationships leading to the downbeat of every measure.

Tempo Markings, Meter Changes, and Passionate Representation

La Barre included one air that refers to revenge in his collection of airs. "Ah! Je sens que mon cœur" (Example 4.11) is the most impassioned of all the airs in his publication. The piece is in minor mode on D and includes several agitated utterances: despair, such as that on "Ah! I feel that my heart" (mm. 1–3); burning fires of love on "The ungrateful Sylvie" (mm. 10–14); and anger on "Love avenge me" (mm. 18–32). Each of these changes in affect is indicated by La Barre with either a tempo indication, change of meter, or both. The chromatically ascending melody on "The ungrateful Silvie" is to be sung slowly ("lentement," mm. 10–15). Here, the melodic chromaticism is not directly associated with "the burning fires of love" (though he still may "burn" for her); instead, La Barre may have set these words in this way as a means of showing that his anger intensifies and builds until it explodes, at m. 16. At this point, the meter changes to $\frac{3}{4}$, accompanied by the indication "gayement." This word does not mean "gay" in the sense of "happily," but rather indicates that the tempo should be faster. The change of beat unit—the smaller quarter-note value—accompanies this frantic pace. From m. 16 on, anger takes over: the frenzied rhythms in both bass and melody continue with few breaks to the end of the piece, the melody remains in the highest register of the air; and major mode on B♭ is stressed. Anger is tempered, however, by reference to love, for throughout these final measures, the word "Love" ("Amour") is accompanied by the bass in parallel tenths and is treated as sighs in mm. 22–23 and mm. 26–27. The tumultuous conflict between feelings of love and anger continues throughout these last few measures.

EXAMPLE 4.11. La Barre, "Ah! je sens que mon cœur," *Airs à deux parties,*
10v.

PAINFUL LOVE: SUMMARY

Airs about painful love demonstrate many characteristic features typical of the repertory. The "object," in this case the beloved's rejection, stimulates more than one passion in each song in this category. The composers' musical settings reflect this "diverse movement of passions" by juxtaposing and combining the various musical devices associated with all the passions suggested by the text. Often the text as a whole necessitates conflicting or seemingly opposite passions. The greater the range of passions embodied in the song text, the more impassioned the air.

Composers also varied mode and meter in response to the text. Generally speaking, they set the more agitated texts in minor mode: the stronger the vocabulary, the more lively the images, the more impassioned the piece. Major mode is used to represent the weaker passions and/or less aggressive actions, particularly resignation. Major modes used within a minor mode piece, however, often accompany the more agitated passions, particularly anger.

Meter alone is not associated with one passion or another, but meter changes and alterations in the unit of beat accompany a change of affect. A change from duple meter (two whole notes per measure) to triple meter (six half notes per measure) represents a change to more agitated passions. A shift from duple meter to triple meter (with three half notes per measure) is associated with a change to weaker passions, particularly tender or sweet love. A change from triple to duple meter ($\frac{3}{2}$ to $\frac{2}{2}$), by contrast, accompanies the appearance of bold expressions. In some cases, as in Lambert's air "Mon ame faisons un effort" (Example 4.1), a metrically free interpretation is warranted following the meter change. As this piece demonstrates, changes in meter may or may not be indicated by the appearance in the score of time signatures. The altered measure is either enlarged or contracted to accommodate syllabic stress and affective representation. In most instances, however, the half-note value remains constant despite the change in unit of beat from one meter to another.

The exception is found in La Barre's song "Ah! je sens que mon cœur" (Example 4.11), wherein the meter changes from $\frac{3}{2}$ to $\frac{3}{4}$. In this case, the singer may wish to establish a proportional relationship between these two meters, with the half note equaling the dotted half (so that the unit of beat in the $\frac{3}{2}$ measure becomes the length of the measure in $\frac{3}{4}$). This would certainly accommodate La Barre's indication that the tempo should increase in speed at this point.

In any case, no matter the meter, the composers invoked the more agitated passions by varying the rhythmic movement from one measure to the next and by using smaller rhythmic values (particularly quarter notes). Upbeats of two quarter notes leading to a large note value on a downbeat are also used for agitated expressions, but when this rhythmic figure appears with weak musical devices, it represents gasps of breath associated with languor. By contrast, the composers used upbeats of three quarter notes for tender expressions.

These few observations apply to all serious airs, whether about painful or bittersweet love. While the composers' general approach to setting the texts was the same for both subject types, the airs from each category are accompanied by different kinds of passions.

Bittersweet Love

As the subject type "bittersweet" suggests, composers were more likely to juxtapose opposite passions in the airs from this category (particularly torment or pain with the pleasure of love) than in those from other categories. There are also more extended tender references in both texts and music in bittersweet airs than in those about painful love. Because minor mode is reserved for the more impassioned texts, the juxtaposition of opposite expressions is most striking in airs set in minor mode on D or G. One of the best examples of a bittersweet air in minor mode is Lambert's air "D'un feu secret," in which burning love representing sexual tension is juxtaposed with relief, presumably in reference to sexual climax. This fascinating air will be discussed at length in chapter 7. A bittersweet air by Bacilly, though in major mode on C and so less passionate, will serve to illustrate the juxtaposition of two antithetical aspects of love: pain and pleaure.

THE INTERCHANGE OF MUSICAL FEATURES
AND TEXTUAL MEANING

Whereas sexual tension and relief are juxtaposed in "D'un feu secret," references to the pain and pleasure of love are presented in Bacilly's air "Dûssay j'avoir mille rivaux," (Example 4.12). Throughout the piece, Bacilly opposes two different kinds of musical gestures: descending patterns primarily of major and minor thirds (associated with tender tones) and ascending major and minor thirds (associated with the more agitated passions, particularly despair). As such, he at first pits pleasure against pain by juxtaposing their musical representation, even on words that carry no particular affective meaning. The piece begins, for example, in a clearly tender manner on the words "Even if I had," achieved by the descending major third and accompanied by the bass in parallel motion by major and minor thirds (m. 1). The reference to "mille rivaux" ("a thousand rivals") in the sec-

EXAMPLE 4.12. Bacilly, "Dûssay j'avoir mille rivaux," *Les Trois livres d'airs,* I:64.

ond hemistich (mm. 3–4), however, is represented as an utterance of despair by an ascending melody, heightened register, predominance of major harmonies, and contrary motion between bass and melody. "Je voudrois estre encor" ("I would still like to be," mm. 4–6), maintains the pattern of moving from "tender" to "desperate," though both expressions are mixed and thus not so clearly juxtaposed. The tender utterance on "I would" is accompanied by the strong repetition of Gs in the bass, while the more agitated expression on "still be" ("estre encor") suggests tenderness in the bass by parallel motion at the tenth and the alternation of major and minor harmonies. "Under Climene's laws" (mm. 6–8), then, is purely tender, as one would expect.

If melodic patterns that descend, particularly by thirds, represent pleasure and those that ascend, pain, the musical setting of "Car le plus grand de tous les maux" ("Because the greatest of all misfortunes," mm. 9–12), presents the pleasure and pain of love simultaneously. The melody is clearly representative of the painful side of love, with its ascent from D to C and sudden drop of the diminished fourth from C to G♯ on the word "misfortunes." The bass line, however, descends from G to A before ascending to E, reminiscent of the opening melody. The pattern is then reversed in the following line: the melody on "Is to have" (mm. 13–14) imitates the "tender" melody from m. 1 and the bass from mm. 9–10, while the bass line at this point is reminiscent of the "desperate" melody in mm. 3–4 and 9–10. "Neither pleasure" (the absence of pleasure, pain), then, is presented as both painful and pleasurable, as is "nor pain" (the absence of pain, pleasure). The first repetition of these last two lines of the poem maintains the juxtaposition and simultaneity of expression (mm. 17–24). The combination of pleasure and pain in love as preferable to no feeling at all is thus presented in every phrase of the piece after the initial four measures, which establish the pattern.

SUMMARY: BITTERSWEET AIRS

In bittersweet airs, oppositions are commonly communicated in the musical setting by establishing a relationship between two contrasting concepts suggested by the text, and by extending the meaning of each concept to other terms and phrases throughout the poem.[41] In "Dûssay j'avoir mille rivaux," Bacilly assigns different musical devices to represent the pain and pleasure of love and their accompanying passions (despair and bitterness in opposition to tenderness) and then manipulates the devices to communicate the relationship between the two. At first, pain and pleasure are juxtaposed and represented as separate entities of love. Then, Bacilly uses devices associated with each simultaneously. By the end of the piece, pain and pleasure are represented as interchangeable: Bacilly treats the word "pleasure" with devices previously associated with pain and "pain" with devices

Music and the Language of Love

originally assigned to pleasure. Unlike his contemporaries' approach to composing airs, Bacilly's placement of the devices associated in this air with pain or pleasure is not affected by specific words or phrases in the text. There is no reason, for example, that the words "Even if I had" (line one) or "Because the greatest" (line three) should imply a tender affect, but Bacilly sets them as such to demonstrate by musical means (that is, specific musical devices and their affective connotations) the relationship between pain and pleasure in matters of the heart. More importantly, by constantly assigning musical devices to words and their accompanying affects, Bacilly demonstrates the relationship between opposing aspects of a single act. By the end of "Dûssay j'avoir," Bacilly has communicated that love is both bitter and sweet.

Enticing Love

The poems in this category are a kind of persuasive discourse: the beloved's presence inspires desire in the speaker, who attempts to persuade her to return his love. His arguments usually appeal to the beloved's reason through a logical association. In some airs, the speaker explains that if the beloved can give love, then she must be capable of receiving it. In others, the speaker assumes that because he loves her, she should love him in return. As noted in chapter 2, several rhetoricians acknowledged that arguments are always imbued with various passions. Thus, the speaker's desire is represented in the airs along with the passions associated with his arguments. In every case, the speaker attempts to convince the beloved with bold tones that love is sweet and desirable.

LIGHT AIRS AND THE REDUCTION OF PASSIONATE REPRESENTATION

In Bacilly's air "Vous sçavez donner de l'amour," Example 4.13, the speaker argues that if the beloved can inspire love, then she should accept his love for her. Since the text is a persuasive discourse, Bacilly imbues the speaker with forceful tones, but as the speaker boldly presents his arguments, he also reveals love as a sweet alternative. As such, in the musical setting of this "light" love song, Bacilly evokes two affects, boldness and tenderness.

Bacilly strategically alternates duple and triple meters to signal one or the other passion: duple meter accompanies a predominantly bold affect, while triple meter is associated with tenderness. Within each

EXAMPLE 4.13. Bacilly, "Vous sçavez donner de l'amour," *Les Trois livres d'airs,* I:68.

type of expression, Bacilly mixes features from the other affect. Line four (mm. 10–16), for example, uses predominantly powerful devices, yet Bacilly also conveys tenderness with sighing figures, such as the descending minor third on "vous ne" and "en" (mm. 13 and 15) and the stepwise descent of a minor third on "prendre" (m. 16) to soften the bold affect.

Although the piece is in minor mode on G, a mode usually reserved for the most serious texts and agitated passions, Bacilly alternates major harmonies on strong beats with minor harmonies on weak ones to minimize the intensity of the minor mode. Bacilly also organizes the melody into conjunct melodic fragments of either major or minor thirds and incorporates "sighing" figures throughout the piece in the form of descending minor and major seconds and minor and major thirds to persuade the beloved that love is sweet.

EXAMPLE 4.14. Bacilly, "Pour la bergere Lisette," *Les Trois livres d'airs,*
I:70.

DANCE AIRS

The dance airs that belong to the category of enticing love project one dominant affect, either tenderness or joy. Most of these are gavottes or minuets in major mode on C or F. "Pour la bergere Lisette" by Bacilly (Example 4.14) is a cheerful gavotte distinguished from other dance airs by its narrative text. The shepherd describes his effort to persuade his beloved and reports the conversation that took place between them. He recalls that she cannot commit herself to him because she already has a "lovable shepherd." But if her beloved becomes unfaithful, she will consider returning the speaker's love. Because the speaker is not fully rejected by the beloved, he has hope for the future, which, judging from the dominant happy affect of the air, pleases him. Isolated words do, however, suggest changes of affect: line one of "Pour la bergere Lisette" (mm. 1–4), for example, is cheerful, but Bacilly treats the word "soupire" ("sigh," m. 3) with tender tones.

The pairing of eighth notes in stepwise descending motion on each syllable is a typical representation of the word "soupire" in cheerful pieces. The second eighth note of the first pair and the first of the second are dissonant, adding a slightly "sweeter" affect in contrast to the cheery disposition of the phrase.[42] The sighing figure appears again on the word "aimable" ("lovable," m. 15).

Bacilly momentarily changes affect as well on the phrase "And tell her about my torment" (mm. 7–8), representing the word "torment" through a number of devices: the melodic descent of a minor sixth over the course of the phrase; the introduction of the B♮ in the bass to form a dissonance with the F in the melody in m. 7; the chromatic movement in the melody from F to E and from D to E♭; the alteration of the E to E♭ in the melody, with the sudden switch to minor mode; the agitated rhythmic movement in the melody in m. 8; the dissonant C and A to the G in the bass in m. 8 (depending on the realization of the harmony); and the emphasis of the descending minor second on "mon" and "tourment" in the same measure. This and other examples demonstrate that when one affect dominates an air, composers are likely to invoke other passions momentarily in response to single words. This holds true for airs belonging to the final category, joyous love, as well.[43]

Joyous Love

The category of "joyous love" contains only minuets and gavottes. All are in major mode, either on C or F, and only two affects are represented in the texts and music, tenderness and/or joy. In every piece, the "object" or stimulus of passion is the beloved one, who inspires the speaker to proclaim his love.

In Bacilly's air "Petite abeille mesnagere" (Example 4.15), the narrator invites the little busy bee to enjoy the sweetness of his beloved. Whereas flowers offer seasonal pleasure, his beloved will satisfy him all year round. Bacilly expresses tenderness in this song to a far greater extent than in other songs from this group. He accomplishes this by the leaps of a third, as in mm. 2 and 3–4, and the stepwise melodic motion outlining thirds in just about every measure. At m. 9, at "Draw near to my shepherdess," the melody leaps up and down by fourths, and in the next several measures the bass also moves by leaps, most likely to represent the flight of the bee. The leaps also make this cheery expression more exciting, in much the same way that agitated passions are intensified in serious airs. Bacilly sets the narrator's description of the

EXAMPLE 4.15. Bacilly, "Petite abeille mesnagere," *Les Trois livres d'airs,* I:58.

beloved's sweet lips, ("Se belle bouche a des douceurs," mm. 17–20) with an expression of intense happiness as well.

Bacilly incorporates many features in this song typical of the lightest airs: the harmonies are simple, the bass line moves primarily by step and follows the rhythmic movement of the melody, creating a homophonic texture. Throughout the piece, the rhythms are straightforward and grouped into recurring patterns in the melody and bass. The song text is entirely in octosyllabic lines, and these are regularly divided into two verbal units of four syllables each, set to eight measures of music. Thus Bacilly achieves simplicity in association with joyous love through simple harmonies and rhythmic patterns, a homophonic texture, and regularity of phrase lengths.

Summary

The composers' approach to composition was the same for every poem, and passion was interpreted according to the kinds of "objects" and "actions" presented in the text. To some extent, composers were also guided by the poet's choice of vocabulary: the more agitated the images, the more agitated the passions; the more subdued the vocabulary or the more references to the beauties of nature, the more modest the expression. Thus, each poem evokes different affects in various combinations and intensities. Even those song texts that share the same objects and actions and imply the same passions differ in some way. These differences inspired the composers to search out a distinctive musical representation for every poem.

Although each piece is unique, composers nonetheless used a common set of musical devices—a conventional musical language—in each setting. Various combinations of the musical devices represented each of the primary passions, and these are the conventions of expression, identifiable as musical entities, that permeate the repertory. Thus it is possible to summarize, as I do below, the conventional features associated with airs within each of the four subject types. This repertory is most remarkable because composers managed to create diversity within the constraints of a highly conventionalized art form. How the composers used the conventions (the way they mixed and juxtaposed the various musical devices) reveals the power of their creative abilities.

Painful Love

1. Each text demonstrates the speaker's reaction to the same "object"—rejection by the beloved—but the speakers react in different ways. The more intense the passions, the more aggressive the act. Declarations of love and threats of revenge result in the most agitated passions, particularly despair, boldness, and anger. Expressions of tenderness usually appear on isolated words, particularly in reference to the speaker's heart, soul, or the beloved. If the speaker reacts with regret (which is a complex passion composed of languor or sorrow and tenderness), the resulting action is resignation. If the more agitated passions are represented in these pieces, they are usually tempered by the use of weak musical devices.

2. An action results from a combination of passions. Often, the passions are contradictory—boldness and sorrow, for example. Different passions are represented from phrase to phrase and within the phrase to underscore the meaning of the text. In this way, composers represented in their musical settings the diverse *mouvements* that typify an impassioned recitation.

3. A passion is made more or less intense by altering certain features, thereby creating a range in the expression of the passion. This is best illustrated by the way textual repetitions are treated in the music. Simply by changing the register of the phrase, the passion either decreases in intensity (in a lower register) or increases (a higher one). A passion is also altered by adding weak devices to representations of agitated passions and strong devices to modest passions. A deceptive cadence, for example, softens a bold or desperate passion. Bitterness within any passion is often represented by dissonance.

4. Mode and subject type are related. Major mode is used more often than minor mode to represent resignation. In "Puisque Philis," however, Bacilly sets a text that expressed vengeance in major mode on F. The composers reserved minor mode on D and G for the most impassioned texts. Bacilly particularly used minor mode on G to express greater agitation ("Vous ne pouvez Iris" or "Au secours ma raison," for example). In these airs by Bacilly, the move from one passion to the next is more erratic, the rhythms are more active, and the harmonies more adventurous.

5. Meter alone is not associated with the representation of passions, but changes of meter and rhythmic unit are. Composers changed from duple to triple meter where the triple measure equals six half notes for more agitated passions. But a change from duple to triple meter where the triple measure equals three half notes represented a change from agitated passions to tender and/or sorrowful expressions. Likewise, the composers changed from triple to duple meter where the half note remains the unit of beat for bold expressions. Composers displaced bar lines without marking time signatures in the score in order to adjust syllabic stress or change affective representation (often to more agitated passions).

6. Of the different dance types, composers included only sarabandes in this category. Their appearance is limited because the representation of the most agitated passions relies upon changes in the size of verbal units, meter, and unit of beat. These are rhythmic features not associated with the sarabande or with any other dance air.

BITTERSWEET LOVE

1. Bittersweet airs share many features with those from the previous category, painful love. Airs in both subject types share a common "object," which is the beloved's rejection. While many of the same

passions of the previous category are represented, the tender side of love is emphasized in bittersweet airs. The action, then, is less decisive. Most airs demonstrate a direct conflict between the pain of rejection and the pleasure of love. The speaker's resignation to the conflict is usually the outcome.

2. The juxtaposition of conflicting passions is most notable in this category, but passions are also represented simultaneously to symbolize that pain and pleasure are one and the same. Recurring musical devices are used to reflect the textual content and/or connect like terms and expressions.

3. Passions are altered in the same manner as in airs from the previous category, painful love.

4. Generally speaking, if the text is impassioned, the piece is in minor mode, as in the previous category of painful love. If minor mode was used for a less impassioned text, composers softened the expressions with weak devices and a greater use of major sonorities within the piece. If resignation is the dominant action and regret the dominant affect suggested by the text, the composers used major mode on C. In these airs, strong devices and minor harmonies are used for the more agitated passions, while an alternation of major and minor sonorities is used for tenderness.

5. Meter changes are used in the same manner as in airs from the previous category, painful love.

6. Of the different dance types, only sarabandes are used in this category.

Enticing Love

1. The "object" is still the beloved in this category, but the speaker has not been rejected; thus, the dominant affect is the speaker's tender desire. Most of these pieces are directly persuasive or recount the attempt of the speaker to persuade the beloved, so the text is an appeal to the beloved's reason and to a lesser extent, her empathy. Composers associated tenderness with the argument because the speaker wants to represent love as pleasurable, but they also invoked boldness as the speaker presents his arguments forcefully.

2. Only two passions, usually tenderness and boldness, are represented in airs from this category. In most dance airs in this category, however, only one affect, tenderness or joy, dominates.

3. If two passions are represented, composers not only juxtaposed the two but often tempered the stronger affect with devices associated with tenderness. If only one passion dominates the piece, the composers isolated the words that suggest another passion and set them with musical devices associated with the different affect.

4. Mode corresponds to the intensity of the passions. Thus composers set pieces that are both bold and tender in minor mode, and set texts that represent one passion in major mode.

5. Composers connected meter changes with the change from boldness to tenderness. Tenderness is associated with triple meter, boldness with duple. A change of meter is not accompanied by a change in the unit of the beat; thus, the change of affect is less abrupt than is usual in more serious airs. The meter does not change when one affect dominates the piece.

6. Many dances are used in this category, particularly if only one affect is represented. Minuets and gavottes are most common.

JOYOUS LOVE

1. The "object" is the beloved. Because she does not reject the speaker, the passions she inspires are joy and tenderness. The action is most often the speaker's simple account of his pleasure. Most airs are cheerful with moments of tenderness.

2. One passion dominates, usually joy, but others may appear in isolation on appropriate words.

3. All pieces are in major mode.

4. There are no meter changes; rhythmic patterns occur regularly; lines are divided into two groups of an equal number of syllables; and the same number of measures, usually eight, is used for each musical phrase.

5. All pieces are either minuets or gavottes.

CHAPTER FIVE

Form and Style: The Organization and Function of Expressions, Syntax, and Rhetorical Figures

Form (Disposition)

The poetry set by composers of airs was a discourse intended to persuade the passions, and as such, subject to the emphasis that rhetoricians placed upon the organization of materials in a discourse. Bernard Lamy stressed that it was not enough to "understand a subject to the bottom"; one also had to put the "[subject] matter in Order in our minds."[1] The organization of a text and its expressions could either intensify the impact upon listeners or fail to move them at all.[2] Marin Mersenne specified that composers, too, must cleverly order the musical materials to accentuate the expressive potential of a piece.[3] And indeed, composers certainly considered in their musical settings the relationship between the variety of expressions, their organization, and their function in unveiling the meaning of the entire poem.

Rhetoricians always addressed the organization of texts. Aristotle believed that there were two parts of a speech: the statement of the case and its proofs. But he conceded that in practice orators often added introductions and conclusions.[4] Other rhetoricians divided a discourse further into seven parts: (1) the introduction (*exordium*); (2) the statement of the case, or setting forth the facts (*narratio* or *praecognitio*); (3) the exposition, or definition of terms and issues to be proven (*propositio, definitio,* or *explicatio*); (4) the outline of the points or steps in the argument (*divisio* or *partitio*); (5) proofs of the case (*confirmatio* or *amplificatio*); (6) the refutation of opposing arguments (*refutatio* or *reprehensio*); and (7) the conclusion (*peroratio* or *epilogus*).[5] Most rhetoricians, though, acknowledged that it was permissible to omit certain parts of the disposition or rearrange the parts in order to best serve the subject. François de Salignac de La Mothe-Fénelon (1651–1715), the celebrated French bishop and author, did not approve of adherence to a strict division of the subject matter: "When you divide [a discourse], it is necessary to divide it simply, naturally. One must have a division that is found ready-made in the very subject itself; a division that clarifies, that puts the materials into classes, that is easily remembered, and that helps one retain everything else; a division, in short, that reveals the size of the subject and of its parts."[6]

The Organization of Expressions in Short Airs

There is no evidence to suggest that composers analyzed the texts they set according to the divisions of rhetorical discourse, but they would have had to interpret the structure, organization, and function of expressions in the song text and set each accordingly. We see that the poems set by composers of airs, while too short to include all seven parts of the disposition, do include up to six types of statements: an introduction (*exordium*), narration (*narratio*), proposition (*propositio, definitio*, or *explicatio*), confirmation (*confirmatio*, or *amplificatio*), refutation (*refutatio*, or *reprehensio*), and conclusion (*peroratio*). These parts most frequently divide the song into four sections. The introduction and narration are almost always combined, and in most airs, this section sets forth the "facts of the case" as a means of introducing the topic under consideration. The proposition is a statement of what is to be proven.[7] The confirmation then sets forth the arguments (or proofs) of the case or amplifies the topic. In several texts there is a refutation of what has been "alleged by the adversary." This is usually part of the conclusion, which is either a recapitulation of the topic or a statement intended to surprise or move the listeners.

The number of lines or length of a song text does not limit the presentation of the usual parts of the disposition; even in the shortest poems, all are represented, as in Bacilly's air "Petits aigneaux," which is made up of two four-verse strophes.

First Strophe

Introduction/ Narration	1. Little lambs if you wander off without a master
	2. In these sad deserts at the mercy of wolves,
Proposition	3. If the shepherd Tircis no longer leads you to graze
	4. Alas, he is still more to be pitied than you.

Second Strophe

Confirmation	5. For having said I love you
	6. He has drawn the rage of his shepherdess,
Refutation/	7. Nothing can soften it, her rigor is extreme
Conclusion	
	8. Alas what could he say to her that was sweeter

In the first strophe, lines one and two serve as both introduction and narration. Here the "facts of the case," typical of the narration, are presented: if the little lambs wander off from their master, they will fall prey to the wolves. Lines three and four prepare and state the proposition, or what is to be "proven": if the shepherd Tircis no longer leads them to graze, he is to be pitied more than they. The reason is demonstrated in the second strophe. In lines five and six, the narrator gives proof (or confirmation) of why the shepherd is in a worse situation than that of the little lambs: Tircis has proclaimed his love for the shepherdess, but this angers her. In the refutation, line seven, the narrator refutes the possible claim that Tircis could have done more to please her. The hopelessness of the situation is the primary point of the conclusion, which is presented as a rhetorical question intended to elicit pity from the auditors. All Tircis did to deserve such cruelty was to declare his love to the beloved. What could have been sweeter?

THE SECOND STROPHE: MUSICAL ALTERATIONS TO ACCOMMODATE SYLLABLE STRESS AND AFFECT

Bacilly's interpretation of overall affect for each section of the first strophe is the same for the corresponding sections of the second strophe, the *double*. The confirmation parallels the introduction/narration in its tragic situation, thereby likening the shepherd to the lambs who "wander off from their master" and the shepherdess to the wolves. The music appropriately represents both strophes, shown in Examples 5.1a and b. Although the expressions for the introduction/narration and confirmation are parallel, Bacilly alters the music in the second strophe to accommodate differences in syllable stress and to underscore, intensify, or change affect on certain words. In the first strophe, Bacilly sets eight syllables of the first ten-syllable line within three measures and extends the last two syllables into the next two measures (Example 5.1a, mm. 4–5; the "-stre" of "maistre" is mute because it appears at the end of the line). In the second strophe, Bacilly sets seven syllables in

'Little lambs if you wander off without a master / In these sad deserts at the mercy of the wolves

EXAMPLE 5.1A. Bacilly, "Petits aigneaux," First Strophe, mm. 1–10, *Les Trois livres d'airs*, I:76.

"For having said I love you / He has drawn the rage of his shepherdess"

EXAMPLE 5.1B. Bacilly, "Petits aigneaux," Second Strophe, mm. 1–10, *Les Trois livres d'airs*.

the first three measures to avoid breaking up the three-syllable phrase "Je vous aime" ("I love you," Example 5.1b, mm. 4–5; the final "-me" of "aime" is also mute). In the ornamented version of the melody, Bacilly places the important word "dit" ("said") on the downbeat of m. 2 and avoids stressing the weak syllable "-le" of "seulement" ("only") by placing it on the weak third beat of m. 2, thereby positioning the strong syllable "-ment" on the downbeat of m. 3. Three of the four syllables of "Je vous aime" are inserted into one measure. The long syllable of the most important word, "ai-" of "aime," falls on the third beat, which is stressed by the trill marked in the score. Bacilly gives this crucial phrase the expressive force it requires by accenting a weak beat and by inserting so many syllables in one measure.

Bacilly's ornaments on the second line of the confirmation in the second strophe, "He has drawn the rage of his shepherdess" (Example 5.1b, mm. 6–10), underscore a most important function of the ornamentation: to intensify the affect, emphasize, and even imitate certain words. The ornaments on "attiré" ("drawn") in mm. 8–9 are "drawn out" or extended by the eighth-note melodic flourish. The diminutions on "attiré" also embody the rage of the shepherdess, particularly by the ascending sixteenth-note movement and the agitated rhythms on "le couroux."

The poem of this piece is constructed so that the meaning of the proposition in the first strophe and the refutation/conclusion in the second strophe also correspond in that they both set up an antecedent/consequent relationship of phrases: even if Tircis no longer leads you to graze, he is still to be pitied more than you (first strophe), and no matter what Tircis has said, he cannot soften the beloved (second strophe). These lines also reveal the parallel "tragedies." In the proposition, the narrator claims that Tircis no longer feeds his flock, and in the refutation, he notes that nothing Tircis can say or do softens the shepherdess's anger. Bacilly's setting conveys that Tircis's situation is more tragic than that of the little lambs.

In line three of the first strophe, Bacilly interprets the first hemistich ("If the shepherd Tircis," mm. 11–13) as a desperate utterance, but concludes the line with bold tones ("no longer leads you to graze," mm. 13–15), shown in Example 5.2a. Although his ornamented version of the second strophe, Example 5.2b, is more agitated than the unornamented strophe, Bacilly softens the affect somewhat on "la" ("her"), which refers to the beloved, a reference which composers set in their airs primarily with descending minor or major thirds (here an E drops to C on "la" within the ornament). Despite this moment, Bacilly maintains the sense of anguish of the greater phrase with a momentary dissonance (the D on the last note of the syllable "la" against the E diminished harmony in first inversion, m. 12), the high register, the diminished chord leading to the F-major harmony (mm. 12–13), and the raised minor second on "-cir" of "doucir." The ornamentation in m. 14 also intensifies the bold affect by the wavering of the sixteenth notes on "est extreme," the high register (in an "extremely" high range), the ascending movement in the bass, and the dissonance between melody and bass on beat three.

The proposition of the first strophe corresponds to the conclusion in the second strophe (mm. 16–21) by antithesis. In the proposition, the

Proposition

'If the shepherd Tircis no longer leads you to graze / Alas he is still more to be pitied than you'

EXAMPLE 5.2A. Bacilly, "Petits aigneaux," First Strophe, mm. 11–21, *Les Trois livres d'airs.*

"Nothing can soften her, her rigor is extreme / Alas what could he say that was sweeter"

EXAMPLE 5.2B. Bacilly, "Petits aigneaux," Second Strophe, mm. 11–21, *Les Trois livres d'airs.*

narrator claims that there is *more* to be pited, and in the conclusion he claims that there is *nothing* sweeter that could have been said. By interrupting the music in the first strophe, with rests between "Alas there is still," and "more to be pitied than you" (Example 5.2a, m. 19), Bacilly attempts to leave listeners in suspense and to intensify the affect on the words "more to be pitied than you." This is further achieved by the agitated rhythms, high register, and tonic/dominant harmonies in mm. 19–21.[8] In the second strophe (Example 5.2b), line eight, "Alas, what could he say to her that was sweeter," warrants no such interruption. By avoiding breaking the phrase with rests, Bacilly implies that there is "no room" for more to be said.

Bacilly's ornamentation in line eight also alters the affect slightly. He sets the corresponding line four in the first strophe, "Alas, there is still more to be pitied than you," with desperate and bold tones, but the ornamentation in the second strophe tempers these affects with tenderness to reflect "what could he say to her that was *sweeter.*" Accordingly, weak devices that evoke tenderness are mixed with strong devices, particularly dissonance. As in the first strophe, the descent of a minor third on "Helas" in the second strophe is tender, yet the C that initiates the exclamation in both strophes is dissonant to the D in the bass (compare m. 16 in Examples 5.2a and b). In the next measure of the second strophe, the B♮ dissonance in the melody that initiates the four sixteenths on "que" against the F in the bass also represents bitterness, even anger. "Pourroit il" (mm. 17–18) is both desperate, by the half-step ascension on "pourroit," and tender, by the "sigh" of a descending half-step on "il." The juxtaposition of despair and tenderness continues to the end of the line. Major and minor thirds in association with tenderness are stressed in the ornamentation, yet there is also dissonance (note particularly the D and F against the E in the bass on the downbeat of m. 19) and agitated rhythmic movement.

The Organization of Expressions in Long Airs
The Extended Confirmation

In most airs, the length of a text affects only the length of the confirmation or means of amplification and not the other sections of the "discourse." Bacilly's "Petits aigneaux" is one of the shortest airs: each section comprises two lines of the eight-line poem. By contrast, his "Mon sort est digne de pitié," eighteen lines in length, is one of the longest pieces from any collection of airs, yet the confirmation comprises most of the piece and is elaborated through *peristasis,* or amplification by detailing circumstances. The sections of the confirmation describe past actions (in the second half of the first strophe) and present actions (second strophe) that failed to release the speaker from his lover. All these comprise the reasons why he is to be pitied. (Note that the proposition and narration are reversed in this example.)

First Strophe

Introduction and Proposition:	1. My fate is worthy of pity
	2. As much as it was worthy of envy
Narration:	3. Since I lost the Affection
	4. Of my adorable Silvie
Confirmation:	5. In vain I believed in order to flatter myself
	6. That I could change like she
	7. My pain only becomes more intense
	8. And although she is unfaithful
	9. My heart could not leave her.

Second Strophe

Confirmation, continued:	10. In vain I want to cure my fires
(Refutation)	11. [But] They consume me all the more
	12. In vain I know that it is shameful
	13. For a loyal heart to love a fickle [heart]
	14. In vain to content myself
	15. I banish it from my memory
	16. My heart loves her so much in spite of me
	17. That it thinks its glory is at stake
Conclusion:	18. When a faithful one loves a fickle one.[9]

ANTITHESIS AND ANAMNESIS IN TEXT AND MUSIC

In addition to the song text's use of elaboration in the confirmation through *peristasis,* "Mon sort est digne" is also unique in its musical setting. First, Bacilly establishes a pattern of associating a particular affect (despair) with the present and another passion (regret) with the past. "My fate *is* worthy of pity" (Example 5.3a, mm. 1–4) is set with tones of despair, while "As much as it *was* worthy of envy" (mm. 4–7) refers to the past with regret. Lines three and four, the narration, follow suit: the speaker is to be pitied (present tense and an expression of despair) because he lost the affection of his adorable Silvie (past tense and an expression of regret). Because the speaker's fate *was* to be envied, he now regrets his loss, which befits Descartes' description of that passion:

"My fate is worthy of pity / As much as it was worthy of envy /
"Since I lost the affection / Of my adorable Silvie"

EXAMPLE 5.3A. Bacilly, "Mon sort est digne de pitié," First Strophe, mm.
1–14, *Les Trois livres d'airs,* I:12.

Regret is . . . a kind of sorrow . . . a bitterness . . . joined to
some despair and to the memory of a pleasure that gave us joy.
For we regret only the good things which we once enjoyed.[10]

"Mon sort est digne de pitié" stands out among other airs for Bacilly's
treatment of the figures *anamnesis,* recalling matters of the past, and
antithesis, the juxtaposition of unfavorable and favorable conditions
(past *and* present, as well as the effort and actions undertaken to be free
of his beloved *and* his failure). Bacilly assigns the same musical material to evoke the same affect on phrases that refer to past events, which
were favorable, and uses other devices to project a different affect on
phrases that refer to the present, which is unfavorable. The same relationship is maintained in the first half of the second strophe, though in
reference to actions taken (despair) which were not successful (regret).
By setting *antithesis* in this way, Bacilly repeated musical material for
different textual phrases, a practice rarely used by composers of airs.

Even though the *double* or confirmation in this air does not alternate circumstances relating to the present and past, as in the first strophe, the expression of despair followed by that of regret is maintained

Music and the Language of Love

"In vain I want to cure my fires / [But] They consume me all the more /
I vain I know that it is shameful / For a loyal heart to love a fickle [heart]"

EXAMPLE 5.3B. Bacilly, "Mon sort est digne de pitié," Second Strophe, mm.
1–14, *Les Trois livres d'airs*, p. 12.

in the corresponding measures and intensified through ornamentation,
as shown in Example 5.3b. (Note that the bass line of the first strophe
needed to be altered to fit the ornaments of the second strophe.) The
first phrase, "In vain I want to cure my fires" (mm. 1–4), evokes the
speaker's futile and desperate attempt to terminate his passion, while
the second phrase, "They [the fires] consume me all the more" (mm.
4–7) is uttered with regret, as if the effort, the burst of energy displayed
in the first phrase in the attempt to "cure" his desire, yields to defeat
and exhaustion. It is extremely interesting that Bacilly set the second
desperate utterance at "it is shameful" (mm. 9–11) with no ornamentation at all. The effect is stunning. It draws attention to and emphasizes
the lover's expression of shame, and extends the portrayal of exhaustion to this declamation of despair.

The second unique feature in Bacilly's setting of "Mon sort est digne" is his use of the musical figure of climax, or *gradation,* in the second half of both strophes, as the narrator recounts with increasing frustration all the reasons why he is to be pitied: (1) he thought he could change, but he was mistaken; (2) despite himself, his desire only intensifies; (3) it is shameful to love a fickle woman; and (4) he tries to banish thoughts of his beloved from his memory, but his heart cannot forget because it believes its glory is at stake. Each statement is intensified through melodic, rhythmic, and harmonic sequence, as well as ascending chromaticism, between the initial statement at m. 15 and the parallel statement at m. 23 (Example 5.4a). In addition, each phrase of the first strophe ends more abruptly than the preceding one: the first phrase ends on the downbeat of m. 18 and is given the value of a dotted whole note; the second ends on the third beat of m. 22 but is preceded by a whole note on the downbeat; and the third statement ends most abruptly on the fourth beat of m. 25, a measure with six half-note beats. In this phrase, the whole note on the fourth beat is preceded by three half notes, and the phrase length is reduced from four to three measures.

In the second half of the first strophe (the confirmation), Bacilly replaces musical repetition, as used in the first half, with sequence (which is also apparent in the second half of the second strophe, Example 5.4b) to intensify the narrator's expression of anguish as he explains that nothing helps him to win back her affection. Sequence is not used to this extent in any other air, particularly in setting different phrases of text (usually sequence is reserved for repetitions of text). The use of sequence in the confirmation becomes all the more intense through ornamentation as the air proceeds from the second half of the first strophe into the *double.* A confirmation is the most passionate part of the musical discourse, but when, as in this air, it starts in the second half of the first strophe, the intensification of affect must begin in the absence of extensive *diminutions.* Bacilly's use of climax, or *gradation,* beginning halfway through the first strophe, nicely builds to the *double,* and the combination of both sequence and ornamentation in the second half of the *double* appropriately expresses with greater and greater force to the end of the piece.

"In vain believed in order to flatter myself / That I could change like she / My pain only becomes more intense / And although she is unfaithful / My heart could not leave her"

EXAMPLE 5.4A. Bacilly, "Mon sort est digne de pitié," First Strophe, mm. 15–30, *Les Trois livres d'airs*, I:12.

"In vain to content myself / I bannish it from my memory / In spite of myself my heart loves her so much / That it thinks its glory is at stake / When a faithful one loves a fickle one"

EXAMPLE 5.4B. Bacilly, "Mon sort est digne de pitié," Second Strophe, mm. 15–36, *Les Trois livres d'airs*, I:12.

Form in Single-Strophe Airs

While most pieces include a second strophe, some airs have only one, such that the first half of the piece is the introduction/narration and proposition, and the second half comprises the confirmation and the conclusion. In these airs, composers usually maintain a correspondence of expression between the introduction/narration and the confirmation, while employing a contrasting affect in the proposition, which ends the first half, as in Bacilly's "Il faut parler."

Introduction/ Narration:	1. One must speak to be done with one's martyrdom (this introduces the primary topic or "case," the facts as the speaker sees them)
Proposition:	2. One loses time sighing (this sets forth what is to be proven)
Confirmation:	3. One must first declare oneself
	4. But especially when Love gives us something to talk about (this sets forth the arguments of the case and reasoning behind the initial statement)
Conclusion:	5. One must speak to put an end to one's martyrdom[11] (this summarizes by repetition the primary topic of the piece)

The introduction/narration (Example 5.5, mm. 1–5) and first part of the confirmation (mm. 8–10) are both statements of necessity that Bacilly sets with bold and agitated tones. As one would expect, however, the confirmation ("One must first declare") is given a much more intensely bold setting. Whereas the introduction places the ten syllables of the first line into four measures, the eight-syllable line of the confirmation is squeezed into two measures. By contrast, the proposition in line two (mm. 6–8) refers to sighing, which Bacilly interprets with tenderness and sighing tones, particularly on the words "son temps" ("one's time," mm. 6–7) and "soûpirer" ("sighing," mm. 7–8). The confirmation extends into line four—"But especially when Love gives us something to talk about" (mm. 11–15)—and parallels the proposition with its tender tones, though in a more passionate manner. Even though this phrase begins in the highest register of the piece with an ascending melodic gesture, the alternation of major and minor harmonies, the extended sigh (the interval of a descending fourth, from

EXAMPLE 5.5. Bacilly, "Il faut parler," *Les Trois livre d'airs,* I:72.

"-tout" of "surtout" to "quand"), and the less agitated rhythmic movement stand in contrast to the bold statements of necessity in the introduction and first part of the confirmation. Line five, the conclusion, is a literal repetition of the introduction, in text and musical setting. The first appearance of "one must speak" (mm. 15–16), however, begins a fourth lower than in the introduction, but by introducing the repetition of the introduction first in this way, the actual return to the original music and text is all the more dramatic and passionate. Indeed, in single-strophe airs, the conclusion is often a textual and musical repetition of the introduction, but with some kind of alteration to increase its affective impact.

The Rhetorical Sections of a Piece: Their Function and Expression

The order and type of expressions suit the function of the different divisions of the text, the utterances being organized to create as much variation of expression as possible. Often the change of section (and function) from introduction/narration to proposition and then again from confirmation to refutation and/or conclusion involves a change of passionate representation. Usually the introduction/narration makes up the first half of the first strophe, and the proposition, the second. If the first half of the piece is predominately forceful or builds to an agitated passion, the second half will often begin with a contrasting passion, usually a weaker utterance. The same is true for the second strophe. In the confirmation, if the first half is more forceful, then the beginning of the conclusion projects a weaker passion, usually intended to inspire pity in the listeners. Often throughout the course of the proposition and the conclusion (first and second strophes, respectively), the passion will either build to the end of the strophe or will show resolution or resignation.

THE INTRODUCTION

Many rhetoricians suggest restraint or "modesty" of expression at the beginning of a discourse because "an orator beginning too high, raises in the hearts of his Hearers a certain Jealousie that disposes them to criticize."[12] Bretteville notes that an introduction "must be pronounced in a mediocre, solemn (or low), and modest voice."[13] To gain the listeners' attention, Lamy notes that one must also begin with "what is most Noble and most Illustrious in the Subject of which we speak."[14] Airs of the most serious type often begin modestly with a sorrowful or languorous affect. Lambert begins "Mon ame faisons un effort" (chapter 4, Example 4.1) with restraint, in that it is predominantly sorrowful, and with courage, in that the speaker boldly asks his soul to make an effort even though his love still burns.

Bretteville points out that there are some exceptions: "One must find exception with this rule in certain Introductions which begin with some agitated passion . . . and which must be pronounced according to the passion that dominates there."[15] Indeed, a few airs begin with angry statements (Bacilly's "Puisque Philis est infidelle," Example 4.10) or with despair (Bacilly's "Mon sort est digne de pitié," Examples 5.3–5.4, just discussed). By contrast, less serious airs often begin boldly or angrily (Bacilly's "Au secours ma raison," Example 4.8), tenderly, or happily (Bacilly's "Pour la bergere Lisette," Example 4.14).

THE PROPOSITION

According to rhetoricians, the proposition should be unemotional, a simple and clear account of what is to be proven.[16] In many airs, composers reiterate the expression of the song's opening statement as the proposition begins the second half of the piece. If the expression of the introduction was sorrowful or languorous, however, the proposition is either a more pathetic rendition, or it expresses a passion of less intensity than that which ended the first half. In "Mon ame faisons un effort" (Example 4.1), Lambert intensifies the passion to the end of the first half of the song, beginning with a restrained statement of the introduction/narration, (mm. 1–8) to the desperate statement at the end of the first half (mm. 8–9) as the speaker unfolds the circumstances of his situation. He burns; he must complain; there is no time to pretend; he is too close to death. But Lambert represents a more restrained affect for the proposition, which begins the second half of the song (m. 11): boldness mixed with tenderness and sorrow.

THE CONFIRMATION

In the confirmation, the speaker must establish the proofs or arguments of the case. Lamy stresses more than any other rule that the confirmation must present clear and exact arguments. Of course, his comments concern discourse in which logic must dictate the type and order of the arguments. Since in vocal music, moving the passions is the means of persuasion, it seems fitting that the confirmation be the most impassioned portion of the song, represented by the most agitated of passions. Indeed, Bretteville notes that "in the confirmation, the voice must be strong and virile in order to give more weight to the reasons, and be varied according to the diversity of the passions and figures which rule in this part of the discourse."[17] Confirmations usually begin the second strophe. Although the affects of the first strophe correspond to the second, the highly ornamented presentation of the confirmation

"My soul let us make un effort"

Mon a - me, fai- sons_____ un ef - fort

3   6   3   3   6   3

EXAMPLE 5.6A. Lambert, "Mon ame faisons un effort," First Strophe, mm. 1–4, *Les Airs de Monsieur Lambert*, p. 4.

"During my last day permit [me]"

Per - met- tez_____ qu'a____ mon_____ der - nier

3   3   6   3

EXAMPLE 5.6B. Lambert, "Mon ame faisons un effort," Second Strophe, mm. 1–5, *Les Airs de Monsieur Lambert*, p. 6.

in the *double* creates a more agitated or intense version of the passion represented previously.

The expressive impact of ornamentation is stressed by both Mersenne and Bacilly, Mersenne claiming that the function of embellishment was to intensify the passionate effect of the poetry,[18] and Bacilly arguing that *diminution* "adds to the expression of a song, especially when the first and second verses are equally strong in their poetic statements."[19] And indeed, Lambert intensifies the bold affect on line seven, "During my last day permit me" in the second strophe of "Mon ame faisons un effort" (compare mm. 1–4 of the first strophe, Example 5.6a, with mm. 1–5 of the second, Example 5.6b). He does so by repeating the Cs on "Permit me" (mm. 1–2), by inserting a short measure (at m. 3, two halves per measure instead of two whole notes as in the first strophe), and by the agitation of the ornament on "my last days," (mm. 4–5).

Line eight of the confirmation, "To show you my martyrdom," is not an utterance of burning love as in the first strophe, so Lambert alters the affect to project the forceful request to declare one's love (Example 5.7). He changes the placement of the bar lines to coincide with the stress on the strongest syllable of the most important word, "-cou-" of "decouvre" ("discover") in m .7.

"To show you my martrydom"

EXAMPLE 5.7. Lambert, "Mon ame faisons un effort," Second Strophe, mm. 6–10, *Les Airs de Monsieur Lambert*, p. 6.

"And at least I dare to say to you / That in dying I die of love"

EXAMPLE 5.8. Lambert, "Mon ame faisons un effort," Second Strophe, mm. 10–15, *Les Airs de Monsieur Lambert*, p. 6.

A lover who declares his feelings is considered a martyr "in the Kingdom of love." The ornamentation of lines nine and ten, "And at least dare say to you / That in dying I die of love," also renders the utterances more intensely bold and desperate than in the corresponding lines of the first strophe (Example 5.8).

The Conclusion

The conclusion, which follows the confirmation, should recapitulate the topic of the song. Lamy reminds prospective speakers that "an orator who apprehends the things that he says, may slip from the memory of his Auditors, is oblig'd to repeat . . . what he said before."[20] The restatement must be no more than a short summary. Lamy also claims that the abridgment "must at the same time awaken the motions that we have excited, and as I may so say, unbind the wounds that we made."[21] Bretteville emphasizes that "the conclusion requires a clear and animated voice: because this is where the orator tries the hardest to move and elevate the hearts [of the listeners]."[22] Conclusions, then, not only review what was said in a text; they must also summarize, in a condensed manner, the passions expressed.

In most airs, the conclusion repeats the proposition. Since the proposition is a statement of what is to be proven or described in the song, its restatement as the conclusion reinforces the primary meaning and expression of the text. Whether conclusions are restatements of the proposition or not, the composers often summarize the passions presented throughout the piece. In "Mon ame faisons un effort," Lambert alters the beginning of the conclusion, as shown in Example 5.9, to parallel the air's opening statement (Example 5.6a, mm. 1–4) with bold and sorrowful tones. The statement begins in F major, as did the introduction, and ends on D, but in this portion of the conclusion, the D sonority is major, not minor (m. 18). Both the introduction and conclusion begin with repeated notes (Cs in the introduction and As in the conclusion, m. 16). There is also a textual link: it is the soul's effort to declare love (line one) that may offend Silvie (line eleven, mm. 16–18, second strophe).

The conclusion also corresponds to the proposition in that Lambert intensifies the tender affect already present in the first strophe by adding sighing figures on the word "pas" and on the syllable "-e" of "vie" (m. 17) and in the bass line (m. 18). In the conclusion, then, the bold and sorrowful affects of line one of the first strophe are made more pitiful, and the tenderness of line five, the proposition, made more intense. By emphasizing a more pitiful version of the passions expressed in lines one and seven, the conclusion successfully recapitulates with greater force. As noted in the previous chapter, Lambert's setting of line six—"If I lose [your] respect I also lose my life"—summarizes all the affects presented throughout the piece: boldness, sorrow, burning

"Do not be offended Silvie / If I lose [your] respect I also lose my life"

EXAMPLE 5.9. Lambert, "Mon ame faisons un effort," Second Strophe, mm. 16–24, *Les Airs de Monsieur Lambert*, pp. 6–7.

love, desperation, and tenderness. Its ornamented repetition also recapitulates these affects, yet pitifully. By ending with a pathetic rendering of the text "I also lose my life" (mm. 22–24), Lambert appeals to listeners to have sympathy for one who, by declaring his feelings, becomes a martyr to love.

Style (Elocution): Poetic Structure, Punctuation, and Rhetorical Figures

In song texts, elements of style concern primarily syntax and figurative language.[23] Syntax is how words combine to form phrases, clauses, or sentences, and figures are generally "any device or pattern of language in which meaning is changed or enhanced."[24] Since the style of airs is neither high (sublime) nor low, but middle (plain), the texts demonstrate a relatively straightforward syntax and moderate use of figurative language. Pierre Perrin's description of his own lyrics is also apt for the poems used by composers of airs: Perrin maintained the sentence in "its natural order, avoided harshness of diction, and kept the sense-groups and the caesuras short, broken up, and precise, containing all the necessary words and purged of all superfluous ones," and "endeavored to make it [the lyric] elevated and poetic, but in moderation, and without exaggerated hyperboles, allusions to too-unfamiliar myths, or far-fetched or uncommon metaphors."[25]

According to theorists Mersenne, Masson, La Voye Mignot, and Saint-Lambert, textual phrases dictate the structure of musical phrases. Likewise, textual clauses, phrases, sentences, and periods warranted various types of musical cadences.[26] Mattheson refers to this as "musical punctuation," or the delineation of the phrase construction of the text by particular devices.[27]

The second aspect of style, rhetorical figures and their musical counterparts, the figures, is not described by French musical theorists. Mersenne, writing earlier in the century, mentions only in passing that composers were to use "all kinds of figures and harmonic embellishments, as does the orator," and only briefly alludes to figures of melodic repetition.[28] David Duncan notes that this is

> an odd omission in light of [Mersenne's] arresting statement from the abortive *Traité de l'harmonie universelle* of 1627 that "rhetoric shows how the subject should be dealt with in order to put it into music and teaches the musician how he must imitate the figures of rhetoric in making various *passage, diminuzione, fuge, consequenze*."[29]

Of importance is Mersenne's reference to musical figures as "embellishments," which we do find in the airs under study. What we do not find with any regularity is the "imitation of rhetorical figures" in music. The distinction between musical figures as embellishments and musical figures that imitate rhetorical figures is significant and will be considered after an examination of textual and musical syntax. I will return to the issue of "musical figures" as *diminutions* in the last chapter of this book as part of an examination of extended ornamentation during Mersenne's lifetime, when ornaments were added indiscriminately to airs, and compare this to the use of ornamentation in the *doubles* of airs. The practice after 1650 to "contain" the ornamentation in airs—that is, to limit their use to the *doubles* to alter syllable stress and accommodate expression—is significant and directly reflects the controversy amongst rhetoricians over the use of figurative language.

SYNTAX

Each line of poetry is called a member (an incomplete phrase), and each hemistich (half of a line) is a measure. In this repertory, two to four members, or lines of poetry, equal a period (a complete sentence), and two or three periods equal a strophe. In short poems of one strophe, each line often serves a different function. In the text of Bacilly's "Qu'il couste cher de voir Silvie," a single-strophe air, each line comprises a complete thought.

FUNCTION	LINE OF POETRY
Introduction/Narration:	1. How much it costs to see Silvie
Proposition:	2. I paid with my heart for the pleasure of my eyes
Confirmation:	3. But alas I am too happy
	4. Even if it costs me my life
Conclusion:	5. Even if it costs me my life
	6. Even if it costs me my life.[30]

In his musical setting of this air, Bacilly observes the textual measures, members, and periods. Line one is eight syllables long and is divided into two measures (see Example 5.10). The division at the hemistich (the measure) is indicated in the music in the first beat of m. 2, "cher," by the relatively large note value (a dotted quarter note) and the chord built on the fifth degree of the mode, A major. The end of the member, on "-e" of "Silvie" (m. 4), indicates the point of repose by the return to D minor on the downbeat, the mode of the piece, and by using the largest note value of the line in *both* melody and bass, a half note.

Bacilly sets line two in a similar manner. He observes the hemistich of the twelve-syllable line on "cœur" (m. 6) with a larger rhythm, the dotted quarter, but unlike the preceding dotted quarter on the downbeat of m. 5, here he emphasizes the point of repose on "cœur" by a return to a D-minor harmony, the mode of the piece. Also noteworthy is the intervallic relationship between the bass and melody at each point of repose. For both lines one and two, the melody and bass form a third (tenth) at the hemistich, while the interval of an octave appears at the end of the first member or line (m. 4) and a fifth (twelfth) at the

EXAMPLE 5.10. Bacilly, "Qu'il couste cher de voir Silvie," *Les Trois livres d'airs*, I:63.

end of the second (m. 8). The fifth forms a stronger intervallic relationship than the third, thereby creating a more forceful resolution at the line. Bacilly treats all other points of repose throughout the piece in the same manner, with large notes on downbeats and important structural harmonies. But he replaces the the fifth between melody and bass with an octave at the end of each member in the second half. The "musical comma" after the exclamation "Mais helas" (mm. 9–10) is quite appropriate, since the octave between melody and bass on "-las" of "helas" (m. 10) helps to strengthen the pause and distinguish it from the following pauses on "suis" (mm. 11 and 13), which Bacilly also set with half notes. Bacilly concludes the piece with the strongest cadence of all, a perfect final cadence from A major to D minor.

In longer airs, the members are frequently grouped to form a complete sense and function together. Lambert's setting of "Que me sert-il" comprises two strophes of six lines each. In this air, three members, or lines of poetry, form a complete thought and function together as one part of the discourse.

FUNCTION	LINE OF POETRY

First Strophe

Introduction/ Narration:	1. Of what use is it to be faithful
	2. To languish night and day for her
	3. If the ingrate does not love me
Proposition:	4. Ah! I am only deceiving myself with vain hope
	5. It is better by a quick death
	6. To put an end to my love and her hate.

Second Strophe

Confirmation:	7. I would be fooling myself
	8. To think that my extreme misfortune
	9. Can move her to pity,
Conclusion:	10. In my condition let us have no other desire
	11. After losing hope
	12. Than that of losing life.[31]

In other airs, the lines are paired to serve a particular function, as in Bacilly's "Pour donner à mon cœur," composed of two quatrains.

FUNCTION	LINE OF POETRY

First Strophe

Introduction/ Narration:	1. In order to give my heart some relief
	2. I have worked to forget the object that possesses it
Proposition:	3. But alas I have only increased my torment
	4. And the ailment is even sweeter than the remedy

Second Strophe

Confirmation:	5. I have tried in vain to forget Philis
	6. Her charms are so sweet that everything must yield to them
Conclusion:	7. And although my torment leads me to death
	8. My torment is even sweeter than the remedy.[32]

The poem is typical in that the first of the paired lines sets up the second by using a preposition and/or conjunction. The "in order to" in line one is completed by line two: *in order to* give his heart some relief, he has worked to forget. The conjunction "but alas" begins the next pair (lines three and four, the proposition) and a new thought, connected by the conjunction "and": *but alas,* he has only augmented his torment, *and* the ailment is even sweeter than the remedy. Even though lines three and four present a new thought, the "but alas" connects them to the first two lines by creating an antecedent/consequent relationship. The speaker has worked to forget his torment (antecedent), but this only increases his suffering (consequent). The lines of the second strophe follow the same pattern as the first.

In most airs, Bacilly reinforces the relationships suggested by the lines of text through his setting and affective interpretation. In "Pour donner à mon cœur," for example, he unites lines one and two to form the first half of the piece (Example 5.11, mm. 1–8). Bacilly observes the point of repose at the hemistich of line one on "cœur" (m. 2), but also pauses after "donner" (m. 1) and "quelque" (m. 3) to divide the line into four verbal units of three, three, two, and four syllables each (indicative of the weaker passions—languor, sorrow, and tenderness). He then concludes the line with the greatest repose on "-ment" of "soulagement" (m. 4). Since the thought begun in line one continues into the next line, Bacilly begins line two on the same pitch (D) that ended the previous phrase (m. 4) and revives the movement of the first line with a smaller note value (quarter note) after the rest. He reinforces the divisions of the twelve-syllable line (four verbal units of three, three, two and four syllables) primarily with larger note values, and concludes the first half of the piece with a strong cadence on of A major to D major.

Just as the meaning of the entire poem unfolds line by line, so too the meaning of the musical setting unfolds phrase by phrase. Bacilly's "Pour donner à mon cœur," like "Dûssay j'avoir mille rivaux" (analyzed in chapter 4, Example 4.12), is a bittersweet poem in which the tender side of love (identified as pleasure in "Dûssay j'avoir") at first *opposes* the torment caused by love (pain in "Dûssay j'avoir"); but by the end of Bacilly's poem, the poetic voice proclaims that the *torment* of love is *sweet* and *preferable* to the remedy of forgetting about or falling out of love with the beloved, just as pleasure and pain become one and the same in "Dûssay j'avoir." In both airs, as well, the relationship between pleasure (sweet love) and pain (the torment of love)

EXAMPLE 5.11. Bacilly, "Pour donner à mon cœur," *Les Trois livres d'airs,* I:44.

is presented, transformed, and revealed through the ways in which Bacilly manipulates musical devices to represent one or the other.

In sum, "musical punctuation" in the air reinforces the organization of the words into phrases, sentences, and periods. The degree of repose in the music always conforms to that of the text. At greater points of repose, the rhythmic values are largest; the notes usually appear on downbeats; the melody and bass form a strong intervallic relationship of a fifth or octave; and the harmonies are structurally important—usually a dominant, major mediant, or chords built on the final of the mode. Composers united or connected by musical means the members, or lines, that functioned together. The second member of a group, for example, may begin in the same measure of music in which the previous member ended. By contrast, composers clearly set apart new groups of members with decisive cadence points that are melodically and rhythmically articulated as well. The passions associated with groups of members are also differentiated in the music. As each line presents more information to clarify the sense of the text, so the significance of the musical devices associated with affect becomes apparent.

THE QUESTION OF MUSICAL-RHETORICAL FIGURES

Of all the parts of rhetoric, the use of figures of speech and their respective "musical figures" have received the most attention from modern scholars, particularly with reference to seventeenth- and eighteenth-century German music. And yet in French sources on music, there is a complete absence of allusions to figures (with the exception of Mersenne from earlier in the seventheenth century, cited above). And as Jonathan Gibson warns in his dissertation "*Le Naturel* and *L'Éloquence:* The Aesthetics of Music and Rhetoric in France, 1650–1715," the imposition of rhetorical figures on an analysis of French music should proceed with great caution. He rightfully points out that even in French sources concerned with both rhetoric and music, particularly Grimarest's *Traité du récitatif,* there is no mention of figures when dealing with music.[33] In this section of the chapter, I will not make the case that the composers themselves were necessarily aware of the figures of speech (by name or otherwise) found in the song texts they set, but rather show how composers *responded* to rhetorical figures in their musical settings. I will first discuss musical-rhetorical figures in German music, as a point of comparison, and then move on to French airs.

Musical figures are generally defined as "a conscious, clearly defined deviation from the simplest mode of writing, intended to establish the expression and to represent a particular meaning or affect contained in the text."[34] The use of musical figures was addressed by many German theorists of the time, among them Johann Mattheson in *Der vollkommene Capellmeister* (1739). Mattheson was not concerned with the representation of *textual* figures in music; rather, he included non-texted musical analogues of the rhetorical figures, which he called "musical figures." In *Tractatus compositionis augmentatus,* Christoph Bernhard included examples of musical figures (presumably those used in vocal and choral music as well as instrumental), but not one of his examples includes a text.[35]

Mattheson identifies two kinds of musical figures, *figurae dictionis* and *figurae sententiae,* which Lenneberg translates as word-figures and phrase-figures, respectively.[36] Mattheson's word-figures are those that have "a great similarity to the alteration of notes, alterations of length, or of rising and falling," while phrase-figures are "concerned with entire phrases, with their changes, alterations, imitations, answers, etc."[37] Mattheson seemed to indicate that both word- and phrase-figures are analogous to textual schemes; that is, the figurative use of language in which the literal meaning of a word remains the same but the arrangement of the phrase is altered in some way. His omission of tropes or metaphors in his explanation of musical figures suggests that schemes are more easily imitated in instrumental music. *Epanorthosis,* or *correction,* for example, is a type of scheme "in which one speaks as if one were correcting something one apparently had said too hastily."[38] Mattheson describes the musical version of this phrase-figure as a "withdrawal . . . [as] found in almost all opposite motion."[39] One of the most common figures is *anaphora,* the repetition of the same word at the beginning of each line of poetry. Mattheson identifies this scheme as a type of musical word-figure and observes: "What is more commonly used in musical composition than *anaphora* which means that a passage already used recurs at the beginning of several successive phrases and thus establishes a . . . relationship."[40] He includes the following example, wherein each musical phrase begins with an upbeat of three sixteenth notes to imitate a textual phrase that would begin with the same word (Example 5.12). Other figures of repetition, such as *anadiplosis,* the repetition of the last word of a phrase as the first word of the next phrase, could also easily be realized in the repetition of musical motives.[41]

EXAMPLE 5.12. Musical *anaphora*

Musical-rhetorical figures such as *anaphora* or *anadiplosis* may have been used by Germans and Italians, but they were not used by French composers of airs during the middle to late seventeenth century. Nor did the poets of French song texts use schemes that emphasized the manipulation of words within a line of text; in French song texts, for the most part, the sentences are maintained in their "natural order," as noted by Perrin.[42] Thus, the motivic imitation of schemes, as in Mattheson's example of *anaphora,* does not exist in the airs by French composers. The most common types of figures in song texts are those that provided the composer with rich images and affective associations, such as exclamations, the "dying" metaphor, or *antithesis* as used in song texts to juxtapose the pain and pleasure of love.

Although musical figures are not addressed by French theorists nor generally used by composers, there are exceptions. Climax, or *gradation*, is the one musical figure used most for immediate textual repetitions. The direct restatement of words or phrases in the song texts was added by the composers, not the poets, who inserted and set textual repetitions to underscore words or phrases and to alter, usually intensify, passion. Composers never repeated the music along with the text, but rather set the restatement to new music or treated it sequentially (an exception, as described above, is Bacilly's "Mon sort est digne de pitié," in which he repeats music set to new textual phrases). Melodic repetitions of this sort (in a different register) were referred to by the Germans as *polyptoton* or *synonymia*.[43] In "Mon ame faisons un effort" (chapter 4, Example 4.1), Lambert repeats the phrase "Si je pers" ("If I lose") not only to indicate the significance of the speaker's loss of the beloved, of respect, and of his life, but also to intensify the sorrowful affect invoked by the speaker's loss.

Another musical-rhetorical figure, *abruptio,* described by Bernhard as an unexpected pause or silence,[44] is used by Bacilly in his setting of "Petits aigneaux" (Example 5.2a), wherein he separates "Helas il est encor" from "plus à plaindre que vous" with rests. Le Camus also employs *abruptio* in several airs. In "Que vous flattez mes resveries," the female poetic voice reveals how she was seduced by a charming shepherd who "troubled" her tranquility. The loss of her tranquility is represented by frequent interruptions within the line by rests, as shown in Example 5.13.

When a line of the poem is repeated as a refrain, as in Bacilly's "Au secours ma raison" (see chapter 4, Example 4.8, 4, mm. 1–5 and mm. 21–24), composers often set the repetition with new additions or ornamentation, called *paronomasia* by Johann Adolph Scheibe.[45]

The musical-rhetorical figures used by German and Italian composers as well as the French, such as climax or *gradation, polyptoton, abruptio,* and exclamation, are those most often applied for affective expression. Mattheson, for example, categorizes several types of exclamations according to the passions they arouse. Those exclamations spoken in astonishment are joyous and should be musically represented by large intervals and fast passages, but yearning or pleasing exclamations are tender or sad. There are also exclamations of fear, horror, and terror. Depending upon the circumstances, they should be represented

"Alas! it was beside your waters / That the charming shepherd far from all that
bores me / Began to trouble. . ."

EXAMPLE 5.13. Le Camus, "Que vous flattez mes resveries," mm. 15–23, *Les
Airs à deux et trois parties,* p. 1.

by uncommon and large intervals or by intervals that are small and
extraordinary.[46]

French composers set expressive figures such as the exclamation
in a different manner than they did other types of figures that involve
alterations, such as the *anaphora*. This parallels in a general way a
distinction between text setting in Italian madrigals and monodies. In
composing madrigals, composers considered the text of fundamental
importance "in terms of the contrived musical reproduction or portrayal of poetic images," while composers of monodies represented
"the manner of delivery and recitation, the communication of the
poet's every feeling in a style of singing that is both beautiful and graceful."[47] This difference between "word-painting" madrigalisms and the
"imitazione delle parole" is particularly demonstrated in Monteverdi's
monodic setting of Ariadne's lament. Monteverdi's "imitation of the
word" was "a powerful musico-rhetorical language, attuned at every
moment to the structure and emotional content of the text."[48] A French
composer's approach to the composition of airs and musical figures is
closer to monodic technique than to a madrigalian "reproduction or
portrayal of poetic images." French composers most often imitated the
tones of voice associated with the figure's affective expression rather
than portray the poetic image itself, and reproduced only those images
that were considered verbalizations of particular passions: sighs as verbal manifestations of tenderness, and sobs as indications of sorrow.

Instead of imitating poetic figures in their musical settings, French composers represented or expressed the passion associated with the figures within the context of the piece. If they manipulated motivic material, as in the bittersweet airs, the musical motives, such as ascending and descending minor and major thirds, are derived from the tones or *accens* associated with an expression of passion and not a result of word painting.

It is possible that French theorists did not consider musical-rhetorical figures in their writings because the musical representation of textual figures changed from setting to setting, depending upon the composer's interpretation of the figure's affective meaning within the context of the poem.[49] The one reference to the composer's "*imitation* [my emphasis] of the figures of rhetoric in making various *passages, diminuzione, fuge, consequenze*" is from Mersenne's *Traité de l'harmonie universelle* and dates from before the middle of the seventeenth century, before the appearance of the new style of air. It might also be possible that he was referring either to polyphonic music or to the "old-fashioned" means of ornamenting an air (as Bacilly indicates in his treatise on singing),[50] in which the composer's *passages* and *diminuzione* were indeed intended as a figurative musical language.

Since the use of musical figures is limited in this repertory (exceptions given above), only a consideration of composers' settings of the rhetorical figures found in the poems is applicable to a consideration of figures and music. Figures were used to intensify the expression of passions; therefore, figurative language is greatest in songs associated with agitated affects. In one of the most passionate song texts, "Puisque Philis est infidelle," from Bacilly's *Les Trois livres d'airs* (chapter 4, Example 4.10), sixteen figures are used; while in "Tantost je suis sous l'Empire," a song about joyous love, there is only one figure, a metaphor. Of the fifty or so figures appearing in the song texts, the most commonly used are considered below, along with examples found in the songs and the passions they help to express. Although there are many examples of each figure, I will only include a few as illustrations.

Exclamations

The exclamation, which represents a sudden exertion of passion, is one of the most frequently used figures in the song texts from the first two subject types: painful love and bittersweet love. Regarding the exclamation, Bernard Lamy notes that when the Soul comes to be distrub'd, and agitated with a furious impulse, the animal Spirits passing through all the parts of the Body, and thronging into the Muscles that are about the Organs of the voice, swelle them up in such a manner, that the passage being streight'ned, the Voice comes forth with more impetuosity, by reason of the Passion that propels it. Every Ebullition of the Soul is followed by an Exclamation.[51]

Indeed, in every piece, the exclamations "Ah!" and "Helas!" signal a change or resurgence of passion. In the vast majority of song texts, the exclamations appear at the beginning of a line. In airs by Bacilly, exclamations occur in the majority of poems at the beginning of the proposition, the confirmation, or the conclusion. In Bacilly's "Pour donner à mon cœur" (Example 5.11), "Mais helas" ("But alas") begins line six, the proposition, and initiates a change to a more intensified expression. In airs by Lambert, Le Camus, and La Barre, the placement of exclamations in the song texts is not as consistent, yet wherever they are placed, the exclamations always begin a new line of text and initiate a change or intensification of passion.

Bretteville and Grimarest both describe the *accens* that accompanies this figure. Bretteville notes that an "exclamation calls for an elevated, firm and vehement tone,"[52] and Grimarest explains that

the exclamation serves to express surprise and astonishment . . . and is almost always accompanied by an interjection, such as Ah!, Oh!, What!, Heavens!, Gods! And a tone which . . . must be elevated, but nevertheless proportionate to that which precedes it and follows it and to the situation . . . and the sentiment which is expressed.[53]

The airs from all collections conform to these explanations and descriptions. With few exceptions, "hélas" is set in the upper register with a descending minor third, filled in or not, usually portraying a sorrowful sigh and initiating a serious or pitiful expression. See Bacilly's "Petits aigneaux," (Example 5.2a, m. 16) or his "Pour donner à mon cœur" (Example 5.11, mm. 9–10).[54]

Composers also set "hélas" with an interval of an ascending or descending fourth when a more agitated expression was warranted. Le Camus sets "hélas" in "Que vous flattez mes resveries" (Example 5.14) with a descending fourth, the exclamation initiating a statement of distress as the female poetic voice claims that she is being seduced by the shepherd.

EXAMPLE 5.14. Le Camus, "Que vous flattez mes resveries," mm. 15–16, *Les Airs à deux et trois parties,* p. 1.

EXAMPLE 5.15. Le Camus, "Amour, cruel Amour," mm. 38–39, *Les Airs à deux et trois parties,* p. 9.

EXAMPLES 5.16. Lambert, "Que me sert-il," m. 13 and m. 15, *Les Airs de Monsieur Lambert,* p. 44.

An extended sigh set to a descending minor sixth appears in one of Le Camus' most passionate airs, "Amour, cruel Amour" (Example 5.15).

The exclamation "Ah" often appears in the highest register of a piece, isolated from the surrounding words in a phrase, as in "Que me sert-il" (Example 5.16, mm. 13 and 15). In this example, as in other airs, the bass line is static, all motion coming to a halt as if the "Ah" signals a moment of reflection before the change of expression.

Doubt, or Aporia

Doubt signals passions that are

> no less changeable and inconstant, than the Waves of the Sea; and they who abandon themselves to the violence of their

"O Gods how is it possible"

EXAMPLE 5.17. Lambert, "O Dieux comment se peut il faire," mm. 1–4, *Les Airs de Monsieur Lambert*, p. 12.

> Passions, are in perpetual disquiet: They will, and they will not:
> They take an Enterprize in hand, and they quit it immediately:
> They approve, and disapprove the same thing in an instant.[55]

Doubt is set by Lambert in his "O Dieux comment se peut il faire" in measures 1–4 (Example 5.17). The musical representation of this phrase corroborates Lamy's description of a person who experiences doubt. The dotted figures and movement of the melody by skips of thirds, fourths, and sixths imitate a "perpetual disquiet" and an "inconstancy of Passion [that] hurries this way and that." The ♯6 chord on A at the end of the line represents a "continual irresolution."[56] The melodic contour also imitates Lamy's metaphor "changeable . . . like the waves of the sea," a musical figure known as *circulatio*.[57] Composers throughout the sixteenth, seventeenth, and eighteenth centuries imitated "waves" and other references to water with melodic alternations of descents and ascents, or the "sine curve."[58]

The entire song text of Bacilly's "En vain j'ay consulté l'amour et le respect" (Example 5.18) is an expression of doubt. The speaker cannot decide whether he should declare his love to his beloved or remain silent; these alternatives are juxtaposed in every line of the text and in Bacilly's musical setting. Bacilly conveys all expressions referring to love (or declarations of love) with more agitation, and all expressions referring to respect (keeping silent) with sorrowful tones.

Antithesis, or Antansgoge

Antithesis, used extensively in song texts belonging to the second category, bittersweet, is a figure wherein two or more favorable and/or unfavorable alternatives or qualities are presented. In the song texts, the favorable and unfavorable aspects are often presented as a paradox —another rhetorical figure—particularly when the pain and pleasure of

EXAMPLE 5.18. Bacilly, "En vain j'ay consulté l'amour et le respect," *Les Trois livres d'airs,* I:18.

EXAMPLE 5.18 CONTINUED

love are referred to as kindred passions. For either antithesis or paradox, each opposing image must be differentiated from the other. Bretteville notes that "antithesis requires two differences in tone, for which the one is more elevated than the other."[59] Grimarest stresses that "the antithesis, which contains violent oppositions, must be pronounced by a firm voice in order to make these oppositions felt all the more . . . [and] by always observing the proper tone of the sentiment that it contains."[60] Grimarest explains that sometimes the oppositions are differentiated by pronouncing the first either weaker or stronger than the other, or by elevating the voice on one or the other.[61] We have seen in two airs analyzed thus far how opposing concepts are represented in musical settings: Bacilly's "Dûssay j'avoir mille rivaux" (Example 4.12), and his "Pour donner à mon cœur" (Example 5.11). Another example, Lambert's "D'un feu secret," is analyzed in chapter 7.

Repetition

Repetition is used for emphasis and is

> very ordinary among those who speak in a heat, or are impatient to make us understand what they mean . . . So in Speaking, if we think our first words not well understood, we repeat them, or explain them another way. Passion having got the Mastery of us, possesses it self of our Minds, and imprints strongly in us those things which have caused it; of which the Mind being very full, no wonder if we speak with emotion.[62]

This rhetorical figure is used by poets most often to stress important phrases. Composers also repeat words and phrases, even when not indicated by the poet, to intensify or diminish passion as well as to stress words and phrases crucial to their interpretation of the poem. Bretteville notes that "repeated words should be pronounced with more force than the others."[63] Force of expression is indeed achieved by composers when intensifying affective expressions. We begin here with the repetitions most commonly used by poets and proceed to those added by the composers.

Repetition takes several forms. Least common is *anacephalaiosis,* or recapitulation, which occurs when the poet repeats the beginning of a poem at the end of each couplet. Most often composers treated these repetitions with musical repetitions as well, as in Bacilly's "Au secours ma raison" (Example 4.8), but Bacilly ornaments the repetition for greater emphasis.[64]

La Barre's "Si c'est un bien que l'esperance" (Example 5.19) reveals another example of *anacephalaiosis:* the phrase "If hope is good" begins and concludes each strophe. La Barre uses the repetition as a refrain and sets the text as a rondeau. The refrain in each strophe is set to the same music without alteration (the second-strophe version, of course, is an ornamented version of the first-strophe refrain).

Epimone, or refrain, is another type of repetition used by poets.[65] In "Puisque Philis" (Example 4.10), the line "Ah! how difficult it is when love is extreme / To banish from one's heart an ingrate whom one loves" is repeated at the end of the second strophe. But as expected, the repetition here is ornamented.

Other forms of textual repetitions were added by composers, who most often chose to repeat a word or phrase immediately in a different or contrary sense, a rhetorical figure called *antistasis.* In doing so, they never repeated music on textual repetitions but rather altered the music, usually by intensifying the affect and occasionally by reducing its intensity. Most commonly, composers intensified the affect of the word or phrase by melodic sequence, as in Lambert's "Mon ame faisons un effort" (Example 4.1) on "si je pers." In "Pourquoy vous offencer" (Example 1.2, mm. 1–7), Lambert reduces the affective impact by placing the repetition of "Beauty for whom I die" ("Beauté pour qui je meurs") in the lowest register of the piece.

In "Mon sort est digne de pitié" (Examples 5.3–4), Bacilly demonstrates another common type of repetition by reiterating the last line of each strophe. In mm. 28–30, the repetition of "Mon cœur ne la sçauroit quitter" ("My heart could not leave her") is almost identical to the first statement, yet the rhythm is changed somewhat in the melody and the bass line has been altered.

EXAMPLE 5.19. La Barre, "Si c'est un bien que l'esperance," *Airs à deux parties,* 5v.

EXAMPLE 5.19 CONTINUED

Maxims, or Sententiae

Many pieces rely upon maxims, or *sententiae,* which are

> Reflexions made upon a thing that surprises, and deserves to
> be consider'd. They consist commonly in few energetic words,
> that comprehend great sense.[66]

Often, maxims are used to explain some negative situation, such as
why it is difficult to forget a love, or why love causes so much suffering. In almost every case, the maxim appears at the end of the air
and is used by the speaker as a way of rationalizing his experience.
The passions represented are always determined by the nature of the
statement in the context of the text. In "Puisque Philis est infidelle,"
for example, Bacilly accompanies the maxim "Ah! how difficult it is
when love is extreme / To banish from one's heart an ingrate whom
one loves" (Example 4.10, mm. 13–27), with languorous (line five) and
bold, angry tones (line six).

The following is a list of maxims that appear in the song texts and a musical description of their musical settings. Most examples appear in song texts used by Bacilly and Le Camus, which suggests that Lambert and La Barre may have purposely avoided setting poems that included maxims.

1. In "Puisque Philis est infidelle," the lover explains why his heart will not revolt against the unfaithful lover. Bacilly sets the first part of the maxim as a lament and the second as an angry utterance: "It is difficult when love is extreme to banish from one's heart an ingrate whom one loves."

2. In Lambert's "Il faut aymer," the narrator's statement that "one must love, it is an inevitable destiny" is set to bold tones.

3. In Bacilly's "Je tasche en vain," the speaker admits that "one can suffer so much even when one loves and is loved." Bacilly sets this maxim with tender tones.

4. In Bacilly's air "Je voy des amans," the maxim only occurs in the final line of the poem. The auditors are left in suspense throughout the piece: what does saying farewell to a lover really mean? Finally, at the end of the second couplet, the speaker explains that death is the only way one can really say farewell. Bacilly sets the first half of the maxim, "To really say farewell in the empire of love," with tenderness, and the second half, "It is death who must say it," with despair.

5. In "Dûssay j'avoir mille rivaux," the speaker claims that "the worst of all misfortunes is to have neither pleasure nor pain." As pointed out in the analysis of this piece in chapter 4, Bacilly represents pain and pleasure in the music as interchangeable so that "pleasure" is treated with strong devices, rather than weak, as in the beginning, and "pain" is treated with weak devices associated with tenderness.

6. In "On est heureux," the narrator proclaims: "Even the bad things in life have their charms." Bacilly sets this maxim with bold and tender tones.

7. In "On n'aime plus dans ces bocages" by Le Camus, the speaker notes that at first love is sweet and pleasing; this is set to tender tones. But "as soon as (Love) introduces itself, / Alas! How cruel it is" is set by Le Camus, as one would expect, with an utterance of despair.

8. Le Camus' air "Il n'est rien dans la vie" is a maxim in its entirety: "There is nothing in life / That tires and annoys one more / When one has no love at all; / And can one without love / Pass a happy day."[67] Le Camus sets this text with tender and sorrowful tones.

9. In La Barre's "Quand une ame est bien atteinte," the narrator claims that when a soul is suffering from love, it is never without fear,

sorrow, or desires. La Barre's setting stresses the tenderness of love as well as the intensity of sexual desire.

Personification

Personification, the application of human characteristics to an inanimate object, occurs in the song texts when the narrator refers to his soul, heart, or reason as if it were a separate human entity. Composers most always represented these words with tenderness and sometimes with sorrow. "Mon ame," from "Mon ame faisons un effort," is treated with sorrow (Example 4.1, mm. 1–2), while "mon cœur," from "Puisque Philis est infidelle," is treated with tenderness (Example 4. 10, mm. 6–7).

In two airs by Le Camus, the lover speaks directly to the forests, and in each case, Le Camus sets the address with bold tones, as shown in Examples 5.20 and 5.21 (though in the first example, the bold affect is softened by the first-inversion harmonies). La Barre also sets the personification of forests in exactly the same manner, in Example 5.22.

EXAMPLE 5.20. Le Camus, "Forests solitaires et sombres," mm. 1–2, *Les Airs à deux et trois parties,* p. 34.

EXAMPLE 5.21. Le Camus, "Forests, lieux écartés," mm. 2–3, *Les Airs à deux et trois parties,* p. 58.

EXAMPLE 5.22. La Barre, "Forests solitaires et sombres," mm. 1–2, *Airs à deux parties,* 3v.

Onedismus

This figure is used when someone is represented as ungrateful or impious. There are many examples of *onedismus* throughout the song texts, as narrators often refer to the one they love as inhumane or unfaithful. The passions associated with this figure vary according to the context of the piece. Occasionally the composers set a statement which contains a reference to the ungrateful one with angry tones, as does Bacilly in "Puisque Philis est infidelle" (Example 4.10).

Interrogation, or Erotesis

Lovers frequently address questions to their beloved, to their heart, soul, sighs, reason, or even to the auditors. Sometimes the phrase will conclude with an upward turn in the music, but often it does not.[68] Like so many other figures, the musical setting of this one depends upon the type of expression, which varies according to the meaning of the overall phrase. In "Pourquoy faut-il belle Inhumaine" (Example 5. 23), for example, Lambert concludes the question with an ascending major second, as one might expect at the end of a question, but the expression is one of despair, which warrants that treatment in any case. Indeed, both Bretteville and Grimarest ackowledge that different circumstances and/or speakers require different *accens*. Bretteville notes that "interrogation must be pronounced in a soft, proud or firm and elevated tone according to the person whom one asks,"[69] and Grimarest explains that when the question serves to "clarify without passion . . . the tone must be soft. . . . When this figure follows an offense, it requires an elevated, quick, and proud tone. . . . When it is full of sorrow, interrogation must be pronounced by a tender and plaintive tone."[70]

Although Lambert interprets the question in "Pourquoy faut-il belle Inhumaine" as a desperate utterance, "Why is it necessary beautiful inhumane one that you are insensitive to my pain?" (Example 5.23), in "Pourquoy vous offencer" he interprets the question with a sorrowful affect (Example 1.1, mm. 1–3) to convey the speaker's knowledge that loving the beautiful one causes his death (mm. 4–7). In La Barre's air "Tristes enfans de mes desirs" (Example 4.4), the lover addresses his sighs and asks, "Why do you escape?," set with tenderness and sighing figures.

Music and the Language of Love

Antonomasis

Antonomasis occurs when the speaker uses a quality in place of a proper name. Often the quality is critical, as in *onedismus*, described above, when the beloved is reproached for being ungrateful or impious. As one would expect, the affect that accompanies this figure varies according to the meaning of the song or phrase. In "Pourquoy faut-il" (Example 5.23), Lambert sets the reference to his "beautiful inhumane one" with sorrowful tones. In Lambert's "Pourquoy vous offencer" (Example 1.1, mm. 3–4), the composer treats the reference to the "beautiful one" with tenderness, but concludes the phrase with anger. Bacilly begins the reference to "the treacherous one" in "Au secours ma raison" (Example 4.8, mm. 5–6) as an emphatic expression but concludes the phrase with sorrow. In "Puisque Philis est infidelle" (Example 4.10, mm. 20–21), Bacilly incorporates the mention of the "ungrateful one" into an angry expression.

EXAMPLE 5.23. Lambert, "Pourquoy faut-il belle Inhumaine," mm. 1–7, *Les Airs de Monsieur Lambert,* p. 40.

Anamnesis

Anamnesis refers to recalling matters of the past. In one of the best examples, Bacilly's air "Mon sort est digne de pitié" (Examples 5.3–4) analyzed earlier in this chapter, present events are described with despair, while past experiences are recounted with regret. The juxtaposition of past and present events and their accompanying affects occur throughout the piece.

Climax, or Gradation

Climax occurs when the disclosure of events, emotions, and their musical portrayal mounts in intensity by degrees. The French referred to this figure as *gradation,* and both Bretteville and Grimarest described the *accens* associated with it as an "elevation of the voice [which] must increase by the same degree by emphasizing the first principal word of each member."[71] The use of *gradation* is closely related to the composer's approach to immediate textual repetition, where the affect is intensified on the restatement by musical sequence.[72] There is only one example of musical climax, or *gradation,* that is not accompanied by textual repetition, Bacilly's air "Mon sort est digne de pitié" (Example 5.3–4). In the second half of this air, Bacilly intensifies the affect on each phrase through melodic, rhythmic, and harmonic sequence, and through ascending chromaticism in the melody, each phrase ending more abruptly than the preceding one.

Metaphor

All metaphors are tropes "by which we put a strange and remote word for a proper word."[73] Many song texts in this repertory are made up of metaphors; the graver the metaphor, the more serious the song. Having said that, it must be stressed that metaphors found throughout the repertory are highly conventional. Rejection in love which causes "death" is used almost exclusively in songs from the first subject type, painful love.[74] As Bacilly's "Vous ne pouvez, Iris" (Example 4.3, mm. 18–20 and 21–22), Lambert's "Mon ame faisons un effort" (Example 4.1, mm. 18–19), and La Barre's "Petit ruisseau" (Example 5.24) show, the three composers treated death caused by the beloved's rejection with sorrowful tones (a melodic descent). But death could also appear within desperate utterances, as in Lambert's "Mon ame faisons un effort" (Example 4.1, mm. 8–10). In other airs, composers set the death metaphor with regret, as in Lambert's "Mon cœur qui se rend" (Example 4.5, mm. 22–24).

Another metaphor, love as martyrdom, appears primarily in bittersweet airs. Because the declaration of love puts an end to martyrdom, one suffers martyrdom when one is unable to declare one's love. References to martyrdom are most often bold, as in Bacilly's "Il faut parler" (Example 5.5, mm. 1–5).

Like martyrdom, love as an illness was frequently represented in bittersweet airs. Even though lovesickness or erotic melancholia was

Music and the Language of Love

EXAMPLE 5.24. La Barre, "Petit ruisseau," Second Strophe, mm. 14–16, *Airs à deux parties,* 26r.

considered a real disease (and so not a metaphor), the "mal" associated with the disease stood for sexual arousal. "Remedy" was also not used as a metaphor, but referred to the true remedy for lovesickness: sexual fulfillment (while death occurred without the remedy).[75] The examination of Bacilly's "Pour donner à mon cœur" (Example 5.11) in this chapter, and Lambert's "D'un feu secret," which will be analysed in chapter 7, demonstrates that illness can be represented as either bitter or sweet within the same air.

The metaphor "Empire of Love" (meaning not only the authority or power of love but also referring to actual maps used allegorically to represent a territory of love[76]) is referred to in several song texts, especially in the less serious bittersweet airs. The metaphor is often treated with tender tones, recalling Madeleine de Scudéry's *Carte de Tendre*—her map of "tender love," or *amitié.*

Another common metaphor highlights the eyes as the essence of the beloved.[77] As Génetiot points out, beautiful eyes, as well as other parts of the body, were often associated with the beloved, whose beauty is idealized in the song texts.[78] In most cases, composers treated the mention of the beloved's eyes with tenderness, as in Bacilly's "Vous sçavez donner de l'amour" (Example 3.7, mm. 4–5). The significance of the beloved's eyes is treated in chapter 7.

Finally, "speaking" represents a declaration of love, while "remaining silent" is a demonstration of respect for the beloved. In either case, the beloved rejects the speaker whether or not he declares his love, which causes the speaker great suffering. Composers most often represented the declaration of love with agitated passions and treated remaining silent with sorrowful, languid, or regretful tones. One of the best examples is Bacilly's "En vain j'ay consulté l'amour" (Example 5.18), briefly described above, in which a declaration of love and remaining silent are directly juxtaposed.

The correlation of musical form, style, and meaning with all aspects of the song text in airs composed during the late 1640s and 1650s was developed primarily by those who attended the most fashionable Parisian salons, the milieu in which airs were composed and performed during this period. As we shall see in the chapter 7, salon culture, which was obsessed with the art of conversation and with matters pertaining to love, determined and conventionalized most aspects concerning the mid-century French air. But before an account of this fascinating literary and musical world is undertaken, an analysis of the air would not be complete without addressing performance issues, for above all, the air was composed to be sung. Every aspect of the analysis so far has shown that airs were written to imitate the tones of voice and rates of speech to be delivered in an impassioned musical "recitation." The organization of phrases and all aspects of style served to enhance the expressive capacity of the musical setting of the text, but all would be lost, despite the composers' best efforts, if the air were sung poorly. The focus in Parisian salons on "orality," that is, on reading out loud and engaging in artful conversation, had an enormous impact upon the performance of the French air.

CHAPTER SIX

L'Art du Chant: Performing French Airs

As Bacilly notes, "Singing is something more considerable than one imagines";[1] thus, describing exactly how French airs should be performed is a difficult task. Even Bacilly, author of the most important seventeenth-century French treatise on the subject, acknowledges that the art of singing must be learned through study with a master who can *demonstrate* proper technique, pronunciation, and ornamentation; in other words, *hearing* proper singing technique and style is paramount. He writes:

> I consider the art of proper vocal style to be one which exists in performance, and I am of the opinion that it consists of the following elements: Proper pitch, proper sustaining of the voice, good carriage and support, the proper performance of *cadences* and *tremblements,* proper throat pulsations [*marquer du gosier*] when necessary (and the omission of this technique when it is not called for; i.e., knowing when to slur over certain notes), the proper performance of *accents* (commonly called *plaintes*), and the proper performance of *passages* and *diminutions.* Since singing scarcely exists without words, in relation to them I must include proper pronunciation, expression, and emotional interpretation, and above all the proper observation of the difference between long and short syllables, which is the principal aim of this work.[2]

But Bacilly also reveals that much can be learned from the kinds of precepts that he offers in his treatise, particularly those pertaining to pronunciation, syllabic quantity, and the proper interpretation and application of ornaments:

> I do know that the student can learn to avoid a thousand mistakes that occur in music, especially regarding pronunciation and syllable-length, and to disassociate himself from the numerous ill-founded concepts which every day insinuate themselves into vocal practice. Thus, it can be said that at least regarding the Theory of Vocal Music this book can be quite valuable, even if not for its Practice.[3]

Despite the difficulty associated with describing performance practice in writing, there are indeed principles to be gleaned from treatises that can serve to guide one's approach to singing this repertory.

Notation, of course, is inexact, and this is especially true for seventeenth-century French music. In addition to a knowledge of pronunciation and syllabic quantity, the singer needs to know when to add "imaginary" dots to prolong certain notes and when not to; when and where to apply ornamentation, which is either marked simply with a "+" in the scores or not marked at all; how to interpret the *diminutions* applied to second verses; what tempo to take; what pitch standard to use (which could have ranged from A4 (A')= 388 to A4=396—the pitch of French organs, or "chapel pitch," before 1680—or A4=404—the pitch of many surviving French woodwind instruments[4]); which temperament is appropriate; and whether or not to transpose a piece. Many of these factors are relevant, of course, for accompanists as well. The lutenist, theorbist, harpsichordist, organist, or gambist needs to know how to interpret figured bass and realize harmonies. Above all, performers of this repertory need to recognize what is being expressed by the text and its musical setting. So many choices regarding performance rely upon a determination of passionate representation. As Bacilly makes clear throughout his treatise, performing a piece according to the composer's intentions is paramount.

It is one thing to recognize that the mid-seventeenth-century air was composed according to the tones of voice and rates of speech associated with a passionate recitation in music; it is quite another thing to be able to know how to put that knowledge into practice. And while nothing can substitute for study with a master, one can at least acquire an understanding about what makes this repertory "tick" in performance. As Bacilly so aptly claims:

> The kind of air which appears common on paper and which may even sound common in the performance of its written notes only, will be entirely relieved of this defect by the ornaments which the singer will add and by the style of their performance.[5]

À *Haute Voix:* The Importance of Orality

In his book *Le culte de la voix au XVIIe siècle*, Philippe-Joseph Salazar demonstrates the importance of orality—the voice—and its intimate link to rhetoric and the passions. He writes:

The orator, wedded to the effects of style, that is, elocution and disposition, must display a science of the passions that grants to the voice this role of mediation which is always his. This supposes an agreement between the orator and the listener on the acoustics of the passions, a meter of the emotions, a recognition; in short, a culture and socialization of the voice.[6]

Seventeenth-century French culture gave voice to the passions through accent, articulation, inflection, intonation, pronunciation, and tone.[7] All of these aspects of vocal production gave recognizable meaning and expression to words, phrases, sentences, paragraphs, and thus, to the entire discourse read out loud, *à haute voix*.

Although no cultural sphere escaped the influence of orality, it was in the intimate setting of the *ruelle,* or salon, that the voice, through the art of conversation, was cultivated with the establishment of particular topics, vocabulary, and meaning being socially accepted or generally agreed upon. Here, the voice mediated between the written word and auditors to establish what Salazar calls "le culte de la voix": an adoration, even worship, of the voice. It was not only the meaning of words that counted but also how they *sounded* when spoken.[8] Literary works of all kinds associated with the salon were written in a style influenced by the spoken word, much of it created to be read *à haute voix,* a phenomenon we have seen in airs which were *composed* as passionate recitation, and as we shall see in chapter 7, as imitations of conversational responses.

Thus, all aspects of recitation were not only applicable to speech but to singing as well, airs being considered and judged as a special type of literary work (poetry) cultivated in the salon, and thus an important manifestation of "le culte de la voix." The importance of "giving voice" to lyric texts—rather than simply reading them to oneself—is aptly expressed in the preface to *Recueil de chansons choisies,* a collection of song texts:

> No matter how agreeable these Chansons [song texts] are when one reads them, it is an entirely different thing when one sings them; it is in this way that all the works here were made for singing.[9]

While singing airs was a common salon activity, airs were also sung as entertainment in private chambers at court, particularly after the beginning of Louis XIV's personal reign in 1661. This intimate space required, even cultivated, a particular singing style that Bacilly himself differentiates from the type of singing necessary for theater productions. He writes:

> Several believe that singing, drawing upon declamation and having as its aim the expression of passions, must be executed with much affectation, which some would call *exaggerated singing*. For me, I believe that this great affectation does not enhance singing and that it has been added to singing for the theater, which is often accompanied by grimaces, if only for recitative. But for singing practiced in salons, I maintain that pleasure is added when one refrains from this manner of bombastic singing that removes all the delicacy and refinement, provided that the pronunciation is not distorted, especially the 'R' which follows or precedes a consonant, and the 'O,' which does not at all need to be exaggerated.[10]

Singing in the salon, then, required a light and delicate approach as opposed to the more exaggerated style required for the theater.[11] Pronunciation in singing, however, is also distinct from ordinary speech. Bacilly insists throughout his treatise that this refined approach to singing requires proper pronunciation, a knowledge and application of syllabic quantity and ornamentation, as well as a good singing voice. As James Stark rightly purports in his book *Bel Canto: A History of Vocal Pedagogy*, a consideration of any vocal repertory requires not just an analysis of the word–music relationship, but also an examination of the intimate connection between word, music, and *tone*.[12] One must consider the voice in an analysis of airs.

The Art of Proper Singing: Tone and Style
BREATH SUPPORT OR MANAGEMENT

The basis of good singing during the seventeenth century was good breath support or management, just as it is today. Seventeenth-century writers from all European countries insisted that proper breath support enables singers to sing in tune, pronounce a text with greater force and accuracy, and sing with expression, all essential to excellent vocal quality.[13] With regard to breathing, Bacilly notes that the singer "will be able to sing without concern over his pitch, on condition that he sings the tones as much as possible from the bottom of the throat or windpipe [*du fonds du gosier;* diaphram?], which is the sole guide to 'correctness' in singing."[14] Mersenne also insists on the importance of the breath. He compares the flow of air through the respiratory tract to the flow of water in a stream: "There is still another quality of the voice which renders it full and solid and which increases its harmoniousness. This can be explained by the comparison with a canal which is always full of water when it flows. . . . Voices which are deprived of this quality are like a thin trickle of water which runs in a large canal."[15]

VIBRATO

Good breath support also contributes to a healthy "natural" vibrato. Most modern scholars agree that a straight tone was not the sound ideal for solo singing during the seventeenth century and that the use of a natural vibrato would have been the desired sound. In his translation of Bacilly's *Remarques curieuses,* Austin Caswell initially defines *cadence* as vibrato, and indeed, Bacilly's use of the word in the initial two paragraphs of Article 2, 'Cadences et tremblements,' is confusing.[16] He notes that some singers "have an acceptable voice without having a *cadence* at all,"[17] while others have a *cadence* that is either too slow or too fast and coarse (*chevrottante,* meaning "goatlike"). From his comments it is impossible to know whether he is referring to the trill alone or to a singer's vibrato. His subsequent discussion of *cadence,* however, clearly refers to its use as an ornament or trill that requires a throat articulation.

Bacilly also uses *cadence,* perhaps in reference to vibrato, in his chapter on different voice types. He differentiates between a pretty voice and a good voice. A pretty voice is pleasing, clear, sweet, and has a nice *cadence* (vibrato?). The good voice lacks sweetness and *cadence,* but it is vigorous, strong, and has a great capacity for expression.[18]

Mersenne also addresses vocal vibrato in the sixth proposition on singing of *Harmonie universelle.* He writes:

> To sing with less imperfection it appears that it is not enough to pronounce the words which one sings . . . unless the voice is beautiful, full, pleasant and mellow, born and guided in a beautiful way and unless the variations and changes are made as undulations of the air in the canal or pipe of the throat without the pit of the stomach, the nose, the roof of the mouth nor the movement of the jaws contributing to it.[19]

Mersenne seems to distinguish between throat articulation (which Bacilly mentions as a type of ornament in itself as well as part of a proper *cadence*) and the natural, or spontaneous, vibrato. As Maria Georgakaradou notes, Mersenne preferred the latter, which is not produced artificially by moving the diaphragm up and down, but through the singer's maintenance of "adequate sub-glottal pressure by willing the diaphragm to recoil very slowly. This type of vibrato is perceived as a series of fluctuations in the intensity of the voice,"[20] and is not the same as the undulations that correspond to the trills played on a keyboard instrument (a *cadence*).[21] According to Mersenne, "equality is holding the voice firmly on the same tone, without its being permitted to vary it by going higher or lower. One can weaken or strengthen it as long as one remains on the same chord."[22] "Thus," writes Georgakaradou, "because vibrato is described as amplitude fluctuation, while throat articulation is a repetition of one note interrupted by extremely brief moments of pitch fluctuation, it is obvious that [Mersenne] distinguishes between frequency and amplitude fluctuation." Therefore, vibrato allows for an increase and decrease in volume while singing on the same pitch.[23]

While a singer's natural vibrato should not be repressed when singing seventeenth-century French airs, it is important to avoid too large a vibrato or fluctuation in tone, as this would obscure not only tuning but also pronunciation and the stress or lack of stress applicable to long and short syllables, respectively. If one is consciously singing in accordance with proper syllable length, or quantity, by lengthening long(er) syllables and delicately singing over short(er) syllables, the execution of one's vibrato would vary. And indeed, in most settings of song texts, short(er) syllables are set with small(er) note values, so there is simply not enough time to allow for the vibrato to sound. In other words, most long syllables, which Bacilly acknowledges could support *cadences,* would be sung with vibrato, particularly if a throat articulation or ornament was not applied, while short syllables, which cannot support any kind of ornament, would and perhaps should be sung without vibrato. This approach would add to the desirable ebb and flow associated with syllabic quantity that would naturally occur when singing stressed and unstressed syllables.

VOCAL REGISTERS

Bacilly does not speak directly about the different vocal registers but rather identifies at least two types of voices, low, or natural, and high, or falsetto:

Some people are proud of their high voices, and others of their low tone, taking the view that a high voice is little more than a screech. Those who have natural voices scorn the falsetto as being artificial and shrill, while on the other hand falsetto singers are usually of the opinion that the beauty of a song is more evident when performed by the shimmering brilliance of their vocal type than when done by a natural tenor, which, although it ordinarily has better intonation, doesn't have the brilliance of the falsetto.[24]

There were theorists, however, who identified three distinct vocal registers within the same voice, presumably for men—high, medium, and low[25]—which later in the eighteenth century, Tosi would identify as chest voice, head voice, and falsetto. Other theorists equated head voice with falsetto and so identified two registers, the natural and the "feigned." Theorists by far preferred the natural voice to the "feigned,"[26] though Bacilly does mention that the falsetto voice is capable of rendering various ornaments in an entirely different, and not necessarily inferior, manner than can the natural tenor voice.[27] There does not seem to be any direct discussion during the seventeenth century about women's voices and register, yet in her discussion of the seventeenth-century voice, Ellen Harris asserts that the natural voice for females and castrati would have been the middle range and the head voice, the upper range.[28]

The most important ramification of the different vocal registers would have been that of vocal color and expression associated with range. It is true that composers of French airs linked register to passionate representation in any given phrase: the lower the register, the more solemn the passion; the higher, the more vehement the expression; while a middle register was used for the more moderate utterances. And yet we also see that the range in many airs is so limited that most women would not have to switch from natural voice (middle register?), to head voice (highest register?) or to chest voice (lowest register). Depending upon the specific female voice and choice of pitch (whether one sings at A4=392 or A4=415, for example), it would be possible to sing some airs entirely in the natural voice. One such air would be La Barre's "Tristes enfans de mes desirs" (Example 4.4), wherein the highest note is E5 and the lowest, F♯4. In most airs, the range is so limited, at just a little over an octave (on average the lowest note is D4 and the highest, E5 or F5), that there would be little opportunity to explore in any radical way different vocal colors.[29] But as Lambert makes clear in the preface to his published airs, it would be possible to transpose any air into a range that best fits any given voice. He explains that he included *basse continue* (figured bass) in his printed airs, rather than tablature for theorbo, for just this reason—in order to facilitate more easily the need to accompany voices by transposition, as is customary.[30] As such, a D4 could be transposed to any lower pitch—a C4, B3, or even A3—that would require most women to move into chest voice.

It should be noted as well that women have another break, or *passaggio,* around E5 in French Baroque pitch (equivalent to an F♯5 in A=440). In those airs that do extend beyond an E5, as does Lambert's "Mon cœur qui se rend à vos coups" which extends from A4 to A5, the singer may need to sing the higher notes in head voice. A more agitated expression in the upper ranges, however, should be sung with greater tension or strength, as Descartes notes, especially in expressions of despair, while more moderate expressions need to be more relaxed, heavier.

In any case, both male and female singers need to consider matching their tone of voice to the expression of a phrase. While modern singers work to diminish the differences required to sing in different registers throughout the voice, both James Stark and Ellen Harris confirm that Baroque singers chose to maintain the distinction in tone quality between low, medium, and high ranges. Mixing tonal production would only take place "on the few notes over the break, thus ensuring a smooth passage."[31] This approach is certainly consistent with rhetoricians, who also advise that orators use different tones of voice to accommodate different expressions.

Ornamentation

Bacilly makes it clear that expression and ornamentation are closely linked, one determined by the other.[32] He also spends a great deal of time explaining that only certain words and syllables can support various kinds of ornaments, and that it is absolutely imperative that the singer understand and take into account the close relationship between ornamentation, vowel sounds, and syllable length.

THE *PORT DE VOIX*

The *port de voix,* literally meaning to "to carry over the voice," involves the movement of the voice from a lower to a higher note.[33] It is one of the most important and expressive ornaments found throughout the repertory and should be applied liberally to any and all airs.[34] Bacilly identifies two types of *port de voix*: the *port de voix ordinaire,* or *plein* (full, complete, or ordinary), and the *demi-port de voix* (partial). He then identifies three ways a singer may facilitate the partial ornament: with the *demi-port de voix,* the *port de voix perdu* (lost), and the *port de voix glissé,* or *coulé* (an added chromatic slide).

Port de voix ordinaire (plein). The ordinary (full or complete) *port de voix* includes three parts: (1) the preparation from below *articulated before the beat* and carried over or sustained across the bar line; (2) the *doublement de gosier,* or throat articulation, which can be interpreted as a mordent, or *pincé;* and (3) the termination or re-articulation of the main note which usually ascends by step. Bacilly gives the following example from Lambert's "Mon ame faisons un effort" (Example 6.1). In most examples, the written version appears on the top staff and the suggested implementation, on the middle staff. Rhythms are approximate. A full *port de voix* is always used at major cadence points, including half cadences, if there is enough time to sing all three parts of the ornament.

EXAMPLE 6.1. *Port de voix ordinaire*

Demi-port de voix. The partial *port de voix* includes only two parts: (1) the preparation from below, as in the complete *port de voix* and (2) the *coup de gosier,* which articulates the upper note but does not sustain it. The difference between the partial and full *port de voix* concerns the length that one holds or sustains the note of termination and the strength of the *coup de gosier,* which should be struck lightly or delicately. The *demi-port de voix* is never used at principal cadence points, but at other less important places in the air. Bacilly indicates in his analysis of "Apres milles rigueurs" that one could perform a *demi-port de voix* on "cruelle" (Example 6.2, mm. 17–18).[35]

L'Art du Chant   193

EXAMPLE 6.2. *Demi-port de voix*

Port de voix perdu. This is similar to the *demi-port de voix* except that the note of preparation is held as long as possible, and the primary (written) note of termination is barely articulated. To sing a *port de voix perdu* on the second syllable of "cruelle" in Example 6.2, one would need to hold the second syllable "-el-" as long as possible and sing the *coup de gosier* very lightly.

Port de voix glissé. Performing the *port de voix glissé* involves sliding over the *coup de gosier* and giving the note of termination a longer value. Bacilly indicates that this can be performed on "hélas," in m. 15 of Caswell's transcription of "Apres milles rigueurs" (Example 6.3). Because this ordinarily involves an ascending half step, the microtone that one would have to sing between the F# and G cannot be notated. The singer, however, would need to glide from the note of preparation to the note of termination.

EXAMPLE 6.3. *Port de voix glissé*

Bacilly notes that all four types of *port de voix* may be applied to intervals larger than a second (particularly the third and fourth), but discourages their use on intervals of a fifth or sixth. He offers the example given in Example 6.4.

Bacilly admits that it is difficult to know where to apply the different kinds of *port de voix* and where another ornament might be more appropriate. He says, however, that the complete *port de voix* should "that it is not always necessary"

qu'il ne faut pas toû - jours

qu'il ne faut pas toû - jours

EXAMPLE 6.4. *Port de voix* (on an interval of a fourth)

absolutely be performed at cadences and half cadences if the final note is approached from below. He also suggests that the different kinds of *port de voix* be used within the same piece so as to give the performance the necessary variety. In addition, some words might require a harsher sort of articulation than that provided by a *port de voix*. He gives as an example the word "attaquer" and also points out that in his air "Au secours ma raison" (Example 4.8), an *animer* would be more appropriate than a *port de voix* on the diphthong "ou" of the word "secours." According to Bacilly, an *animer* is like the *coup d'archet* played on violin. A "bold vocal stroke," but imperceptibly repeated, is articulated on the note for strength. Bacilly's examples remind us that certain vowels and diphthongs simply cannot support certain kinds of ornaments.[36]

THE CADENCE, OR TREMBLEMENT

Bacilly describes the *cadence, tremblement,* or trill as comprising three parts: (1) the preparation, which is the pitch above the note to be ornamented, which may or may not be notated; (2) the actual trill, or *battement du gosier;* and (3) the *liaison,* or termination, lightly singing the note which follows that which was ornamented.[37] This sort of *cadence* is only performed on long syllables, most often on the penultimate syllable of a feminine word found at the end of an air or at the ends of important phrases within an air. Bacilly cites the following example from Lambert's "Mon cœur qui se rend à vos coups" (Example 6.5).

Bacilly notes that the singer should linger slightly on the preparation, begin the alternation of notes of the *cadence* slowly and accelerate slightly to the end, and touch the *liaison* (termination) lightly with the "[that I had] foreseen"

EXAMPLE 6.5. *Cadence, or* tremblement

voice. He also warns of a *cadence* that is either too slow or too fast, which is too compressed and sharp. One may "acquire a *cadence* by practicing in the necessary manner; i.e., by alternately singing the two notes of which the *cadence* is composed rapidly and with a certain equality, one after the other."[38]

This type of *cadence* would not be performed on the penultimate syllable of most masculine words (that is, words that do not end with a vowel),[39] but on the final long syllable. In the Example 6.6, the *cadence* is sung on the last syllable of the masculine word "soûpirer" and the *liaison* sung on the second-to-last syllable of the phrase, "pour," the phrase ending on the long syllable "vous."

"To sigh for you"

EXAMPLE 6.6. *Cadence and* liaison

In many instances it is impossible to add the *liaison,* particularly if one performs a *cadence* on the last syllable of a masculine word or on a single long monosyllable. Bacilly, however, warns against the overuse of the *cadence* in this way.

Bacilly acknowledges as well that the *liaison* is sometimes intentionally omitted by the composer, as in the second strophe of Lambert's "J'aymerois mieux souffrir la mort" (Example 6.7). Here, the prepara-

Music and the Language of Love

tion is the G on "-bel-" moving to the F (the *battement de gosier*), and instead of singing the *liaison* on E on the syllable "-bel-," one sings the final syllable, "-le," and then moves to the D to conclude the phrase. Bacilly warns that because the *liaison* creates an insipidness associated with its sweetness, composers remove it purposefully to lend strength to certain expressions.

re - bel - le____

3-4

EXAMPLE 6.7. *Cadence* without the *liaison*

Bacilly also warns that like the *liaison,* a preparation which is held in performing every trill can also be annoying. Only at primary cadence points in the air are all three parts of the *cadence* imperative. Even then, the *liaison* occurs in those places where the penultimate note is a second away from the final, not a third; thus, the *liaison* strikes the final note of the cadence of the piece.

The performer needs to take care to vary the types of *cadences* used, and Bacilly suggests that one may also add a type of trill which is done at the base of the throat and is quite "tight and short" ("fort serré et fort court").[40] He gives as an example the second strophe of his own song "Puisque Philis est infidelle," on the phrase "Mon cœur" (Example 6.8). Here, as an alternative, one could perform a very short "throat *tremblement*" on the B, prepared by the C on which "Mon" begins. A fuller *cadence* would be performed on the long masculine syllable "cœur," of course without the *liaison*.

Bacilly describes three other types of *cadence*: the *tremblement étouffé*, the *flexion de voix,* and the *double cadence.* The *tremblement étouffé* is explained in this way: "After having sung the *appuy,* which

"my heart"

Mon_____ coeur

6

EXAMPLE 6.8. "Tight and short" *cadences*

L'Art du Chant

is the note which precedes and prepares the *cadence* or *tremblement,* the voice starts to *trembler* [tremble] but actually only seems to as if only wanting to *repeat* the note on which it would ordinarily make a complete *cadence*";[41] see Example 6.9.

EXAMPLE 6.9. *Tremblement étouffé*

The *flexion de voix* dispenses with all parts of the normal trill except the *battement de gosier.*[42] The *double cadence,* as Guinamard notes in her article on Bacilly's *Remarques curieuses,* is not at all well explained by Bacilly. Guinamard supposes it to literally mean a double *cadence,* wherein two trills are performed in succession, one being the *cadence étouffé* and the other short with little to no preparation or *liaison,* as shown in Lambert's "J'aymerois mieux souffrir la mort," second strophe, mm. 17–18 (Example 6.10).[43]

EXAMPLE 6.10. *Double cadence*

THE *ACCENT, ASPIRATION,* OR *PLAINTE*

The *accent* is to be placed only on long syllables and occurs solely between notes that are repeated or descend by step, as in the example from La Barre's air "Tristes enfans de mes desirs," mm. 10–11 (Example 6.11). Instead of giving the *accent* (the A) the full quarternote value, one could cut the note short to an eighth note, followed by a rest.

"righteous sighs"

EXAMPLE 6.11. *Accent*

THE *DOUBLEMENT DU GOSIER*

The *doublement du gosier* is the "repetition which the throat makes on a single note"[44] and is never used on a short syllable. The ornament is so slight that auditors often cannot tell whether the singer has performed one or two notes. Bacilly likens the *doublement du gosier* to a device used by viol players called the *animer,* meaning that it is intended to give "motion to the note" ("donner le movement").[45] This ornament can only be used on long syllables, particularly monosyllables that cannot support *tremblements* or *accents.* Bacilly notes that a *doublement du gosier* may be combined with an *accent* and gives as an example the first few measures of Lambert's "Puisque cette Ingrate Beauté," shown in Example 6.12. Here the *doublement du gosier,* labeled (1), appears on the first syllable of "Ingrate." The *accent,* labeled as (2), is sung immediately following. Bacilly suggests placing a small *tremblement* on "-gra-," labeled (3). Guinamard explains that the *doublement du gosier* can be performed either as a note repetition or as mordent (*pincé*) and that the difference would be imperceptible to auditors.[46]

PASSAGES, OR *DIMINUTIONS*

Passages, or diminutions (the terms are synonymous, according to Bacilly) are sung in both first and second strophes but are used to a greater extent in the *doubles.* Both terms refer to breaking up the length of a note into smaller note values. Bacilly explains that "a '*diminution*' is any melodic device added to the simple melodic notes as they appear in notation on the printed page."[47] This would include the simpler ornaments described above—the *port de voix, cadences,* and so forth—used when singing the first verse or *simple,* as well as the more extended *passages* found in the printed second strophes or *doubles.*

L'Art du Chant   *199*

"Since this ungrateful Beauty"

EXAMPLE 6.12. *Doublement de gosier*

Bacilly identifies three considerations pertaining to diminutions: (1) their invention takes much talent and long practice; (2) their application to a vocal text requires a knowledge of syllabic quantity, thus the singer needs to know which syllables can support this or that ornament; and (3) their performance requires "an excellent and natural constitution of the throat so that the voice is supple enough to perform any delicacy the singer may wish."[48] Bacilly defends the use of diminutions, claiming that if simplicity and smoothness are beautiful, then embroidery and decoration are all the more so, as long as they are applied correctly. Thus diminutions, if placed and sung properly, will show off to good advantage a beautiful and simple melody. He also indicates that ornamentation must *add* to the expression of a text and certainly should not detract from it. Part of the secret to the proper application of diminutions is knowing where to add ornaments and where to suppress their use. Additionally, the proper placement of *passages* should never obscure the pronunciation of the words but serve to readjust the syllable length where necessary.

Before offering specific advice on performing diminutions, Bacilly notes that the only way to learn how to sing *passages* is to associate with skillful singers and ask for their guidance. One must also study the published *doubles* found particularly in editions of airs by Lambert and by Bacilly himself, and compare the first strophe of an air to the second.

Bacilly includes the following specific advice concerning the application of diminutions:[49]

> 1. The syllables "on" or "ou" cannot support extensive ornamentation.

Music and the Language of Love

2. *Coulements* or *roulements,* the movement from a high to a low note, usually by octave, are most appropriate for the bass voice and are rarely used in the treble.

3. *Passages* should *never* be performed with the tongue.

4. Practice should at first include performing the throat accents as heavily and slowly as possible, and once vocal control is established, the singer may perform the diminutions at the proper tempo.

5. In a series of notes that make up a diminution, the singer needs to dot or observe the dot added to the note that precedes an ascending leap. Bacilly gives the following example from his own air, "Je fais ce que je puis" (Example 6.13).[50]

EXAMPLE 6.13. Dotting a note that precedes an ascending leap

6. Several notes written as equal must be sung as if dotted or unequal, one being interpreted with a dot while the other is not (*inegalité*). The dot is never written in, because the singer would sing the dotted note in too jerky a manner. Rather, this note should be sung as delicately as possible. The example Bacilly offers is by Lambert, "J'ay juré mille fois" (Example 6.14).[51]

7. A note following a *cadence* or *tremblement* on the same syllable which serves as a *liaison* to connect the note of the *tremblement* to the note that follows should not be

EXAMPLE 6.14. Inequality within a passage

long, even though its rhythmic value is the same as the notes that preceded it. As in any *liaison* that concludes a trill, it should also be sung as delicately as possible.

8. The upper note that begins a descent of any length should be given an adequate throat accent.
9. Throat accents need not be equally applied to each note in a passage. Some should be sung without accent or firmness. Bacilly gives the example by Lambert, "J'aymerois mieux" (Example 6.15),[52] indicating that the final three notes of the ornament (the ascending dotted eighth and two sixteenths) should not be accented.

EXAMPLE 6.15. Unaccented passage

10. Descending *passages* require a distinct accent on each note.
11. Within a given *passage,* singers should lengthen (or dot) two notes in a row to add grace to an extended diminution to avoid sounding like a "hurdy-gurdy." From Bacilly's explanation, it is impossible to know exactly where the singer might lengthen certain notes in *passages* and not others, but it does seem that this practice is related to accentuating notes in descending, not ascending *passages.*

The Pronunciation of Seventeenth-Century French

Even though Bacilly begins his treatise with a general discussion on singing followed by a consideration of vocal ornamentation, he acknowledges that proper pronunciation is the most important aspect of effective and beautiful singing. The gravity and weight that one gives to singing a text adds to the performance energy (*l'énergie*), a word used by Caccini, Purcell, and others to describe the sung delivery of a text that attains the desired expressive impact.[53] Since singing is a type of declamation, singing a text should be quite different from pronouncing words in familiar speech: one should strive for greater strength and vigor, not only to make the text understandable to listeners but also to express and excite different passions. At the same time, however, sung declamation should not use the more exaggerated style associated with the theater.

Although there are a number of seventeenth-century sources that deal with French pronunciation,[54] the present account depends almost solely upon Bacilly's explanation, for he bases his comments exclusively on the performance of his airs and those by Lambert, La Barre, and Le Camus—airs composed and sung in Parisian salons and at court. This portion of the chapter focuses only on those French sounds (words) that are not pronounced in the same way today as they were in the seventeenth century. It is therefore highly recommended that anyone wishing to sing this repertory study Bacilly's treatise with great care, because he speaks at length about exceptions to rules. Whether or not a singer chooses to use modern or seventeenth-century French pronunciation, he or she must at least know about these differences and understand that for the seventeenth-century singer and auditor, proper pronunciation not only affected poetic rhymes but also comprehension.

Oi or *Oy*

One of the greatest differences between old and modern forms of French regards the diphthong *oi* (or *oy*), as in the words *toi, moi,* or *foi (toy, moy, foy)*. *Oi* and *oy* were pronounced as the semi-consonant/vowel combination [wê],[55] like the English word "way" (without adding the y to the sound), so that *moy* would be pronounced [mwê], or "mway." A good example of this diphthong is found in La Barre's setting of "Ah! je sens que mon cœur" (Example 4.11), where *foy* [fwê] in m. 16 rhymes with *moy* [mwê] in mm. 20 and 22. Words like *tesmoins* (Example 4.4, m. 6) and *espoir* (Example 4.5, mm. 15–16) should also be pronounced as [têmwên] and [espwêr], respectively.

Bacilly describes the diphthong in this way: "*Oi* . . . is made up of two successive sounds, one being the 'o' (almost as ou) and the following 'i' being pronounced like the wide-open 'e,' or rather an 'ai.'"[56] He stresses that the singer needs to pass quickly from the first part of the diphthong on to the *ai* sound. The exception to the rule occurs when *oi* is followed by an *n,* as in the word *point.* Here the diphthong is pronounced using these sounds in succession: first the *ou,* then *ai* (or *i*), and finally *n,* to sound like *poüeint.*[57]

Verb forms and other words that include the *oi* combination that are today spelled with *ai*, however, are pronounced as in modern French. In Example 7.2, Lambert's setting of "D'un feu secret," *pourrois* in mm. 17–18 would be pronounced [pourrês] (modern spelling is "pourrais"). Bacilly notes an exception: the singer needs to alter certain pronunciation practices to accommodate rhymes. He gives as an example the word *reconnois* (which in modern French is pronounced as "reconnais"). Here, the singer should pronounce *reconnois* as [reconnwê] so that it rhymes with *fois* [fwê].[58] A modern pronunciation—"reconnais" and "fois"—would not constitute a proper rhyme.

An and En

During the seventeenth century, an *a* or *e* followed by an *n* to create a nasal sound was pronounced as a closed *a* [â], as in *pâte*, with the nasalization occurring at the end of the vocal emission.[59] According to Bacilly, this rule also applies to words with *en* pronounced like *an*, as in *tourment*. He states that "the 'n' should not be pronounced at all until the end of the final note has been reached since the 'n' cannot be sung in any way other than with a nasal tone. . . . 'never sing through your nose.'"[60]

Words that include the *en* combination that is not pronounced as *an* (as in *bien, ancient,* and so forth) require a different approach.[61] Here, the *e* is pronounced as an open [e], as in *bête*, which is then followed by the nasalization or *n* sound. All other nasal-vowel combinations (*in, on,* or *un*) are pronounced as they are in modern French, with an immediate nasalization.[62]

The Mute E

In seventeenth-century pronunciation, all mute and/or feminine *e*'s would have been pronounced (as in "une belle fille");[63] however, as Bacilly notes, the pronunciation is different from other *e*'s. He suggests pronouncing the mute *e* by mixing an *e* and *u* sound, as in the diphthong *eu*. This applies to all feminine words, including monosyllables like *de, ne, me,* and so forth.

The R

All *r*'s are rolled. Double *r*'s should be rolled with greater force than single *r*'s (a rolled *r* would apply to seventeenth-century spoken

French as well, since the modern *r* pronunciation became standard-ized practice during the nineteenth century).[64] The singer can roll the *r* with greater force if it begins the word or appears either before or after another consonant (*rien, grace,* or *prendre*), but if the *r* appears between two vowels or at the end of a word, it must be struck more softly or gently (*rare,* or *accabler*).[65]

Bacilly notes, however, that *r*'s appearing before another con-sonant (*pourquoy*) must be pronounced with greater strength than those that come after a consonant (*agréable*). He also emphasizes that the singer must match the strength of the *r* to the meaning of the word within the text. "The singer must take care to give the proper emphasis to the 'r' according to the context and meaning of the words in which it is found rather than being guided by grammati-cal rules."[66] In words containing an *r* which belong to a phrase that demands a more vehement recitation, the *r* should be struck with greater strength. Bacilly gives as examples the phrases "Pourquoy faut-il belle inhumaine?" and "Si l'ingrate ne m'aime pas" in airs by Lambert. Words like *cruelle* or *tourment* would almost always require a stronger pronunciation.

In dealing with the *r* as a final consonant, Bacilly advises that it should most likely be pronounced gently (this applies to both verb infinitives like *finir* or *aimer,* as well as nouns like *berger* or *soûpir*), though he recognizes that the issue is controversial. He admits that without an audible final *r,* a word may sound "flat" or "feeble" and warns that failure to pronounce a final *r* may lead to confusion in meaning. To illustrate, he notes that on the phrase "vous sçavez donner de l'amour," if one "were to slur over 'sçavez' in addition to dropping the infinitive 'r' [of 'donner'] the result would be 'vous avez donné de l'amour' ['you have given love'] rather than 'vous sçavez donner de l'amour' ['you know how to give love']."[67]

THE ASPIRATED *H*

In modern French, the difference between a mute and aspirated *h* still exists, though not in pronunciation (both are mute). One would, for example, elide a previous consonant with a mute *h,* as in "l'hôpital," whereas no elision would take place before an aspirated *h,* as in "le haricot." During the seventeenth century, aspirated *h*'s were pronounced as they are in English. One of the most prevalent examples of an aspirated *h* is the word *hélas*—a word found in just about every air— wherein the *h* is pronounced. For many English speakers singing this repertory, the only way to make sure an *h* is aspirated or not would be to consult a French dictionary.

The *L*

All *l*'s that appear between two vowels (even the double *l*) must be pronounced lightly (*celer* or *belle*), while all *l*'s that precede a consonant should be pronounced as if doubled or with greater strength, as in *malgré* or *revolter,* though these two words would require a more vehement pronunciation in any case due to their meaning. By contrast, the *l* in *Silvie* should be struck lightly.[68]

Gronder

Bacilly devotes an entire chapter to *gronder,* or "growling" consonants. He defines this effect as emphasizing "certain consonants before sounding the vowels which follow by prolonging or suspending them." This is used "when a singer wants to give a greater force of expression to a word."[69] The consonant most likely to be "growled" (and easiest as well) is the letter *m,* particularly on words that express more vehement passions such as *mourir* (death), *malheureux* (unhappy), or *misérable* (miserable). Bacilly notes, however, that strict attention should be paid to the use of these words in negative sentences. The *m* that begins *mourir* in the phrase "Je ne veux mourir" ("I do *not* want to die"), for example, should not be "growled." The *m* that begins the word *malaisé* in "Ah! qu'il est malaisé" ("Ah! how difficult it is") from Bacilly's air "Puisque Philis est infidelle" (Example 4.10, mm. 14–15) would require the extended *m*. To "growl" an *m* requires that the singer hold the lips together a little longer before sounding the vowel that follows.[70] Other consonants to be suspended in the same way are the *f,* as in *infidelle* (unfaithful) and *n,* as in *non* (no). The *s* may also need to be extended on words like *severe,* the *j* in *jamais* (never), or the *v* in *volage* (flighty one). Bacilly stresses, however, that "there must be an actual emotion expressed by the device, not just a supposed one. Nothing could be more ridiculous than to use this device on the "v" of "vous" [you], "vos" [your], and "volage" every time they occur."[71]

Final Consonants

When singing a text in seventeenth-century French, it is necessary on some occasions to pronounce the final consonants. These include the *r, n, l, s, x,* and *z.* First and foremost, these final consonants are to be pronounced when they are essential to proper understanding of a text.[72] This especially applies to the *s* and *x* in plural forms that are followed by words beginning with vowels. In Lambert's air "Mon ame faisons un effort" (Example 4.1), the *s* at the end of "faisons" in line one, "Mon ame, faisons un effort," should be pronounced like a *z* and elided to "un." In the third phrase of this same air, "Parlons il n'est plus temps de feindre" ("Let us speak there is no time to pretend"), the *s* at the end of "parlons" must be sounded and elided to "il," while the *s* at the end of "temps" should not. In the line "Si je pers le respect, je pers aussi la vie" ("If I lose [your] respect, I also lose my life"), only the *s* in the "pers" that precedes "aussi" need be pronounced.

One should not pronounce either the *r* or *s* in plural words like *bergers* (shepherds) or *toûjours* (always) if these words are followed by a consonant and not a vowel. Bacilly does note, however, that in the singular form of *berger* or *rocher,* the *r is* pronounced whether the word precedes a vowel or not.[73] Although Bacilly gives other exceptions to rules that govern the pronunciation of final consonants, he most especially explains that the plural forms of nouns must be articulated when the plural is unclear. In "Fleurs qui naissez sous les pas de Silvie," for example, the *s* must be pronounced to show clearly that the plural form of *fleurs* (flowers) is intended. This holds true as well for *arbres* (trees) and *rochers* (rocks) in the phrase "Arbres, rochers, aimable solitude" ("Trees, rocks, lovely solitude").

Of most importance, Bacilly notes, is that a final consonant be pronounced before a "catch-breath" or pause to make the meaning of a phrase clear, as in "Arbres, rochers, . . ." cited above. This also applies to rhymes at the hemistich (mid-way through a verse or line of poetry) and at the ends of poetic lines. As Eugène Green notes: "At the rhyme, and before all other breaks in the voice, a final consonant must be articulated. The consonants in this case have a muted sound: d and t = [t]; g and c = [k]; s, z, and x = [s]. When a consonant which is normally articulated is followed by another that one must pronounce according to these rules, one will [pronounce] both, but when several latent consonants follow one another, one only [pronounces] the last one: *mort* [mort], but *morts* [mors]."[74]

The articulation of final consonants is sometimes left to the interpretation of the singer. Bacilly gives as an example the phrase "Je veux briser mes fers je veux finir" ("I want to break my bonds I want to finish"), wherein one may wish to pronounce the *s* at the end of *fers* if choosing to pause after this word, even if the *mes* which precedes *fers* does identify this word in its plural form. The final consonant for unmodified plural words, however, should *always* be pronounced.

In considering the final *t,* Bacilly notes that it should not be pronounced if a break or pause is taken after a word like *content* (happy), even if it is followed by a word beginning with a vowel, as in "Je parois si content Iris" ("I appear so content Iris"). The *t* in *content,* however, *should* be pronounced if the singer connects the word to the following *Iris.*[75]

Vocal Technique and the Pronunciation of Vowels and Diphthongs

Although Bacilly gives no advice about how to generate a good vocal sound in general, he does relate certain vocal techniques to pronunciation, particularly when singing certain vowels. He begins this section on pronunciation with the complaint that teachers of singing mistakenly profess that all good singing requires an open mouth. "Even when it is a question of correcting a faulty pronunciation of a consonant, they [teachers] have no other secret—no other counsel than this: 'Open your mouth.'"[76] Bacilly insists, however, that different vowels require a different shape of the mouth, for while it is true that singers must open their mouths when singing certain vowels, other vowels and diphthongs require the mouth to be held nearly shut. The following is a list of his suggestions:

A

1. There are different ways and degrees of opening the mouth, even for the same vowel. When singing a *port de voix* on *a,* for example, the singer must take particular care. He must begin by opening the mouth slightly and then "after the throat has performed the accent which is necessary in order to carry the first note over to the last, he must open the mouth wider, not all at once, but rather little by little so that the tone quality gradually becomes more agreeable."[77]
2. The mouth must also open gradually when singing an *a* on a long note.
3. Just how wide the mouth should open when singing an *a* depends upon the passion expressed. The more vehement the passion, the more open the mouth when singing the this vowel.

4. When singing an *a* for expressions of joy, the mouth must be open "in a way similar to a smile with the emphasis on width."[78]
5. When singing *an* or *en* (if it is pronounced like *an*), the mouth should be open and the *n* pronounced at the last moment.

E

1. In most situations, the *e* must be sung with an open mouth, just as the *a* is.
2. "The more open the vowel, the more open the mouth."[79]
3. When singing *en* as in *bien,* which is pronounced with an open *e* and the *n* pronounced at the last minute, the mouth should be open.
4. The silent (mute or feminine) *e* should be pronounced like the diphthong *eu* with the lips nearly closed.

I

1. The *i* must be pronounced with refinement so one should avoid singing this vowel in too sharp and piercing a manner.
2. One should not sing an *i* through the nose.
3. The *i* sound should be formed by using the throat as much as possible, though not as much as one would for the *o,* which is formed farther back in the throat.

O

1. The *o* is a guttural vowel and pronounced in the throat.
2. The throat must be open when pronouncing an *o.*
3. When an *o* is followed by either an *n* or *m,* one must add a *u* sound to it so that one pronounces *boune* and *coume* instead of *bonne* or *comme.*[80]
4. One should never apply diminutions to syllables that contain *on* or *om.*

U

1. Bacilly suggests that it is wrong to close the mouth too much when singing the *u.*
2. One should also avoid making the *u* sound like *eu.*

Ai and Au

1. The *ai* sound is identical to the open *e*.
2. The *au* sound is identical to the *o*.
3. There is a slight difference between the *ai* in *aimer* and that in *faire*. The first is pronounced with a semi-open *e* sound, the second with a completely open *e*.

Eu

1. The *eu* sound should be pronounced with lips close together.
2. The *eu* must be pronounced in the front of the mouth.
3. One must avoid pronouncing the *e* and *u* separately.

Ou

1. The *ou* must be pronounced in the palate, so at the back of the throat and not in the front of the mouth.

Ai or Ay

1. The *a* and *i* or *y* that make up the diphthong *ai* or *ay* should never be pronounced equally, but rather, the singer should move to the [ê] sound as soon as possible.
2. The final [ê] sound is made in the front of the mouth.

Syllabic Quantity

In addition to singing with proper pronunciation, the ability to discern syllable length is extremely important to singing French airs. By doing so, the singer is not only able to apply the proper ornaments on particular syllables, but is also able to give to the pronunciation the necessary energy and weight through the combination of long and short syllables (and those in between). A reference to reciting poetry *à haute voix* and the application of syllabic quantity to reciting *and* singing is stressed by Bacilly:

> One must certainly agree . . . that French poetry takes no cognizance of the length of syllables *insofar as it is written* as long as some rhyme is maintained; but when it comes to the question of *reciting, singing, or declaiming* [emphasis mine] some verse in a proper fashion, it is obvious that differing syllable-

length must be observed not only in poetry but also in prose. As a matter of fact, in this regard there is no difference between the two types of literature.[81]

Although the application of syllable length and one's ability to ascertain which syllables are long, which are short, and which syllable lengths are altered in context seem quite complicated, it is important for singers to recognize that a master composer would have accommodated rhythmic values to syllable length. As Bacilly notes, "It must be stressed that even though these rules [of syllabic quantity] are applied to the *performance* of language, for this precise reason they must also be applied to the *composition* [emphasis mine] of a piece of music which utilizes a French text."[82] Even so, singers need to understand how to discern syllable length for a variety of reasons: (1) to sing long(er) syllables with greater force through length or addition of ornaments, and short(er) syllables lightly with simpler ornaments (or none at all) to create a certain ebb and flow to the performance; (2) to apply proper ornaments on appropriate syllables with regard to vowel sounds and thus length; and (3) to understand and recognize why certain *passages* or diminutions and ornament types have been added to certain syllables in second strophes or *doubles*.

Although skilled composers consider syllable length in their musical settings, Bacilly warns that often a composer

> will write a short note over a long syllable, leaving the solution of the resulting problem to whatever singer has a perfect enough knowledge of syllable-length to cope with it. . . . This sort of thing crops up most often in airs which have a strict rhythm such as *Sarabandes, Gavottes, Bourées,* etc. In this sort of air, the composer is obligated to work within a fixed rhythm of short and long notes in order to establish the accepted dance patterns, even though the syllables underneath the notes don't always correspond to the rhythms.[83]

Thus, a singer needs to know when to stress long syllables even if they are assigned smaller rhythmic values, as one may find in dance airs. When it comes to adding ornaments to any type of air, including dance songs, Bacilly does stress that singing a long syllable "a little longer" is often enough, though "one doesn't have to sing them long enough to be able to use a final or mediant *cadence* on them nor a long *tremblement* either. One need only use an *accent* or a repetition of the throat to establish the proper length or perhaps its semi-length."[84] One simply must not pass lightly over long syllables.

Bacilly designates basically three quantities: long, semi-long or semi-short, and short. Syllabic quantity refers to the duration of the syllable and does not mean that a long syllable need be accented or necessarily stressed in any way (though one could add an ornament to the syllable). The precise length assigned to any syllable is not addressed by Bacilly, and so it is impossible to state that a long syllable be held twice as long as a short syllable, and so forth. In other words, syllable length is not quantifiable. As we have seen as well, syllable length has less to do with emphasizing or accenting certain words over others and more to do with creating patterns of *stress by length* to accommodate the expression of an entire phrase, period, and even complete piece.

The following account of syllabic quantity is based solely upon Bacilly's treatise, wherein he organizes his treatment of the subject according to the number of syllables that make up various words. He states that syllabic quantity is generally determined by certain indications of length (such as the appearance of the letter *n* in a word or syllable), the place of the syllable in a word, and the place of the word in a phrase. He also spends a great deal of time explaining the "principles of symmetry," the most difficult aspect regarding quantity, which he defines as the alteration of the "normal" length of a syllable according to the type of syllables that surround it.

It is important not to become overwhelmed by all the rules, but rather to consider the text of one air at a time, perhaps marking which syllables in words would most likely be long (aided by the composer's choice of rhythms) and then move on to more ambiguous syllables, keeping in mind that a singer's own interpretation, then and now, is extremely important. I include in this section of the chapter a relatively brief explanation of quantity and encourage readers to study Bacilly's treatise to learn which words are usually long, short, or semi-long/semi-short, how to apply principles of symmetry, and the kinds of ornaments that syllables in words can support.

SYMMETRY

A syllable which is either naturally short or long can be altered in length, depending upon the syllables surrounding it. An application of the principles of symmetry usually creates an alternation of long(er) and short(er) syllables, counting backwards from the last long syllable. Normally, for example, the monosyllable *de* would be short, though it becomes long if it precedes a two-syllable masculine word. Thus, the *de* in "de l'aimer" becomes long (while *l'ai*- is short and *mer* is long). The syllable *ny*, which is usually short, would also be made long if it precedes *de* as in "ny de mesme." Here the *ny* is long, the *de* is short, and the *mes*- of *mesme*, long, creating a long–short–long–short pattern.

In Lambert's air "Que me sert-il" (Example 6.16), we see how Lambert sets the phrase according to Bacilly's description of symmetry and what happens with a series of monosyllables that precede a masculine word like *flatter*. In this example, the long syllables are clearly *Ah, se,* and *-ter* of "flatter." *C'est* is short and *trop* semi-long. *Ah!,* the exclamation (exclamations are always long), is properly set as a long syllable in both appearances of the phrase. *C'est,* a short syllable, however, is given the same rhythmic value as the semi-long syllable *trop* in the first statement, but made appropriately short in the second. In singing this phrase, one may wish to sing the first *c'est* more like the second (either extending the *Ah!* a bit longer or taking a catch-breath or short pause after the exclamation). The shortest syllable of all, *flat*-, appears short in both statements. *Trop,* though slightly shorter than *se* in this example, needs to receive emphasis by adding either a ornament (most likely a *demi-port de voix*), while the longer syllable *se* (made long through the principle of symmetry) would warrant emphasis by adding a *tremblement* or trill.

"Ah [I] am only deceiving [myself]"

EXAMPLE 6.16. Lambert, "Que me sert-il," mm. 14–19, *Les Airs de Monsieur Lambert,* p. 44.

QUANTITY

The following lists outline the most common principles pertaining to syllable length.

Long Monosyllables

1. Monosyllables with an *s* (including *x* or *z* when pronounced like an *s*) are long if the last or second-to-last letter is long (*temps* or *beaux*).
2. Monosyllables with an *n* or *m* after a vowel, with another
   letter that follows, are long (*temp* or *donc*).
3. Monosyllables with diphthongs are long (*oi/oy, ou, eu,
   ui/uy,* or *ai/ay*) but can easily be altered. Words with *au*
   (*beau*), however, are almost always long.
4. All monosyllables on the rhyme or caesura or immediately
   preceding a point of punctuation, including interjections
   followed by an exclamation mark, are long (*Ah!*).
5. All interjections (*Dieux!*), exclamations (*Ha!*), interrogati-
   ves (*Quoi?*), and imperatives (*Va*) are long.
6. In masculine words with two or more syllables, the final
   syllable is always long (*aimer*), but is subject to the principle of symmetry depending upon the quality of the
   penultimate syllable, which may be naturally longer. In
   longueur, lon- is longer than *-gueur* because is contains an
   n. In masculine words, the final syllable can also be made
   short if it is followed by a word that begins with a vowel
   (*l'amour est*).
7. In feminine words with two or more syllables, the penultimate syllable is always long, but subject to symmetry
   (*mesme*).
8. Particles and pronouns are long, but are easily subject to
   the principles of symmetry (*les, vos,* or *ces*).

Bacilly also explains that two monosyllables in a row might both be
long. "Mon cœur" and "vos coups," for example, from Lambert's air
"Mon cœur qui se rend à vos coups" (Example 4.5, mm. 1–2 and 3–4,
respectively) are all long. In his description of the first four measures of
this air, Bacilly makes it clear that the singer's interpretation is important, and that within certain limits, singers can decide for themselves if
a syllable of questionable length is long, short, or in between.

Bacilly explains the passage in this way:

> The first two monosyllables are both naturally long ["Mon
> cœur"]; the first because it contains an *n,* and the second
> because it is contained in the table of long monosyllables, and
> both of them because neither one of them precedes a vowel.

If either one of these did precede [a word that begins with] a vowel, it would become short. The third [syllable, "qui"] can be long if the *singer wants to treat it so* [emphasis mine] (but is not so in its essence) because it precedes one which ought to be short in this context since it (se) is followed by one which is very long and is unchangeable (rend). . . . The sixth monosyllable is short (à) because it precedes the word "vos" which is essentially long since it ends with an *s*.[85]

Bacilly concludes the chapter on monosyllables by insisting that in serious airs, the rules for syllable length take precedence over considerations of rhythm.[86] As such, when a singer encounters equal rhythms set to words of differing length, as in the setting of "Qu'il couste cher de voir Silvie" (see Example 5.10, m. 1), or in several measures throughout "Mon sort est digne de pitié" (Examples 5.3a and 5.4a), it is perfectly acceptable to bend rhythmic values, either by subtly shortening rhythms set to short monosyllables or by lengthening rhythms on long monosyllables.

Semi-Long Monosyllables

Monosyllables that contain an *r* or *l* with another consonant are semi-long (*perd*). Bacilly explains that when singing a syllable of this kind, one may "slow down a bit to give them proper emphasis on the 'r.'"[87] Even though singers should not apply long ornaments on these syllables, it is acceptable to add a half-*tremblement* or *accent*.

Short Monosyllables

1. Monosyllables ending with an *e* are always short (*de*).
2. Usually the penultimate syllable in masculine words is short.
3. Usually the final mute *e* in feminine words is short, unless it appears at the hemistich or at the end of a line.

Consecutive Short or Long Syllables or Monosyllabic Words

1. In any word, there are never two consecutive short syllables. Neither can there be two short monosyllabic words in a row. Either one of them is allowed to be long in order to preserve retrograde symmetry.

2. In multi-syllabic words or in a string of monosyllables, there can be consecutive long syllables (*mon cœur* or *vos coups*).

Up to this point, aspects of performance that pertain specifically to singers have been addressed. The last portion of this chapter treats tempo, *mouvement,* repeats, and basso continuo accompaniment, which pertain to both singer and accompanist.

Tempo

The tempo of the tactus, or beat, for any given piece is determined by a number of factors: the meaning of the text, the time signature (and its association with affect), the rate of rhythmic movement within the given beat, and the complexity of the second-verse diminutions. In his *Methode claire, certaine et facile, pour apprendre àchanter la musique,* Jean Rousseau explains that common time, or *la Majeur* (C), indicates four "heavy" or *grave* beats per measure, and cut time (C with a slash through it), or *le Mineur,* designates two slow (*lent*) beats. *Le Binaire* (2) indicates two fast (*vite*) beats, while *le Trinaire* (C3) specifies three slow beats.[88] *Le Triple simple* (3) equals three light (*leger*) beats, and *le Triple double* ($\frac{3}{2}$) designates three slow beats per measure.[89] If the unit of beat is the half note, the tempo (the speed of the tactus) is slower; if the unit of beat is a quarter note, the tempo is faster. In almost all serious airs in the four collections under study, the half-note beat is the unit of beat, and the most common time signature is *le Trinaire* or *le Mineur;* thus, an indication that the tempo of the beat in most airs ought to be rather slow.

A performer must also keep in mind that in the more serious airs, the tempo can vary within. Bacilly is very clear on this and even defines an air as "a song in free meter," as distinct from dance airs.[90] He adds that even though most dance airs can be sung more slowly than their instrumental counterparts, the character of the dance must never be lost. He writes:

> [In] pieces of vocal music which have a fixed meter, it is entirely permissible to perform them more slowly than usual, but it is always necessary to maintain the metric proportions so as not to alter a Minuet or a Sarabande to such an extent that it becomes a song in free meter, such as is usually implied by the term "Air."[91]

Bacilly also indicates, however, that there are certain types of old gavottes which "demand a greater degree of expression and tenderness," in which the "dance meter is broken in order to give the air more refinement and to bring to it hundreds of stylistic changes."[92]

Thus, if the air is a dance—the minuet, gavotte, or sarabande being the most common—the character and tempo of the dance should be maintained, though the singer is permitted to slow down and even vary the tempo if need be to accommodate expression.

Le Mouvement

Within his section on ornamentation, Bacilly includes a very brief account of *le mouvement,* which we, for a lack of a better word, will translate as "movement." A better sense of the meaning might be "expression" or "emotion," in reference to the movement of animal spirits within the body that causes an emotional response, as described in chapter 3. Bacilly defines *le mouvement* as "a certain quality which gives spirit to a song . . . called *mouvement* because it evokes . . . or excites the attention of the listener . . . [and] inspires the hearts of listeners with whatever passion the singer might wish to evoke and mainly the passion of tenderness."[93] *Mouvement* has little to do with tempo, so it is not the same as *mesure,* nor should it be confused with *airs de mouvement* or the rapid skipping style associated with gigues, minuets, or other dances, which are quite different from slower, more expressive airs.

Jean Rousseau addresses *mouvement* at the very end of his *Methode claire.* He, like Bacilly, distinguishes between *mouvement* and *mesure. Mesure* refers to the number of beats in a measure, the rate of which must be subjected to and animated by *mouvement,* the "soul of the music" ("l'esprit de la Musique") and the "expression of the piece" ("l'expression de la Pièce"). In recitative, he notes, "one rarely beats the *mesure,* because the equality of the beats would often distort the *mouvement* and the soul of the passion."[94] This statement applies to most serious airs as well.

Although a good deal of this book has been devoted to illustrating how composers set airs to represent their interpretation of affect—through notation or the musical composition itself—Bacilly reminds us that it is the singers' responsibility to "animate" their voices to accommodate passionate expression. A large part of this is accomplished through the application of vocal *agréments.* Sadness and grief require *plaints, accents,* and "certain *langueurs* which are realized in a descending pattern from one long note to another supporting the voice very lightly."[95] Doleful expressions also require *tremblements étouffé,* slow *cadences, "demi-ports de voix* which are executed while ascending by imperceptible degrees,"[96] and *gronder,* or "growling" (extending certain consonances, such as *m*). One must also sustain final notes in a languorous manner, rather than cutting the phrase off too abruptly. Joyful expressions require *doublements de gosier,* "a single note articulated twice rather than once . . . performed so lightly and delicately that it hardly appears so."[97] This ornament should only be used on long syllables and never on short ones in cheerful utterances.

Repeats

It is often assumed that the singer should repeat both the first ("A") and second ("B") parts of the air within a given strophe, but in fact, repetitions are indicated in a number of ways in the score. While Rousseau in his treatise makes it clear that repetitions are designated by the sign we use today, most airs from the 1660 publications either employ just a double bar or a double bar with dots within, as shown in Figure 1.3, "Vous demandez pour qui mon cœur soupire" by La Barre. All airs by Le Camus show clearly marked repeats; there is always a first and second ending, separated by a double bar with dots inside. La Barre's airs most commonly indicate repeats by a double bar with dots, as in Figure 1.3, but some also include first and second endings, such as his setting of "Tristes enfans de mes desirs" (Example 4.4), while in many, no second ending is indicated. Both procedures are observed in Lambert's airs. In the vast majority of pieces (twelve of the twenty), the double bar (filled in with dots) is followed by a second ending (see Example 4.5, "Mon cœur qui se rend à vos coups"), and in only a few (six) are there no second endings, but just the double bar (Example 4.1, "Mon ame faisons un effort"). Of the two remaining airs in Lambert's collection, one is a dialogue ("Philis j'arreste en fin"), which would logically not include any sectional repetitions, and the other is "J'ay juré mille fois" (Example 6.17). In this air, however, we see that a "petite reprise" is indicated at the end.

Bacilly rarely indicates a second ending, but when he does, there is only a double bar separating the two. He will indicate the last syllable of the first half normally, "mé" of "consumé," for example, but repeat the last syllable of this word on the other side of the double bar line and enclose the syllable within two slashes: con-su-mé // /mé/.

EXAMPLE 6.17. Lambert, "J'ay juré mille fois," *Les Airs de Monsieur Lambert*, p. 48.

EXAMPLE 6.17 CONTINUED

Most often, only a double bar is used to separate the two halves of an air in Bacilly's publication, and more often than not, the final note of the first half is given enough length to allow for both a repetition of the first half and time to move on to the second half, as in "Qu'il couste cher de voir Silvie" (Example 5.10). In these airs with no repeat sign or notated second ending, one should repeat at least the first half. Proof of this practice may be gleaned, perhaps, from Bacilly's air "Il n'est parlé." Here, there is no second ending nor a repeat sign, but there is a second text that must be sung to the melody of the first half.[98]

In some of Bacilly's airs, there is no double bar line to separate the parts of the air, as in "Mon sort est digne de pitié" (Example 5.3–4) or "Au secours ma raison" (Example 4.8). Does this mean that one should not repeat one or both sections? "Mon sort est digne de pitié" is quite long, so perhaps it would make sense not to repeat each half, and yet the other pieces without double bar lines are exactly the same length as the majority of airs. Additionally, in all these pieces, there is a clear cadence that separates the air into two halves. There are no other features common to each of these airs to distinguish them from the others wherein repeats are indicated. It might be that Bacilly felt that no sectional repetition was necessary in these airs, for he clearly could have indicated repeats, but chose not to.

Basso Continuo Accompaniment

As Bacilly notes in the fourth chapter of his treatise, he prefers the theorbo or lute to accompany airs, but acknowledges that the harpsichord and viol are also acceptable even though these two instruments lack the "grace and accommodation found in the theorbo."[99] This is because the "sweetness of the theorbo adapts itself to weak and delicate voices, while the other instruments tend to obscure such a voice."[100] Interestingly, Bacilly makes no mention of a bass-line vocal accompaniment even though his airs, as well as Lambert's and La Barre's, include texted bass lines, as we have seen. Additionally, he does not mention what exactly the bass viol would play. Should the viola da gamba play chords, as Jean Rousseau suggests in his *Traité de la Viole* of 1687, or the bass line along with the harpsichord or theorbo?

It is doubtful that a viola da gamba would have played the bass line along with the theorbo or harpsichord, for as Paul O'Dette and Jack Ashworth note, the addition of a bowed bass not only obscures the "transparent texture over which to deliver the text clearly," which is facilitated by the decay of the plucked sound of the theorbo or harpsichord, but also, "the fewer performers involved the more flexible the performance can be."[101] A bowed bass might be added to the accompaniment if the bass line is especially active (as some are), or if the performance space requires that a stronger bass be heard.[102]

Bacilly also addresses the nature of an accompaniment. He writes that "one must not doubt that the beauty of a song appears greater when it is accompanied by an instrument instead of [several] voices, which in order to make the harmony perfect, could be joined with the voice singing *le sujet,* in other words, the melody of an air." The accompaniment, however, must not include confusing figuration, but should "merely sustain the voice pleasantly without detracting from either its beauty or its delicate features."[103]

Although in his treatise on accompanying (1690), Denis Delair does not address specifically how to accompany serious airs, his comment on using a lighter accompaniment in the recitative might also be relevant to mid-century French airs: "Very few chords are played in fast pieces and in slow recitatives, where chords are separated by some silence in order to feature the voice."[104]

Anyone with much experience in singing and accompanying this repertory will agree with Bacilly's warning (and Delair's) to avoid confusing figuration. Generally speaking, chords need to be lightly voiced, especially when accompanying on the harpsichord. It is best to play as simply as possible and then begin to add non-chord tones or figuration where appropriate.

Most importantly, the accompanist needs to provide the sort of accompaniment that supports the expression of the text. Thus, as Jack Ashworth and Paul O'Dette point out, the essence of continuo playing is to provide harmony and rhythm, and to provide gestures that match or complement the solo part(s). Continuo players need to shape and inflect lines. . . . The playing should be spontaneous, inventive, and interactive. Continuo playing that strives merely to stay out of the soloist's way actually makes it more difficult for singers . . . to create the kinds of affects required in early Baroque music, since a flat, neutral shape counteracts a highly inflected one. At the same time, hyperactive continuo playing diverts attention from the solo parts and usually works at cross purposes.[105]

And indeed, seventeenth-century treatises on accompaniment stress that chords may be filled in with non-harmonic tones and that the texture of the chords should vary according to an individual passage. In many of his examples, Delair shows the addition of sevenths, ninths, and elevenths to the "natural" chords and also indicates the practice of playing the chord with a *coulé* (notes added to fill in the intervals that make up a chord). While the notes of the chord should be held, the inserted *coulé* should be struck and released.[106]

The nature of the chords is determined by the text. An accompanist might want to play fuller chords to support long syllables and strong beats, or a two-note chord or no chord at all on short syllables and weak beats. One should also "vary the speed and pattern of arpeggios, mixing them with block chords according to metric placement, rhythmic function, note values, and so forth."[107] The accompanist also must place the bass note firmly on the beat and roll the chord after the bass sounds.[108] This is especially crucial when the singer performs a *port de voix* which begins before the beat and should form a dissonance to the chord on the downbeat. The singer needs time before the beat to begin the *port de voix* and then time after the beat for its resolution.

The voicing and register of the chord is also important and must be linked to text expression. Sorrowful utterances require chords in lower registers that are more tightly voiced in order to accommodate a voice that descends to the lowest register of the piece, while agitated affects such as despair or anger could be accompanied by chords in higher registers and fuller textures.[109] But even then, the chords should vary from one beat to the next to accommodate syllabic quantity and to achieve the ebb and flow necessary to a successful performance of this repertory. Such voicing and register choices also prevent doubling the voice part, which should be avoided if at all possible. As Ashworth and O'Dette point out,

Figures [are] frequently "descriptive" of the harmonies in solo parts and not necessarily "prescriptive" of what the continuo player should play. However, beware of the "table-scraps" school of continuo player, an approach that forbids the doubling of all dissonances and thirds and requires the accompanist to avoid all notes in the solo part(s), playing only what is left over. . . . While exposed thirds and dissonances are often better left to the soloist, habitually avoiding them leaves the continuo player with the fewest notes to play at the moments of greatest tension, the opposite of what is musically required.[110]

Another problem facing the continuo player accompanying airs is realizing the figures, which are often incomplete or confusing, a situation not at all unusual for seventeenth-century music.[111] The performer needs to make many decisions, not only regarding how to play chords but also which chords to play. Bacilly's air "Vous ne pouvez Iris" (Example 6.18) illustrates three of the most common problems encountered when interpreting figures: (1) no indication to help distinguish between major and minor chords; (2) incomplete figures; and (3) incorrect figures.

The following is a list of problems posed by the various figures given in this piece:

m. 1: There is no figure for the F in the bass, beat 3. Should one play a D-minor chord or F-major chord? Is there a "6" missing that would indicate one should play a first-inversion chord over this F?

m. 2: Should one play a C-minor or C-major chord on beat 2?

m. 3: Should one play a D-minor or D-major chord on beat 1? Should one play a G-minor or B♭-major chord over the B♭, beat 3?

m. 4: Is a ♯6 over the A in the bass, beat 1, correct? Or is this a second- inversion chord (a "6" chord often refers to a second-inversion chord and not a first inversion).

mm. 4, 5, and 6: Note that no figure is needed to show the major version of the chord because it is evident from the melodic alteration that major chords need to be played.

m. 5: The F♯ requires a first-inversion figure and is not in root position.

m. 7: On beat 3, should the accompanist play an F-major chord followed immediately by a D-minor chord, or

EXAMPLE 6.18. Bacilly, "Vous ne pouvez Iris," *Les Trois livres d'airs*, I:60.

should a D-minor chord be played throughout the beat? What chord should be played over the E on beat 2—C major, A minor, E minor, or F⁷?

m. 8: On beat 3, a 4–3 figure is missing over the F.

m. 14: The A on beat 1 is missing a figure; it should be a first-inversion chord.

m. 15: Should one play a C-major or C-minor chord on beat 2?

m. 16: Should one play a D-major or D-minor chord on beats 1 and 2? What chord should be played on beat 3 over the E?

m. 17: A figure to indicate that a third-inversion chord should be played over the E♭, second half of beat 1, is missing.

m. 18: Should the chord on beat 2 be a third-inversion chord (E♭⁷) or a second-inversion chord (G minor)? Does the chord played over the C (with the A in the melody) include an E♭ or E♮?

m. 20: The B♮ in the bass should have a figure to indicate that the chord is in first inversion.

m. 21: Should one play a D-major or D-minor chord over the D on beat 2? In this case, because the D is forming a cadence to G, a major chord would be the obvious choice.

One can see from this air that there are certainly choices that the accompanist needs to make regarding inversions of chords and their quality, major or minor. The most obvious example of an incomplete figure is the absence of the sharp to indicate that one would need a D-major chord in cadences to G minor. This is especially true at the end of the piece, wherein a 4–♯3 suspension would have been taken for granted. While some airs do indicate the 4–3 suspension, just as many do not. The use of the major version of any chord at major cadences was almost universally applied.[112]

We can also assume that the need to turn a minor chord into its major version would have been necessary in other measures of the air. One might play a D-major chord on beat 2 of m. 1 to establish the mode (minor mode on G) and create the cross-relation of F♯ (in the D-major chord) to F♮ (the F-major chord) on beat 3. This would set up a series of cross relations that appear throughout the piece—caused, for example, by the shift from G minor to G major (end of m. 1 to downbeat of m. 2) or from G minor on beat 1 to G major (m. 20, beat 1 to beat 3).

A knowledge of affective representation in this repertory can certainly inform the choice of major or minor chords. Thus a D-major chord would be fitting on the downbeat of m. 3 on "Iris." The musical setting of a beloved's name is typically "sweet," so alternation of minor and major chords would be appropriate here —the G-minor chord on beat 3 of m. 2 moving to D major on beat 1 of m. 3. On beat 1 of m. 16, the player may also wish to play a D-major chord to better represent the word "plaints" ("complaint"), even though the melodic gesture at that point is sorrowful.

There are also chords that appear to be major but might be better played as minor. This especially affects those chords that incorporate the sixth scale degree in minor modes. In m. 2, for example, a C-minor chord might be more appropriate than C major, given the sorrowful melodic phrase and reference to Iris's harsh treatment.

Many other problems arise in considering how to accompany this piece. What chord would one play on beat 2 of m. 3 over the C? Should one play an A-minor chord? An A-diminished? Or perhaps a D^7 chord in third inversion? Because the phrase refers to harsh treatment, perhaps the dissonance at this point created by either a D^7 chord in third inversion or an A-diminished chord would be the best choices. We see this pattern in other measures of the piece. In m. 17, for example, the E♭ in the second half of beat 1 forms a seventh to the F-major chord, and the C in the second half of beat 2 forms a seventh of the D-minor chord. In m. 6, instead of playing a different chord on the second quarter note of beat 1, the player should allow the F to form the seventh of the G-minor chord (as a passing note to E♭). The second beat in m. 7 also causes pause. A C-major chord might be more appropriate here instead of A minor (the only other option) due to the agitation of the passage in reference to the lover's suffering.

Whereas the problems facing performers when accompanying airs by Bacilly also apply when playing airs by Le Camus and La Barre, fewer problems arise in airs by Lambert, which tend to be more accurately and clearly figured. In "Mon ame faisons un effort" (Example 4.1), for example, the final cadence is marked with figures 4–3. Lambert also indicates where sevenths are to be added to chords, as in m. 7, or where passing tones are to be played, as in m. 6, wherein a "melodic" movement from D to E leading to an F♯, middle m. 6, is indicated by the figure 5–6 over the G in the bass. We also see in "Mon ame" that Lambert often places a "3" under a bass note not to indicate that the chord is in root position but to show that the third above the bass needs to be included in the chord. In m. 5, for example, the "3" under the B♭ does not indicate a B♭-major chord but shows that a D must be played, along with the B♭ and G (in the treble), to form a G-minor chord in first inversion. The "4" that follows indicates that an E needs to be played, forming an E-diminished chord on beat 2 of this measure. A similar example occurs in Lambert's "Mon cœur qui se rend à vos coups"

EXAMPLE 6.19. Lambert, "Mon cœur qui se rend," mm. 1–2, *Les Airs de Monsieur Lambert*, p. 32.

(Example 6.19) in m. 2, beat 1, wherein the figure allows for no other alternative than to play a G-major chord in first inversion and not a root position B-diminished chord.

Returning to "Mon ame faisons un effort" (Example 4.1), we see that the final beat of m. 9 has a 4–3 figure over the D in the bass. Here, it seems likely that the 4–3 indicates that the continuo player needs to move from the G above D (the "4") to an F ("3") in the chord to form a B-diminished chord. The diminished chord on the final beat of this measure forms a dissonance against the A in the treble, an appropriate reference to the pain at "being close to death."

In airs by Bacilly and La Barre wherein the texted bass line is the *only* bass line given (as opposed to Lambert's airs, which include a separate bass line for voice and instrument), the continuo player should feel free to exclude notes in the bass notated to accommodate the syllables of the text, as many seem awkward and cause problems in determine what kinds of chords to play where. Examples of this problem appear in mm. 3, 5, 8, 10, 11, 15, 16, 17, 18, and 21 of "Vous ne pouvez Iris" (Example 6.18). With the exception of m. 5, all these are places where either a quarter or eighth note appears as a repetition of the preceding note located on a primary beat of the measure. Thus the bass note D in m. 3 could be played as a half note (Example 6.20, A and B).

We see that in Lambert's air "Mon ame faisons un effort," as in all his airs, he replaces note repetition to accommodate syllables in the texted bass with a single note (Example 6.21, m.4). He also adds a note of anticipation moving from C to D on "ef-fort" in m. 3, as we find in Bacilly's "Vous ne pouvez Iris" on the word "souf-frir" (Example 6.18, mm. 8–9).

The interaction between singer and accompanist is extremely important and can make or break a successful performance. A great deal of useful information can be found in F. T. A. Arnold's *The Art of Accompaniment from a Thoroughbass*, Peter Williams's *Figured Bass*

EXAMPLE 6.20. Bacilly, "Vous ne pouvez Iris," mm. 2–3, *Les Trois livres d'airs*, I:60.

EXAMPLE 6.21. Lambert, "Mon ame faisons un effort," mm. 1–4, *Les Airs de Monsieur Lambert*, p. 4.

Accompaniment, and Jack Ashworth and Paul O'Dette's essay "Basso Continuo," in *A Performer's Guide to Seventeenth-Century Music.* Most notable is the bibliography of original sources that concludes Ashworth and O'Dette's essay. Next to studying various primary and secondary sources on playing basso continuo, the best teacher is experience.

In addition to reading about performance practice and studying on one's own, a successful performance of this repertoire requires listening to and working with master performers. In my opinion, the best recording to be used as a guide is by Stephan Van Dyck, tenor, and Stephen Stubbs, lute, performing airs by Joseph Chabanceau de La Barre.[113] One's own experience and experimentation are also imperative. Because so much of the secondary literature on seventeenth-century performance covers music from all over Europe and tends to focus on Italian and German works, there is much to be gained from an application of what French writers like Bacilly, Mersenne, and others have to say about singing. French music requires a special sensitivity and great attention to details, particularly to pronunciation, text stresses (related to syllabic quantity—singing rhythms with flexibility within the pulse), and ornamentation. Perhaps more than any other seventeenth-century repertory, French serious airs require a declamatory, not especially lyrical, approach to singing that is subtle, not overdone, intimate, and yet expressive and sensitive—in a word, *tendre*.

CHAPTER SEVEN

Salon Culture and the
Mid-Seventeenth-Century French Air

The French Air and Conversation

The development of the French air after 1650 cannot be separated from a consideration of the Parisian *ruelle*.[1] The salon was a most important milieu for cultivating proper social interaction and promoting artistic activities, particularly between 1650 and 1670.[2] *Ruelles* were conceived as entities separate from court society and served as a kind of escape from the distractions of courtly politics. Although members of elite society moved freely between court and private residences, the environment of the salon served to set apart a select group of people, both nobles and non-nobles. Indeed, the segregation of salon participants was increasingly necessary as members of and visitors to the courts of Louis XIII and Louis XIV grew steadily more diverse.[3] During the seventeenth century, then, the salon served to establish a sense of exclusivity for its participants, who considered themselves part of an elite group of people who were "in the know," particularly regarding codes of behavior, modes of conversation, topics of discourse, and current fashion. Accepted into this select group of people were the most talented French artists who, within the security of the salon setting, worked together to create significant works of art associated with seventeenth-century salon culture. Novels, books of gallant and moral conversations, poetry, and published volumes of love letters were among the products of this fruitful and inspired environment.

The most important musical genre associated with the salon was the serious air. Both the creation and performance of songs were an indispensable part of salon activity, and the airs themselves embodied in a unique manner the mores of France's most elite group of men and women. Composers and poets capable of creating the finest airs—artists able to internalize and express salon codes of behavior through their works—were welcome members of this prestigious enclave of polite society. Among them were France's most important creators of airs:

composer-performers Michel Lambert, Jean-Baptiste Lully, Bénigne de Bacilly, Jean-Baptiste de Boësset, Joseph Chabanceau de La Barre, and Sébastien Le Camus; and poets Isaac de Benserade, Pierre Corneille, Jean-Baptiste Molière, Philippe Quinault, Madeleine de Scudéry, La Comtesse de La Suze, Paul Pellisson, and Pierre Perrin, among others.

Airs were not only created and performed in the *ruelles,* but the air's musical and poetic structure, style, and topics were also determined by salon participants, specifically by the air's link to the most influential literary model of the time, promoted by salon devotees: polite conversation. The art of conversation was not only practiced in salons but was also a central literary form, a parent to many of the most important French literary genres of the seventeenth century.[4] The style of language used in most forms of seventeenth-century literature, including poetry set to music, was founded upon conversation, with its natural turns and its improvised and spoken quality.[5] Indeed, poems intended to be set to music were an important part of a specific kind of salon activity—*un grand jeu littéraire,* "a grand literary game that assumed not only the rules of dialogue, choreography . . . , but also scenery . . . , accessories (such as clothing, hair styles, and jewelry), body language, expressions, and writings that bring to life the dialogue and intrigue."[6] An air's value and function were derived from its association with the dialogues and intrigues acted out by salon participants. Airs were inserted into conversations on all sorts of topics and used to give voice to an imaginary and pleasurable discourse of seduction between men and women, a dialogue that would have been forbidden in any other situation. Dialogues were not only acted out in the salon, but for this elite group of people, the airs that made up the imaginary intrigues had a particular meaning and served a distinct function. Indeed, the great majority of airs written during mid-century, even the most serious and passionate, reflected the *jeux d'esprit,* or "games of wit," that characterized literary conversations, themselves idealized imitations of the verbal interchange so artfully practiced in seventeenth-century salons.

If Madeleine de Scudéry's literary works present an account of what actually transpired in the *ruelles,* the creation of airs seems to have been a salon activity. In her study of song texts, Anne-Madeleine Goulet found that Scudéry included lyrics as part of the narrative in her novels *Clélie, histoire romaine* (1658) and *La Promenade de Versailles* (1669).[7] An air that is actually notated appears in *Clélie,* volume 8.[8] The inclusion of airs in Scudéry's novels as well as in her *Conversations morales* of 1686 illustrates specifically how airs (song texts) were incorporated into exchanges between characters. In her *Conversations morales,* for example, several members of polite society are engaged in conversations on various philosophical issues that explore different emotional and psychological or emotional states, such as hope, love, or idleness. At some point in each of the conversations (often toward the end), several of the participants recite or sing *chansons* to summarize their particular points of view. The *chansons,* or song texts, most frequently appear in clusters that constitute a sort of "conversation in verse" that parallels the primary "conversation in prose."[9] In Conversation One, "On Hope," for example, the participants agree that hope is a sentiment that is always associated with love.[10] But one individual, Philiste, points out that while this is true, hope often causes deception. To encapsulate this thought, she offers this *chanson:*

> *Sing [about] what indifference*
> *Has that is sad and languishing,*
> *The pleasures of a new love,*
> *With its secret charms the seductive hope,*
> *In the midst of the longest torments*
> *Deceives gullible lovers.*[11]

Her *chanson* inspires others to offer their opinions in the form of song, so that by the end of this conversation, four song texts have been recited by the various participants, each offering a slightly different explanation of the relationship between love, hope, and deceit.

The use of clusters of airs that respond to conversation topics in Scudéry's works also demonstrates that the composition of song texts was a cooperative effort that involved everyone in the group, the creation of texts becoming the focus of all participants' attention. In some conversations, one person begins by creating a first strophe or substituting a new text into a pre-existing song.[12] Someone else then composes a second strophe that presents a slight variation on the point presented in the first.[13] Other participants alter certain words or phrases, while others offer a different song text altogether that either complements or contrasts with those already included.[14]

The musical repertory itself offers evidence to support Scudéry's literary representation of the cooperative process of creativity. In his *Recueil des plus beaux vers,*[15] Bénigne de Bacilly shows that more than one composer and poet participated in the creation of various airs. He indicates, for example, that both Le Camus and Lambert composed the music to "J'ay si bien publié vos attraits."[16] Bacilly also specifies that as many as four people took part in the composition of "Je fais ce que je puis": two composers, Le Camus and Bacilly, and two poets, the author of strophe one designated only as M. F., and that of strophe two, Pierre Perrin.[17]

> I do what I can to love you no longer,
> And weary of so much rejection,
> I want to break my chains, I want to finish my pains:
> But my revolt, alas! lasts only a moment,
> I cannot live without my chains,
> Nor escape my torment. (text by M. F.)

> Often Despair, Spite, Reason,
> Try to break out of my prison,
> And in order to heal me, in vain make a thousand attempts:
> But their revolt, alas! only lasts a moment,
> I cannot live without my chains,
> Nor escape my torment. (text by Perrin)[18]

Mlle de Scudéry herself worked with other poets and various composers to create airs.[19] In his *Recueil,* Bacilly indicates that Scudéry created a third strophe written in the form of a response to the air "A quoy pensiez-vous, Climène."[20]

> What were you thinking, Climène,
> What were you thinking when you fell in love?
> Did you not realize the pain
> That suffers a heart which allows itself to be inflamed
> What were you thinking, Climène,
> What were you thinking when you fell in love?

> When with all its charms
> Love comes to inflame us,
> One must give in to its weapons,
> One must languish, one must be consumed,
> When with all its charms
> Love comes to inflame us.

Response by Mlle de Scudéry

One does not think, Silvie
When one begins to love,
And without desiring it,
In a moment one becomes inflamed;

You who made everyone else burn with desire,
You burn with desire yourself;
Your beauty equal to none
Has felt the power of love;
You who made everyone else burn with desire,
You burn with desire yourself.[21]

The cooperative effort that went into the composition of an air applied as well to its performance. Indeed, in Scudéry's discourse on idleness, two participants sing alternate strophes of one air in dialogue.[22] The relationship between verses in many airs found throughout the repertory also suggests that Scudéry's representation of cooperative performance is realistic, for in performing Le Camus' "A quoy pensiez-vous, Climène," given above, there could have been as many as three or four singers: Silvie and Climène to sing strophes one and three, respectively, and one or two others, presumably men, to sing strophes two and four. In the first strophe, Silvie asks Climène: "What were you thinking when you fell in love?" Climène responds to Silvie's question in strophe three: "One does not think when one begins to love." The second strophe serves as a commentary on the dialogue between Silvie and Climène. Here, the poetic voice claims that love eventually inflames everyone. The fourth strophe repeats the message given in the second, but apparently addresses one or both women: "You who made everyone else burn with desire, you burn with desire yourself."

Additional proof for "singing in dialogue" appears in a discourse incorporating several airs in the anonymous treatise *Entretiens galans* (1681). In the chapter entitled "Music," the character Berelie and her lover, Philomon, sing songs to one another about love. After the performance, their friend Celinde remarks that they have just created a "longue scène en musique."[23]

These examples illustrate that a strophe or an air, presented as part of a conversation in song, could function either as a response to the primary conversation in prose or as an autonomous musical dialogue.

Whereas many examples of the air as a response are spread throughout Ballard's *Livres d'airs de différents autheurs,* only a few airs published within the collections by Lambert, Bacilly, La Barre, and Le Camus could be construed as responses to a topic of conversation. One exception appears in Le Camus' *Airs à deux et trois parties:* the first three airs could have served as responses to a conversation about the dangers of giving in to a man's seduction and the pain caused by his absence and then rejection. In the first of these airs, the female poetic voice recounts to the peaceful streams how she came to love her shepherd:

> *How you delight my reveries!*
> *How I love your flowering banks,*
> *Clear and peaceful streams,*
> *Alas! It was on the bank of your waters*
> *That the charming shepherd, far from all that which bores me,*
> *Began to disturb my peaceful life;*
> *All favored his desires,*
> *Zephyrus and Flora*
> *Attracted in these premises amorous pleasures;*
> *But his gazes and sighs*
> *Were more amorous still*
> *Than Flora and the zephyrs.*[24]

In the second air, she asks Aurora to extend the night in order to hide the sorrow she feels by her shepherd's absence:

> *Allow the night to last, impatient Aurora,*
> *It helps me to hide my secret sorrows,*
> *And I have not yet shed enough tears;*
> *For my pain, alas! Are there nights too dark?*
> *Since my shepherd left this beautiful place,*
> *Ah! I cannot suffer the bright light of day;*
> *Leave me then to weep under the cover of the darkness*
> *As long as his love wishes.*[25]

In the third air, the beloved angrily recounts how her lover seduced her in "this dangerous place" and then left her with "cruel memories":

> *Ah! let us escape this dangerous place,*
> *These green umbrages,*

These sweet shores,
Where Tircis made me see so much love;
Let us turn our flocks away from these woods
Where the ungrateful one lured me a hundred times;
But my heart against my rebellious intentions
Cannot banish
This cruel memory:
Alas! An unfaithful one made me love these premises,
And in spite of my diversions
I come here always.[26]

The vast majority of airs published by these composers more easily form autonomous musical dialogues, though each air presents only
half of the conversation, the male poetic voice addressing his thoughts
and pleas to his beloved. Other airs would then serve as a response. In
Lambert's *Airs de Monsieur Lambert*, we find what could be construed
as a two-air dialogue, wherein the only air with a female poetic voice
in his collection, "J'ay juré mille fois" (Example 6.17), is followed by
a response, "Puisque chacun doit aymer a son tour." Here, in "J'ay
juré," the speaker claims that she tried not to fall in love with Tircis,
but underestimated love's power:

I swore a thousand times never to love,
And did not believe that anything could entice me,
But when I made this rash plan,
Tircis, you had not yet undertaken to please me:
My reason against you no longer does its duty,
And finally I know Love's power.

Alas! I learn of my error too late,
I thought that this god subjected to his laws
Only those who do not know how to defend themselves from
his arrows;
But I feel that my heart in spite of myself will surrender.
My reason against you no longer does its duty,
And finally I know Love's power.[27]

As if to put her mind at ease and persuade her to give in to the power of
love, the speaker in the following air responds by saying that everyone
must love, so she should give it a try:

Since everyone must love in turn
Philis why do you resist it,
If you have eyes in order to give love
You have a heart for accepting it.

If it is an affliction it is a charming one
And it gives extreme pleasure,
In order to test it Philis you need only
To love me as I love you.[28]

Musical Seductions

The nature of the airs published by Lambert, Bacilly, La Barre, and Le Camus, as well as other airs found throughout the repertory, correspond closely to one specific seventeenth-century genre of literary discourse: *galant* conversation. René Bary's *L'Esprit de cour, ou les conversations galantes divisées en cent dialogues,* first published in 1662, offers some of the best examples.[29] Most of Bary's exchanges are dialogues of seduction, or *jeux d'amour,* in which a man attempts to seduce an *honnête fille,* a proper young woman, who vigorously resists him.[30] Bary represents the seduction as a process that involves particular steps: the man's improper advance, his use of flattery, the beloved's rejection, his complaint of her indifference, his perseverance, the breakdown of her resistance, their shared love, and eventually acts of infidelity.[31] When comparing the subjects of song texts represented in the vast majority of airs with Bary's seductive dialogues, we find that different airs correspond to the different steps in the seduction process, making it possible to classify the airs accordingly. Groups of airs that belong to each stage in the process not only share the same literary topic, they also share similar musical features that represent particular types of passions. As such, in writing and setting each type of song text, both poets and composers worked to realize the primary aesthetic ideal of salon culture—to write as they spoke—and thus strove to capture the spontaneity of verbal conversation in their texts and musical settings. As has been demonstrated in the preceding chapters, in musical representations of a speaker's passions the shape of the melody, its placement in different registers of the piece, the quality of harmonies and their relationships, the type of rhythmic movement, and the alteration of meter appear in various combinations to imitate the tones of voice and rate of speech associated with the different emotional states appropriate to each phase of the seduction.

The first stage in this process is the improper advance, wherein a man approaches a woman without permission from her parents. In Bary's conversations, the pretext for such an improper advance is often the man's attraction to her physical beauty. The first several conversations are, in fact, entitled "Beautiful Hands," "Beautiful Eyes," "Beautiful Hair," "Beautiful Breasts," and so forth, and in each of these conversations, the man attempts to seduce his beloved with false compliments.

The use of flattery as a pretext for an improper approach finds its counterpart in many airs throughout the repertory. As in the conversations, the man refers either to the beloved's eyes, her charms, her voice, or her mouth, as in Bacilly's "Petit abeille mesnagere" (Example 4.15). The musical settings of texts that represent the improper advance are not usually overly passionate. At this point in the conversation, the man wants to appear sincere, proper, and polite, so he dare not overwhelm the object of his affection with the full force of his feelings and intentions. Instead, the expression is usually limited to tenderness, represented most often in the music by rounded melodic contours, alternating major and minor harmonies, melodic phrases that outline major and minor thirds, repeated rhythmic and melodic patterns, sequencing, and a predominance of first-inversion chords. Occasionally, strong musical devices such as melodic and harmonic repetitions, a melody that moves in disjunct motion by fifths or fourths, harmonic movement by fifths, or dissonances are introduced into the musical setting to represent the boldness of the man's attempt.

A typical woman in Bary's conversations is insulted by the man's bold approach and his obsession with her physical attributes. She complains that he is drawn to her for the wrong reasons and recognizes his compliments as false, a pretext for the improper advance and a guise to hide his real intention, seduction. This "courtly wit that makes one speak lies," as Bary puts it,[32] is a common theme throughout the conversations—a sentiment that is also expressed in several songs. In many of these airs, the beloved responds aggressively to the deception, as illustrated in Example 7.1, "On n'ayme plus dans ces boccages," by Le Camus. The aggressive response in this air is expressed in the first part of the piece to measure 12 and is achieved primarily by a quasi-recitative style, erratic rhythmic movement by small values, and the use of expressive intervals in the melody. The images presented in the second part of the air (mm. 13–26)—the bird songs, the freshness of the

EXAMPLE 7.1. Le Camus, "On n'ayme plus dans ces boccages," *Les Airs à deux et trois parties*, p. 15.

EXAMPLE 7.1 CONTINUED

shade, the sound of the streams, and the sweetness of nascent love—however, elicit tender and sorrowful tones. In the third portion of the air, mm. 27–47 followed by a return to the first part, the woman's utterances become more and more frantic as she describes love's cruelty.

Since the woman in Bary's conversations is insulted and angered by the man's inappropriate behavior and concerned about her reputation, she has no choice but to reject him. He, in turn, blames her for his misery and is often aggressive, expressing himself with great passion. He insults her; she is harsh and cruel in her refusal to "heal" him. His reaction to her rejection is the most widely represented stage in the seduction found throughout the musical repertory. These airs are the most passionate, often expressing more than one emotional state in a single air. They include the most violent passions—despair, the burning fires of love, and boldness—as well as the more moderate sentiments such as sorrow and languor. In these airs, the lover may ask to be healed, as in Bacilly's "Pour donner à mon cœur" (Example 5.11); he may complain of her cruelty, as in Bacilly's "Vous ne pouvez Iris" (Example 4.3); or he may admit that his love for her is so strong that he must declare it outright, even if she finds this offensive, as in Lambert's "Pourquoy vous offencer" (Example 1.1).

The passions expressed in these pieces may or may not be sincere, but by expressing his torment, the man hopes to soften the beloved's response by eliciting her pity. In "Beaux yeux, que voulez-vous me dire," which was published in Ballard's *Livre d'airs de différents autheurs* (1667), the speaker even admits to this strategy. This is part of the game he plays—his game of seduction:

> Beautiful eyes, what do you want to say to me
> By your charming and sweet glances:
> If I give in, if I surrender to your blows,
> Will you someday pity my martyrdom?[33]

But the man's display of over-sentimentality is exactly what disturbs a woman the most.[34] When love is violent, she claims in Bary's conversations, modesty must preserve it; if passion enlivens it, virtue must cool it.[35] Many women claim that they do not want to be cruel, they are only doing what they must: the words "je fais ce que je dois" appear throughout Bary's conversations as well as in several airs.[36]

Despite being initially rejected by the beloved, the man could eventually win her heart either by "maintaining respect"—by avoiding a bold and passionate declaration of his love—or with "perseverance"—

by continuing to love her and serve her despite her discouragement and cruel treatment. Although maintaining respect and perseverance were still part of the game of love, the means to an end, the man had to suffer long and hard in order to prove to the woman that his love was constant and true.[37]

In many airs throughout the repertory, the man acknowledges the importance of maintaining respect. Contrary to those airs in which he boldly and passionately declares his love, maintaining respect is associated with the representation of more moderate passions, particularly tenderness, languor, or sorrow, as demonstrated by Lambert's setting of "Mon cœur qui se rend à vos coups" (Example 4.5). In the game of love, no matter how cruel the beloved's treatment, the man must not complain if he hopes to win her affections. He must practice restraint, as any expression of the more agitated passions is offensive. An air published by Sébastien de Brossard in 1696, "Soyez tendre, soyez fidelle," perfectly summarizes this tact:

> Be tender, be faithful,
> Persevere to the end:
> Lover, you will touch the heart of your beautiful one,
> That time will come.[38]

In a number of conversations and airs, the diligent lover finally wins his beloved's heart, and the lovers proclaim the pleasures of their shared love, as in Bacilly's air "Petit abeille mesnagere" (Example 4.15). As one might expect, these airs express happy and tender passions, represented in music most often by the major mode, simple harmonies, the repetition of melodic and rhythmic patterns, a homophonic texture, and regular melodic phrases.

The pleasures of love, however, do not always endure, for in the conversations and in many airs, both men and women lament the unfaithful lover. This complaint results in some of the most passionate airs in the repertory. Even though Bacilly's song "Puisque Philis est infidelle" (Example 4.10) is directed toward the lover's heart and not Philis, it is one of the most passionate airs in the repertory, the first half presenting one of the rare musical representations of anger as he tries to convince his heart to "revolt against her." In La Barre's "Ah! je sens que mon cœur" (Example 4.11), the lover also vows revenge in angry musical tones.

Even the most serious and passionate airs were not meant to represent real interactions between men and women. Given the *galant* aesthetic that governed salon activities, conflict amongst participants and the expression of great passion were absolutely not permitted in salon culture. In reality, a man's seduction of a woman, particularly if it were indiscreet, would have been highly inappropriate. Indeed, women were warned of the threat of seduction; surrendering to temptation would mean the ruination of reputation and place in society. The representation of seduction in song, however, allowed men and women within the safety of a closed and protected environment to "play the game of love" without consequences. A grave social impropriety and the intensity of passion associated with love were thus mitigated within the dimensions of a *mise-en-scène,* in the guise of playful activities, in conversations, and *jeux d'esprit,* or games of wit. The pastoral setting and the conventionalized characters and metaphors of love (typical features of seventieth-century French airs) helped to disengage the participants from the reality of life. By expressing the most powerful of passions in song, the intensity of real human emotions was diminished. Through song, men and women were permitted to make fun of the many social restrictions that kept them in bondage, break through those constraints, and even enjoy the pleasures of forbidden love, albeit vicariously. Indeed, the world created in these airs may have been based in reality, but it offered an outlet for dealing with its harsh limitations. A woman could flirt, or "say" and "express" what she dare not in other circumstances, and allow the man to seduce her without fear of repercussions. Likewise, a man could flirt and emote without being less of a man. As we shall see, this repertory, filled with erotic references, underscores an obsession with love as demonstrated not only in literary works associated with salon culture but also in treatises by doctors, Catholic leaders, moralists, and pornographers.

Galanterie and the Air:
Undercurrents of Eroticism and Lessons of Morality

One of the best accounts of the *galant* aesthetic, which governed literary works around mid-century, is found in Scudéry's novel *The Story of Sapho* (*Histoire de Sapho*). Here, Scudéry maintains that through the art of conversation, "we may recount a love affair to the most censorious of women and make a trifle agreeable to the solemn and serious. . . . There ought to be a certain *joie de vivre* that reigns [and] inspires in the hearts of the whole company a disposition to be amused by everything and bored by nothing."[39] Thus, at the heart of salon literature, and therefore applicable to song texts and airs, was an aesthetic that promoted a style both "serious" and "playful," which enabled writers like Scudéry to include lighthearted poems within the context of serious philosophical discussions. As Alain Viala explains, "The fundamental seme of 'galant' (galer = to play, to amuse oneself) is thus the basis for a conception wherein the opposition between the learned and the entertaining can be surpassed, or where the learned is transcended by worldly embellishments."[40] Jean-Michel Pelous similarly notes that "it is the essence of galanterie always to mix the serious and the amusing and to approach any subject, no matter how serious, only under the guise of an 'agreeable fiction.'"[41]

Thus, the ability to express artfully that which could not be expressed directly embodied the essence of salon culture. This approach enabled Scudéry and others to convey controversial opinions on governance, civility, or women's issues, cloaked as entertaining stories about love. Scudéry's *Artamène, ou, Le grand Cyrus* (written between 1649 and 1653), for example, a historical novel set in ancient Greece, is really an account of the French uprising known as the Fronde (1648–53), its characters representing the actual participants in the rebellion: the Prince de Condé, the Duchesse de Longueville, and the Duchesse de Montpensier (la Grande Mademoiselle). Through this work, Scudéry was able to play both sides of the conflict—to express her support for the *frondeurs* and their cause, while at the same demonstrate her loyalty to the young king. In her novel *Clélie,* set in ancient Rome, Scudéry draws parallels between proper interactions between men and women, particularly in matters of the heart, and ideal relations between king and state. By doing so, she conveyed her own vision of a woman's right to choose her husband, to take part in cultural endeavors, and to participate in government.[42]

Suggestions of eroticism are also typical of a *galant* aesthetic which allowed for undercurrents of meaning that blur the distinction between proper (non-physical) love and improper (physical) love.[43] Even though Scudéry's works include detailed examinations of love, revealing that proper love begets both individual and civic tranquility while improper love gives way to personal and public chaos, there are descriptions of lustful attraction that occur between heroes and heroines. Scudéry's views of proper love appear in her novel *Clélie* and are demonstrated by the rivalry between Aronce and Horace to win the hand of Clélie. Aronce overcomes his lustful attraction for Clélie and demonstrates personal virtue and respect for his beloved, thus earning her devotion, while Horace breaks every rule of civility with his brutish and manipulative behavior. The chaos caused by this love triangle is juxtaposed in the novel by a fight for control of Rome, which causes civic chaos. In her novels and conversations, then, Scudéry equates non-physical love with concord, tranquility, and a moral high ground, and sexual love with animal-like brutality. And yet there are always hints at the erotic force of attraction between men and women, even when their love is presented as proper. This is best exemplified in her novel *Histoire de Sapho,* wherein the attraction between Phaon and Sapho is palpable.

This obsession with love is not only typical of salon poetry, conversation treatises, and novels, it is also the focus of medical, religious, and emblematic treatises as well as erotic novels. Each presents a variety of theories about love's nature, its manifestations, and/or how its evils may be cured. In medical, religious, and emblematic treatises, writers address real-life struggles with love, either as an illness or as a matter of morality. Other sources reflect or comment upon fictionalized representations of love.

Most authors corroborate Dr. Jacques Ferrand's classification of love as either heavenly or earthly (even vulgar).[44] For doctors, earthly love, if unrequited, could develop into a serious disease called erotic melancholia or lovesickness, whereby sexual desire causes violent reactions in the body and, if left untreated, death.[45] For pornographers, physical love was "the greatest pleasure on earth."[46] But for theologians, earthly love was appropriate only for procreation within marriage; feelings of sexual desire had to be redirected toward love of Jesus and God, converting earthly desires toward the heavens.[47] Through her writings, Scudéry created a third category of love in addition to the heavenly and earthly by adding *amitié,* a sort of civic morality associated with an intimate yet non-physical friendship between man and woman.

Differences between earthly love, heavenly love, and *amitié* are explained and illustrated in Albert Flamen's *Devises et emblèmes d'Amour moralisez,* first published in 1653. Figure 7.1 shows a stream running between two intertwined palm trees, representing the male and female. The worldly explanation indicates that lovers who are physically joined together are so drawn to one another that they cannot be kept apart by any force of nature. By contrast, the moral explanation frames physical love within the bonds of marriage and a sanctioned, holy union of two souls. In Figure 7.2, Flamen's emblem shows a stream running between two palms that lean toward each other but do not touch. Here Flamen defines and illustrates *amitié,* a love between two

FIGURE 7.1. Flamen, *Devises et emblèmes,* pp. 110–12. Emblem XXVIII.
Love Joins Them Together (*"Jungit Amor; L'Amour les joint"*).

people that does not involve any physical contact but is a noble and
honorable friendship.

The airs, though products of salon culture, do not represent *amitié*
but rather men who are seemingly suffering from lovesickness and are
attempting to seduce proper young women—the men to be feared and
avoided in Bary's *Conversations galants.* Song lyrics portray the lover
as overwhelmed with passion; he is indiscreet and disrespectful, even
nasty and treacherous. We see in Scudéry's famous *Carte de Tendre*
(Figure 7.3), from her novel *Clélie,* that a man's negative traits and

FIGURE 7.2. Flamen, *Devises et emblèmes*, pp. 114–16. Emblem XXIX. They Love without Touching Each Other ("*Non Tangunt Et Amant; Elle* [sic] *s'aiment sans se toucher*").

behaviors, as represented in the airs, are depicted as villages where rejected lovers are sent. Villages that lead to "The Sea of Hostility" (*Mer d'Inimitié*) are Indiscretion (*Indiscrétion*), Disloyalty (*Perfidie*), Malicious Gossip (*Médisance*), and Malevolence (*Meschanceté*). The villages that lead to "The Lake of Indifference" (*Lac d'Indifférence*) are Negligence (*Négligence*), Inequality (*Inesgalité*), Half-Heartedness (*Tiédeur*), Fickleness (*Légèreté*), and Negligence (*Oubli*). If a potential lover behaves badly, he follows the paths either to the beloved's hostility (*inimitié*) or to her indifference, rather than the paths that lead to her acceptance of him.

Scudéry's *Carte de Tendre* is a geographical representation of how a man could properly win the heart of a virtuous, well-bred young woman. The man's goal is to arrive at "Tendre-sur-Estime" (love based on esteem) and/or "Tendre-sur-Reconnoissance" (love based on gratitude). To do so, he must pass through various villages that depict what he must do to deserve her devotion. A lover begins at "Nouvelle amitié" (new friends), and to arrive at "Tendre-sur-Estime," he must demonstrate social and civil prowess by writing pretty verses and gallant love letters, by showing her respect, and so forth. To arrive at "Tendre-sur-Reconnoissance," he must demonstrate submission to her through kindness, sensitivity, and obedience.

Lovers who do not follow the correct "routes" lose the beloved and take the paths to negligence, inequality, unfaithfulness, and treachery, among other places. An interpretation of the airs according the *Carte de Tendre* demonstrates a man's improper or immoral behavior as it contrasts with a man's proper comportment. A comparison of opposites was a means of moral education commonly used by religious leaders during the seventeenth century and adopted here by Scudéry. We know what is right by knowing what is wrong.[48] Thus, juxtapositions of moral/proper and immoral/improper behavior facilitate direct comparison.

Most airs, however, represent much more than just a man behaving badly, for several critics considered this repertory to be dangerously erotic, particularly for women and the young. Even Bénigne de Bacilly, composer of these "erotic" airs, warns that most song texts are "lascivious" and inappropriate for women.[49] By the end of the seventeenth century, critics were going so far as to claim that airs threatened the moral fabric of society, not just because of their effects on women but also on youths, who were thought to be especially susceptible to love sickness.[50] Jean Racine, for example, complains that "our most beautiful airs [are] set to words that are extremely soft and effeminate, capable of making harmful impressions on young minds."[51] In *Histoire de la Comédie et de l'opéra*, Ambroise Lalouette argues that "one of the most disastrous effects of these songs is to place in the heart a very great disposition for crime and libertinism; with the result that those who love them and who make them their recreation, easily allow themselves to engage in disorder and impiety."[52] In a satire dedicated

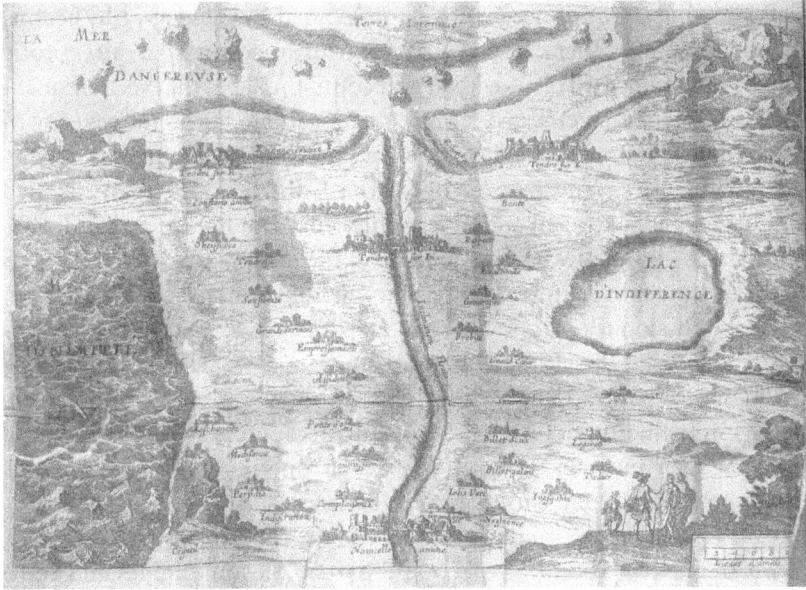

FIGURE 7.3. *Carte de Tendre,* in Madeleine de Scudéry, *Clélie, histoire romaine* (Paris: A. Courbé, 1656), vol. 1, p. 179. *Reproduced by permission of Brown University Library.*

to Nicolas Boileau, Pierre Bellocq condemns songs through which all worship pleasure:

> *What disturbed spirit, what blind mania,*
> *Incessantly desires to consecrate heresy with Harmony?*
> *Godless singers, will I always hear*
> *You praising Bacchus and Love in your songs?[53]*

Bellocq believed that profane airs were so decadent they threatened religious belief and social mores which would lead to moral decay and public chaos:

> *It is the God of Love, it is the God of Wine*
> *Whose praises are heard everywhere;*
> . . .
> *Why are these frivolous songs all the rage?*
> *Must one see among us the triumph of idols?*
> *And into the hideous abyss of the false cult,*
> *Will the universe plummet in our day?[54]*

The vulgar and indecent love condemned by Scudéry, physicians, theologians, and others, however, is not overtly expressed in airs. Erotic references are instead cloaked beneath commonplaces that seem innocuous, but are, in fact, charged with sexual meaning. Given the severity of the criticism, there can be little doubt that erotic undercurrents permeated the repertory and were recognized as such. The use of an encoded language in polite society—that is, polite words and phrases that denote vulgarities—is openly discussed in one of the most popular erotic novels of the seventeenth century, *L'École des filles*, first published in 1655.[55] In a series of dialogues that include graphic descriptions, Suzanne divulges the secrets of lovemaking to her cousin, Fanchon. A common theme throughout the novel is the differentiation between public and private behavior, including the way that socially acceptable words are used in place of their more vulgar equivalents. At one point, Fanchon claims that when she is alone with her lover, he insists that she use dirty words like *vit* or *con* (cock or cunt), but otherwise, she is to use their proper, more "refined and honorable" counterparts.[56] Suzanne agrees and adds: "when in polite company, in place of *foutre* [fuck] or *chevaucher* [to straddle], one could use *baiser* [to kiss], *jouir* [to enjoy], *embrasser* [to kiss or embrace], or *posséder* [to possess]."[57] François Sarasin, poet and participant in Scudéry's salon, also acknowledges the use of metaphors as a kind of amorous language that "passes from generation to generation"[58] and eventually become "pure convention"—conventional, yes, but nevertheless, ripe with meaning.[59]

Two of the most frequently used metaphors in airs concern fire, heat, or burning, and death, as in Lambert's "D'un feu secret" (Example 7.2 and 7.3) and "Mon ame faisons un effort" (Example 4.1). In these two song texts, the poetic voice claims that he is so consumed by fire that he will surely die. These conventional references, in fact, are not necessarily metaphors, but describe the real symptoms associated with lovesickness. In his treatise on erotic melancholia, Dr. Ferrand's medical explanation of the disease demonstrates the connection between heat and sexual desire. He notes that unlike "natural melancholy," which results from a cold and dry nature, erotic melancholy is caused by hot and dry humors through the excessive burning, or adustion, of yellow bile and blood such that "melancholiacs are subject to incessant sexual desire."[60] "Those who are melancholy from adust humors . . . are hot and dry and produce within a variety of flatulent vapors that tickle them, driving them to extremes of lasciviousness."[61]

Other sources use the same terminology to connect fire with sexual arousal. In *L'École des filles,* for example, Suzanne tells Fanchon that

Music and the Language of Love

at night when her lover comes to see her, he takes off his clothes and climbs into bed with her. His gentle words and sweet caresses heat both of them up.[62] They then experience "the greatest pleasure in the world" ("le plus grand plaisir du monde"). Emblematic treatises also illustrate this correlation. Even though the explanations use acceptable terminology, the provocative images associate the words with their erotic connotations, specifically with male arousal. The emblem in Figure 7.4, from Flamen's *Devises et emblèmes d'Amour,* shows an erupting volcano that resembles a penis in the midst of ejaculation.[63] The text that accompanies this image describes the intensity of the fire that consumes the lover and its violent physical manifestations, made explicit by the image of a volcano erupting. Figure 7.5 is from Otto Van Veen's treatise *Amorum emblemata,* first published in Antwerp in 1608 and subsequently in 1615 and 1660. This emblem also makes explicit the connection between a man's genitalia and the fire (arousal) caused by rubbing objects together.

The explanation in Van Veen's emblem (Figure 7.5) states that merely the *sight* of a beautiful woman causes a "fire burning in his soul." The important role of the eyes in causing and spreading lovesickness is also noted in the lyrics of airs, such as Bacilly's "Vous sçavez donner de l'amour":

> You know how to inspire love
> The power of your eyes makes this clear
> But your heart Iris shows me more and more each day
> That you do not know how to receive it.

The role of the eyes in exciting the passions also has its medical explanation. Dr. Ferrand cautions that "the eyes are the windows by which love enters to attack the brain."[64] Love, being contagious, was spread, thus delivered and received, through the eyes:

> Once love deceives the eyes, which are the true spies and gate-keepers of the soul, she slips through the passageways, traveling imperceptibly by way of the veins to the liver where she suddenly imprints an ardent desire for that object that is either truly lovable, or appears so. There love ignites concupiscence and with such lust the entire sedition begins.[65]

One erotic reference prevalent in airs and other literary sources which is a true metaphor is combat, used to signify the aroused lover's pursuit of the beloved, as in Lambert's "Superbes ennemis du repos de mon ame":[66]

FIGURE 7.4. Flamen, *Devises et emblèmes,* pp. 98–100. Emblem XXV. More Inside Than Outside ("*Mas Dentro Que Fuera; Plus dedans que dehors*").

> *Superb enemies of my soul's peace*
> *Whose brilliant flame*
> *Makes all hearts tremble under the effort of their blows,*
> *Do not be offended beautiful eyes if I sigh*
> *It is nothing but martyrdom*
> *To keep from sighing.*

Here the song text refers to the beloved's eyes as the enemy which make all hearts tremble under the effort of their blows. Flamen's emblem

FIGURE 7.5. Van Veen, *Amorum emblemata,* pp. 134–35. The Shock
Enflames (*"Le chocq enflamme"*).

"Combat maintains it [love]" (Figure 7.6) refers to the effects of combat on the body and makes explicit its reference to sexual arousal. The
emblem shows a bow and quiver filled with arrows on a table, the quiver
resembling an erect penis and the bow, its testicles. The first explanation, referring to earthly or improper love, states that even the slightest
dispute or resistance fortifies and intensifies feelings of love. The image
shows what cannot be said: the beloved's resistance causes an intensification of love and renders a man ready and eager for lovemaking.

In *L'École des filles,* Suzanne and Fanchon also refer to combat and
sexual arousal. Here we learn that the word dart or arrow is used to
mean penis and that lovemaking is a "natural combat" that involves
"blows."[67] Thus, the same words used in *L'École des filles* to describe
actual lovemaking are used in the emblems and song texts to describe
sexual arousal in the absence of the actual act.

The connection between lovemaking and death is found in all
sources and can take on either a metaphorical or literal meaning: in

FIGURE 7.6. Flamen, *Devises et emblèmes,* pp. 186–88. Emblem XLVII. Combat Maintains It [Love] ("*Certamine Durat*; *Le Combat l'entretient*").

erotic novels, sexual climax is referred to as "death," while in medical treatises unrequited love causes "death." Often it is difficult to know which sort of "death" is being referred to, particularly in song texts. Yet in this dialogue, written by Pierre Perrin and set to music by Perdigal, death and sexual climax are directly connected:

> *Sylvie:*   *Ah! Tyrsis, it is time, my Tyrsis.*
> *Tyrsis:*   *My Silvie*

Music and the Language of Love

> *Are you going to die?*
> Sylvie: *I am dying!*
> Tyrsis: *And I am losing my life.*
> Both: *In this charming death,*
> *Where love brings us together,*
> *Let us not be divided,*
> *Let us die together.*
> Sylvie: *O sweetness, O pleasure, I languish!*
> Tyrsis: *I am overcome,*
> *I can no longer go on,*
> *Sylvie.*
> *Helas!*
> *And I am going to surrender my soul.*
> Both: *Together.*
> *In this charming death.*[68]

Sexual climax or "death" was also considered a cure for erotic melancholia, though not recommended by Dr. Ferrand outside of marriage.[69]

Whether love is considered pleasurable, sinful, or painful, all sources give advice on how to avoid and/or overcome illicit love. In the moral explanation to the emblem shown in Figure 7.6, for example, Flamen counsels readers to ignore this troublesome passion, proclaiming that love can survive without combat. Flamen's account matches the advice given by Scudéry and doctors on how to fight lovesickness. For Scudéry, particularly as exemplified in her novel *Clélie*, a woman's resistance should not excite the lover but rather should give both the lover and beloved a chance to get to know each other, and the man an opportunity to prove that his love is pure, not lustful. In his treatise on erotic melancholia, Dr. Ferrand recommends that anyone suffering from lovesickness should seek diversion, turning thoughts of love to other things.[70] He explains by quoting a passage from Ovid's *Remedies of Love:* "Love gives way to business; / If you're seeking an end to love, keep busy and you'll be safe."[71] This advice seems to have been heeded in the air "Au secours ma raison," by Bénigne de Bacilly (Example 4.8). Here, the poetic voice refers to combat in love and asks reason to overcome this passion as he attempts to divert his thoughts. In Bacilly's air, however, the lover is ultimately unable to resist the beloved's charms.

While the texts of many airs refer to eroticism through an encoded language, the music, with its own set of expressive conventions, represents the physical manifestations of erotic melancholia and reinforces the experience of a loss of self-control or excessive display that accompanies this intensely passionate state.[72] Dr. Ferrand warns that "the many vexations and perturbations that torture the soul of the passionate lover bring about greater harms to men than all the other affections of the mind."[73] As chapter 4 showed, musical settings of the most serious airs, when considered in their entirety, underscore this loss of emotional control by representing different passions in succession. The musical setting of the first strophe of "D'un feu secret" (Example 7.2) represents a rapid alternation or juxtaposition of the pain and the pleasure of love, which "consists of several contrary motions."[74] Expressions of sexual arousal—"I feel consumed by a secret fire," "the power," or "the pain that possesses me"—are accompanied by musical devices that create and maintain tension—an ascending chromatic melody and decisive rhythmic movement in mm. 1–4; the ascending minor second in the highest register of the piece at mm. 6–7; the dissonance on beat two of m. 9; and the repetition of the note F, the decisive rhythms, and the strong authentic cadence on F in mm. 10–11. Expressions that create tension contrast and alternate with expressions of "relief," "consummation," and "being healed," accompanied by musical devices that release tension, particularly the melodic descent of a third in flowing quarter notes in mm. 4–5 and 7–8. In the second half of this first strophe, musical devices that represent sexual tension continue to alternate with musical devices that represent relief.

Many song texts and musical settings, when viewed as a type of discourse subject to certain rhetorical principles, represent an impassioned speaker suffering from lovesickness, whose discourse is unequal, interrupted by the diverse movements of the passions, and devoid of regular cadence and moderate tones of voice. The parts of a discourse (*dispositio*) would also have been applicable to the formal arrangement of airs. As we have seen, the *double*, or second verse of the air, coincides with what rhetoricians identified as the *confirmatio* (confirmation) and *peroratio* (conclusion) of a discourse. Here the "musical orator" presents the "proofs of the case" and his final "argument." In the second strophe to "D'un feu secret" (Example 7.3), the lover explains that he must continue to love even if it results in death. He then concludes with an impassioned summary of the situation—"When people learn, Philis, that I have stopped loving / They will know that I have stopped living." For someone in the midst of lovesickness, approaching death, the final stage of the illness, is accompanied by the greatest agitation of the passions. In airs, the confirmation and conclusion are always

EXAMPLE 7.2. Lambert, "D'un feu secret," First Strophe, *Les Airs de Monsieur Lambert*, p. 60.

the most impassioned portions of the song. It is no wonder that at this point in the air singers were to present highly ornamented versions of the original melody, either as notated by the composer or improvised. Florid ornamentation served not only to adjust the music to a new set of syllabic stresses, it also intensified passion.[75] In "D'un feu secret," we see that the actual "healing" or culmination of this fantasized sex

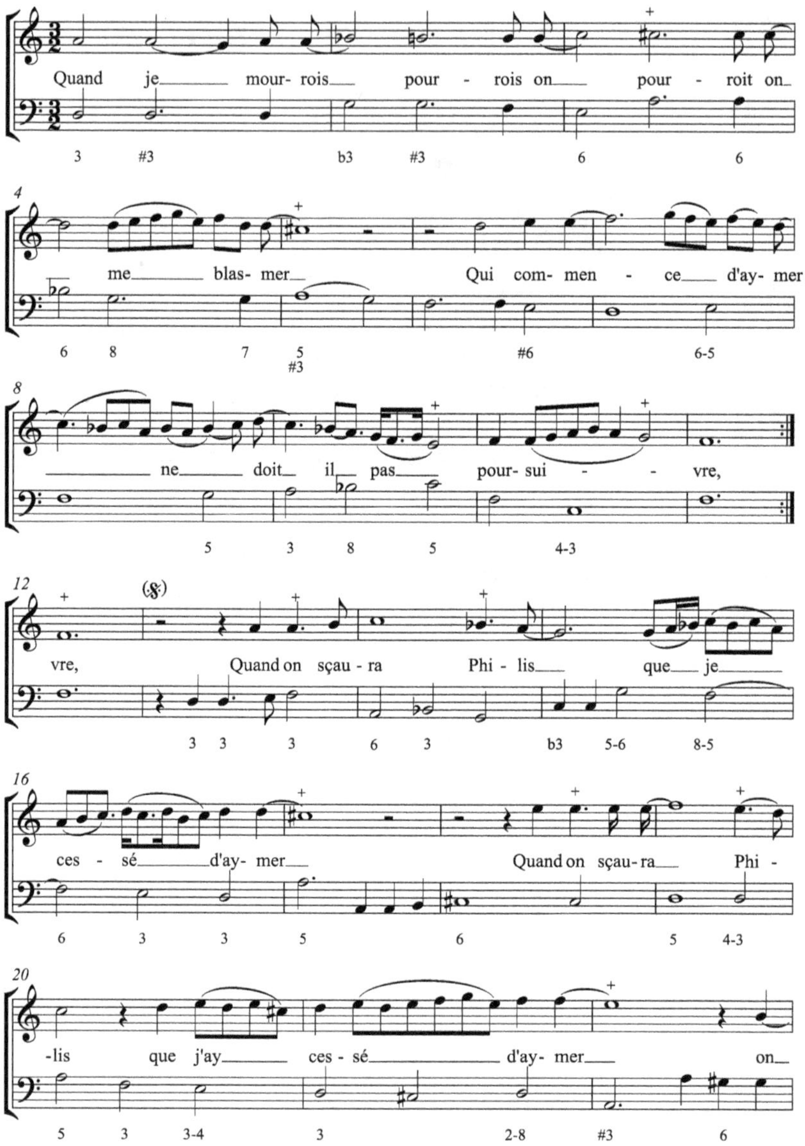

EXAMPLE 7.3. Lambert, "D'un feu secret," Second Strophe.

EXAMPLE 7.3 CONTINUED

act occurs at the end of the air, where we find the greatest number of ornaments, particularly in accompanying repetitions of the word "cessé" ("stopped"), which progressively climb to the highest register of the piece (mm. 15–28).

These final few measures represent both meanings associated with death—the pain of one's demise, the final stage of erotic melancholia—as well as the screams of delight that accompany sexual climax—the cure that could be fantasized or real. For as Dr. Ferrand explains, some felt that even a fantasized sex act could cure lovesickness. He then imparts a story told by Plutarch of a young Egyptian

> who was lost in his love folly for the courtesan Theognis. One night, as it turned out, this poor lover merely dreamed that he slept with his Theognis. But upon waking he realized that the ardor threatening to consume him had been allayed [and he was] contented with the imaginary pleasure.[76]

In one song text, set by Sébastien Le Camus, reference to the "relief" brought about by ejaculation is expressed in an unusually direct manner:

> *When love wants to end the pains of a lover,*
> *One single moment*
> *Discharges easily*
> *The harshest torment.*
> *O sweet moment! O sweet fruits of loves,*
> *O sweet moment! That creates happy days,*
> *O sweet moment by which unjust law*
> *Were you not made for me?*[77]

Women Singing Airs as Men

When viewed as a genre of literature written according to a *galant* aesthetic, airs present a serious and/or moral message—men behaving badly—under the guise of an "agreeable fiction."[78] When men sang airs, the songs were an entertaining way to poke fun at and yet draw attention to their unacceptable behavior. But women also sang these same airs. This is an intriguing contradiction, considering that literary works, particularly those written by Scudéry and her entourage, promoted notions of non-physical love and controlled discourse, and yet also inspired this sensuous music that set a man's eroticized utterances, all the while allowing women to sing as men when they were otherwise forbidden by propriety to express such base feelings.[79]

Proof that women sang airs written in a male poetic voice is found in editions of religious or devotional airs. Father François Berthod, for example, makes explicit in the prefaces to his three *Livre[s] d'airs de devotion à deux parties,* published in 1656, 1658, and 1662, that his sacred parodies of popular airs are to be sung by noble women, nuns, and schoolgirls, and yet he never uses a female poetic voice in his parody texts. Most of his texts are gender neutral, meaning that there is no reference whatsoever to gender, be it through addressing a particular person (Philis, Iris, or Tircis),[80] referring to oneself (as an *amant*—male lover—or *bergère*—shepherdess), or using adjectival forms (*heureux* or *heureuse*—the male and female forms of "happy"). However, in a few texts Berthod employs a male poetic voice. Bénigne de Bacilly also specifically states in the prefaces and postscripts to his editions of spiritual airs that his pieces are to be sung by women and schoolgirls, and yet a female poetic voice is conspicuously absent from the song texts. All poems are either gender neutral or use a male poetic voice.

It seems that convention dictated that profane song texts from the middle of the century use either a gender neutral or male poetic voice, particularly in association with the expression of erotically charged language. Of the airs published during the 1660s by Michel Lambert, Bénigne de Bacilly, and Joseph Chabanceau de La Barre, the vast majority are composed to texts with a male poetic voice.[81] Of the ninety-three airs published by Lambert, Bacilly, and La Barre, seventy-four (79.5 percent) include a male poetic voice, sixteen (17.2 percent) are gender neutral, and three (3 percent) use a female poetic voice. Of the seventy-five airs included in the collection *Airs de Monsieur Lambert non imprimez,* which includes many airs written during the middle of the century, forty-eight (64 percent) include a male poetic voice, twenty-three (30.6 percent) are gender neutral, and four (5.3 percent) use a female poetic voice. We see the same phenomenon represented in Ballard's *Livres d'airs de différents autheurs* between 1658 and 1668, in which less than 2 percent of the songs use a female poetic voice.

Even though there are songs from the middle of the century written in a female poetic voice, it is only later, after 1680, that the "I" in song texts increasingly refers to a woman.[82] The absence of the female voice in song texts from the middle of the century suggests that proper women were to remain silent on topics pertaining to love. And indeed, through the character of Sapho, even Scudéry suggests that women should rarely speak their minds *directly*, especially in matters of the heart.[83] When a woman did "speak" through mid-century airs, her words differed significantly from those of her male counterpart.[84] In Bacilly's air "Il est vray je suis rigoureuse," for example, the female speaker admits that she is cruel. She loves seducing men, but she never returns their love. In this way, she can live happily and in peace:

> It is true, I am harsh
> But my severity will enable me to live in peace:
> There is nothing to make me more happy,
> Than to be lovable but never love.[85]

In lyrics that represent women who cannot help but fall in love, the speaker expresses her feelings directly and avoids erotic references. The only air with a female poetic voice in Lambert's publication is "J'ay juré mille fois" (Example 6.17). In this song, the speaker claims that she did everything she could to resist love, but love's power conquered her heart after all.

Unlike song texts with a female poetic voice, the majority of gender-neutral texts include the same erotic metaphors as those with a male poetic voice. A good example is Lambert's "Superbes ennemies du repos de mon ame" (Example 4.7). Here, there are references to combat ("enemies" and "blows"), sexual desire and arousal ("brilliant flames" and "dying"), and other allusions that would pertain specifically to women ("beautiful eyes" and maintaining "respect"). Even if women were not singing airs written in a male poetic voice but limiting themselves to airs that are gender neutral, they would still have been singing "as men." But this does not seem to be the case with the use of the male poetic voice in Bacilly's spiritual airs, which were composed to be sung by women.

Not everyone felt it was appropriate for women to sing airs that were full of erotic references. Bénigne de Bacilly, for one, claimed that modesty should prohibit women from singing profane airs.[86] In the preface to his first book of spiritual airs, he notes that even though songs are "an exercise very useful in social interactions (*commerce du monde*)," there is nothing "innocent" about them. He had dreamt for a long time about rectifying the situation by "correct[ing] the bad use that one makes of [melody] in French chansons (which are ordinarily filled with only lascivious words) by replacing them with words of piety that inspire feelings of love for God alone."[87] Thus, women should more appropriately express feelings of love toward God, rather than man, through their singing.[88] To this end, Bacilly composed his spiritual airs in the same style as serious airs to replace their worldly counterparts.

Bacilly did not consider, however, that salon activities included literary games. Dialogues, choreography, scenery, costumes, and music brought to life literary intrigue.[89] Women writers such as Scudéry could write about forbidden lust through their characters, both male and female. She could "speak" through writing in either a masculine or feminine voice. It was a kind of cross-dressing that was not uncommon in the theater and in literary representations at the time. Female-to-male cross-dressing was, in fact, much more common than male-to-female.[90] Even though not literally *dressing* as men, women who wrote or sang like men were *acting* like men. In his book *Hidden Agendas: Cross-Dressing in 17th-Century France,* Joseph Harris does not speak directly to the phenomenon of women writing or singing as men, but he does consider the issue generally, showing that narrative cross-dressing "suggests that women can only acquire agency 'as' men."[91] Interestingly, Dr. Ferrand also mentions in his treatise on erotic melancholy that some believe lovesickness turns women into men: "Hippocrates seems to attribute to passionate love the power to transform women into men." Ferrand then goes on to say that this "metamorphosis was one of behavior and complexion only and not of sex."[92] Thus, the phenomenon of women "acting" like men was associated with feelings of impassioned love, either in real life (according to doctors) or in literary representations.

In salon culture, what was true for the written word was also applicable to the sung word. Women could sing airs of seduction as men because there was a disconnection between the real and imagined. This detachment is addressed in Scudéry's *Clélie* when the main character,

Clarinte, notes that women who sing do not have to worry about their honor. Although a woman "sings in a passionate manner, . . . she sings however as a person of condition, that is to say, without staking her honor on it, . . . and she [sings] so gallantly that she becomes all the more attractive."[93]

Even though inappropriate passions could be expressed in socially acceptable ways, there was surely an ambiguity, a fine line, between fantasy and reality, for as Joseph Harris points out, "the driving force behind narrative agency [females dressing as males] remains masculine in nature,"[94] such that "the female-to-male cross-dresser appears to have been a particularly eroticized figure in seventeenth-century theatre."[95] We find the same phenomenon at work when applied to female singers. Singing was directly associated with love, youth, beauty, and desire, and as Dr. Ferrand asserts, "what caressing and naughty voice does not excite?"[96] He then maintains that even "tiny birds who, pricked by love, make great effort to render their songs and chatter more charming and melodious than usual in order to excite their mates."[97] The same applies to the singing human voice, which has great powers for "exciting the spirit."[98]

We see in the following three descriptions that women who sang airs did indeed excite men, who noticed their red lips and white teeth as much as the beauty of their voices.

I.

L'Abbé: They prefer . . . a beautiful voice all alone

Le Chevalier: Assuredly, especially if this beautiful voice emanates from a crimson mouth and passes between perfectly white teeth, clean and nicely arranged.[99]

2.

She sang them [the airs] with pleasure . . . and while singing them, she showed the most beautiful and well-arranged teeth in the world. If one applauded her voice, one also admired the beauty of her teeth.[100]

3.

When we contemplate the coral of [women's] lips, we would never want to see them open, but when singing reveals to us the ivory of their teeth which maintains the air which passes through them, we never want to see [these women] close their mouths.[101]

So strong was the physical appeal of a woman who sang that she could even attract a husband with her voice.[102] In the following poem, L'Abbé Bertaut asks the question that perhaps any potential husband might have had on his mind as he listened to a woman sing:

You know how to sing like Hilaire [Dupuis],[103]
Write prose and verse,
Perform airs
On a thousand different instruments:
It is more than is necessary
In order to charm;
But could one inquire
If you know how to love?[104]

Singing was seductive, and there is no question that women could be both intentionally alluring and sexually aroused. Flamen's emblem "He cannot safeguard himself from all the heat," shown in Figure 7.7, portrays a woman and man in a secluded woods. The woman holds one of her hands out to him, while the other touches her exposed breast. The explanation warns that he cannot protect himself from the sparks of love emanating from the woman that enter his eyes.[105] Ferrand warns of this same phenomenon in his treatise on lovesickness: "The lady of incontestably perfect beauty . . . wounds the heart through the eye more quickly than the feathered arrow, and from the eye love darts and glides into the vital organs." Ferrand goes on to explain that "the lover, in a sense, melts away as he looks upon and contemplates the beauty of his lady, as though he would fuse himself with her."[106]

Not only is the reference to the beloved's eyes important in this emblem, but the location of the seduction in the forest or countryside also has special significance in French airs from this period. Many airs describe men and women seeking out secluded forests when suffering from unrequited love, which, according to Ferrand, is the worst thing a lover can do: "Solitude brought no better relief to Phyllis, Echo, Pan, and many others. . . . Indeed I would disapprove it as a cure for this disease," for those left in solitude and seclusion will be carried away by lust. "Society, on the contrary, diverts the mind of the frantic lover, cheers him, and brings him to a recognition of his error."[107]

FIGURE 7.7. Flamen, *Devises et emblèmes*, pp. 170–73. Emblem XLIII. He Cannot Safeguard Himself from All the Heat ("*Non Sic Omnis Vitabitur Ardor; Il ne se garantit pas de tout le chaux*").

Pastoral settings in song texts also reveal the place where men and women find solitude and privacy in order to engage in lascivious activities, as described in this air from Robert Ballard's *Livre d'airs de différents autheurs* (1663):

> *Underneath the green ferns,*
> *Tircis with his shepherdess,*
> *Devote the day to love:*

Ravished by an extreme pleasure,
They take turns sighing!
Ah how sweet it is when one loves,
To pass the day in this way.

In the shade next to the shore,
Where in the midst of a thicket,
During the heat of the day:
In order to augment their flame,
They court each other:
How sweet it is when one is enflamed,
To love in this way.[108]

The ultimate irony presented by the airs is that while the texts largely revolve around the actions and feelings of men, doctors and theologians considered women to be most susceptible to erotic melancholy and more likely to seduce men than the reverse case.[109] Considered especially dangerous were noble women living lives full of leisure.[110] When women sang, even as men, their music could accompany and stand for expressions of love. It did not matter that a woman sang as a man, her suitor was seeing *her* and listening to *her*. While the airs appeared on the surface to be innocuous, both men and women would have recognized the connection to actual lovemaking, especially when listening to the sensuous music that accompanied the erotically encoded texts.[111] And indeed, religious leaders and doctors warned that certain kinds of music functioned as an aphrodisiac.[112] Explicit displays of sexuality, while forbidden in public, of course, could have secretly transpired in the most private of all spaces, the mistress's bedroom in the middle of the night, or in the seclusion of a wooded grove. But first, a man had to prove himself worthy of his beloved. According to Scudéry's *Carte de Tendre*, it was possible for an honorable suitor to pass beyond "Tendre-sur-Estime" or "Tendre-sur-Reconnoissance." Was the act of singing an air like an invitation—a ticket—that enabled the suitor to cross "La Mer dangereuse" on his way to "La terre inconnuë"—the dangerous sea of seduction and foreplay to reach the unknown land, the greatest pleasure in the world? Composed according to a *galant* aesthetic, airs not only mixed the serious and the amusing, they also combined the public with the private or secret, surely inspiring in the hearts of all a *joie de vivre*.

As we will see in the final chapter, this *joie de vivre* was precisely what offended moralists and church leaders, who feared that by singing "frivolous songs," by "worshiping pleasure," the universe would "plummet into the hideous abyss" of the "false cult."[113] The potential for the creation of a godless world seemed to intensify once the composition and performance of airs was taken out of the safety of the salon and made readily available to a larger, more diverse group of people through the Ballard publication of airs and other sources. What is especially interesting is that rhetoric was the central issue in the attacks leveled against the air. The power of the word, the illicit references to pleasure, could all too easily penetrate the souls of both singers and listeners, move the wrong sorts of passions, and lead "those who love them [airs] to engage in disorder and impiety,"[114] which would eventually trigger moral decay.

CHAPTER EIGHT

The Late-Seventeenth-Century Air and the Rhetoric of Distraction

If there were any doubt that the French air was considered a type of rhetorical discourse, the crusade launched by church leaders and moralists toward the end of the century to replace the secular air with a sacred counterpart eliminates any such uncertainty, for rhetoric and eloquence were the grounds on which the air was attacked. At the heart of this condemnation was the air's expression of pleasure and its allusions to concupiscence (sexual desire), which were seen as infiltrating the minds and imaginations of impressionable youths and weak-minded women through the medium of persuasive, erotically charged texts and music. This criticism became all the more urgent with the proliferation of profane airs through publications like Ballard's *Livres d'airs de différents autheurs*, which after 1694 became *Livres d'airs sérieux et à boire*, and the *Mercure galant*, which reached a relatively large public in the provinces as well as in Paris.

The Air after 1670

When airs were composed and sung within the exclusivity of the salon, the identities of the poets and composers were known to a select few. In this way, the exclusivity of an elite group of people who were "in-the-know" was maintained. The autonomy and insularity of the group were also perpetuated by avoiding the publication of airs. By transmitting airs orally or by passing around manuscript copies of songs, one could control who was privy to the latest works. When Ballard began publishing collections of songs in 1658, airs became available to a larger and more diverse public on a regular basis. Ultimately, the greater accessibility of airs would alter and affect their nature, as "public taste" began to rule the marketplace.

When Robert Ballard began publishing serious airs, he intended to reach as wide an audience as possible. He promised to publish the latest, newest, and best airs written by the most prestigious composers and poets of the day. What mattered was that the publications would sell. Not only were the airs in Ballard's collections obtained against the wishes of the most important composers, but the teachers and singers who used his publications may not have had the advantage of having heard the composers and/or trained singers perform the repertory properly. Bacilly, in fact, complains at length that too many teachers started with second-rate or inferior versions of airs to teach their students and then proceeded to teach them poorly by an inferior example.[1] Thus neither the composition nor performance was in accord with composers' intentions.[2]

Around 1670, the nature of airs appearing in the Ballard editions began to undergo a transformation. It was not so much that the airs changed radically, but rather that a certain type began to dominate, characterized by musical features associated with lighter songs like Bacilly's "Petite abeille mesnagere" (Example 4.15). The musical phrasing is regular, with phrases divided into two groups of an equal number of syllables; fewer passions are represented; there are few, if any, meter changes; and rhythmic and melodic patterns occur more regularly. Almost every air includes pastoral images: of the thirty-four airs in Ballard's edition of 1675, for example, twenty make reference to nature in some way—to spring, birds, forests, and so forth. In "C'est aux amans que la saison" (Example 8.1), the poetic voice complains that spring, flowers, and beautiful days are only for lovers, while for an ungrateful and rebellious heart, winter always endures. Despite the negative sentiment of the text, the music is more typical of airs which celebrate the joys of mutual love. Thus, while the song *texts* still express the same range of passions found in the airs published during the 1660s, the *music* is simplified by a more limited expressive range.

In addition, more and more song texts are gender neutral, and, particularly after 1680, the number of texts in a female poetic voice increases. It is quite possible that Ballard chose to include these types of airs because they would have been more appropriate for women to sing outside the "safe" confines of the salon and easier to sing by those with less facility. Even though many airs include a second strophe, there are no notated *doubles,* and while singers were supposed to improvise the ornaments of the second couplet, it is doubtful whether most could do so. In every publication, then, there would have been airs that just about *anyone* could sing. And sing they did. Singing secular airs was all the rage—for nobles, for bourgeois, for men and women of all ages.

One could speculate that the increased attacks leveled against the air are themselves evidence of the increasing popularity of the songs.

EXAMPLE 8.1. "C'est aux amans que la saison," *Livre d'airs de différents autheurs* (Ballard, 1675), 4v.

Church leaders and moralists were greatly concerned about the effects that singing and listening to airs would have on French society and feared that souls would be contaminated by the lascivious nature of song texts. Poets incorporated a certain kind of rhetoric in their lyrics that was thought to distract vulnerable women and youths away from truth and inspire acts of a sinful nature.

Songs and the Rhetoric of Distraction

The discipline of rhetoric in seventeenth-century France underwent major transformations which, as we shall see, are reflected in general assessments of the air. For some, particularly the Jesuits, rhetoric was an admirable discipline. But for others, like Descartes, it was considered a means to distort the truth, to persuade by empty eloquence. While Descartes acknowledges that the original purpose of rhetoric was noble—a civilizing force—"it passed into the hands of base men who, despairing of winning the assent of the audience in open battle and with only truth as a weapon, had recourse to sophisms and empty verbal tricks."[3]

Jansenists Antoine Arnauld and Pierre Nicole and the Oratorian Nicolas Malebranche formulated theories of rhetoric which were to serve as the basis for the condemnation of profane airs. Whereas Descartes blamed childhood as the time when false notions are acquired and then maintained by habit throughout one's life, Arnauld, Nicole, and Malebranche took a theological stance and blamed Adam's fall from grace.[4] Persuaded by the serpent's false rhetoric, Adam turned away from God and gave in to the pleasures of the flesh, which distracted him from the true source of happiness. Adam's fall left an imprint upon the brain that was passed down from parent to child, generation after generation; the eternal transmission of original sin.[5]

Using Descartes' psychophysiology of the passions, Malebranche explains that sense perceptions and passions cause constant turmoil within the body, making it impossible to recognize, focus on, and follow truth:

> Pleasure is in the soul: it touches and modifies it. This diminishes our freedom; it makes us love the good through a love based on instinct and transport instead of through a love based on reasoned choice; it carries us away, so to speak, toward objects that can be perceived by the senses.[6]

Consequently, as Carr explains in his book *Descartes and the Resilience of Rhetoric,*

> Once Adam had opted for the sensible pleasure of the body instead of the light found in his duty to God, he discovered that his union to his body and to God was irrevocably transformed. The senses and passions . . . occupied the capacity of the mind with such intensity that it could no longer be properly attentive to God. Thus, the body exercises a greater attraction on the mind than its union with God. . . . The loss of this ability of control over the senses and passions and the consequent weakening of freedom of the will constitute concupiscence.[7]

Thus, people who are weak-minded are easily infected by pleasure and by an appeal to sensations. False eloquence, which appeals only to the senses, not to reason, moves auditors through a superfluously ornamented language that misguides and misdirects. It is a "rhetoric of distraction"[8] that prevents people from focusing on God and living a devout life.

Malebranche asserts that false eloquence functions on three levels: (1) on a level of individual psychophysiology, wherein the commotion of animal spirits in the brain dulls the attention which the mind requires to attain truth; (2) in the social dimension, wherein humans are transformed into mindless machines persuading each other mechanically through their bodies; and (3) on the level of expression, wherein the speaker's words or delivery—the air, the tone, or spoken words—form a complex medium which bypasses pure understanding.[9] We see all three of these levels at work in profane airs: (1) performers and listeners are moved by the music on the individual psychophysiological level, the airs being, in fact, composed to do so; (2) the textual and musical expressions are conventional, thus imitated from one piece to the next and transmitted through social interactions; and (3) music reaches the soul through the expressive tones of voice and rates of speech used in the musical recitation of a text.

In this light, attacks on profane airs of all kinds, including opera airs, make sense and take on greater significance. The focus of condemnation was the pleasure derived from performing and listening to airs, as well as the references, veiled or otherwise, to the pleasures of love—concupiscence. Pierre Bellocq was not exaggerating his outrage when he asked, "What disturbed spirit, what blind mania, / Incessantly desires to consecrate heresy with Harmony? / Godless singers, will I always hear / You praising Bacchus and Love in your songs?" Singing songs was a kind of heresy, leading the weak-minded toward pleasure and away from God. Love's maxims, so clearly accompanied in airs by "concerts and rhymes," "deceive reason" and create "by an innocent charm a mortal poison." Bellocq sarcastically refers to "beautiful hymn[s]" placed "in the mouths of women"; these songs are "shameful confessions of their secret flames." The mockery continues as he exclaims that the air is "a marvelous secret for shaping youth." Songs mock reason, treat it "disparagingly." All are subject to the "law" of pleasure.[10] But he doesn't stop there. He asks, "Why are these frivolous songs all the rage?" and despairingly notes that this "idol," if it triumphs, will send all "into the hideous abyss of the false cult," a chasm into which the entire universe will "plummet."[11]

These seemingly simple airs, many of which become musically less and less impassioned and more and more conventional as the century progresses, nonetheless had texts that appealed to the imagination and imprinted passions associated with pleasure upon the soul—promoting physical love between man and woman—and thus distracted minds away from God. Youths were especially vulnerable, for many critics felt that "children's attention is naturally attracted to outward sensible appearances, a condition that many adults never outgrow."[12] Jansenist Pierre Nicole warns that "[a child's] whole application is always directed toward pleasing manners. . . . They only use their minds to study what delights and the art of pleasing, as well as the things that flatter concupiscence and the senses."[13]

The solution was to make available to the general public spiritual or devotional airs written in the style of popular songs.[14] François Berthod's devotional airs, published in 1656, 1658, and 1662, are parodies or contrafacta, his newly written sacred texts set to pre-existing love songs by the most prominent mid-century French composers.[15] Below is the text of an air by Michel Lambert, followed by Berthod's parody of the same air. Here we see just how close the original and parody texts are, though the beloved is Philis in Lambert's original and Jesus in Berthod's parody.

Michel Lambert, "Depuis que j'ay veu vos beaux yeux,"
Rés. Vma. ms 854, p. 70.

Since I have seen your beautiful eyes,
Philis, I search for you everywhere,

Absent from you, my pain is extreme;
As for me I believe, Philis, that I love you.
You cost me a thousand sighs,
You cause me a thousand desires,
I think of you much more than myself
As for me I believe, Philis, that I love you.

(Depuis que j'ay veu vos beaux yeux, / Philis, je vous cherche en tous lieux, / Absent de vous ma douleur est extreme; / Pour moy je croy, Philis, que je vous ayme. // Vous me coustez mille soupirs / Vous me causez mille desirs, / Je pense à vous beaucoup plus qu'à moy-méme / Pour moy je croy, Philis, que je vous ayme.)

François Berthod, "Charmé des regards de vos yeux," Livre d'airs de dévotion (1656), ff. 6r–7v.

Charmed by the glances from your eyes,
Jesus, I search for you everywhere,
Absent from you my pain is extreme;
Because I feel strongly, great God, that I love you.
You cost me a thousand sighs,
You cause a thousand desires,
I think of you much more than myself
And I feel strongly, great God, that I love you.

(Charmé des regards de vos yeux, / Jesus, je vous cherche en tous lieux, / Absent de vous ma douleur est extresme; / Car je sens bien, grand Dieu, que je vous ayme. / / Vous me coustez mille soupirs, / Vous me causez mille desirs, / Je pense à vous beaucoup plus qu'à moy-mesme, / Et je sens bien, grand Dieu, que je vous ayme.)

Bénigne de Bacilly published his *airs spirituels* in two volumes in 1672 and 1677, which were then edited and both reissued in 1688.[16] His spiritual airs are not parodies but the first sacred songs composed in the style of the serious air and set to newly composed religious texts by L'Abbé Jacques Testu, who became director of the Académie Française in 1674.[17] Testu's *Stances chrétiennes sur divers passages de l'escriture*, published in 1669, are sacred verses that resemble lyrical poetry written in a *galant* style, meant to be used by members of the social elite for meditation and prayer. All imagery relating to concupiscence and other worldly pleasures, however, has been avoided. For even though there are certain familiar *galant* words and phrases, there is no immediate secular referent as there would be in a parody. Like Testu's *Stances,* Bacilly's musical settings were written in a style accessible to the laity and so a perfect replacement for their profane counterparts.[18]

Example 8.2 is Bacilly's setting of "D'où vient cette sombre tristesse," from his *Airs spirituels* (1688). Here we see that there are no illicit images in Testu's text as there were in Berthod's lyric ("a thousand sighs," "a thousand desires"). Instead, the poetic voice urges the soul to arm itself with God's holy joy. Only in this way will the soul enjoy a profound peace.

Most fascinating is Bacilly's use in his spiritual airs of musical conventions associated with passionate expression in profane songs to represent the opposition between heavenly virtue and earthly vice. In this way, he manipulates the conventions of expression to suit the important function served by these sacred airs: to imprint upon the souls of singers and listeners the message that earthly desires are to be rejected in favor of a life lived in the service of God. In the opening phrase, "Where does this somber sorrow come from" (mm. 1–4), for example, Bacilly uses musical representations of sorrow to accompany references to worldly suffering or desires rather than the loss of a beloved as in profane airs. Frustration is expressed at being devastated by earthly sorrow, not by the burning fires of love or sexual arousal, in the phrase "that you allow to devastate you" (mm. 4–6). Intense joy represents references to heaven or to God's glory, not the union of mortal lovers: "You whom God must fill with a holy joy" (mm. 8–11). A more modified sorrow, even tenderness, is associated with earthly suffering and not the delight associated with pleasant thoughts of the beloved in "What can you fear upon the earth" (mm. 16–19). And finally, noble indignation is represented when condemning worldly pleasures, not despair, in response to a beloved's rejection: "From this divine hope, arm yourself from now on" (mm. 19–23). There is also obvious word painting: references to heaven ascend in pitch and appear in the highest range of a piece (mm. 8–11 and 13–15), while allusions to being here on earth descend and are set in a low register (mm. 16–19).

Pleasure, Airs, and the New Rhetoric

Despite Bacilly's manipulation of the conventions of expression found throughout the profane repertory, his spiritual airs are nonetheless passionate, with affective representation important to their success. Arnauld, Nicole, and Malebranche would not have objected.

EXAMPLE 8.2. Bacilly, "D'où vient cette sombre tristesse," *Airs spirituels* (1688), Part 2, p. 2.

EXAMPLE 8.2 CONTINUED

mon-de^en-tier   te   li - yre-roit   la guer - re   Tu joü - ir - as   tou-jours

6   6#   b   6   5   4

d'u - ne   pro - fon - - - - de   paix   Tu

7

joü - ir - ras_____   tou - jours   d'u - ne   pro - fon - de   paix.

4

Manipulation through eloquence was acceptable if used to promote truth and persuade the weak-minded to live a life devoted to God. Even in purely speculative matters, Arnauld and Nicole held that reason itself requires accompanying *mouvements* and came up with the notion of accessory meaning (the passionate associations) of words and phrases as important in persuasion, a concept developed by Bernard Lamy in the many editions of his *L'art de parler*.[19] As Arnauld and Nicole explain: "When the topic one treats is such that one should be reasonably touched by it, to speak of it in a dry, cold manner without stirring is a failing because it is a failing not to be touched by what should touch."[20] Arnauld, Nicole, and Malebranche believed in incarnation, that the human soul could be saved and Adam's fall rectified. Incarnation was viewed as "a rhetorical act, using the senses to make known the intelligible, [such that] the recourse to the sensible to strengthen the attention and to fortify the will's resolve to do good gains legitimacy."[21] Thus, Malebranche asserts that

> the Order that must reform us is too abstract to serve as a model for base minds. . . . Let it therefore be given a body: make it accessible to the senses; dress it in various manners to make it loveable to the eyes of carnal men; let it be incarnated so to speak.[22]

The suspicion in religious circles surrounding eloquence and their promotion of the proper use of figured language has its profane equivalent, particularly in descriptions of *honnêteté*. Nicolas Faret, for example, insists that an *honnête* man arrives at a *juste milieu* (a happy medium, or middle ground) in all he undertakes: a middle ground between ignorance and erudition; prodigality and avarice; insensitivity and volatility; obsequiousness and brashness.[23] He also attacks affectation and exaggerated eloquence and interestingly associates mannered speech with effeminacy, a word used to attack airs as well.[24]

The attack upon figured language and affectation also has its parallel in writings about music and in the music itself, and could explain the preference for the simpler, more "natural" air exemplified in the Ballard collections from later in the century. But even in profane airs published during the 1660s, ornamentation—the musical equivalent to flowery or figured speech—was reserved for a specific function and all the more controlled after the 1670s. This is most dramatically exemplified by comparing accounts of ornamentation in both Mersenne's *Harmonie universelle* and Jean Millet's *La Belle méthode, ou l'Art de bien chanter* with that by Bacilly in his treatise *Remarques curieuses*. Millet, in particular, describes musical figures or ornamentation without a consideration of text. Millet promotes the addition of diminutions to various kinds of melodic patterns found throughout the repertory, what Bacilly refers to as the former style of ornamenting old-fashioned airs. Bacilly writes:

> It is incorrect to assume that contemporary musical style alone dictates the addition of melodic ornaments and that this practice is merely following in the static tradition of former times. It is true that in former times it was considered a crime to allow any syllable to pass by without ornamenting it and that without the slightest regard for long or short syllables, it was the practice to *fredoner* [ornament with diminutions] indiscriminately and at random, even at the expense of pronunciation (which was evidently held in little esteem).[25]

He goes on to say that "the single difference [between then and now] lies in the fact that today's singer uses ornaments and *diminutions* only where the text will allow them and only where there is no other consideration to oppose their use."[26] By definition, Bacilly stresses, an air is "natural" only if the vocal line is well-suited to the words: "Le Chant convienne bien aux Paroles."[27] Thus, *diminutions* of any extent were only acceptable when applied to second verses of airs, and then only on long syllables. Even though ornamented *doubles* continued to be pub-

Music and the Language of Love

lished at the end of the century, they do not appear with any regularity.[28] There are no *doubles* in the Ballard publications (though Ballard does include ornamented second couplets in his three volumes of *Brunetes* published during the first decade of the eighteenth century). And it is a well-known fact that Lully did not approve of *doubles* for his opera airs and refused to allow singers to ornament to any great extent.[29]

The desire for less-elaborated music seems to parallel the trend shaping rhetoric at the end of the century, that is, the movement away from a more figured language (unless properly employed in the service of truth) toward a direct, clear, and natural expression. Bacilly was thinking along the same lines when he noted that song texts written for the new, post-1650 style of air "can accept only sweet, flowing terms and familiar expressions."[30] He goes on to say that composers should avoid setting words that are "coarse" (*paroles rudes*) and "insipid" (*paroles plates*) and that "above all, it is necessary that they [song texts] have good meanings without puns or ambiguities."[31]

Was Bacilly unaware of the double meaning of the erotically charged metaphors and commonplaces typical in French airs, even his own? This is doubtful, since he absolutely believed that women and especially girls should not sing his or anyone else's profane airs. In the prefaces to his first two volumes of spiritual airs and in the postscript to his 1688 edition, he calls profane airs lascivious and insists that his spiritual airs were written especially for girls learning how to sing in "les Maisons de Religion" and thus the only vocal repertory that should be used in a girl's musical instruction. He writes:

> I was urged to compose these sorts of spiritual airs by my own inclination and by people of first-rate quality, who, seeing with pain that in the religious houses, young girls were being taught how to sing with profane airs (in order not to say lascivious). [32]

Thus it is clear that Bacilly was well aware of the erotic associations that permeated airs to the end of the century.

What about the music? Did the music itself, without its text, carry specific meaning? We have seen how Bacilly manipulated the musical conventions associated with setting profane texts to suit his settings of Testu's sacred texts. But for those who advocated sacred parodies of popular airs or opera airs, music did *not* have meaning in and of itself. As early as 1597, Le Père Michel Coyssard claimed that music can function independently of a text—music is not inherently good or bad—an opinion that persisted throughout the seventeenth century, as least for some church leaders and moralists.[33] Pierre Bellocq echos this sentiment in his defense of sacred parodies in 1695:

> If of softening of the heart music is guilty,
> The sound is innocent [emphasis mine], the verse is guilty;
> All harmony by itself raises my mind [spirit].
> The poet himself alone lowers me and instills in me
> that tender feeling of love.[34]

Bacilly, however, would seem to disagree, as he promoted his *airs spirituels* as *newly* composed music set to *new* sacred texts. If Bacilly had believed music didn't have meaning, he might not have been so careful to use musical conventions in his settings of the sacred texts with the hope that the new textual expressions would alter the associated meaning of those very conventions. That Lambert, Bacilly, Le Camus, and La Barre believed in the power and meaning of the music is evident by the similarity of musical devices used again and again throughout their publications in association with specific textual expressions. If musical sounds themselves did not have meaning there would have been no conventions of expression. Composers would not have used particular musical devices to express a text's accessory meaning.

The Legacy of Lambert, Bacilly, Le Camus, and La Barre

By the end of the seventeenth and into the eighteenth century, serious airs composed in the mid-century style of Lambert, Bacilly, Le Camus, and La Barre were out of fashion, and yet Lambert, in particular, continued to be acclaimed by many writers into the eighteenth century. His name appears several times in the *Mercure galant*,[35] and his works are praised as exemplifying all that is good about French style in *Mémoires de Trévoux* (November 1704, pp. 1881–1896, April 1716, p. 607).[36] In addition, Lecerf de la Viéville praises Lambert throughout his *Comparaison* of 1704.[37] It is interesting to note, however, that Lecerf seems to be familiar only with Lambert's lighter airs written later in the century.[38] This would explain why he insists that expression in Lambert's airs was limited:

> Thus Lambert, who never expressed very strong passions in his airs, was not obligated to search out such piercing expressions. He was able to dedicate himself more to pleasing the ears; and his great merit was in knowing how to give to anything said a delectable pleasure by the happiest tones possible.[39]

It could be that Lecerf chose particular airs by Lambert on purpose to demonstrate that French music, in the hands of master-composer Lambert, was more natural and thereby superior to Italian music. But as Catherine Massip points out, while Lecerf praises Lambert's airs and even his ornamented second strophes throughout his *Comparaison*, he contradicts himself by claiming that *doubles* are more characteristic of the Italian style than the French. He then praises Lully for his rejection of *doubles* and excessive ornamentation.[40]

Lambert's airs continued to be published later in the century as well long after his death. Many appeared periodically in several of the Ballard publications, including several volumes of *Livres d'airs de différents autheurs* (between 1658 and 1692), Bacilly's *IIII. Livre de chansons pour danser et pour boire*, seven editions of *Recueils de chansonnettes de différents autheurs* (between 1676 and 1686), twelve editions of *Recueils d'airs sérieux et à boire* (between 1695 and 1721), and three editions of *Brunetes ou Petits airs tendres* (1703, 1704, and 1711). Lambert's airs also appeared in two collections of Ballard's *Meslanges de musique latine, françoise et italienne*, published in 1725 and 1730.[41]

Bacilly also continued to receive homage throughout the late seventeenth century and into the eighteenth. Bacilly is mentioned several times by Lecerf in his *Comparaison*, particularly in reference to aspects relating to his singing method and his ability to compose *doubles*.[42] In addition to appearing in Ballard's *Livres d'airs de différents autheurs*, *Livres de chansons pour danser et pour boire*, *Recueils de chansonnettes*, and various manuscript sources,[43] Bacilly's airs continued to be published in the *Mercure galant* throughout the century.[44] Christophe Ballard also honored him by publishing a number of his airs in the three volumes of *Brunetes ou petits airs tendres*. But here again, it was Bacilly's lighter, dance-like airs that were chosen by Ballard to be published into the eighteenth century.

Le Camus' name appears alongside that of Lambert's in several sources, while La Barre's name does not.[45] The *Mercure galant,* for example, claims that Madame la Dauphine not only sings airs by Lambert, but also those by Le Camus.[46] Antione Furetière's famous rant against lyric poetry in his *Le Roman bourgeois* (1666) also mentions Le Camus together with Lambert as composers whose musical settings make even the worst of poems tolerable.[47] Lecerf also identified Le Camus as one of France's most prestigious composers. As well, Le Camus is praised for his delicate and moving airs in *Mémoirs de Trévoux* (November 1704).[48] Like Lambert and Bacilly, his airs continued to appear throughout all of Ballard's publications and in manuscript sources.[49]

While various writers praised Lambert, Bacilly, and Le Camus as champions of French musical style, critics, even those without a religious agenda, berated the poets of song texts for the emptiness of their ideas and criticized lyric poetry for its common images which were repeated from poem to poem. Bacilly, himself both a poet and composer, recognized the banality of song texts: the phrases and words not included in lyric poetry are those that are "often the very expressions which bear the greatest weight and expressive profundity in the art of poetry."[50] In his novel *Le Roman bourgeois,* Furetière observes with disgust that lyrical poetry is "rubbish." But when set to music by the masters (he mentions Lambert, Le Camus, and Boësset) and sung by "the most beautiful mouths at court," these texts are so esteemed that their creators become "men of beautiful verses."[51] Thus, music enhanced the worth and emotional appeal of even the crudest of poems.

In the hands of a masterful composer, the quality of the music surpassed that of the song text. Even though the musical tones associated with affective representation were "identifiable entities," the composers cleverly juxtaposed and combined devices to conform to a general interpretation of poetic content. Composers worked with the same musical tools (their songs use the same "musical language"), but their application of the tools often differed in ways so that each could be said to have forged his own individual style within this highly conventional art form.

The conventions of expression provide a framework for the comparison of composers' works, for particular composers tended to favor certain devices over others. Bacilly's predilection for dance airs (and lighter songs), for example, distinguishes his collections. Unlike Lambert, he tended to organize musical phrases into a regular number of measures, avoid frequent meter changes, and limit the number of passions represented in a piece. Many of his most serious airs are sarabandes, such as "Si je vous dis" (Example 4.2) or "Mon sort est digne de pitié" (Figures 5.3–4). In the former example, he limits the affect to sorrow and tenderness (with one expression of despair). Bacilly was also more apt than Lambert, Le Camus, or La Barre to use musical figures akin to those described later by German theorists. He was inclined to repeat musical material with different texts, to use musical sequence to a greater extent, and to construct pieces on musical motives that are repeated and manipulated throughout the piece to stand for larger concepts presented in the text, as in "Mon sort est digne de pitié" or "Dûssay j'avoir mille rivaux" (Example 4.12). These features appear to some extent in airs by other composers but primarily in "hybrid" pieces, the songs that mix features from both the serious and the light.

La Barre's airs are generally more graceful than Bacilly's. His rhythms are supple and his bass lines fluid, as many of his airs resemble the more lyrical recitative developed later by Lully in his operas. A good example is "Ah! Je sens que mon cœur" (Example 4.11), in which he not only changes meter to indicate a different *mouvement* but also uses written directions to indicate an alteration in tempo and expression: *lentement* (slowly) and *gayement* (lively or quickly). In "Ah! Je sens que mon cœur," the slower tempo on the words "ungrateful Silvie has betrayed me" serves to emphasize this most important phrase of the text, while the lively tempo is used to intensify the angry expression of revenge on "for her infidelity, Love, avenge me." Tempo markings, not in conjunction with a change in meter, also appear in other airs which are more tuneful. In "Si c'est un bien que l'esperance" (Example 5.19), La Barre indicates in mm. 26–28 that the interjected sighs "Helas!," which express sweet sorrow, are to be sung slowly (*lentement*). He then indicates that the next phrase be sung *gayement* on the words, "Let one ask these hearts in love / Who because they have nothing but hope / Are not any happier for it / If hope is good." He also indicates changes in tempo and affect in the passacaglia, "Quand une ame est bien atteinte":[52] *lentement* on the words "All groan, all sigh," to express sweet sorrow, and *gayement* on "And yet this empire [of lovers] grows every day." Both the theme of the rondeau "Si c'est un bien que l'esperance" and the first twenty-seven measures of the passacaglia "Quand une ame est bien atteinte" are composed in a more lyrical style and sweet tone, while all other portions of the two pieces are recitative-like. This variation in *mouvement* within a single piece is a preview of Lully's frequent alteration between lyrical and speech-like moments within a single operatic scene.

La Barre also experimented with form; his "Rondeau sur le movement de la chaconne" ("Si c'est un bien que l'espérance," Example 5.19), for example, combines formal procedures associated with both the rondeau and the chaconne, but neither form is completely represented. The rondeau theme in the voice returns when the first section of the piece is repeated and then again at the end, mm. 38–41. The chaconne pattern in the bass reappears in variation but not throughout the air—a very different approach to this form than Lambert or Lully employed in their rondeaux, wherein the ostinato bass persists through-out the piece.[53] In the passacaglia "Quand une ame est bien atteinte," the bass line pattern is presented as an instrumental introduction and then only once again to accompany the first vocal phrase of the air.

Le Camus' airs differ in a number of ways from those by Lambert and La Barre, but like Bacilly, his publication includes the longest and the shortest of airs, though there are no *doubles* or second verses. As in Bacilly's editions, Le Camus' son also included in his father's posthumous publication light *chansonnettes* in lively triple time, as exemplified by "Je passais de tranquilles jours," alongside serious airs such as "On n'ayme plus dans ces boccages" (Example 7.1). The melodies of his serious pieces are like Lambert's in their flexibility, speech-like quality, and supple rhythms. Airs like "On n'ayme plus dans ces boccages" are exquisitely dramatic and rival some of Lully's most powerful and pas-sionate operatic moments. Many of Le Camus' airs are expanded by lengthy instrumental introductions and interludes, which, as Catherine Massip points out, may be related to his prowess as a viola da gam-bist and theorbist.[54] It is telling, as Massip explains, that his airs and Lambert's were sometimes confused. Lecerf de la Viéville, for example, thought that "Je veux me plaindre" was by Lambert, bringing it up as an example of a superior song text set by the venerable composer. The air, however, was actually set to music by Le Camus.[55]

Lambert was clearly the most masterful of the four composers. While La Barre and Le Camus, in particular, favored musical represen-tations of the more moderate passions, Lambert seemingly preferred a much wider range of expression. He was a master of the serious air and attempted with every piece "to translate the complexity of the expressed or subjacent sentiments."[56] Lambert's settings reflected every subtle gradation of affect suggested by the text; juxtaposing and combining devices associated with the passions was a means of unify-ing and varying musical materials. In "Mon ame faisons un effort" (Example 4.1), Lambert mixes devices associated with boldness and sorrow, burning love and boldness, despair with reference to death, sorrow and tenderness, and concludes the piece by mixing elements of all these passions. Bacilly, Le Camus, and La Barre, by contrast, were more apt to juxtapose devices associated with the passions than com-bine them. Bacilly, in particular, tended to limit the number of passions in his airs, so he achieved affective variety by intensifying and diminish-ing the same passions, often by abrupt changes in tessitura, by motivic sequence, by a change in the rate of harmonic and rhythmic movement, or by leaps of expressive intervals, such as the tritone.[57] Lambert, La Barre, and Le Camus also used these expressive devices, but to a lesser extent and with greater subtlety.

Even though the subtle and expressive style of the serious air established by these four composers no longer dominated the repertory at the end of the seventeenth century, their influence cannot be underestimated. In her article "Michel Lambert and Jean-Baptiste Lully," Catherine Massip notes that

> in the field of Lully scholarship, there yet remains an important area to be investigated—that of stylistic analysis. It would be desirable for such a study to be undertaken in a "comparatist spirit," and for the musical contributions of Michel Lambert to be weighed objectively: Lully developed an important part of his language in the *comedies-ballets,* even more so than in the ballets, and thus the years 1664–1670 represent a crucial period that must be evaluated in its entirety.[58]

The conventions of expression identified in this study provide a criterion for assessing Lully's style, and that of other French composers, in a "comparatist spirit." According to Massip, Lully's music could not express emotional intimacy in miniature forms because he was writing for the stage.[59] His music had to fit into a great "architectural" scheme; his style was simpler and more *recherché* than Lambert's.[60] Yet Massip also notes that Lully's and Lambert's music, in particular, share common elements as well:

> The links between the two spheres of creation of [Lully's opera and the air as exemplified by Lambert] remain: nurtured by the air, the *tragédie en musique* remained submissive to the constraints of that closed form. . . . Inserted into a dramatic and musical continuum, the air remained for a long time one of the most original elements of French opera and of vocal art. Lully's genius capitalized on Lambert's remarkable gifts—therein lies one of the principal keys to the evolution of Lully's art.[61]

The similarlity of Lully's music, even his recitatives, to the French air was a point often commented upon, sometimes in a critical tone, throughout the seventeenth and eighteenth centuries.[62] Lully's music reflected the current French taste, already inherent in the French air. He could not have successfully created his operas without a clear understanding of French musical style and aesthetics. Lecerf de la Viéville's comments regarding the limited expression evident in Lambert's airs were made only after he and all of France had already experienced *tragédies en musique* at the hands of Jean-Baptiste Lully. Through the dramatic medium of opera, a wider range of emotion and musical expression could be explored and promoted.

There is no doubt that at the point in time at which the French serious air reached its apex, during the 1650s and 1660s, composers and poets were working under established restrictions regarding the composition of serious airs. With few exceptions, love was the only topic suitable for songs. The pastoral setting of the poems presented vague and conventionalized characters (shepherds and shepherdesses) in amorous situations that had long been used in musical composition. French audiences accepted singing shepherds and shepherdesses and readily associated the emotions provoked by the amorous situations with musical imitation.[63] The lover (the poetic voice) was a "type," the personification of particular emotional states, who "spoke" in impassioned tones, despite the narrow range of expression.

When one considers the limitations that restricted Lambert, Bacilly, Le Camus, and La Barre, it is all the more impressive that they were able to compose such miniature masterpieces. In the hands of a skilled composer, the quality of the music surpassed that of the song text. Writers demanded that the music be "well composed with regard to the text and its meaning."[64] Yet in practice the musical setting enhanced and added to the meaning and appeal of the text. Composers of airs at mid-century were to apply "to the words [of a song text] tones so proportioned, that the poetry is blended and reborn in the music: it carries to the bottom of the heart of the listener what the singer says."[65] While the goal of the composer—to move the passions and thereby captivate the listeners—was founded upon a rational system of rhetoric and the theory of artistic imitation, the success of a work was based upon its appeal to the senses, to the "heart of the listener." The conflict between the rational and the sensual was at the core of the seventeenth-century controversies over ancient and modern models, the profane and the religious, and of the eighteenth-century dispute over French and Italian music.[66] Although that debate was played out largely in writings about opera (pitting Lully and Quinault's *tragédies en musique* against spoken tragedies, and Rameau's operas against Italian operas), the sensual appeal of the French air was a point of contention long before Lully's first opera, *Cadmus et Hermione*, was performed in 1673. The "musical competition of 1640" between Ban and Boësset was, in fact, a debate about musical expression and national style. Ban's composition exemplified the Italian method, and Boësset's, the French. Mersenne grappled with the "language" and meaning of music and wrote many letters to Descartes and others on the subject. Descartes eventually admitted that effects of music were not subject to rational measurement.[67] The absence of a particular musical theory to guide composers during the seventeenth century attests to the impossibility of rationalizing music's effects. Seventeenth-century intellectuals had difficulty justifying an art form that appealed so strongly to the senses.[68]

While the song text and the rhetorical devices found therein inspired composers in their settings, music acquired its own rhetoric, its own system of connoting meaning. Furetière's contention that lyrical poetry was "rubbish" until set to music by the masters and sung by expert singers demonstrates music's capacity to signify meaning beyond the text, and underscores the importance of music as a sensual language with its own set of conventional symbols: its own rhetoric, its own language of love.

Appendix: Translations for
Musical Examples and Emblems

Example 4.1 Lambert, "Mon ame faisons un effort," *Les Airs de Monsieur Lambert*, p. 4.

> My soul let us make an effort / Since I burn I must complain / Let us speak it is no longer time to pretend / We are too close to death, // Do not be offended Silvie / If I lose [your] respect I also lose my life.

Example 4.2 Bacilly, "Si je vous dis," *Les Trois livres d'airs*, I:52.

> If I tell you that I love you / Why Philis so much severity // Ah! I see only too much for my extreme unhappiness / That one must not always tell the truth.

Example 4.3 Bacilly, "Vous ne pouvez Iris," *Les Trois livres d'airs*, I:60.

> You cannot Iris show yourself more severe / When you order me to be quiet / What you make me suffer // In the excess of torment of whose blows I feel / To defend myself from the rightful complaints / Is to command me to die.

Example 4.4 La Barre, "Tristes enfans de mes desirs," *Airs à deux parties*, 19v.

> Sad children of my desires / Innocent witnesses of my flame, / Sad and righteous sighs, // Sweet relief of my soul: // Why do you escape me, / Alas, what harshness forces you to burst forth from my heart.

Example 4.5 Lambert, "Mon cœur qui se rend à vos coups," *Les Airs de Monsieur Lambert*, p. 32.

> My heart which surrenders to your blows / Will not complain Philis of the heavens nor of you / I will die a death that I had foreseen // I have lost in my misfortunes all hope of being healed / And as soon as I saw you / I had to dream of dying.

Example 4.7 Lambert, "Superbes ennemis de repos de mon ame," *Les Airs de Monsieur Lambert*, p. 20.

> Superb enemies of my soul's peace / Whose brilliant flame / Makes all hearts tremble under the effort of their blows, // Do not be offended beautiful eyes if I sigh / It is only because of the martyrdom / To not dare sigh for you.

Example 4.8 Bacilly, "Au secours ma raison," *Les Trois livres d'airs*, I:28.

Help my reason rescue my heart / The treacherous one surrenders without resistance / And gives in to the laws of its victor / Seduced by the vain appearance / Of a false sweetness / Help my reason rescue my heart.

Example 4.10 Bacilly, "Puisque Philis est infidelle," *Les Trois livres d'airs*, I:4.

Since Philis is unfaithful / Let us avoid death my heart / Let us revolt against her // But you do not agree to it / Ah! how difficult it is when love is extreme / To banish from one's heart an ingrate whom one loves.

Example 4.11 La Barre, "Ah! Je sens que mon cœur," *Airs à deux parties*, 10v.

Ah! I feel that my heart / Is going to die of languor // Ungrateful Silvie betrays me // For her infidelity Love avenge me.

Example 4.12 Bacilly, "Dûssay j'avoir mille rivaux," *Les Trois livres d'airs*, I:64.

Even if I had a thousand rivals / I would still like to be under Climene's laws // Because the greatest of all misfortunes / Is to have neither pleasure nor pain.

Example 4.13 Bacilly, "Vous sçavez donner de l'amour," *Les Trois livres d'airs*, I:68.

You know how to inspire love / The power of your eyes makes this clear // But your heart Iris shows me more and more each day / That you do not know how to receive it.

Example 4.14 Bacilly, "Pour la bergere Lisette," *Les Trois livres d'airs*, I:70.

For the shepherdess Lisette / I sigh in vain / In vain I look to find her alone / And to tell her about my torment // Don't you know she says / That I cannot commit myself / How could I be unfaithful / To my lovable shepherd.

Example 4.15 Bacilly, "Petite abeille mesnagere," *Les Trois livres d'airs*, I:58.

Little busy bee / If you are only looking for flowers // Draw near to my shepherdess / You will be able to satisfy yourself / Her beautiful mouth has pleasures / That one does not find elsewhere.

Example 5.5 Bacilly "Il faut parler," *Les Trois livres d'airs*, I:72.

One must speak to be done with one's martyrdom / One loses time sighing // One must first declare oneself / But especially when Love gives us enough to talk about / One must speak to put an end to one's martyrdom.

Example 5.10 Bacilly "Qu'il couste cher de voir Silvie," *Les Trois livres d'airs*, I:63.

How much it costs to see Silvie / I paid with my heart for the pleasure of my eyes // But alas I am too happy / Even if it cost me my life.

Example 5.11 Bacilly, "Pour donner à mon cœur," *Les Trois livres d'airs,* I:44.

In order to give my heart some relief / I have worked to forget the object that possesses it // But alas I have only increased my torment / And the ailment is even sweeter than the remedy.

Example 5.18 Bacilly, "En vain j'ay consulté l'amour et le respect," *Les Trois livres d'airs,* I:18.

In vain I have consulted love and respect / In order to know if I must speak or keep silent / One has always been suspect to me / The other I see offends you // Alas Philis to heal myself / Teach me what I must do / May I speak must I be silent / As for me I believe I must die.

Example 5.19 La Barre, "Si c'est un bien que l'esperance," *Airs à deux parties,* 5v.

If hope is good, / It should alleviate my suffering, / And yet I hope, and I am not any better: // No, it is only a false appearance of pleasure? / Alas! let one ask these hearts in love / Who because they have nothing but hope / Are not any happier for it: / If hope is good.

Example 6.17 Lambert, "J'ay juré mille fois," *Les Airs de Monsieur Lambert,* p. 48.

I swore a thousand times never to love / And did not believe that anything could entice me / But when I made this rash plan / Tyrsis you had not yet undertaken to please me / My reason against you no longer did its duty / And finally I know the power of Love.

Example 6.18 Bacilly, "Vous ne pouvez Iris," *Les Trois livres d'airs,* I:60.

See Example 4.3 above.

Example 7.1 Le Camus, "On n'ayme plus dans ces bocages," *Les Airs à deux et trois parties,* p. 15.

One no longer loves in these glades, / All the shepherds are liars and fickle, / Let us flee love, shepherdesses, it causes too much pain; / Let us love only the song of the birds / The freshness of the shades, / And the sweet sound of our streams. / When love wants to surprise us, / It appears sincere and tender, / And we think that it must be eternal; / It is sweet and flattering when it begins to be born; / But as soon as it makes itself known, / Alas! It is cruel.

Figure 7.1 Flamen, *Devises et emblèmes,* pp. 110–12. Emblem XXVIII. Love Joins Them Together ("*Jungit Amor; L'Amour les joint*").

Explanation: Those who have learned the secrets of Nature, say that there is an inclination so perfect and reciprocal between these male and female trees, that they cannot live far from each other, that they lower their palms, and curve their trunks to be joined together, without the rivers that separate the two being able to stop them from doing so; that if one is sick, the other feels it and many other qualities, that would cause the most reasonable *amities* to blush.

Moral: Come all as many as you are, that the holy bond of love has united, come and take a lesson from these palm trees, that tell you secretly, Now two harmonious souls will die as one. Although we are two in reality, love nevertheless has us joined together so well, that it seems that we have only one soul.

Explication: Ceux qui ont approfondy les secrests de la Nature, disent qu'il y a une inclination si parfaite & reciproque entre ces Arbres masles & femelles, qu'ils ne peuvent vivre éloignez les uns des autres, qu'ils abbaissent leurs palmes, & courbent leurs troncs pour se joindre, sans que les Riveieres qui passent entre eux, les en empeschent; que si l'un est malade, l'autre s'en ressent, & beaucoup d'autres proprietez qui feroient rougir les amities les plus raisonnables.

Moralité: Venez tous tant que vous estes, que le Saint noeud de l'Amour a unis, venez & prenez leçon de ces Palmiers, qui vous disent secretement, Nunc duo concordes anima moriemur in una

Quoy que nous soyons deux en effet, l'Amour neantmoins nous a si bien joints, qu'il semble que nous n'ayons plus qu'une ame.

Figure 7.2 Flamen, *Devises et emblèmes,* pp. 114–16. Emblem XXIX. They Love without Touching Each Other (*"Non Tangunt Et Amant; Elle* [sic] *s'aiment sans se toucher"*).

Explanation: Although these two palm trees can never touch, they nonetheless love each other, and represent perfectly those true friendships, that have an object more noble than sensual or brutal.

Moral: The goal of love must not be possession; as long as it remains a reasonable appetite, one calls it affection; when it descends into the sensual, it is satisfied under the name of passion: and if it wants to pass for true friendship, it must rely on virtue, it must base itself on *l'honnesteté,* or else renounce the first law that Cicero prescribes, . . . that is, that we must never ask of our friends or do anything for them except that which is honorable (*honneste*).

Explication: Quoy que ces deux Palmiers ne se puissent jamais toucher, ils ne laissent pas neantmoins de s'aimer, & representent parfaitement ces amitiez veritables, qui ont un objet plus relevé que le sensible & le brutal.

Moralité: Le but de l'Amour ne doit point estre la possession; tant qu'il reside dans l'appétit raisonnable, on le nomme affection; quand il descend dans le sensitif, il se contente du nom de passion: & s'il veut passer pour veritable amitié, il faut qu'il s'appuye de la vertu, il faut qu'il s'établisse sur l'honnesteté, ou qu'il renonce à la premiere Loy que luy prescrit Ciceron, lib.r.de.Amie. Hecigitur prima lex amicitae sanciatur, ut ab asmicis honesta petamus, amicorum causa honesta faciamus; c'est à dire que nous ne devons rien demander à nos Amis, ny rien faire à leur occasion que d'honneste.

Figure 7.4 Flamen, *Devises et emblèmes,* pp. 98–100. Emblem XXV. More Inside Than Outside ("*Mas Dentro Que Fuera; Plus dedans que dehors*").

Explanation: One cannot understand the fervor of the fire that consumes a lover; what he contains in his chest is much more violent than what he exhales with his sighs; this illness is felt, and can express itself: all that one can say, is that it burns all the more because it is hidden: The more the fire is hidden, the more it, having been hidden, burns. And its least spark is a mark of a very great fire.

Moral: This illicit love that you nourish in your breast, throws some flames that insensibly win your guts, its fire creeps into your arteries, and destroys as a result all the parts of your miserable body, that the most malicious plants will be those that set down the deepest roots. Ovid is proof of what I propose. Meanwhile they silently crawl in(to) the inner flame(s), and the evil tree drives (its) roots deeper.

Explication: On ne conçoit pas l'ardeur du feu qui consomme un Amant; ce qu'il renferme dans sa poitrine est bien plus violent, que ce qu'il fait exhaler par ses soûpirs; ce mal se ressent, & se peut exprimer: tout ce que l'on en peut dire, est qu'il brûle d'autant plus qu'il est caché: Quoque magis tegitur, tectus magis aestuat ignis. Et sa moindre étincelle est une marque d'un fort grand embrasement.

Moralité: Cet Amour illicite que tu nourris dedans son sein, jette des flâmes qui gagnent insensiblement tes entrailles, son feu se glisse dans tes arteres, & détruit en sorte toutes les parties de ton miserable corps, que les plus méchantes Plantes seront celles qui y jetteront les plus profondes racines: Ovide sera caution de ce que j'avance. Interea tacite serpunt in viscerflamme, Et mala radices altius arbor agit.

Figure 7.5 Van Veen, *Amorum emblemata,* pp. 134–35. The Shock Enflames ("*Le chocq enflamme*").

Wood rubbed together sparks an intense flame.
Man in the same manner, who with his face and eyes
Meets a beauty, in this sweet shock,
Feels soon after a fire burning in his soul

Le bois entrefrotté jette une drüe flame.
l'Homme pareillement, qui du front & des yeux
Une beauté rencontre, en ce chocq doucereux,
Sent embraser bien tost un feu dedans son ame.

Figure 7.6 Flamen, *Devises et emblèmes*, pp. 186–88. Emblem XLVII.
Combat Maintains it [Love] (*"Certamine Durat; Le Combat l'entretient"*).

Explanation: Little disputes, slight oppositions, discouraging gestures, and all these little disguised insults maintain love: Combats either real or imaginary that one engages in against one or the other fortifies it; and these great assaults that our appetites force upon us, serve only to establish its throne more solidly.

Moral: If you want to heal yourself of this agreeably troublesome passion, ignore it, do not imagine that it possesses you, do not enter the fray even to destroy it, (and I assure you according to Ovid) it will not torment you for long. Love consumes [you] in battle if you do not remove it completely. Because it is indubitable that love cannot survive without combat.

Explication: Les disputes moderées, les legeres oppositions, les jeux de main, & toutes ces petites piquoteries entretiennent l'Amour: Les combats ou veritables ou imaginaires que l'on rend au dehors contre les uns & les autres le fortifient; & ces grands assauts que se livrent nos appétits en nous mesmes, ne servent qu'à y établir plus solidement son trône.)

Moralité: Si donc vous voulez vous guerir de cette passion agreablement importune, negligez la, ne songez point qu'elle vous possede, n'entrez pas en lice mesme pour la détruire, [& je vous donne parole apres Ovide,]. . . qu'elle ne vous tormentera pas longs-temps. Non bene si tollas praeliadurat amor. Car il est indubitable que l'Amour ne peut subsister sans combat.

Example 7.2 Lambert, "D'un feu secret," First Strophe, *Les Airs de Monsieur Lambert*, p. 60.

I feel myself consumed by a secret fire / Without being able to relieve the pain that possesses me, // I could well be healed if I stopped loving / But I prefer the pain to the remedy.

Example 7.3 Lambert, "D'un feu secret," Second Strophe, *Les Airs de Monsieur Lambert*.

Even if I were to die could one blame me / Whoever begins to love should he not continue, // When people learn Philis that I have stopped loving / They will know that I have stopped living.

Figure 7.7 Flamen, *Devises et emblèmes,* pp. 170–73. Emblem XLIII. He Cannot Safeguard Himself from All the Heat ("*Non Sic Omnis Vitabitur Ardor; Il ne se garantit pas de tout le chaux*").

> Explanation: The man whom you see in the shade of this tree, does not avoid the greatest heat; the thickness of its leaves and the abundance of its branches, can safeguard his body from the rays of the sun; but they are not capable of protecting his heart from the sparks of the fire of love, since imperceptibly they creep in through his eyes.
>
> Moral: While this man works to protect himself from the ardor of the sun, which is only capable of burning his skin a little, he ignites by the illegitimate gaze of this woman a fire in his breast, which after having destroyed all parts of his body, will make his soul burn eternally in Hell, without after ages to come ever seeing its end.
>
> Explication: L'Homme que tu vois à l'ombre de cet Arbre, n'évite pas la plus grande chaleur; l'épaisseur de ses feüilles & l'abondance de ses branches, peuvent garantir son corps des rayons du Soleil; mais elles ne sont pas capables de mettre son cœur à l'abry des étincelles du feu d'amour, puis qu'insensiblement elles se glissent par ses yeux.
>
> Moralité: Pendant que cet Homme travaille à se garantir de l'ardeur du Soleil, qui n'est capable que d'échauffer un peu sa peau, il allume par le regard illegitime de cette Femme un feu dans son sein, qui apres avoir détruit toutes les parties de son corps, fera brûler eternellement son Ame dans les Enfers, sans que la suite des Siecles en voye jamais la consommation.

Example 8.1 Ballard, "C'est aux amans que la saison," *Livre d'airs de différents autheurs* (1675), 4v.

> It is for lovers that the new season / Gives the flowers and the beautiful days, / It is sweet and beautiful / Only in favor of lovers; // For an ungrateful and rebellious heart / Winter always endures.

Example 8.2 Bacilly, "D'où vient cette sombre tristesse," *Airs spirituels* (1688), Part 2, p. 2.

> Where does this somber sorrow come from / That you allow to devastate you /
>
> My soul who can trouble you / You whom God must fill with a holy joy. // If you take Him for your support / And if you hope only in Him / What can you fear upon the earth! / From this divine hope arm yourself from now on / And even if the whole world were to wage war against you / You will always enjoy a profound peace.

Notes

Introduction

1. A few airs are also rondeaux, chaconnes, passacaglias, and dialogues.

2. The term "salon" was not used during the seventeenth century but has been adopted by scholars today in reference to the *ruelle* or *alchôve,* among other names, derived from the place in a room between the hostess's bed and the wall, where people would gather. The term "salon" has been adopted particularly by English-language scholars because there is not a proper translation for *ruelle.* As such, I will also use "salon" throughout this study, keeping in mind that the term, while anachronistic, is nonetheless useful.

3. Michel de Saint-Lambert was not the same individual as Michel Lambert.

4. Throughout this book, I will use the words "passion," "affect" ("affection"), and, less often, "sentiment" to refer to the seventeenth-century understanding of "emotional states." Of all these terms, "passion" is most accurate in referring to the emotions felt in reaction to a stimulus. (This "process" is described at length in chapters 3 and 4, according to Descartes' treatment of passions in his book *The Passions of the Soul (Les Passions de l'âme,* 1649). Definitions of affection and sentiment are more limited and refer to a desire for that which pleases us ("affection") or to a feeling of affection or love toward an object ("sentiment"). See Antoine Furetière, *Le Dictionnaire universel* (1690) for specific definitions of the terms "passion," "affection," and "sentiment."

5. Throughout the book I make many references to Dr. Jacques Ferrand's treatise on lovesickness entitled *De la maladie d'amour ou melancholie erotique* published in 1623. This was Ferrand's second treatise on the subject, the first, *Traité de l'essence et guérison de l'amour ou mélancholie erotique,* published in 1610. Ferrands encyclopedic treatise of 1623 on lovesickness draws on 2,000 years of writings on the subject from the ancients to the Latin and Arabic Middle Ages. His sources would have been written in Latin, Greek, Italian, Spanish, and French and would have included contemporary as well as ancient treatises. Ferrand relied on extremely diverse sources, including writings by Avicenna (the great Arab physician), Plato, Galen of Pergamum, and Hippocrates, as well as more immediate predecessors and contemporaries François Valeriola, Levinus Lemnius, Francesco Valles, Cristobal de Vega, Luis Mercado, Rodrigo de Castro, Marsilio Ficino (his translations on and commentaries of Plato's works), Pietro Capretto, Battista Platina, Giovan Battista Fregosos, Mario Equicola, André Du Laurens, and Jean Aubery, among many others. Ferrand's approach was to incorporate different views on lovesickness into a rational medical and philosophical system; thus incorporating, for example, both Plato's view of love as

a disease which affects the blood along with the Galenic classification of humors. His constant references to past authorities reflect cumulative scholarly writings on lovesickness typical of encyclopedic humanism, an approach which began to wane early on and throughout the seventeenth century. For a thorough commentary regarding a history of medical accounts on lovesickness and their influences on Ferrand, see the introduction to the English translation of the treatise, *A Treatise on Lovesickness*, by Donald A. Beecher and Massimo Ciavolella. The information given above was reduced from the preface, p. xi and p. xii, and the introduction, pages 5–8 and 98. For a thorough account of medical interpretations of the disease leading up to Ferrand's analysis, see Mary Frances Wack, *Lovesickness in the Middle Ages: The* Viaticum *and Its Commentaries* (Philadelphia: University of Pennsylvania Press, 1990).

6. Studies published before 1994 that address the relationship between rhetoric and French music are Duncan, "Persuading the Affections"; Ranum, "Audible Rhetoric"; Mather, *Dance Rhythms;* and Pinson, "L'expression dans la musique de chambre." The most important studies after 1994 to consider rhetoric and French music are a dissertation by Gibson, "*Le Naturel* and *L'Éloquence,*" and his recent article, "'A Kind of Eloquence.'"

7. Two books that consider song texts from the middle of the seventeenth century are Auld, *The Lyric Art of Pierre Perrin,* and Génetiot, *Les genres.* Although Auld concentrates on opera, he provides information about lyric poetry in general. Of particular value is the inclusion in Auld's book of Perrin's introduction to his "Recueil de paroles de musique," a manuscript dated 1667.

8. The three books of *Brunetes ou petits airs tendres* were published by Christophe Ballard in 1703, 1704, and 1711. In the *Advertissement* to the first collection, Ballard identified two types of *brunetes:* "airs simples ou passionnés," and "airs de mouvement" (simple or expressive airs, and dance airs). Both are defined as simple airs concerning pastoral matters, usually love, often playful, written in a *galant* and natural style. Any kind of air, be it serious, popular, a drinking song, or dance air, could be called a *brunete* if the subject matter were pastoral.

9. Massip, "Michel Lambert (1610–1696)"; Caswell, "The Development of the 17th-Century French Vocal Ornamentation"; see also Massip, "Michel Lambert and Jean-Baptiste Lully."

10. See also Perella, "French Song in the 1660s," and Perella, "Bénigne de Bacilly."

11. Facsimiles of airs by Bacilly, La Barre, Lambert are available, as well as modern editions of works by Le Camus and Lambert. See Bénigne de Bacilly, *Les Trois livres d'airs,* ed. Jean Saint-Arroman; Joseph Chabanceau de La Barre, *Airs à deux partis avec les seconds couplets en diminution,* ed. Jean Saint-Arroman; Michel Lambert, *Airs from* Airs de différents autheurs, ed. Robert Green; Michel Lambert, *Les airs de M. Lambert non imprimez,* ed. Jean Saint-Arroman; and Sébastien Le Camus, *Airs à deux et trois parties,* ed. Robert Green.

12. I have found that the influence of the Lully-Quinault *tragédies lyriques* on the song texts and music is especially evident in airs published during the 1680s and 1690s; see Gordon-Seifert, "Strong Men—Weak Women."

13. As Marin Mersenne argues, "the most captivating airs are those that are well composed with regard to the text and its meaning"; quoted in Walker, "Joan Albert Ban," 253.

14. The remaining component of rhetoric established by rhetoricians of classical antiquity is memory (*memoria*).

15. "Un des effets funestes de ces Chansons, est de laisser dans le cœur une tres-grande disposition au crime & au libertinage; en sorte que ceux qui les aiment & qui en font leur divertissement, se laissent facilement engager dans le désordre & dans l'impiété," Lalouette, *Histoire de la Comedie*, 71.

1. Music and Texts

1. The following eighteenth-century writers cite the French serious air as exemplifying French musical style: Lecerf de la Viéville, *Comparaison*, Pt. 1, 302 ; Grimarest, *Traité du récitatif*, 203–32; Montéclair, *Brunetes*, unpaginated preface; and Dandrieu, *Principes de l'Accompagnement du Clavecin*, 4.

2. The term *air de cour* continued to be used in various sources later in the century, though in a more generic fashion and not specifically to indicate actual court airs from the late sixteenth and early seventeenth centuries; see Goulet, *Poésie*, 19–24.

3. Gérold, *L'art du chant*, vii. Despite his influence on an entire generation of composers, only one air by Nyert has survived and appears in the manuscript Paris, Bibliothèque nationale de France, Rés. Vma. ms 854: "Si vous voules que je cache ma flame."

4. Perrin, *Recueil de paroles de musique*, translated in Auld, *The Lyric Art*, 2:29.

5. Ibid., 2:30. Another type of light air, the *chanson à boire*, or drinking song, does not appear in the collections under examination.

6. Ibid., 2:29–30.

7. In addition to the yearly publication of serious airs, Ballard also published a series of *Airs bachiques* (beginning in 1672), *Livres d'airs pour danser et pour boire*, and *Recueils de chansonnettes* (beginning in 1675). For a wealth of information pertaining to the Ballard family publications, see Goulet, *Poésie*.

8. The *Airs sérieux et à boire* collection first appeared in 1690 but was not published monthly until 1695.

9. Unless otherwise stated, all musical examples from and references to Michel Lambert's airs are from the 1666 edition of *Les Airs de Monsieur Lambert* in facsimile (Minkoff, 1983), though all three editions are extremely similar.

10. Of the other editions published before 1670 that are devoted to a single composer, none consist exclusively of two-part serious airs. Editions of airs in four parts include those by François de La Roche (1655 and 1658), Mathieu Quinot (1662), Jean Mignon (1664), and Étienne Moulinié (1668).

Editions of drinking songs (some mixed in with serious airs) include those by Robert Cambert (1665) and Jean Sicard (1666–83). Charles Hurel published his *Meslanges* in 1687.

11. For a list of manuscript sources for Lambert's airs and others, see Massip, *L'Art de bien chanter,* 316–27.

12. "Bien que mon Inclination n'ayt jamais esté portée a rien donner au public, Je me laisse toutes fois emporter aux persuasions et aux raisons de mes Amis, dont la plus forte est qu'il y a un nombre considerable de mes Airs ou Imprimez ou qui courent le monde qui ne sont pas selon mon Intention." Lambert, *Les Airs de Monsieur Lambert* (1666), foreword.

13. Charles Le Camus, Sébastien's son, makes reference to this in the note to the reader (translated by Robert Green): "The reputation of my late father was the reason that his airs were printed with so much eagerness that they were filled with a thousand faults and always deprived of their true bass." Le Camus, *Airs,* ed. Robert Green, x.

14. For a fascinating account of printing practices by Ballard and others, see Guillo, "La diffusion"; Guillo, *Pierre I Ballard,* 32–57; and Goulet, *Poésie,* 35–135.

15. For more biographical information on Michel Lambert, see Massip, *L'Art de bien chanter,* 27–97.

16. Tallemant des Réaux, *Historiettes,* 2:525.

17. Lecerf de la Viéville, *Comparaison,* 2:77. See also Tillet, *Le Parnasse françois;* La Borde, *Essai sur la musique;* and Tallemant des Réaux, *Historiettes,* 2:523–25.

18. In addition to Austin Caswell's dissertation, "The Development of the 17th-Century French Vocal Ornamentation" (1968), other sources on Bacilly include Gudrun Ryhming's article, "L'art du chant français" (1982); Lisa Perella's dissertation, "Mythologies of Musical Persuasion," which treats to some extent Bacilly's published editions of drinking songs; and Perella's article on Bacilly as editor, "Bénigne de Bacilly" (2000). The only study devoted to Bacilly's musical style is Gordon-Seifert, "The Language of Music in France." Catherine Guinamard, in "L'art du chant fin XVII siècle" (master's thesis, 1983) and "Les *Remarques curieuses*" (1989), treats Bacilly's treatise on singing; Elena Lorimer, "A Critical Study and Translation" (doctoral dissertation, 2002) is a second English translation of the treatise. It was Sébastien de Brossard who claimed that Bacilly was "a priest from Lower Normandy" ("un prestre de Basse Normandie"); cited by Lescar in the introduction to the facsimile edition of Bacilly's airs, *Les Trois livres d'airs* (Fuzeau, 1996).

19. Poole, "The Sources," 17 and 34. Many of Bacilly's pieces were so popular that Christophe Ballard included them in the three collections of *brunetes* published in 1703, 1704, and 1711.

20. Bowers, "La Barre, Chabanceau de." See also Gérold, *L'art du chant,* 117, 126–28, 149–51; Tiersot, "Une famille," 1–11, 68–74; Hardouin: "Notes"; Benoit, *Versailles et les musiciens du roi;* Massip, *La vie des musiciens;* and Hurel, *Airs à deux parties,* ed. Jean Saint-Arroman, 3–32.

21. Gustafson, *French Harpsichord Music.*

22. Bowers, "La Barre, Chabanceau de."

23. Robinson, "Le Camus, Sébastien." See also Dufourcq, "Autour de Sébastien Le Camus"; Benoit, *Versailles et les musicens du roi;* Green, "The Treble Viol"; and Le Camus, *Airs,* ed. Green, ix–xi.

24. Robinson, "Le Camus, Sébastien."

25. Ibid.

26. Ibid.

27. The Ballard family had monopolized music printing in France since the mid-sixteenth century. Their privilege, however, did not extend to engraving; thus, Lambert and Bacilly were able to have their collections engraved by Richer. Engraving, though more expensive, made it easier to print in score format and to incorporate the most recent developments in music practice, but the copper plates that were used allowed only a few hundred copies to be made (between 250 and 300). The Ballard method of movable type was more practical and less expensive, yet it did not allow for the more complex notational practices apparent in the engraved collections; see Poole, "The Sources," 27–28. It was not until 1685 that Ballard began to print his *Livre[s] d'airs de différents autheurs* in score format. Even though the *Livre[s] d'airs* were published with the treble and bass printed on separate pages, Ballard did have the capability to print in score format, as he published both La Barre's and Le Camus' airs in this manner.

28. Lambert claims in the preface to all editions of *Les Airs de Monsieur Lambert* that figured bass would facilitate the transposition of the accompaniment if the singer needed to alter the given pitch.

29. The ambiguity between a contrapuntal orientation (both the melody and bass conceived as independent melodic lines) and a truly homophonic texture (in which the bass line provides harmonic support for the melody) is typical of seventeenth-century French music and demonstrates a transition to a system whereby chords were viewed as a series of progressions rather than the result of several lines sounding simultaneously. Schulenberg, "Composition before Rameau."

30. Bacilly recommended the theorbo as the instrument of preference but also claimed that the viol or harpsichord were used "to sustain the voice." Bacilly, *Remarques,* 17–18, and *A Commentary,* 11.

31. Bacilly, *Remarques,* 20, and *A Commentary,* 12.

32. "Les basses ne sont quasi propres qu'à exprimer celle de la Colere, qui est rare dans les Airs François. Ainsi ces sortes de Voix se contentent de Chanter en Parties." Bacilly, *Remarques,* 45–46, and *A Commentary,* 23.

33. "Vous observerez aussi que la pluspart des Airs à trois parties se peuvent chanter en Basse & Dessus sans la troisiesme Partie, & se joüer en Symphonie avec la Basse, & le Dessus de Viol, ainsi que je l'ay pratiqué dans quelques Concerts." Cambert, *Airs à boire,* l'avis au lecteur [preface]; Goulet, *Poésie,* 102.

34. Bacilly, *Remarques,* 27, and *A Commentary,* 15.

35. Goulet, *Poésie,* 81.

36. Bacilly, *Remarques,* 27, and *A Commentary,* 15.

37. The importance of novelty is discussed at length in Goulet, *Poésie,* 176–78 and throughout the book.

38. Quoted in ibid., 81.

39. In Auld, *The Lyric Art,* 2:30.

40. Génetiot, *Les genres,* 54. Génetiot notes that while seventeenth-century definitions of *lyrique* (given by Furetière in 1690 and the *Dictionnaire de l'Académie Française* in 1694) identified the lyric as poetry to be set to music, the poets he considers in his book used the word *chansons* to designate song texts. Génetiot, *Les genres,* 15.

41. For a comprehensive study of reactions to lyric poetry during the seventeenth century, see Goulet, *Poésie,* 221–58.

42. "Etudier les modèles littéraires des poèmes mondains consiste donc à évoquer la multiplicité des traditions qui informent cette poésie d'imitation, sans perdre de vue toutefois que leur influence ne peut être que diffuse, indirecte, et sous la constante médiation d'un goût galant puis classique, qui ne cesse de les adapter, les transformer et les mélanger pour finalement se les approprier." Génetiot, *Poétique,* 37.

43. See Winegarten, *French Lyric Poetry,* 1–10, 48–92; and Génetiot, *Les genres,* 85.

44. Auld, "Text as Pre-Text," 65–67.

45. "Il est certain que dans les Paroles Françoises . . . il faut qu'il y ait du bon sens, sans pointe & mesme sans équivoque, ce qui ne se pratiquoit pas de mesme au temps jadis, où l'on aimoit les pointes par dessus les plus belles pensées." Bacilly, *Remarques,* 113–14; my translation.

46. "On appelle Chanson un certain petit Ouvrage en Vers, tourné d'une maniere simple, aisée & naturele, que l'on chante sous diferens airs, suivant le caractere de Vers, & dont chaque Stance s'appelle 'Couplet.'" La Croix, *L'Art de la poësie françoise,* 290.

47. Ibid.

48. Génetiot, *Les Genres,* 20–22, 171–90. For more general information on the seventeenth-century French salon, see Beasley, *Salons;* Craveri, *The Age of Conversation;* DeJean, *Tender Geographies;* Denis, *La muse galante;* Goldsmith, *Exclusive Conversations;* Goulet, *Poésie;* Harth, *Cartesian Women;* Lougee, *Les Paradis des Femmes;* Lilti, *Le monde des salons;* Maître, *Les précieuses;* Picard, *Les salons littéraires;* and Timmermans, *L'accès des femmes à la culture.*

49. Massip, "Michel Lambert," vol. 1, introduction.

50. Some of these dates listed in Goulet's bibliography are not indicated on the *Recueils* but were derived from the publication dates of airs contained therein; Goulet, *Poésie,* 763–65.

51. For the most comprehensive survey of poets of song texts, see Goulet, *Poésie,* 495–511. See also Gérold, *L'art du chant,* 133–37; and Génetiot, *Les genres,* who considers the works of Voiture, Sarasin, Scarron, and Charles Vion d'Alibray.

52. Gérold, *L'art du chant,* 134 and 166; Massip, "Michel Lambert," 1:175–76.

53. Génetiot, *Les genres,* 83.

54. In Auld, *The Lyric Art,* 2:27.

55. "Les Airs François . . . ne souffrent que des mots doux & coulans & des Expressions familieres." Bacilly, *Remarques*, 93, and *A Commentary*, 43. The influence of feminine taste on the transformation toward a more refined style of language is mentioned by Robert Ballard in the preface to Bacilly's *XXII. livre de chansons* of 1663.

56. Lougee, *Le Paradis des Femmes*, 35–38, and Génetiot, *Les genres*, 85–110, 171–91. For more information on the representation of love by salon members during this period, see Pelous, *Amour précieux*.

57. Poetry written in a female voice appears more frequently in the Ballard collections during the 1680s and 1690s. The only air in either the Lambert or Bacilly collections with a female poetic voice is "J'ay juré mille fois" from *Les Airs de Monsieur Lambert* (all editions), which is addressed to the shepherd Tyrcis.

58. Génetiot also distinguishes between the painful or serious and light or frivolous texts. He and Jean-Michel Pelous note that those texts concerning tender love (*amour tendre*) are serious; those concerning gallant love (*amour galant*) are "frivolous," to use Génetiot's term. By contrast, Winegarten does not distinguish between the two. She classifies both as *la poésie galante* (gallant poetry). She therefore differentiates between all genres of poetry as either *poésie galante* or *poésie sérieuse*. The highest genres of poetry were serious and included the ode, elegy, sonnet, eclogue, and *stance;* see Winegarten, *French Lyric Poetry*, 48ff and 104ff.

59. La Croix did not distinguish between tender and gallant love. By the 1690s, when his *L'Art de la poësie françoise et latine* was published, there was little difference between the two types of texts and the musical representations.

60. Génetiot's observations parallel my own. He labels "les souffrances de l'amant" (the lover's suffering) as part of "le code amoureux" (the code of love) and notes that this theme is common to other genres of poetry besides the *chansons* or song texts; Génetiot, *Les genres*, 93ff.

61. In the lyrics that follow, all punctuation marks are indicated exactly as found in the originals. In Lambert's collection, a comma appears at the end of the verse which concludes the first half of the poem, and a period appears at the end of the lyric. In the works by Bacilly, there are no punctuation marks except a period at the end of most texts. In airs by La Barre and Le Camus, both published by Ballard, punctuation marks abound. Commas appear within phrases, colons are used at the ends of the first half of the texts, and periods appear at the end. A double slash is used in translations to divide the first half of the air from the beginning of the second. Other aspects of the texts I cite remain true to the original, particularly spelling and capitalization, but I have spelled out any words that originally appeared in shorthand. For example, in "Mon sort est digne de pitié," the word "mon," line seven, appears as "mo" in the original. My translations are as literal as possible in order to preserve the original sense and order of the words. Even though the English translations lack poetic elegance, this kind of translation is necessary to maintain the proper alignment between portions of the text

and the musical setting to demonstrate the original correlation between text and musical meaning.

62. Génetiot and Pelous categorize the texts into two groups, as representing either "tender" or "gallant" love, and claim that the salon members themselves differentiated the texts in this way; Génetiot, *Les genres*, 85–87 and 106–10; Pelous, *Amour précieux*, 79–80 and 143–45. My categories fit their scheme: painful and bittersweet love are both representations of tender love, while enticing and joyous love are *galant*, My use of four categories instead of two, however, more accurately reflects the differences in the composers' approach to setting each type of song text.

63. "Utilise un nombre fini de lieux communs, de thèmes et de motifs qui emportent avec eux toujours les mêmes images et le même langage figuré et qui servent précisément à definir le 'genre amoureux,' genre sérieux par excellence." Génetiot, *Les genres*, 85.

64. Ibid., 88–96. As mentioned in the introduction, these song texts differ from earlier examples of the courtly love song. In seventeenth-century texts, the male poetic voice does not necessarily worship the woman but is insulted by her harsh treatment and indifference.

65. Ibid., 106; Pelous, *Amour précieux*, 145.

66. "Le discours galant rétablit l'équilibre entre les hommes et les femmes en refusant la tradition qui plaçait par avance l'amant aux pieds de sa dame." Génetiot, *Les genres*, 107.

67. Ibid., 97; Pelous, *Amour précieux*, 154–59.

68. Génetiot, *Les genres*, 97; Pelous, *Amour précieux*, 159.

69. "Sensibilité du cœur & de l'ame. La delicatesse du siecle a renfermé ce mot dans l'amour & dans l'amitié. Les amans ne parlent que de *tendresse* de cœur, soit en prose, soit en vers; & même ce mot signifie le plus souvent *amour;* & quand on dit, J'ay de la *tendresse* pour vous, c'est à dire, J'ay beaucoup d'amour." Furetière, *Dictionnaire universel*.

70. "Qu'elle [la qualité du mouvement] inspire dans les cœurs telle passion que le Chantre voudra faire naistre, principalement celle de la *Tendresse*." Bacilly, *Remarques*, 200, and *A Commentary*, 100.

71. "Le legereté donne au Chant, ce qui s'appelle le *tour galant;* mais la pesanteur donne la force aux Pieces serieuses, & qui demandent beaucoup d'expression." Bacilly, *Les Remarques*, 5, and *A Commentary*, 10. I have changed the word "style" in Caswell's translation to "tone" to better reflect the phrase "le *tour galant*." I believe that Bacilly is speaking here about the level of strength given to an expression and not to the style of a piece.

72. Poole, "The Sources," 35; Masson, "Les Brunettes," 349. In addition to the Italian and French pastorals, Génetiot gives other influences, including the *eclogues* and *bucolics* of Greek and Roman antiquity and works by Petrarch, Bembo, Marino, and other Neoplatonists in France. Génetiot, *Les genres*, 85–88.

73. This song text appears as track 17 in René Jacobs, *Airs de Cour*, compact disc, Harmonia Mundi, 'Musique d'abord' 1901079, 1981. The source of the song is not given in the program notes.

74. Ferrand, *A Treatise on Lovesickness*, 352.

75. La Croix, *L'Art de la poësie,* 138; Auld, *The Lyric Art,* 2:28–29.

76. Perrin wrote: "For the sake of brevity, and because serious matters easily become tiring, the *Air* is given only a second verse or a second stanza." In Auld, *The Lyric Art,* 2:29.

77. Bacilly laments, however, that "the entire poetic force is usually couched in the first verse so that the second is nothing but a restatement of the contents of the first" ("la force dans des Paroles estant d'ordinaire toute entiere sur le premier; & le second, n'estant qu'une redite foible de ce qui est dans le premier." Bacilly, *Remarques,* 213, and *A Commentary,* 106.

78. For more information about rhyme in lyric poetry, see Auld, *The Lyric Art,* 2:28, 104–11.

79. La Croix, *L'Art de la poësie,* 66.

80. Abraham, "Aperçu de la versification," 59; Guiraud, *La versification,* 34; Grammont, *Petit traité,* 35.

81. An exception is "aabb" (for a quatrain), because it does not demonstrate closure or a return to the original rhyme; Grammont, *Petit traité,* 78–80. For other types of rhymes, see La Croix, *L'Art de la poësie,* 51–70.

82. This is a type of *rime embrassée,* more frequently illustrated as "abba." Two rhymes in a row, "aa" or "bb," are called *rimes plates;* Grammont, *Petit traité,* 35; Guiraud, *La versification,* 34; and Abraham, "Aperçu de la versification," 59.

83. La Croix, *L'Art de la poësie,* 138.

84. Ibid., 327 and 328.

85. The longest air is La Barre's "Depuis quinze, jusqu'à trente" (*Airs à deux parties*), made up of three strophes and nineteen lines. Most airs, however, range from four to twelve or fourteen lines in length.

86. Auld, *The Lyric Art,* 2:96–99; and Génetiot, *Les genres,* 61–64.

87. "On doit entendre par les Chansons une espece de Vers irreguliers, qui ne sont propres qu'à chanter, à cause qu'ils ont un nombre de silabes diferents." La Croix, *L'Art de la poësie,* 133.

88. Abraham, "Aperçu de la versification," 55.

89. La Croix, *L'Art de la poësie,* 29–32.

90. "La cesure est un certain Repos, qui coupe ou separe le Vers en deux parties dont chacune s'apelle Hemistiche ou demi-vers." Ibid., 39.

91. Lamy, *The Art of Speaking,* IV.3.5–IV.3.4; cited in Harwood, *The Rhetorics,* 327–29.

92. Genre was an important factor in the determination of style; thus, the style of a poet should differ from that of a historian or orator; see Lamy, *The Art of Speaking,* IV.3.5; Harwood, *The Rhetorics,* 325–28.

93. "Des caracteres des agitations de l'ame, . . . ces figures sont . . . violens & propre à combattre & convaincre les esprits qui sont opposées de la verité." La Croix, *L'Art de la poësie,* 105.

94. Ibid., 105–106.

95. Lanham, *A Handlist,* 116.

96. Ibid. Lamy uses the word "figure" specifically to mean schemes; see Lamy, *The Art of Speaking,* II.2.3; Harwood, *The Rhetorics,* 224.

97. "Mon sort est digne de pitié" is treated at length in chapter 5. All musical examples serve as illustrations and are not for performance; see "Note on Quotations, Translations, and Musical Examples" at the beginning of this volume.

98. Lambert, "Que me sert-il," *Les Airs de Monsieur Lambert,* p. 44.

99. Lanham, *A Handlist,* 116.

100. Symptoms associated with the erotic melancholia include recklessness, immodesty, lust, inordinate desire, sorrow, fear, pain, and excessive display; Ferrand, *A Treatise on Lovesickness,* 226–27. Claims that extreme cases of lovesickness would lead to death if left untreated extend back to ancient literary and medical sources. Ovid, in his *Metamorphoses,* for example, wrote that Narcissus, who falls in love with himself, eventually dies: "Death closed the eyes that once had marveled at their owner's beauty." Quoted in the introduction to Ferrand, *A Treatise on Lovesickness,* 53.

101. See the analysis of "D'un feu secret" in chapter 7.

102. "The empire of love" can also be defined as the power or domination of love. See Furetière, *Dictionnaire de musique,* "Empire."

103. The use and significance of these and many other schemes and tropes will be addressed in conjunction with the musical settings in chapter 5.

104. Kibédi-Varga refers to the transference of rhetorical precepts to poetics, particularly regarding the three classifications of style, as the "rhetorization of poetics." Kibédi-Varga, *Les poétiques,* 14.

105. Lamy, *The Art of Speaking,* IV.2.1; Harwood, *The Rhetorics,* 312.

106. "Dignité de la matiere remplissant l'ame du Poëte . . . d'estime & d'admiration, son discours ne sauroit être égal, il doit être interrompu par les divers mouvemens, dont son esprit est agité." La Croix, *L'Art de la poësie,* 117.

107. Ibid.

108. Lamy, *The Art of Speaking,* IV.2.1; Harwood, *The Rhetorics,* 312; La Croix, *L'Art de la poësie,* 117.

109. Lamy, *The Art of Speaking,* IV.2.3; Harwood, *The Rhetorics,* 317.

110. In Auld, *The Lyric Art,* 2:27.

111. Ibid.

112. Perrin wrote: "I have maintained the sentence in its natural order, so that the mind would in no way have difficulty understanding it; and accordingly I have made its order correspond to the order to human thought and ordinary discourse." In Auld, *The Lyric Art,* 2:26.

113. La Croix, *L'Art de la poësie,* 72–73.

114. Lamy, *The Art of Speaking,* III.3.3; Harwood, *The Rhetorics,* 271.

115. "La poésie est aussi avant tout une seconde rhétorique, qui joint les ornemens du style et de la fable à propos dont le but premier est, comme toute pièce d'éloquence, d'avoir un effet sur l'auditeur, quand bien même il ne s'agirait que de lui plaire." Génetiot, *Poétique,* 274.

116. Ibid., 275.

2. Rhetoric and Meaning in the Seventeenth-Century French Air

1. The following summary of the Neoplatonic academies is based on Yates, *French Academies*, and Isherwood, *Music*, 1–54. See also Walker, "Musical Humanism," 1–13, 55–71, 111–21, 220–308, and Walker, "The Aims of Baïf's Académie."

2. Yates, *French Academies*, 80.

3. Ibid., 36.

4. Ibid., 21.

5. For more information concerning *musique mesurée*, see Durosoir, *L'air de Cour*, 15–74; Walker, "The Aims of Baïf's Académie," and "The Influence of *Musique mesurée*"; and Auld, "Text as Pre-Text."

6. Yates, *French Academies*, 36; Isherwood, *Music*, 29–33.

7. Yates, *French Academies*, 295–302; Desan, "The Worm," 26–30.

8. See Naudin, *Evolution*, 112–29. Naudin provides several reasons why seventeenth-century scholars, particularly those later in the century, no longer felt music was an important academic topic. The scientific discoveries of the seventeenth century destroyed the Pythagorean-Platonic theory of the harmony of the spheres; thus, music was no longer viewed as the symbol of the universe. Another reason was the absence of music from the curriculum in Jesuit institutions, where most scholars were educated. The *Ratio studiorum*, established in 1598, included five years of study devoted to classical languages, literature, and rhetoric. During the last two or three years (reserved for those entering the priesthood), students studied philosophy.

9. Cowart, "Inventing the Arts," 213; see also Auld, "Text as Pre-Text." I refer here particularly to the aesthetic function of the air and not that of opera.

10. Winegarten, *French Lyric Poetry*, 48–92, and Auld, "Text as Pre-Text," 55–68.

11. Naudin, *Evolution*, 120. Kibédi-Varga also notes the "relative discredit given to profane poetry" throughout the course of the seventeenth century; see *Les poétiques*, 12–13.

12. Fumaroli, *L'âge de l'éloquence*, 687.

13. Crampé, "De Arte Rhetorica," 260.

14. Carr, *Descartes*.

15. Scholars began to consider the aesthetic of music only after the appearance of the Lully-Quinault *tragédies en musique*, because they were perceived as a genre of tragedy; even so, the comments concerned primarily the libretti and not the music; Norman, "Ancients and Moderns," 179–82.

16. Desan, "The Worm," 26–30.

17. Bary, *La Rhétorique*, unpaginated preface. The identity of "Monsieur Le Grand" is not revealed in the treatise.

18. Ibid.

19. La Croix, *L'Art de la poësie*, 619–27. Isherwood gives several references to universal harmony found in the *Mercure galant* during the last half of the seventeenth century; see his *Music*, 37–40.

20. "Si essentiel, qu'on ne sauroit bien traiter de l'une séparément de l'autre." La Croix, *L'Art de la poësie,* 617.

21. "Le raport merveilleux qu'il y a entre la nombre & nôtre ame." Ibid., 652–58.

22. "La Musique vocale est une espece de langue, dont les hommes sont convenes, pour se communiquer avec plus de plaisir leurs pensées, & leurs sentimens." Grimarest, *Traité,* 195–96.

23. Ibid., 202 and 207.

24. Yates, *French Academies,* 295–302; Isherwood, *Music,* 1–3, 12, 30–37; and Walker, "Musical Humanism," 4. See also Vignes, "L'*Harmonie universelle.*"

25. Mersenne, *Questions harmoniques,* 15. "Elle est bien plus difficile que l'on se l'imagine & qu'il faut savoir toutes les autres sciences pour la comprendre parfaitement." Translated in Duncan, "Persuading the Affections," 162.

26. Walker, "Joan Albert Ban," 253. See also Isherwood, *Music,* 1–3, 12, 30–37.

27. "Ce qui aidera grandement à perfectionner toutes sortes de Chants, qui doivent en quelque façon imiter les Harangues, afin d'avoir des membres, des parties, & des periodes, & d'user de toutes sortes de figures & de passages harmoniques, comme l'Orateur, & que l'Art de composer des Airs, & le Contrepoint ne cede rien à la Rhetorique." Mersenne, "De la musique accentuelle," in *Harmonie universelle,* 1:365; translated in Duncan, "Persuading the Affections," 153.

28. Mersenne, *Traité,* 1:191; Duncan, "Persuading the Affections," 153.

29. Mersenne, "Des consonances," in *Harmonie universelle,* 4:106; Duncan, "Persuading the Affections," 153.

30. Mersenne, "De la composition," *Harmonie universelle,* 4:316; Duncan, "Persuading the Affections," 154.

31. Mace, "Marin Mersenne," 4–5.

32. Georgia Cowart provides a detailed explanation of the increasing importance given to musical sound over language in "Inventing the Arts."

33. An exception is Parran's *Traité* (1639), which included a Neoplatonic account of *musique universelle.* See also the collection of lute pieces by Gaultier, *La Rhétorique des dieux,* which includes a brief reference to *musique universelle.*

34. La Voye, for example, only mentions that musicians must subordinate themselves to the expression of the text; La Voye Mignot, *Traité,* 90. Masson also points out that music must be expressive of a text, but offers no more explanation; Masson, *Nouveau traité,* 27–28.

35. "J'avois plusieurs fois fait réflexion, que quoique nous ayons en nôtre langue assez de Traitez de Musique, nous n'en avons point qui entre dans une discussion des beautez de nôtre composition. Ce ne sont que des traitez de méchanique & d'artisan, si je puis parler ainsi: des Tratitez qui enseignent à sentir le cas qu'on doit faire des Piéces où les régles sont pratiquées: desquels aucun ne conduit les honnêtes gens à juger en gros du prix d'une simphonie & d'un air. Je concevois qu'il y auroit quelque mérite ou quelque gloire à donner

le premier des Traitez de ce genre-ci." Lecerf de la Viéville, *Comparaison,* 1:1–13; translated in Cowart, *The Origins,* 54. Lecerf's treatment of rhetoric and music is thoroughly investigated in Gibson, "*Le Naturel* and *L'Éloquence,*" wherein he deals extensively with "theories" of rhetoric and music on a philosophical level. He then analyzes select excerpts from Lully's operas.

36. Either the relationship was taken for granted, or, as Lorenzo Bianconi suggests, writers lacked a competent means of writing about music. See Bianconi, *Music,* 61–62.

37. Even though Saint-Lambert's treatise concerns harpsichord playing, he did not distinguish between vocal or instrumental music in the following comments. Gibson points out the significance of Saint-Lambert's statement—that an oration resembles more a piece of music—claiming that music had become the model for oratory, rather than the reverse. Several rhetoricians made the same observation. Fénelon observes that the action and voice in discourse are "a kind of music: all its beauty consists in the variety of tones, that rise or fall according to the things they must express." Cited in Gibson, "*Le Naturel* and *L'Éloquence,*" 319.

38. "Une pièce de Musique ressesmble à peu prés à une Pièce d'Eloquence, ou plûtot c'est la Pièce d'Eloquence qui ressemble à la Pièce de Musique: Car l'harmonie, le nombre, la mesure, & les autres choses semblables qu'un habile Orateur observe en la composition de ses Ouvrages, appartiennent bien plus naturellement à la Musique qu'à la Rhétorique." Saint-Lambert, *Les principes,* 14.

39. "Une Pièce d'Eloquence a son tout, qui est le plus souvent composée de plusieurs parties; Que chaque partie est composée de périodes, qui ont chacune un sens complet; Que ses périodes, qui ont chacune un sens complet; Que ses périodes sont composées de membres, les membres de mots, & les mots de lettres; De même le chant d'une Pièce de Musique a son tout, qui est toûjours composé de plusieurs reprises. Chaque reprise est composée de cadences, qui ont chacune leur sens complet, & qui sont les périodes du chant. Les cadences sont souvent composées de membres; les membres de mesures, & les mesures de notes. Ainsi, les notes répondent aux lettres, les mesures aux mots, les cadences aux périodes, les reprises aux parties, & le tout au tout." Ibid., 14.

40. "Sçavoir bien Chanter & bien Declamer tout à la fois." Bacilly, *Remarques,* 62–63, and *A Commentary,* 30.

41. "Mais s'il est question de reciter agreablement des Vers, les Chanter, mesme les declamer, il est certain qu'il y a des longues & des bréfves à observer, non seulement dans la Poësie, mais aussi dans la Prose." Bacilly, *Remarques,* 328–31, and *A Commentary,* 175–76. Bacilly also notes that although related, singing and declaiming are not entirely the same, specifying that "beyond the general rules of syllable-length there are specific rules that apply to vocal music" ("outre les observations des Regles generales de la Quantité, il y en a de particulieres pour le Chant").

42. Bianconi, *Music,* 83.

43. "La Théorie et la Pratique font bande à part et il semble meme que ce soit deux sciences touttes différentes." Étienne Loulié, Paris, Bibliothèque

nationale de France, N.a.fr. ms 6355, f. 251v (ca. 1700). Translated and quoted in Ranum, *Harmonic Orator*, xvii.

44. Bianconi, *Music*, 57–64.

45. In his treatise *The Passions of the Soul* (1649), Descartes asserts that although works of art may stimulate even the darkest and most violent of passions, we experience a sense of pleasure resulting from activities that do not harm us in any way; Descartes, *The Passions*, 362.

46. Kibédi-Varga, *Les poétiques*, 15; see also Naudin, *Evolution*, 147–48.

47. Bary, *Méthode*, prologue.

48. Bretteville, *L'Éloquence*, preface.

49. In his dissertation, Jonathan Gibson demonstrates convincingly that treatises on rhetoric and eloquence from later in the seventeenth century are more relevant than earlier treatises for our understanding of that period's musical aesthetic. The primary difference is that in later treatises, authors had moved away from a classically based Latin rhetoric to an emphasis upon *actio* and passionate expression. Gibson shows that "the stark differences between [René] Bary's two primary treatises (*Rhétorique* [1653] and *Méthode* [1679]) epitomize the changes taking place in French rhetorical practice between 1653 and 1679"; see Gibson, "*Le Naturel* and *L'Éloquence*," 14. Other transformations in the French approach to rhetoric and eloquence included an insistence upon a more "natural," unornamented approach to writing and discourse and a more flexible use of rhetorical principles (such as the ordering of materials) to suit the subject of the discourse and to serve in representing Truth. See also Wilbur Samuel Howell's introduction to his translation of Fénelon, *Dialogues on Eloquence*.

50. For Aristotle's treatment of the passions, see Aristotle, *Rhetoric*, 92–121.

51. Bretteville, *L'Éloquence*, 321–450; Bary, *Méthode*, 101–57; Grimarest, *Traité*, 119–55. See also Le Faucheur, *An Essay*, originally *Traité de l'action de l'orateur* (1657).

52. We will see in chapter 5 that rhetorical figures were minimally used by poets of song texts and that their musical equivalents—musical-rhetorical figures—were not used by French composers in the same way as by their German or Italian counterparts.

53. Lamy belonged to the Congregation of the Oratory of Jesus and was trained at Port Royal, a Jansenist organization opposed to Jesuit doctrine. He taught philosophy at the College of Anjou but was later stripped of his teaching position and moved to the Convent of Saint Martin de Misère near Grenoble because he openly promoted Cartesian principles. He was greatly influenced by Descartes, particularly Descartes' view of the passions and his physiological explanations for rhetorical effects, i.e., what happens in the body in response to various qualities of sound (published in Descartes, *The Passions* [*Les Passions*, 1649] and *Compendium musicae* [1618], respectively). Because Lamy's ties to Descartes were controversial, he published his first edition of *L'art de parler* outside of France. Harwood, *The Rhetorics*, 131–64.

54. Lamy's treatise *De L'art de parler* appeared anonymously in Paris in 1675. In 1688, the treatise was again revised and published as *La Rhétorique, ou l'art de parler*. *L'art de parler* was first translated into English (*The Art of Speaking*) in 1676.

55. Lamy, *The Art of Speaking*, V.I.I.; trans, in Harwood, *The Rhetorics*, 343. All material quoted from Lamy's treatise comes from the seventeenth-century English translation of *L'art de parler* included in Harwood, 165–377.

56. The following consideration of the figures is from Lamy, *The Art of Speaking*, II.3.2–3; quoted in Harwood, *The Rhetorics*, 227–40. See also Waite, "Bernard Lamy," 390–91.

57. Lamy, *The Art of Speaking*, II.3.3; Harwood, *The Rhetorics*, 361.

58. Lamy, *The Art of Speaking*, II.3.1; Harwood, *The Rhetorics*, 361.

59. Descartes, *Compendium musicae*, 11–13. For an account of Lamy's interpretation of Descartes, see Waite, "Bernard Lamy."

60. Lamy, *The Art of Speaking*, III.2.7; Harwood, *The Rhetorics*, 266; and Waite, "Bernard Lamy," 392.

61. "Pour rendre le Son agreable & donner ainsi l'art de plaire par le dis-cours ou par la Musique, on doit observer sept choses, comme autant de Regles." La Croix, *L'Art de la poësie françoise*, 645–46.

62. Ibid., 652. See Lamy, *The Art of Speaking*, III.5.1; Harwood, *The Rhetorics*, 291. For a brief explanation of numbers according to Plato, Pythagorus, and Saint Augustine, see Isherwood, *Music*, 5–7 and 13–14.

63. Lamy, *The Art of Speaking*, III.4–7; Harwood, *The Rhetorics*, 289–90.

64. La Croix, *L'Art de la poësie*, 102–105; Lamy, *The Art of Speaking*, III.5.2–4; Harwood, *The Rhetorics*, 291–302.

65. "On apelle nombre, dans l'Art de parler et de chanter, tout ce que les oreilles aperçoivent de proportionné . . . soit suivant la proportion des mesures du tems, soit selon une juste distribution des intervalles de la respi-ration." La Croix, *L'Art de la poësie*, 652–53.

66. "L'Accent . . . est une inflexion ou modification de la voix, ou de la parole, par laquelle l'on exprime les passions & les affections naturellement, ou par artifice." Mersenne, "L'Art de Bien Chanter," in *Harmonie univer-selle*, 1:366. For a consideration of *nombre* and *accens*, see Mace, "Marin Mersenne," 15–21.

67. Mersenne, "L'Art de Bien Chanter," in *Harmonie universelle*, 1:366–76; considered in Mace, "Marin Mersenne," 15–21. Furetière defines *accent* in music as "an inflection or modification of the voice, or of the word, for expressing passions and affections, either naturally or by artifice" ("l'accent en musique est une inflexion ou modification de la voix, ou de la paroles, pour exprimer les passions & les affections, soit naturellement, soit par arti-fice"). *Nombre* in music, in poetry, and in rhetoric was defined as "certain measures, proportions or cadences which render an air, a verse, [or] a period agreeable to the ear. There is a certain *nombre* which renders periods harmo-nious" ("Nombre, en musique, en poesie, en Rhetorique, se dit de certaines mesures, proportions ou cadences qui rendent agreable à l'oreilles un air, un

vers, une periode. Il y a un certain nombre qui rend les periodes har-
monieuses"). Furetière, *Dictionnaire de musique.*

68. Lamy, *The Art of Speaking,* III.5.1–3; Harwood, *The Rhetorics,*
291–302; and La Croix, *L'Art de la poësie,* 71–74. For more information on
rhythmic movement in French poetry, see Pineau, *Le mouvement rythmique.*

69. "Qu'il s'agit de rendre les nombres conformes aux choses qu'on
exprime, pour exciter avec succés les mouvements que l'on veut, & c'est le
moien de reüssir dans toutes les parties de la Musique, & dans l'Art de plaire
& persuader." La Croix, *L'Art de la poësie,* 658; Lamy, *The Art of Speaking,*
III.5.2; Harwood, *The Rhetorics,* 293.

70. Mersenne's statement here is reiterated by rhetoricians as well. René
Rapin, for example, writes that "'tis not enough for a preacher to say great
truths, but he must say them well and heartily, and with an air of decent passion and concern." Rapin, *Les Réflexions,* 75; quoted in Gibson, "*Le Naturel*
and *L'Éloquence,*" 107.

71. "Ce qui arrive particulierement lors que le Compositeur est luy
mesme frappé du sentiment qu'il desire imprimer dans l'esprit de ses auditeurs . . . comme il arrive que l'orateur a plus de puissance sur son audience,
quand il se sent esmeu & entièrement persuadé des ses raisons." Mersenne,
"Embellissement des chants," *Harmonie universelle,* 1:363; in Duncan,
"Persuading the Affections," 154.

72. "Il faut considerer la lettre toute entière, & le dessein ou l'intention
de ce qu'elle contient . . . qu'estant chantée elle ait du moins autant de force
sur les auditeurs, comme si elle estoit recitée par un excellent Orateur."
Mersenne, "Embellissement des chants," *Harmonie universelle,* 1:363;
Duncan, "Persuading the Affections," 154.

73. Lamy, *The Art of Speaking,* V.3.2; Harwood, *The Rhetorics,* 364.

74. Lamy, *The Art of Speaking,* V.3.2; Harwood, *The Rhetorics,* 364.

75. Lamy, *The Art of Speaking,* V.3.2; Harwood, *The Rhetorics,* 364.
Lamy derives this notion of accessory meaning specifically from the Port
Royalists Antoine Arnauld and Piere Nicole; see Carr, *Descartes,* 71.

76. Lamy, *The Art of Speaking,* I.3.3; Harwood, *The Rhetorics,* 201.

77. Quoted in Walker, "Joan Albert Ban," 253. Walker includes only the
English translation, not the original French.

78. Bacilly, *Remarques curieuses,* 200, and *A Commentary,* 100. Bacilly
adds that by matching the expressive content of the text, one discovers the
correct *mouvement* as a certain quality which gives a soul to a song.

79. "L'Expression du Chant pour répondre à celles des paroles, dépend
de l'invention & du juste discernement du compositeur; Cette expression
étant soûtenuë & prefectionnée par une judicieuse diversité du mouvement
de la mesure, a la force & la vertu de faire passer l'ame d'une passion à une
autre; ce qui est une preuve naturelle de la perfection d'un Ouvrage."
Masson, *Nouveau traité,* 28.

80. Mersenne, *Traité de l'harmonie universelle,* 189–90; Duncan,
"Persuading the Affections," 153. Masson also insists that composers pay
attention to the punctuation of the text; see his *Nouveau traité,* 26. La Voye
Mignot, in his *Traité de musique* of 1666, directs that "one never pause in

the middle of a word, nor even in the middle of a complete thought; . . . the pauses in music are the periods and the commas in an oration and discourse" ("Il est à mesme hors d'un sens parfait; . . . les pauses soient dans la Musique ce que sont les points & les virgules dans l'oraison & dans le discours." La Voye Mignot, *Traité de musique,* 8.

81. Mersenne, *Traité de l'harmonie universelle,* 191; Duncan, "Persuading the Affections," 153.

82. Bacilly, *Remarques curieuses,* 185, 201–203, and 310, and *A Commentary,* 94, 101–102, and 162. This was a technique that Bacilly referred to as *gronder,* or "growling," the consonances (see chapter 6).

83. "La première raison est pour faire entendre toute la dureté & pour donner par là une expression triste & lugubre à la Chant, soit qu'il ait des paroles, soit qu'il n'en ait point. La seconde raison est pour contribuer à la beauté de Chant, en ajoûtant une note qui en fait l'ornement, & qui luy donne de l'agrément." Masson, *Nouveau traité,* 59.

84. Grimarest makes the same observation thirty-nine years later: "I think I should warn the composer not to strive, from affection, to make his music convey the meaning of a word. There is not a rule that decrees melismas on words such as *coulez* [flow], *volez* [fly], or held notes on words such as *éternelle* [eternal], *repos* [repose]. The words alone . . . do not express a sentiment, but the Expression as a whole does, and these musical diversions alter the passion and are more revealing of the musician than of the witty man." Quoted and translated in Gibson, "*Le Naturel* and *L'Éloquence,*" 76.

85. "Il en est d'autres qui croyent qu'un Chant est mal appliqué aux Paroles, s'il n'exprime le sens de chaque mot en particulier, & mesme qui pretendent qu'il y a des marques de Musique qui sont précisément affectuées pour la signification, & pour l'expression tendres & passionnées; de sorte qu'ils n'hesitent point à traiter d'ignorant un Compositeur qui aura manqué à mettre une de ces marques sur les mots de 'langueur, martyre, pleurer, gemir . . . ' ou tout au contraire s'il a mis les marques de Dioses & du b mol, sur des mots qui ne signifient rien de passionné." Bacilly, *Remarques curieuses,* 121–22, and *A Commentary,* 54–55. It should be noted that there are exceptions to this rule. We find that when composers set second strophes, in particular, they did employ word or text painting. See chapter 5 for examples.

86. Bacilly, *Remarques curieuses,* 121–22, and *A Commentary,* 54–55.

87. Walker, "Joan Albert Ban." See also Pirro, *Descartes,* and Anthony, *French Baroque Music,* 352–53.

88. As one might imagine, national pride had a lot to do with the outcome of the competition. Ban was a foreigner, representing the Italian approach to composition, which the French believed was inferior to their own methods. Pirro, *Descartes,* 93, 96–102, 112–20.

89. Walker, "Joan Albert Ban," 249.

90. Ibid. Even though the air begins in duple meter, the meter actually changes from duple to triple throughout the piece (from two whole notes per measure to three halves). Descartes refers to a point in the air where the meter changes to six half notes per measure from an alternation of two

whole notes and three halves per measure. The analysis of the repertory in the following chapters does indeed show that a change to triple meter (six half notes per measure) from duple (two whole notes per measure) indicates a change to a more agitated affect.

91. Lamy also devotes a portion of his treatise to the customary use of language; see Lamy, *The Art of Speaking*, II.4.2; Harwood, *The Rhetorics*, 205.

92. "Sçavoir si c'est sans raison, ou avec fondement que cela se pratique, c'est ce qui n'est pas encore decidé; & comme il semble que c'est une rigueur trop grande que cette exclusion de ces sortes de termes & d'expressions, qui hors la Chanson sont non seulement bonnes, mais qui sont mesme souvent de grand poids & de grande consideration dans la Poësie. . . . Il faut donc en cela suivre l'usage present, jusques à ce que la suite du temps en ait autrement ordonné." Bacilly, *Remarques curieuses*, 94, and *A Commentary*, 43.

93. Bacilly, *Remarques curieuses*, 95, and *A Commentary*, 44.

94. "Comment donc le Musicien peut-il s'empescher d'employer souvent des mesmes Nottes, lors qu'une fois il les a appliquées aux Paroles avec tant de succez, qu'il semble que l'on ne pouvoit presque pas faire autrement?" Bacilly, *Remarques curieuses*, 103, and *A Commentary*, 47.

95. Bacilly, *Remarques curieuses*, 103, and *A Commentary*, 47.

96. "Un Air ne doit pas estre censuré, pour estre de Pieces Rapportées . . . emprunté des autres Airs; car outre qu'on ne peut rien dire qui n'ait esté dit, & que toute la Musique ne roule que sur six ou sept Nottes, on croit souvent un Chant emprunté, qui ne l'est point dans l'intention de l'Autheur . . . que quand mesme cela seroit, il vaut souvent mieux copier sur ce qui est bon, que de vouloir mal à propos faire l'Original & l'Inventeur." Bacilly, *Remarques curieuses*, 108–109, and *A Commentary*, 49.

97. This was a subject that greatly interested Mersenne. Particularly in his correspondence with Descartes, he reveals his search for a means of scientifically or mathematically determining a hierarchy of beauty among the consonances. Descartes' response is that what is agreeable in music cannot be determined by math or science because, unlike math and science, these sorts of judgments are subjective. An assessment of music is not a matter for reason but for taste. It is not based on the intellect but in the temperament of individuals and nations. See Mace, "Marin Mersenne," 8–10; Pirro, *Descartes*, 96.

98. Walker, "Joan Albert Ban," 254.

99. "Les exemples qu'on peut voir dans les bons Autheurs feront connoître la pratique de ces regles." Masson, *Nouveau traité*, 27.

3. Musical Representations of the Primary Passions

1. "Diferens airs, suivant le caractere de Vers." La Croix, *L'Art de la poësie*, 290.

2. "L'Expression du Chant pour répondre à celles des paroles, dépend de l'invention & du juste discernement du compositeur; Cette expression étant soûtenuë & perfectionnée par une judicieuse diversité du mouvement

de la mesure, a la force & la vertu de faire passer l'ame d'une passion à une autre; ce qui est une preuve naturelle de la perfection d'un Ouvrage." Masson, *Nouveau traité*, 28.

   3. In Auld, *The Lyric Art*, 2:25–26.

   4. Ibid., 2:26.

   5. Ferrand, *A Treatise on Lovesickness*, 53.

   6. Forests solitaires & sombres, / Sejour du silence & des ombres, / Lieux affreux steriles desert: / Aprenez le sujet de mon douleur mortelle. // Helas! je suis trahy de celle que je sers, /Mon Iris est une infidelle. La Barre, "Forests solitaires et sombres," *Airs à deux parties,* 3v.

   7. Buelow, "The *Loci Topici*," 162.

   8. Ibid., 163.

   9. In the introduction to Chaïm Perelman's *The Realm of Rhetoric,* Carroll Arnold refers to Perelman's use of the term "liaison" as that which "connotes a joining, a conjunction, a connection, an acquaintance." In Perelman, *The Realm of Rhetoric,* xiv–xv.

   10. Mersenne identifies several passions appropriate for representation in music, such as love, hate, sadness, desire, joy, hope, audacity, boldness, anger, fear, and despair; see Duncan, "Persuading the Affections," 161.

   11. This concept was recognized by several theorists writing about music. A pertinent quote by Bacilly was given in chapter 2. Mersenne also underscores this point within the context of his criticism of Ban's setting of the air "Me veux-tu voir mourir": "One must not regard each diction [word] in order to give it the accent or the passionate movement. Because one must first see what the entire subject of the discourse within the air aims toward, and then what each period contains" ("Ce n'est pas à chaque diction qu'il faut avoir esgard, pour luy donner l'accent ou le mouvement de passion. Car il faut premièrement voir à quoy butte tout le sujet du discours compris dans l'air, et puis ce que contient chaque période"). Quoted in Pirro, *Descartes,* 117. Grimarest also asserts that "terms alone do not express sentiment; but the entire expression, and its musical diversions alter the passion" ("Les termes seuls, . . . n'expriment point un sentiment; mais l'expression entiere, & ces divertissemens de musique alterent la passion." Grimarest, *Traité,* 210.

   12. We shall see that in some cases the affective representation of a word receives isolated treatment, particularly in the musical settings of certain words in second strophes, to be considered in chapter 5.

   13. These four rhetoricians provide information on the passions that is most applicable to considerations of music.

   14. Although the goal of oratory was not always to move auditors to take some action, it is the one goal that is most often associated with discourse. Many seventeenth-century rhetoricians were influenced by Saint Augustine's contention that "just as the listener is to be delighted if he is to be retained as a listener, so also is he to be persuaded if he is to be moved to act." Saint Augustine, *On Christian Doctrine,* 136–37.

   15. Descartes' book *The Passions of the Soul* (1649) was widely influential in the seventeenth and eighteenth centuries. Early in his life, Descartes theorized about music in *Compendium musicae* (1618) and in the letters he

wrote about music, primarily to Mersenne and Huyghens. He specifically influenced two authors of sources used in this study: Bernard Lamy and Phérotée de La Croix.

16. Descartes, *The Passions,* 349.

17. Ibid.

18. Bretteville describes twelve passions (love, friendship, hate, desire, hope, despair, boldness, fear, anger, compassion, envy, and sadness); Bary, eleven (love, sorrow, pity, emulation, indignation, envy, hope, shame, anger, fear, and boldness); and Grimarest, fourteen (love, hate, desire, flight [*fuite*], joy, sadness, hope, despair, fear, envy, jealousy, indignation, compassion, and anger).

19. Descartes considers each of these (and many of the other passions that Bretteville, Bary, Le Faucheur, and Grimarest treated) in *The Passions,* part 3, "Specific Passions."

20. Descartes, *The Passions,* 361.

21. Ibid., 360–61.

22. Ibid., 362.

23. Ibid., 381.

24. Descartes, *Compendium musicae,* 11.

25. Duncan, "Persuading the Affections," 160–61, a paraphrase from Mersenne's "De la voix," in *Harmonie universelle,* 1:81.

26. Bretteville, *L'Éloquence,* 321.

27. In 1704, Viéville specifically identified music as an imitation of poetry; that is, an imitation once removed (an imitation of an imitation of nature). Lecerf de la Viéville, *Comparaison,* 1:168–69.

28. Descartes, *Compendium musicae,* 11.

29. I use the word "primarily" because strength of voice requires not only strong harmonies but rhythmic accents as well. Accordingly, rate of speech is not only accomplished by rhythmic means but by the rate of harmonic movement; thus, it is a combination of devices that conforms to the desired tones of the voice.

30. Descartes, *The Passions,* 363.

31. Ibid., 363, 365, 367.

32. "Le desespoir . . . est un mouvement violent & impetueux par lequel l'ame s'éloigne d'un bien qu'elle ne peut posseder, après l'avoir recherché avec ardeur." Bretteville, *L'Éloquence,* 381.

33. Grimarest, *Traité,* 144.

34. Descartes, *Compendium musicae,* 11 and 44.

35. "Des mouvements pesans et tardifs des airs tristes, qui représentent une vie interrompue et mourant." Mersenne, "Les Chants," in *Harmonie universelle,* 1:172; quoted in Pirro, *Descartes,* 93. Here Mersenne was comparing "gay" songs, particularly dances, with sad airs. It should be noted that those writers who considered affect and music contrast only happy and sad sentiments as separate poles of expression. I have found that many devices associated with happy expressions were also used for agitated expressions, except in reference to tempo. Faster tempos, which were considered appropriate for happy songs (Descartes, *Compendium musicae,* 15), would

not have been appropriate for serious airs wherein one finds reference to the agitated passions.

36. These musical features are identified as "strong" by many seventeenth-century music theorists; see Rivera, "The Seventeenth-Century Theory of Triadic Generation."

37. In the following analyses, airs are identified by mode rather than key. For more information concerning modality and tonality during the seventeenth century, see Tolkoff, "French Modal Theory"; Schulenberg, "Composition before Rameau"; and Atcherson, "Key and Mode." Even though the pieces under consideration are essentially modal, the number of modes actually in use was small. This was typical of works written at this time and was supported by such theorists as Mersenne, Denis (*Traité*, 1650), and Nivers (*Traité*, 1667). Most of the pieces in the four collections under consideration are either in the natural Dorian mode on D, transposed Dorian mode on G (transposed because there is a B♭ in the "key signature" and the emphasis is on the dominant D instead of B♭), natural Ionian on C, and transposed Ionian on F (transposed because there is a B♭ in the "signature" and C is stressed as the dominant instead of A), and occasionally transposed Lydian on B♭. I refer to these as minor mode on D or G and major mode on C or F, respectively.

38. Seventeenth-century theorists state that second-inversion chords are weaker than root-position chords. Henrius Baryphonus, in his *Pleiades musicae* (1630), notes that "when the third or fifth of the triad usurps the place of the basis, the sonority turns languid." Quoted and translated in Rivera, "The Seventeenth-Century Theory of Triadic Generation," 67 and 76.

39. Minor modes (in which the chord on the final tone contains a minor third) were considered less forceful and thus appropriate for sad affects, while the major modes were considered more forceful and appropriate for either joyful and vehement or agitated affects. Pirro, *Descartes*, 95 and 115; and Walker, "Joan Albert Ban," 240–249. One note: even though chord relationships like V–I or V–i are more typically tonal than modal, for clarity, I will use terms proper to tonality (i.e., dominant to tonic) from here on to describe them.

40. La Croix, *L'Art de la poësie*, 102–105; Lamy, *The Art of Speaking*, III.5.1–3; Harwood, *The Rhetorics*, 291–302.

41. Descartes, *Compendium musicae*, 11 and 44.

42. Ibid., 24.

43. Descartes, *The Passions*, 391.

44. Bretteville, *L'Éloquence*, 389ff.; and Grimarest, *Traité*, 145.

45. Descartes, *The Passions*, 389.

46. "La Hardiesse est un mouvement de l'ame, qui l'assure à la veue du peril, & qui fait qu'elle s'élance contre le mal, pour le combattre, & pour le vaincre." Bretteville, *L'Éloquence*, 389.

47. Grimarest, *Traité*, 145.

48. Le Faucheur, *An Essay*, 80.

49. Cohen, "'La Supposition' and the Changing Concept of Dissonance."

50. Pirro, *Descartes,* 119; Duncan, "Persuading the Affections," 155.

51. Descartes, *Compendium musicae,* 24.

52. Genétiot, *Les genres,* 93–96.

53. Rasmussen, "Viols, Violists and Venus in Grunewald's Isenheim Altar." Rasmussen also points out that in paintings from the sixteenth century, Venus was often accompanied by images grouped into threes, particularly three musicians. It is not certain if this practice continued into the seventeenth century.

54. Several theorists perceived a difference between the major and minor third, major being strong and minor being weak. Keppler, for example, describes minor thirds as "feminine and mournful" and major thirds as "viril and vehement" (quoted in Pirro, *Descartes,* 95). Indeed, Mersenne quotes Keppler in his *Harmonie universelle,* "Les Genres," regarding the difference between major and minor thirds; see Walker, "Joan Albert Ban," 248–49.

55. The figures are often incomplete (and even incorrect) in these editions, so the accompanist has some latitude.

56. Descartes, *The Passions,* 360.

57. Ibid.

58. Ibid.

59. Ibid., 373.

60. Bretteville, *L'Éloquence,* 471.

61. Grimarest, *Traité,* 142; Le Faucheur, *An Essay,* 79; Bary, *La Rhétorique,* 101.

62. Descartes, *The Passions,* 375. According to Descartes, this is caused by lungs, which are swollen by the abundance of the blood that enters them. The air they contained is thus expelled. As the air rushes out through the windpipe, it produces the groans and cries that accompany weeping. As explained above, sighs are produced when the lungs are partially empty and are associated with milder forms of sadness.

63. In their assessment of Boësset's "Me veux-tu voir mourir," the judges in the competition between Joan Albert Ban and Antoine Boësset (see chapter 2) agreed that falling intervals are appropriate for weakness and expressions of sorrow. See Walker, "Joan Albert Ban," 248.

64. Mersenne, *Harmonie universelle,* 2:172; Pirro, *Descartes,* 93.

65. Neither Bretteville, Grimarest, nor Descartes distinguishes languor from sadness.

66. See Lambert's air "Mon cœur qui se rend à vos coups" (Example 4.5), mm. 1–4, for a representation of languor on the words "my heart which surrenders to your blows," even though this passion is not identified in the phrase.

67. See also Bacilly's setting of "Au secours ma raison" (Example 4.8), mm. 9–13, on "And gives in to the laws of its victor."

68. I use the word "tender" here not to designate the *tendre* genre of airs, which includes all the passions associated with love, as explained in chapter 1, but to mean "sweet."

69. Descartes, *The Passions,* 375.

70. Bretteville, *L'Éloquence,* 471; Grimarest, *Traité,* 135–36; Le Faucheur, *An Essay,* 79.

71. Translated in Reilly, "Georg Andreas Sorge's *Vorgemach der musicalischen Composition,*" 179–80; cited in McClary, *Feminine Endings,* 11.

72. Walker, "Joan Albert Ban," 245; Pirro, *Descartes,* 117.

73. See, for example, La Barre's air in "Un feu naissant vient d'enflamer" on "A sweet languor" (*Airs à deux parties,* 17v), and Le Camus' "Parmi le verd naissant" on the phrase "all it [the new season] has for me that is tender and sweet" (*Airs à deux et trois parties,* 25).

74. Descartes, *The Passions,* 360, 363, and 365.

75. Ibid., 365.

76. Le Faucheur, *An Essay,* 79

77. Mersenne and Descartes characterize joyous airs as using major mode, frequent major thirds, and equal and perpetual movement; Pirro, *Descartes,* 93 and 96. The use of major harmonies in the major modes, as in cheerful airs, has a different effect than the use of major harmonies in the minor modes, as in serious airs.

4. Setting the Texts

1. "Il faut . . . voir à quoy butte tout le sujet de discours compris dans l'air." Pirro, *Descartes,* 117.

2. Descartes, *The Passions,* 343–47. Charles Le Brun, who was influenced by Descartes' theories of the passions, incorporates the three-step emotive process (object–passion–action) into his explanation of "expression"; see Le Brun, *A Method.* See also Van Wymeersch, *Descartes.*

3. Descartes, *The Passions,* 343.

4. Ibid.

5. Descartes implies these three assertions in the following statements: (1) a husband who mourns the loss of his wife may feel sadness, but also may feel "remnants of love or of pity . . . [and] at the same time a secret joy" (this is what Descartes calls an internal passion, as distinct from those passions "which always depend on some movement of the spirits"); (2) only extreme joy may cause fainting, or only a mild feeling of sadness when mixed with love can produce tears; and (3) regret is a kind of sadness "joined . . . to the memory of a pleasure that gave us joy." *The Passions,* 381, 371, 374, and 402; see also Le Brun, *A Method,* preface.

6. Descartes, *The Passions,* 402.

7. Lamy, *The Art of Speaking,* IV.2.1; Harwood, *The Rhetorics,* 312.

8. La Croix, *L'Art de la poësie,* 117.

9. Duncan, "Persuading the Affections," 160.

10. Descartes, *The Passions,* 391.

11. The second couplet, or *double,* of "Mon ame fasions un effort" will be considered in chapter 5. I consider only the first strophe here because composers wrote music to accommodate the first strophe and not the second; thus, there is a special relation between musical devices chosen in association with the first strophe of the text that does not necessarily exist for the second.

12. Rosand, "The Descending Tetrachord"; and Rosand, "Lamento."

13. Rosand, "The Descending Tetrachord," 349 and 357.

14. Although Bacilly makes it clear that airs are songs in "free meter" (Bacilly, *Remarques,* 108, and *A Commentary,* 49), the proportional relationship of changing meters in the air has not been fully explored by scholars. Metrical change, however, is considered in various articles on French operatic recitatives. Lois Rosow asserts that the placement of bar lines was to accommodate the accents at the hemistich and end rhyme, unless the meaning of the phrase warranted otherwise. She then suggests that the performance of the recitative was meant to be free, with little or no consideration of proportion between the changing meters. Rosow, "French Baroque Recitative," 471–472; see also Wolf, "Metrical Relationships."

15. Bacilly, *Remarques,* 108, and *A Commentary,* 49.

16. Rosow, "French Baroque Recitative," 469 and 472. See also Massip, "Michel Lambert," 1:31–39.

17. In his treatise, Bacilly clearly asserts that strong syllables are to be stressed no matter where they fall in the measure. Although all monosyllablic words ending with an "s" are long, monosyllabic words that end with a combination of consonants, such as "mps," are even longer. Bacilly, *Remarques,* 331–32 and 356–68 and *A Commentary,* 176–77 and 188–91.

18. Normally "de" is a short monosyllable but according to the principle of symmetry, in the phrase "de la mort," "de" is made long and "la" short, because "mort" must be long. See chapter 6.

19. Buelow, "Rhetoric and Music," 796.

20. Descartes, *The Passions,* 402.

21. Resignation to one's fate was endorsed by Descartes as a valid action. In his evaluation of Boësset's air, "Me veux-tu voir mourir," Descartes notes that most of the text concerns "submission on the part of the lover to his cold mistress . . . a resigned acceptance of death." He then noted that in the last few verses, the speaker's resignation turned to a "hope of posthumous revenge for this suffering." Walker, "Joan Albert Ban," 249.

22. Bary, *La Rhétorique,* 101.

23. Descartes, *The Passions,* 402.

24. The interpretation of bass line figures is considered in chapter 5.

25. Walker notes that Mersenne, Joan Albert Ban, Descartes, and the judges of the musical competition of 1640 all agreed that leaps were associated with more agitated passions. Walker, "Joan Albert Ban," 239–40.

26. Mersenne indicates that minor mode is generally more appropriate for expressions of sadness and major mode for joy, but he also notes that major mode is used for "masculine and courageous acts" ("Les actions masles & courageuses," cited in Duncan, "Persuading the Affections," 156), as revealed in the air "Mon ame faisons un effort."

27. In his assessment of the Boësset air at the 1640 competition, Descartes notes that significant words within a text were given a "similar musical identity" in order to connect them textually and musically. Walker, "Joan Albert Ban," 250.

28. Both Bretteville and Descartes agree that anger incites revenge. Descartes, *The Passions,* 399; and Bretteville, *L'Éloquence,* 416.

29. Descartes, *The Passions,* 399.

30. Ibid.

31. "La colere est un mouvement turbulent de l'Ame, par lequel elle s'éleve contre la cause du mal & de l'injure qu'elle ressent, avec un desir violent de s'en vanger." Bretteville, *L'Éloquence,* 416.

32. Ibid., 471.

33. Bary, *La Rhétorique,* 101; Grimarest, *Traité,* 154.

34. In the musical competition of 1640, Ban had interpreted the text as vengeful, so he chose Lydian mode for his setting of the piece. The differences of opinion between Ban and the judges concerning the setting of "Me veux-tu voir mourir" had to do with Ban's affective interpretation. The French interpreted the text as pathetic, not indignant; thus, Boësset's choice of Dorian mode was more appropriate than Lydian. Walker, "Joan Albert Ban," 245.

35. Quoted and translated in Walker, "Joan Albert Ban," 245; also quoted in Pirro, *Descartes,* 117.

36. Descartes identifies these same actions and passions in "Me veux-tu voir mourir" and notes that the change to revenge takes place at the end of the piece. Walker, "Joan Albert Ban," 249.

37. Joan Albert Ban associated the use of wide intervals with "violent or vehement affects," while Mersenne associated iambs and anapests with angry expressions. Walker, "Joan Albert Ban," 238; Mersenne, "Les chants," *Harmonie universelle,* 1:99; Duncan, "Persuading the Affections," 158.

38. Descartes, *The Passions,* 399.

39. These two verses are repeated at the end of the second strophe. German theorists refer to the repetition of a closing section at the end of another section as *epistrophe;* see Buelow, "Rhetoric and Music," 795.

40. Mersenne, *Harmonie universelle,* "Embellissement des chants," 1:371; Duncan, "Persuading the Affections," 155. In his *Réflexions critiques,* Abbé Jean-Baptiste Dubos describes the singer Champmeslé's style of theatrical declamation, as taught to her by Racine, and notes that she raised her voice an octave higher on the words "Seigneur, vous changez de visage" from where she had ended the previous phrase "Nous nous aimions" "for showing Monime's confused thoughts in the instant when she realized that her easy trust of Mithridate . . . had just put her and her lover into extreme danger." Quoted and translated in Rosow, "French Baroque Recitative," 473. Rosow explains that Lully imitated this effect in his recitative. My analysis shows, however, that it was already used quite effectively in the certain airs several years before the performance of Lully's first opera.

41. The German theorist Athanasius Kircher identifies the *antitheton* as a kind of musical figure that contrasts one musical idea with another in order to express opposites that occur successively or simultaneously. Buelow, "Rhetoric and Music," 798.

42. Charles Masson claims that in lighter airs, dissonance adds to the beauty of the melody, making it all the more agreeable. Masson, *Nouveau*

traité, 59; see also Cohen, "'La Supposition' and the Changing Concept of Dissonance."

43. Another air belonging to this category of enticing love is Le Camus' "Parmi le verd naissant," in which happy and tender tones dominate. There is only one expression of sorrow, in mm. 16–21, as the lover appeals to the shepherdess to pity him: "But, shepherdess, I feel that such a beautiful season would not please me without you."

5. Form and Style

1. Lamy, *The Art of Speaking,* V.II; Harwood, *The Rhetorics,* 343.
2. Ibid.
3. Mersenne, "Des consonances," *Harmonie universelle,* 1:106; Duncan, "Persuading the Affections," 153.
4. Aristotle, *Rhetoric,* 199 (Book III.13.1414a.30ff.).
5. Lanham, *A Handlist,* 106–107; Corbett, *Classical Rhetoric,* 23.
6. Fénelon, *Dialogues,* 61.
7. According to Lamy, the narration and proposition were the same; both set forth the "thing of which we speak." Lamy, *The Art of Speaking,* V.4.1; Harwood, *The Rhetorics,* 370. In most songs, however, there seems to be a difference between stating the facts of the situation described in the song (the narration) and what is to be proven or amplified upon in the remaining sections of the piece (the proposition).
8. The German theorist Christophe Bernhard referred to this sort of musical device as *abruptio.* It is a general pause or silence where it is not expected. Buelow, "Rhetoric and Music," 798.
9. For original text in French, see Examples 5.3–4.
10. Descartes, *The Passions,* 402.
11. For original text in French, see Example 5.5.
12. Lamy, *The Art of Speaking,* V.4.1; Harwood, *The Rhetorics,* 371.
13. "L'Exorde doit être prononcé d'une voix mediocre, grave, & modeste." Bretteville, *L'Éloquence,* 480. The combination of introduction and narration does not contradict what is required in an introduction. Bretteville notes that "the narration must be pronounced according to the nature and quality of the actions and the events about which one recites," which in these airs *is* the introduction ("La narration se doit prononcer selon la nature & la qualité des actions & des évenemens dont on fait le recit"; Bretteville, *L'Éloquence,* 482).
14. Lamy, *The Art of Speaking,* V.4.1; Harwood, *The Rhetorics,* 370.
15. "Il faut excepter de cette regle certains Exordes qui se sont par quelque mouvement prompt . . . & qui se doivent prononcer selon la passion qui y domine." Bretteville, *L'Éloquence,* 481.
16. Lamy, *The Art of Speaking,* V.4.1; Harwood, *The Rhetorics,* 371. Bretteville did not include the proposition in his consideration of the passions that accompany the parts of a discourse.
17. "Dans la Confirmation, il faut que la voix soit forte & male, pour donner plus de poids aux raisons, & qu'elle varie selon la diversité des Passions & des Figures qui regnent dans cette Partie du Discours." Bretteville, *L'Éloquence,* 482.

18. Mersenne, "Embellissement des chants," *Harmonie universelle,* 1:372; Duncan, "Persuading the Affections," 156.

19. "Mais on leur dit que tant s'en faut que l'Expression soit aneantie par les Passages du Chant, elle est mesme augmentée, pourveu que les Paroles soient également fortes dans un premier & second Couplet." Bacilly, *Remarques,* 213, and *A Commentary,* 106.

20. Lamy, *The Art of Speaking,* V.4.4; Harwood, *The Rhetorics,* 375.

21. Lamy, *The Art of Speaking,* V.4.4; Harwood, *The Rhetorics,* 376.

22. "La Peroraison demande une voix eclantante & animé: parce que c'est la où l'Orateur tâche le plus d'émouvoir & d'enlever les cœurs." Bretteville, *L'Éloquence,* 482.

23. René Bary defined elocution as that which "regards words, phrases, periods, and figures" ("L'Elocution regarde les mots, les phrases, les periodes, & les figures"; Bary, *La Rhétorique,* 228).

24. Lanham, *A Handlist,* 116.

25. Perrin, *Recueil;* quoted and translated in Auld, *The Lyric Art,* 2:26–27.

26. Mersenne, *Traité de l'harmonie universelle,* 189–90, noted in Duncan, "Persuading the Affections," 153; Masson, *Nouveau traité,* 26; La Voye Mignot, *Traité de musique,* 18; Saint-Lambert, *Les principes,* 14.

27. Lenneberg, "Johann Mattheson, 206.

28. "Toutes sortes de figures & de passages harmoniques, comme l'Orateur." Mersenne, "De la musique accentuelle," in *Harmonie universelle,* 1:365; in Duncan, "Persuading the Passions, " 153 and 157.

29. "La Retorique enseigne comme il faut disposer le sujet pour le mettre en Musique & apprend au Musicien comme il faut imiter les figures de Retorique, en faisant divers passages, diminutions, fugues, consequences." Mersenne, *Traité de l'harmonie universelle,* 21; in Duncan, "Persuading the Passions,"157.

30. For original text in French, see Example 5.10.

31. First Strophe: "Que me sert-il d'estre fidelle / De languir nuit et jour pour elle / Si l'ingratte ne m'ayme pas, // Ah c'est trop de flatter d'une Esperance vaine / Il vault mieux par un prompt trespas / Finir mon Amour et sa hayne."

Second Strophe: "Ce seroit me tromper moy mesme / De penser que mon mal extreme / A la pitié peut la mouvoir, // En l'estat ou je suis n'ayons plus d'autre envie / Aprés avoir perdu l'espoir / Que celle de perdre la vie."

32. First Strophe: "Pour donner à mon cœur quelque soulagement / J'ay tasché d'oublier l'objet qui le possede // Mais helas je n'ay fait qu'augmenter mon tourment / Et le mal est encor plus doux que le remede."

Second Strophe: "Pour oublier Philis j'ay fait un vain effort / Ses attraits sont si doux qu'il faut que tout leur cede // Et bien que mon tourment me conduise à la mort / Mon tourment est encore plus doux que le remede."

33. Gibson, "*Le Naturel* and *L'Éloquence,*" 37. See also Gibson, "'A Kind of Eloquence."

34. Kirkendale, "Circulatio-Tradition," 69.

35. Bernhard, *Tractatus compositionis.*

36. Lenneberg, "Johann Mattheson," 200–206.

37. Ibid., 202–204.

38. Ibid., 202. Lenneberg cites Gottsched as the source for this definition.

39. Ibid.

40. Ibid., 203.

41. Ibid.

42. Auld, *The Lyric Art*, 2:26.

43. Mauritus Vogt referred to the repetition of a melodic idea in a different register as *polyptoton*, while Johann Gottfried Walther called the repetition of a melodic idea on different notes in the same part a *synonymia*. Buelow, "Rhetoric and Music," 796.

44. Bernhard, *Tractatus compositionis*, 115; Bernhard explains that *abruptio* is best suited to pieces in the *stylus theatralis*.

45. Buelow, "Rhetoric and Music," 796.

46. Lenneberg, "Johann Mattheson," 221.

47. Bianconi, *Music*, 15.

48. Tomlinson, "Madrigal," 89.

49. Duncan suggests that Mersenne did not consider the relation of textual and musical figures because he respected the composer's ingenuity and inspiration; "Persuading the Affections," 167.

50. Bacilly, *Remarques*, 225–26, and *A Commentary*, 114. As mentioned above, this issue is dealt with in more detail in the chapter 8.

51. Lamy, *The Art of Speaking*, II.3.2; Harwood, *The Rhetorics*, 227. Bary simply noted that exclamations are used "to express some astonishment, sorrow, or passion" ("cette figure consiste à exprimer quelque étonnement, quelque douleur, quelque passion"; Bary, *La Rhétorique*, 317). Auld also cites Lamy's explanation of this figure and considers its use in the works of Perrin; Auld, *The Lyric Art*, 2:57–58.

52. "L'Exclamation . . . demande un ton élevé, ferme & vehement." Bretteville, *L'Éloquence*, 477.

53. "L'Exclamation sert à exprimer la surprise & l'étonnement . . . [et] est presque toujours acompagnée d'une Interjection, comme Ah!, Oh!, Quoi!, Ciel!, Dieux! & le ton qui . . . doit être fort élevé, mais neanmoins proportionné à ce qui precede, & à ce qui suit, & à la situation . . . [et] le sentiment que l'on exprime." Grimarest, *Traité*, 169–70.

54. See also Lambert's "Pourquoy vous offencez," m. 20, or "J'ay juré mille fois," m. 1; La Barre's "Un feu naissant," mm. 13–16; and Le Camus' "Non, il n'est pas en mon pouvoir," mm. 13–14. There are also examples of "hélas" set to a repeated tone (as in Le Camus' "Vous m'aimez," mm. 13–14, or La Barre's "Forests solitaires," m. 25) or a descending major or minor second (Le Camus' "Vous serez les témoins," mm. 19–20).

55. Lamy, *The Art of Speaking*, II.3.3; Harwood, *The Rhetorics*, 227. See also Bary, *La Rhétorique*, 429. Grimarest and Bretteville did not consider this figure.

56. Mattheson considers doubt in his examination of interrogation. True doubt (he notes that some questions do not arise from doubt) is best represented by "imperfect consonances," particularly phrases that end on an

interval of a sixth (rising and falling) between bass and melody (Lenneberg, "Johann Mattheson," 220).

57. Kirkendale, "Circulatio-Tradition," 70–74.

58. Ibid.

59. "L'Anthithese demande deux differences de ton, dont l'un soit plus élevé que l'autre." Bretteville, *L'Éloquence*, 472–73.

60. "L'Antithese, qui renferme des opositions violentes, doit être prononcée par une voix ferme, pour faire sentir advantage ces opositions . . . [et] en observant toujours le ton propre au sentiment qu'elles renferment." Grimarest, *Traité*, 166.

61. Ibid., 167.

62. Lamy, *The Art of Speaking*, II.3.3; Harwood, *The Rhetorics*, 230. For a consideration of Perrin's use of repetition, see Auld, *The Lyric Art*, 2:64–66.

63. "Dans la Repetition, les mots repetés doivent être prononcés avec plus de force que les autres." Bretteville, *L'Éloquence*, 477–78.

64. Johann Adolph Scheibe refers to this as *paronomasia,* the repetition of a musical idea on the same notes but with additions or alterations for emphasis; see Buelow, "Rhetoric and Music," 796. Mersenne notes that ornamentation should be used to intensify affect, as it does in this example (Mersenne, "Embellissement des chants," *Harmonie universelle*, 1:372, and Duncan, "Persuading the Passions," 156). Furthermore, it is the entire phrase that is repeated in this example, not just a short musical idea as implied by Scheibe.

65. This was called *epistrophe* by the Germans; Buelow, "Rhetoric and Music," 795.

66. Lamy, *The Art of Speaking*, II.3.3; Harwood, *The Rhetorics*, 235.

67. "Il n'est rien dans la vie / Qui ne lasse et qui n'ennuy / Quand on n'a point d'amour; / et peut-on sans aimer / Passer un heureux jour."

68. Mattheson also acknowledges that questions may or may not end with a melodic ascension, depending upon the context. Scheibe evidently did not make such a distinction. He defined interrogation as a musical question represented in music by melodic ending or entire harmonic passage that ends by a second or some other interval higher than the previous note or notes. Buelow, "Rhetoric and Music," 798.

69. "L'Interrogation doit se prononcer d'un ton doux, fier, ou ferme & élevé, selon la difference des personnes à qui on la fait." Bretteville, *L'Éloquence*, 474.

70. "Eclaircir sans passion . . . le ton doit être doux. . . . Quand cette figure est la suite d'une offense, elle demande un ton élevé, vif, & fier. . . . Lorsqu'on est rempli de la Douleur, l'Interrogation doit être prononcée d'une voix tendre & plaintive." Grimarest, *Traité*, 160–61.

71. "L'Elevation de la Voix [qui] doit croître par les memes degrés, en pesant sur le premier mot principal de chaque membre." Bretteville, *L'Éloquence*, 477; see also Grimarest, *Traité*, 173–75.

72. Climax, or *gradation,* was also frequently mentioned in German treatises (Buelow, "Rhetoric and Music," 795).

73. Lamy, *The Art of Speaking,* II.1.2; Harwood, *The Rhetorics,* 215–16.

74. Génetiot notes that this is one of the most common metaphors in the lyric genre, and points out that it is also hyperbolic; Génetiot, *Les genres,* 93. Death can refer to actual death, the final outcome of what people viewed as a real disease: lovesickness. This will be discussed at length in chapter 7.

75. Ferrand, *A Treatise on Lovesickness,* 234.

76. Madeleine de Scudéry's *Carte de Tendre* is perhaps the most famous of "love maps." This will be discussed in chapter 7.

77. It was thought that love was spread and received through the eyes; see Ferrand, *A Treatise on Lovesickness,* 232 and 252.

78. Génetiot, *Les genres,* 88–92.

6. *L'Art du Chant*

1. "Il est donc vray de dire que le Chant est quelque chose de plus considerable que l'on ne s'imagine." Bacilly, *L'Art de bien chanter* (1679), 7; my translation.

2. "Je parle de l'Art de bien Chanter, comme Practique, & je dis qu'il consiste à bien entonner les tons dans leur justesse ; à bien soûtenir la Voix ; à la bien porter; à bien faire les Cadences & Tremblements; à bien marquer du gosier quand il le faut; à ne pas tant marquer quand il ne le faut pas, mais glisser certains tons à propos; à bien faire le Accens, que l'on appelle vulgairement *plaintes,* à bien former les Passages & les Diminutions: Et comme le Chant ne se pratique gueres sans Paroles ; à les bien prononcer; à les bien exprimer, ou passionner à propos; & sur tout à bien observer la quantité des syllabes longues ou bréves, qui est la principlae fin de cét Ouvrage." Bacilly, *Remarques,* 5–6, and *A Commentary,* 6.

3. "Je sçay que l'on peut apprendre du moins à eviter mille fautes qui se pratiquent dans le Chant, particulierement pour les prononciations, & pour la quantité des paroles, & se desabuser de bien des opinions mal fondées qui se glissent tous les jours dans le commerce du Chant; ainsi l'on peut dire que du moins pour la Theorie du Chant cet Ouvrage pourra estre fort utile s'il ne l'est pour la Pratique." Bacilly, *Remarques,* unpaginated avant-propos, and *A Commentary,* xvi.

4. This information was gleaned from accounts given by Marin Mersenne and Georg Muffat. See Cyr, *Performing Baroque Music,* 63–64; Bruce Haynes and Peter R. Cooke, "Pitch."

5. "Ces sortes d'Airs, qui paroissent communs sur le papier, ou qui le sont en effet, sont bien relevez de ce defaut par les ornemens que l'on y adjouste, & par la maniere de les executer." (Bacilly, *Remarques,* 104, and *A Commentary,* 47).

6. "L'orateur, conjointement aux effets de style, c'est-à-dire d'élocution et de disposition, doit déployer une science des passions qui accorde à la voix ce rôle de méditation qui toujours lui revient. Cela suppose un accord de l'orateur et de l'auditeur sur une acoustique des passions, une métrique des

émotions, une reconnaissance, bref une culture et une socialité de la voix." Salazar, *Le culte de la voix*, 89–90.

7. Ibid., 90.

8. Ibid., 198–200.

9. "Quelques agréables que soient ces Chansons lors qu'on les lit, c'est tout autre chose lors qu'on les chante; il en est ainsi de tous les Ouvrages qui sont faits pour le chant." *Recueil de chansons choisies,* quoted in Goulet, *Poésie* (1694), 168.

10. "Plusieurs s'imaginent que le Chant tenant de la Declamation, & ayant pour but d'exprimer les Passions doit estre executé avec beaucoup d'affectation que d'autres appelleroient *Outrer le Chant;* Pour moy je tiens que ce n'est pas avoir adjoûté au Chant que cette grande affectation qui souvent est accompagnée de grimace, si ce n'est pour le Recitatif, je veux dire pour le Theatre; mais pour le Chant qui se pratique dans les Ruelles, je soûtiens que c'est adjoûter de l'agrément que d'en retrancher cette façon de chanter trop ampoulée qui en oste toute la mignardise, & toute la delicatesse, pourveu que la Prononciation n'y soit point interessée sur tout des R, qui suivent ou qui precedent une consone, & des O, qui ne veulent point du tout estre flattez." Bacilly, *L'Art de bien chanter,* 11–12; my translation.

11. Bacilly, *Remarques curieuses,* 248–49, and *A Commentary,* 129.

12. Stark, *Bel Canto,* xxv.

13. Harris, "Voices," 99.

14. "L'on prenne les tons autant que l'on pourra du fonds du gosier, qui est le seul gouvernail de la justesse du Chant." Bacilly, *Remarques curieuses,* 58, and *A Commentary,* 28.

15. "Il y a encore une autre qualité de la voix qui la rend plaine, & solide, & qui augmente son harmonie, ce que l'on peut expliquer par la comparaison d'un canal qui est tousjours plain d'eau, quand elle coule, . . . les voix qui sont privées de cette qualité, sont semblables à un filet d'eau qui coule par un gros canal." Mersenne, *Harmonie universelle,* 2:354. Translated by Maria Georgakarakou in "Marin Mersenne." I would like to thank Maria Georgakarakou for generously allowing me access to her paper.

16. Bacilly and others mention as well that *cadence* also refers to the harmonic progression that takes place at the end of a phrase or different parts of a musical composition: "*cadences* that are the result of musical compositions" ("des Cadences qui sont affectées au Traité de la Composition de Musique"). Bacilly, *Remarques,* 164, and Caswell, *A Commentary,* 82.

17. "Il y a donc beaucoup de Personnes qui ont la Voix, sans avoir nulle Cadence." Bacilly, *Remarques,* 164–65, and Caswell, *A Commentary,* 83–84.

18. Bacilly, *Remarques,* 38, and Caswell, *A Commentary,* 20.

19. "Or pour chanter avec moins d'imperfection, il semble qu'il ne suffise pas de prononcer les paroles qu'on chante . . . que la voix soit belle, pleine, douce & moëlleuse portée & conduite d'une belle maniere et que toutes les Variations, ou Changemens se fassent ainsi que des roulemens d'air au canal ou tuyau du gosier sans que le rang l'estomac, le nez, la voûte du palais ny le mouvement des machoires y contribuent." Mersenne, *Harmonie universelle,* 2:341; quoted and translated by Georgakarakou, "Marin Mersenne."

20. Georgakarakou, "Marin Mersenne."

21. Mersenne, *Harmonie universelle*, 2:355.

22. L'égalité est la tenuë, & stable de la voix sur une mesme chorde, sans qu'il soit permis de la varier en la haussant ou en la baissant, mais on peut l'affoiblir, & l'augmenter tandis que l'on demeure sur une mesme chorde." Ibid., 2:353. My translation; see also Georgakarakou, "Marin Mersenne."

23. Georgakarakou, "Marin Mersenne."

24. "D'autre se vantent d'avoir la Voix plus haute; & d'autres qui l'ont plus basse, disent que de Chanter haut c'est *Glapir.* Ceux qui ont la Voix naturelle, méprisent les Voix de Fausset, comme fausses & glapissantes; & ceux-cy tiennent que le fin du Chant paroist bien plus dans une Voix éclatante, telle que l'ont ceux qui chantent en Fausset, que dans une Voix de Taille naturelle, qui pour l'ordinaire n'a pas tant d'éclat." Bacilly, *Remarques,* 35–36, and *A Commentary,* 19. Also quoted in Harris, "Voices," 101.

25. In 1638, for example, Monteverdi denotes these three registers in the foreword to his *Madrigali guerrieri ed amorosi* (Venice, 1638). Quoted in Harris, "Voices," 101; translation in Strunk, *Source Readings,* 413.

26. Harris, "Voices," 101; from Tosi, *Observations on the Florid Song,* 24.

27. Bacilly, *Remarques,* 47, and *A Commentary,* 23.

28. Bacilly does discuss the female voice, but only in his description of various voice types. Bacilly *Remarques,* 38–47, and *A Commentary,* 20–23.

29. A few airs are exceptional. Lambert's "Mon cœur qui se rend à vos coups" (Example 4.5) extends from A4 to A5, which would suit only high voices unless the air were transposed.

30. "Il m'auroit esté facile d'ajoûter la tablature du Teorbe telle que je l'ay composé, mais je n'ay mis a dessein que les basses continues pour la facilité des voix que l'on pourra plus aisement accompagner en transposant quand il le faudra a la maniere accoutumée." Lambert, *Les Airs de Monsieur Lambert,* avant-propos (all editions).

31. Harris, "Voices," 101.

32. The application of ornaments in vocal music is one of the most commonly addressed and thoroughly covered performance-related topics. Here I recount only what Bacilly has to say on the subject as it relates to the French serious air.

33. Bacilly, *Remarques,* 137, and *A Commentary,* 65.

34. Rousseau indicates that when a note is approached from below, this is indication that a *port de voix* must be sung. Rousseau, *Methode claire,* 49.

35. Bacilly, *Remarques,* 159, and *A Commentary,* 79–80. Bacilly's air "Apres milles rigueurs" is transcribed in *A Commentary,* 80–81.

36. Bacilly, *Remarques,* 152–53, and *A Commentary,* 75.

37. Rousseau indicates that one should trill on a note when it is slurred from above. Rousseau, *Methode claire,* 49.

38. "On peut acquerir de la Cadence en exerçant de la maniere qu'il faut, c'est-à-dire en battant souvent du gosier sur les deux Nottes dont la Cadence est composé, dans une certaine égalité, & l'une apres l'autre." Bacilly, *Remarques,* 165, and *A Commentary,* 83). Like Mersenne, Bacilly

then goes on to say that the vocal *cadence* resembles the trill played on the harpsichord wherein two fingers alternate between two two keys.

39. I should distinguish here between words which are masculine by virtue of their gender, like *le garçon,* and those that are masculine by virtue of their endings, like *porter.* The same distinction exists between a feminine word, like *la femme,* and a word with a feminine ending, like *rime.* Here, of course, the discussion concerns masculine and feminine endings.

40. Bacilly, *Remarques,* 184–85, and *A Commentary,* 93.

41. "[Le tremblement étouffé] se fait lors qu'ayant formé l'appuy, c'est à dire la Notte qui precede & prepare la Cadence ou Tremblement, le gosier se presente à trembler, & pourtant n'en fait que le semblant, comme s'il ne vouloit que doubler la Note sur laquelle se devoit faire la Cadence." Bacilly, *Remarques,* 187–88, and *A Commentary,* 95. Based on but slightly different from the example in Guinamard, "Les *Remarques curieuses,*" 78.

42. Based on, but slightly different from, the example given in Guinamard, "Les *Remarques curieuses,*" 79.

43. Example 6.10 is my example.

44. "Le Doublement de la mesme Notte qui se fait du gosier, si promptement." Bacilly, *Remarques,* 196–97, and *A Commentary,* 99.

45. Bacilly, *Remarques,* 196–97, and *A Commentary,* 99.

46. Guinamard, "Les *Remarques curieuses,*" 80. Guinamard also describes two ornaments not mentioned by Bacilly, the *chute* and the *coulé de tierce.* The *chute* is an anticipation of a note that descends and must be sung lightly, while the *coulé de tierce* is an ornamental note that fills in the interval of a descending third.

47. "Tout ce qui s'ajouste à la simplicité des Nottes marquées sur le papier en Caracteres de Musique." Bacilly, *Remarques,* 206, and *A Commentary,* 103.

48. "L'Execution qui procede d'une disposition naturelle du gosier, qui est souple à faire tout ce qu'on veut." Bacilly, *Remarques,* 209, and *A Commentary,* 105.

49. Bacilly, *A Commentary,* 115.

50. The complete air is in Bacilly, *Les Trois livres d'airs* (1668), I:78.

51. Lambert, *Les Airs de Monsieur Lambert* (1666), 51.

52. Ibid., 58.

53. Rohrer, "'The Energy of English Words.'"

54. See for example Maugers, *French Grammar;* Mersenne, *Harmonie universelle;* Millet, *La Belle méthode;* or Hindret, *L'Art de bien prononcer,* to name but a few.

55. Green, *La parole baroque,* 281.

56. "*Oi* ou *oy* qui se pronounce presque comme un *o,* mesme un *ou,* & un *e* fort ouvert, ou plutost un *ai.*" Bacilly, *Remarques,* 283, and *A Commentary,* 147.

57. Bacilly, *Remarques,* 284, and *A Commentary,* 147.

58. Bacilly, *Remarques,* 286, and *A Commentary,* 148.

59. Green, *La parole baroque,* 282.

60. "Il ne faut prononcer l'*n*, que lors que l'on est prest de finir, autrement ce seroit Chanter du nez. . . . *Qu'il ne faut point Chanter du nez.*" Bacilly, *Remarques,* 261, and *A Commentary,* 136.

61. Bacilly, *Remarques,* 263–64, and *A Commentary,* 137–38.

62. Green, *La parole baroque,* 282–83.

63. Ibid., 284.

64. Ibid., 283.

65. Ibid., 283–84.

66. "Il faut, dis-je, bien prendre garde si l'expression est veritable pour le sense, comme on void par les exemples precedens, & non pour le mot." Bacilly, *Remarques,* 293–94, and *A Commentary,* 152.

67. "Pour peu que l'on neglige la prononciation de *sçavez,* comme cela se peut facilement, on entendra *vous avez donné de l'amour,* au lieu de *vous sçavez donner de l'amour,* si l'on manque à prononcer l'*r* de donner." Bacilly, *Remarques,* 296, and *A Commentary,* 153.

68. Bacilly, *Remarques,* 298, and *A Commentary,* 154.

69. "Donner plus de force à l'éxpression, on apuye de certaines Consones, avant que de former la Voyelle qui les suit." Bacilly, *Remarques,* 307; *A Commentary,* 159.

70. Bacilly, *Remarques,* 307–308, and *A Commentary,* 159.

71. "Il y a quelque expression veritable & non apparent; car il n'y auroit rien de plus ridicule que de prononcer toûjours l'*v* de *vous,* de *vos,* & de *volage,* avec affectation." Bacilly, *Remarques,* 311, and *A Commentary,* 163.

72. Bacilly, *Remarques,* 313–12, and *A Commentary,* 164.

73. Bacilly, *Remarques,* 317, and *A Commentary,* 166.

74. "A la rime, et devant tout autre arrêt de la voix, une consonne finale doit s'articuler. Les consonnes sonores ont dans ce cas une valeur sourde: d et t = [t]; g et c = [k]; s, z, et x = [s]. Lorsqu'une consonne normalement articulée est suivie d'une autre qu'on doit prononcer selon ces règles, on entendra les deux, mais lorsque plusieurs consonnes latentes se suivent, on ne fait entendre que la dernière: *mort* [mort], mais *morts* [mors]." Green, *La parole baroque,* 284–85.

75. As in modern French, the final consonants in proper names such as Iris, Tircis, or Philis, commonly found throughout the repertory, are also always pronounced.

76. "Mesme quand il est question de corriger le defaut de la Prononciation d'une consone, ils n'ont point d'autre secret, ny d'autre conseil à donner, que celuy d'*ouvrir la bouche.*" Bacilly, *Remarques,* 256, and *A Commentary,* 133.

77. "Premierement dans le Port de Voix où il se rencontre un *a,* il faut ouvrir la bouche bien moins dans la premiere Notte que dans la derniere, c'est-à-dire que d'abord il ne faut ouvrir la bouche qu'avec mediocrité; & lors que le gosier a marqué ce qu'il faut pour porter la premiere Notte sur la derniere, pour lors il la faut ouvrir davantage, non pas tout d'un coup, mais peu à peu, afin que le son de la Voix s'insinuë plus agreablement dans l'oreille de l'Auditeur." Bacilly, *Remarques,* 258, and *A Commentary,* 134.

78. "Il faut ouvrir la bouche en soùriant, & plus en large qu'en long." Bacilly, *Remarques*, 260, and *A Commentary*, 135.

79. "Selon que l'*e* est plus ou moins ouvert, il faut plus ou moins ouvrir la bouche." Bacilly, *Remarques*, 264, and *A Commentary*, 138.

80. Bacilly, *Remarques*, 275, and *A Commentary*, 142.

81. "Il faut demeurer d'accord avec eux, que la Poësie Françoise n'a aucun égard à la Quantité des syllabes, quant à la composition, pourveu que la rime soit conservée, mais s'il est question de reciter agreablement des Vers, les Chanter, mesme les declamer, il est certain qu'il y a des longues & des brèsves à observer, non seulement dans la Poësie, mais aussi dans la Prose; de sorte qu'elles n'ont en ce rencontre aucune difference l'une de l'autre." Bacilly, *Remarques*, 328, and *A Commentary*, 175.

82. "Il faut aussi remarquer que bien que ces sortes d'Observations se doivent pratiquer non seulement dans l'execution du Chant, mais à plus forte raison dans la composition d'une Piece de Musique faite sur des paroles Françoises." Bacilly, *Remarques*, 331, and *A Commentary*, 176.

83. "On n'est pas toûjours si exact à marquer sur le papier les Nottes longues & brèves, conformémens à celles qui se rencontrent dans le langage, que pour la grace de la mesure on ne marque quelquefois une Notte brèsve, qui toutesfois répondra à une syllabe longue, laissant à celuy qui a une connoissance parfaite de la Quantité, à remedier à cet incovenient. . . . Cela se rencontre particulierement dans les Airs qui ont leur mesure reglée, comme sont les Sarabandes, Gavottes, Bourées, &c. à la composition desquelles on est obligé de mettre certaines longues ou brèsves pour venir dans les Cadences, quoy que les syllabes ne s'y rapportent pas toûjours." Bacilly, *Remarques*, 331–32, and *A Commentary*, 176.

84. "S'ils ne sont pas longs du poinct de souffrir une Cadence finale ou mediante d'un Air, ou autre long tremblement, on peut y faire du moins un Accent ou un Doublement du gosier, qui sont marques de longues, ou du moins de demy longues pour ainsi dire." Bacilly, *Remarques*, 337, and *A Commentary*, 179.

85. "Les deux premiers Monosyllables sont longs naturellement, l'un à cause qu'il contient une *n*, l'autre parce qu'il est contenu dans la Table, & qu'ils ne precedent ny l'un ny l'autre une Voyelle; car en ce cas ils auroient pû estre brefs: le troisième est encor long, si le Chantre le trouve à propos (& non pas naturellement) parce qu'il en precede un qui doit estre bref necessairement, puis qu'il tombe sur un autre qui est tres-long & qui ne peut jamais estre bref. . . . Le sixiéme Monosyllabe par la mesme raison est bref, parce qu'il precede le mot *vos,* qui est essentiellement long, à cause de la Lettre *s* qui le finit." Bacilly, *Remarques*, 344, and *A Commentary*, 182.

86. Bacilly, *Remarques*, 354, and *A Commentary*, 187.

87. Bacilly, *Remarques*, 368, and *A Commentary*, 192.

88. In my musical examples, I was unable to indicate *le Trinaire* and *le Triple simple*. Instead, I resorted to using $\frac{3}{2}$ for *le Trinaire* and $\frac{3}{4}$ for *le Triple simple*.

89. Rousseau, *Methode claire*, 35–36.

90. Bacilly, *Remarques,* 108, and *A Commentary,* 49.

91. "Pour les autres Chansons qui ont leur mesure reglée, il est bien permis de la rendre plus lente; mais il faut toûjours en conserver la proportion, & ne pas faire d'un Menuet, ou d'une Sarabande, un Chant qui soit d'une Mesure libre, comme font ceux que nous appellons précisement *Airs.*" Bacilly, *Remarques,*108, and *A Commentary,* 49.

92. "Pour les rendre plus tendres . . . dans lesquelles on rompt la Mesure de la Danse, afin de leur donner plus d'éclat, & les tourner de cent manieres l'une plus agreable que l'autre." Bacilly, *Remarques,* 106–107, and *A Commentary,* 48–49.

93. "Le mouvement est donc tout autre que ce qu'ils s'imaginent; & pour moy je tiens que c'est une certaine qualité qui donne l'ame au Chant, & qui est appellée Mouvement, parce qu'elle émeut, je veux dire elle excite l'attention des Auditeurs, mesme de ceux qui sont les plus rebelles à l'harmonie; si ce n'est que l'on veüille dire qu'elle inspire dans les cœurs telle passion que le Chantre voudra faire naistre, principalement celle de la *Tendresse.*" Bacilly, *Remarques,* 200, and *A Commentary,* 100.

94. "On peut encore remarquer que dans le recitatif on bat rarement la Mesure, parce que l'égalité de ses temps préjudicieroit souvent au mouvement & à l'esprit de la passion." Rousseau, *Methode claire,* 86.

95. "Certaines Langueurs qui se font en descendant d'une longue sur une autre, sans appuyer du gosier que fort legerement." Bacilly, *Remarques,* 201, and *A Commentary,* 101.

96. "Les demy-Ports de voix qui se font en montant par degrez imperceptibles." Bacilly, *Remarques,* 201, and *A Commentary,* 101.

97. "Quant au Mouvement des Expressions gayes & enjoüées, rien n'y contribuë tant, comme le Doublement du gosier . . . qui se fait comme j'ay dit, d'une Notte que l'on frape deux fois, au lieu d'une ; mais si legerement, & si delicatement, que cela ne paroist point." Bacilly, *Remarques,* 202–204, and *A Commentary,* 101–102.

98. See Bacilly, *Les Trois livres d'airs,* I:32.

99. "La grace [et] la commodité qui se rencontre dans le Theorbe . . ." Bacilly, *Remarques,* 17, and *A Commentary,* 11. Goulet indicates the term "theorbo" could have referred to any lute-like instrument capable of playing the bass line and/or adding harmony; Goulet, *Poésie,* 108.

100. "Le Theorbe, qui est propre pour accompagner toutes sortes de Voix, quand ce ne seroit que par la seule raison de sa douceur, qui s'accommode aux Voix foibles & delicates; au lieu que les autres Instrumens les offusquent." Bacilly, *Remarques,* 17–18, and *A Commentary,* 11. Bacilly also recommends that it is best that the singer be capable of playing theorbo in order to accompany himself/ herself; Bacilly, *Remarques,* 19, and *A Commentary,* 12.

101. Ashworth and O'Dette, "Basso Continuo," 272.

102. Ibid.

103. "[Le] Theorbe ne fait que soûtenir agreablement la Voix sans en diminuër la beauté, ny la delicatesse des traits." Bacilly, *Remarques,* 18, and *A Commentary,* 11.

104. Delair, *Traité d'acompagnement,* 47; Delair, *Accompaniment,* 15.

105. Ashworth and O'Dette, "Basso Continuo," 275.

106. Delair, *Accompaniment,* 47, 101.

107. Ashworth and O'Dette, "Basso Continuo," 277.

108. Delair, *Accompaniment,* 13.

109. Delair notes that most master accompanists play chords in the lower register of their instruments (in the tenor and alto ranges); ibid, 18.

110. Ashworth and O'Dette, "Basso Continuo," 281.

111. Delair himself points out that the figure "6" especially causes problems, as it can refer to either 6/3 or 6/4 chords; Delair, *Traité d'accompagnement,* 22.

112. Ashworth and O'Dette, 283.

113. Stephan Van Dyck and Stephen Stubbs, *Joseph Chabanceau de La Barre: Airs à deux Parties,* compact disc, Ricercar, 2000.

7. Salon Culture and the Mid-Seventeenth-Century French Air

1. Much of this chapter comes from my article "'La Réplique galante.'" According to Eric Walter, by the year 1660, there were about 40 salons and about 800 participants. Walter, "Les autheurs"; in Goulet, *Poésie,* 590.

2. During the first few decades of the seventeenth century, Marquise de Rambouillet established the first and perhaps most important salon, which became the model for subsequent salons throughout the century. Génetiot divides salon activities into three periods. The first, between 1598–1630, gave witness to the process of civilizing society in France; the second part, from 1630–61, includes the triumph of the Rambouillet salon and the "glory years" (particularly of the Scudéry salon) during the decade 1650–60; and finally, post-1661, which Génetiot identifies as the development of "classicism" in France and the decline of the influence of salon culture. Génetiot, *Poétique,* 116–27.

3. For more information on the nature, function, and transformation of the seventeenth-century salon, see Beasley, *Salons;* Craveri, *The Age of Conversation;* DeJean, *Tender Geographies;* Denis, *La muse galante;* Goldsmith, *Exclusive Conversations;* Goulet, *Poésie;* Harth, *Cartesian Women;* Lougee, *Les Paradis des Femmes;* Lilti, *Le monde des salons;* Maître, *Les précieuses;* Picard, *Les salons littéraires;* and Timmermans, *L'accès des femmes à la culture.*

4. Fumaroli, *La diplomatie,* 303. See also Génetiot, *Poétique* and Goulet, *Poésie.*

5. Fumaroli, *La diplomatie,* 304. See also Denis, *La muse galante;* Goldsmith, *Exclusive Conversations;* Pessel, "De la conversation"; and Strosetzki, *Rhétorique de la conversation.*

6. "Un grand jeu littéraire, qui suppose non seulement des règles du dialogue, des figures chorégraphiques . . . , mais des décors et des lieux appropriés . . . , une foule d'accessoires (vêtements, coiffures, bijoux), une gestuelle, un jeu d'expression et de regards, et des écrits propres à faire rebondir le dialogue et l'intrigue." Fumeroli, *La diplomatie,* 307.

7. Airs were also included in Mme Gomez de Vasconcellos's *Le Galant nouvelliste* (1693) and Paul Tallemant's *Le Second voyage de l'île d'amour* (1664) and were set to music and published, along with those from Scudéry's novels, in Ballard's *Livres d'airs de différents autheurs* between 1659 and 1693. Goulet, *Poésie*, 639–41.

8. Scudéry, *Clélie*, f. 1048, in Goulet, *Poésie*, 640.

9. It was a common practice to mix literary genres in what Alain Viala calls "l'esthétique galante"; thus, prose and poetry could appear within a single work. Pellisson, *Discours*, 30–34.

10. Scudéry, *Conversations morales*, 29.

11. "Chante ce que l'indifférence / A de triste & de languissant, / Les plaisirs d'un amour naissant, / Par quels secrets appas la flateuse espérance, / Au milieu des plus longs tourmens / Trompe les crédules Amans." Scudéry, *Conversations morales*, 67.

12. See Ibid., "De la paresse," 159–75.

13. Ibid., "De l'amitié," 927–31.

14. Ibid., "De l'amitié," 999–1004.

15. Several volumes of *Recueil des plus beaux vers* were compiled by Bénigne de Bacilly and published between 1661 and 1680.

16. Setting by Lambert and Le Camus in *Livre d'airs de différents autheurs* (Paris: Ballard, 1658), f. 28v–29; *Recueil des plus beaux vers* (Paris: Ballard, 1661), 241.

17. Setting by Bacilly and Le Camus in *Livre d'airs de différents autheurs*, 1668, f. 2v–3r; *Recueil des plus beaux vers*, 1668, p. 474.

18. "Je fais ce que je puis pour ne vous aymer plus, / Et lassé de tant de refus, / Je veux briser mes fers, je veux finir mes peines: // Mais ma revolte, helas! ne dure qu'un moment, / Je ne puis vivre sans mes chaisnes, / Ny me passer de mon tourment. [M.F.]

Souvent le Désespoir, le Dépit, la Raison, / Taschent de forcer ma prison, / Et font pour me guérir, mille entreprises vaines: // Mais leur révolte, helas! ne dure qu'un moment; / Je ne puis vivre sans mes chaisnes, / Ny me passer de mon tourment. [Perrin]" *Recueil des plus beaux vers* (1668), 474.

19. For more information about Madeleine de Scudéry's involvement in the creation of song texts, see Goulet, "Les divertissements musicaux du Samedi."

20. *Livre d'airs de différents autheurs* (1661), f. 20v–21r; *Recueil des plus beaux vers* (1661), p. 10. Music by Le Camus and Perdigal.

21. "A quoy pensiez-vous, Climène, / A quoy pensiez-vous d'aimer? / Ne sçaviez-vous pas la peine / Que souffre un cœur qui se laisse enflâmer? / A quoy pensiez-vous, Climène, / A quoy pensiez-vous d'aimer?

Alors qu'avec tous ses charmes / Amour vient nous enflâmer, / Il faut ceder à ses armes, / Il faut languir, il faut se consumer, / Alors qu'avec tous ses charmes / Amour vient nous enflâmer."

"On n'y pense pas, Silvie / Quand on commence d'aimer, / Et sans en avoir envie, / En un moment on se laisse enflâmer; / Vous qui brûliez tant le monde, / Vous brûlez à vostre tour; / Vostre beauté sans second / A ressenty le pouvoir de l'Amour; / Vous qui brûliez tant le monde, / Vous brûlez à vostre tour."

22. See Scudéry, *Conversations morales,* 175.

23. "La Musique," in *Entretien galans,* 27–30.

24. "Que vous flatez mes resveries! / Que j'ayme vos rives fleuries, / Clairs & paisibles ruisseaux, / Helas! ce fut sur le bord de vos eaux / Que l'aymable Berger, loin de qui tout m'ennuye, / Commença de troubler le repos de ma vie; // Tout favorisoit ses desirs, / Zephirs & Flore / Attiroient en ces lieux les amoureux plaisirs; / Mais ses regards & ses soûpirs/ Estoient plus amoureux encore / Que Flore & les Zephirs." Le Camus, *Airs à deux et trois parties,* 1.

25. "Laissez durer la nuit, impatiente Aurore, / Elle m'ayde à cacher mes secretes douleurs, / Et je n'ay pas encore assez versé de pleurs // Pour ma douleur, helas! est il des nuits trop sombres? / Depuis que mon Berger quitta ce beau sejour, / Ah! je ne puis souffrir le vif éclat du jour; / Laissez-moy donc pleurer à la faveur des ombres / Autant que voudra mon amour." Le Camus, *Airs à deux et trois parties,* 4.

26. "Ah! fuyons ce dengereux sejour, / Ces verds ombrages, / Ces doux ravages, / Où Tircis me fit voir tant d'amour; // Détournons nos troupeaux de ces bois / Où l'ingrat m'attira cent fois; / Mais mon cœur à mes desseins rebelles / Ne peut bannir / Ce cruel souvenir: / Helas! un infidelle me fait aymer ces lieux, / Et malgré mes detours / J'y viens toûjours." Le Camus, *Airs à deux et trois parties,* 7.

27. "J'ay juré mille fois de ne jamais aymer, / Et je ne croyois pas que rien ne pust charmer, / Mais alors que je fis ce dessein temeraire, / Tircis, vous n'aviez pas entrepris de me plaire: // Ma raison contre vous ne fait plus son devoir, / et de l'Amour, enfin, je cognois le pouvoir.

Helas! de mon erreur trop tard je m'apperçois, / Je pensois que ce Dieu ne rangeoit sous ses loix / Que ceux qui de ses traits sçavent mal se deffendre; / Mais je sens que mon cœur malgré moy se va rendre. / Ma raison contre vous ne fait plus son devoir, / et de l'Amour, enfin, je cognois le pouvoir." Lambert, *Les Airs de Monsieur Lambert,* 48. The text to this piece was written by Henriette de Coligny Comtesse de La Suze; Goulet, *Paroles de musique,* 215.

28. "Puisque chacun doit aymer a son tour / Philis pourquoy vous en defendre, // Si vous avez des yeux pour donner de l'amour / Vous avez un Cœur pour en prendre.

Si c'est un mal que c'est un mal charmant / Et qu'il donne un plaisir extreme, // Pour l'esprouver Philis vous n'avez seulement / Qu'a m'aymer comme Je vous ayme." Lambert, *Les Airs de Monsieur Lambert,* 52.

29. Bary, *L'Esprit de cour.* Bary's conversations are different from Scudéry's. In one hundred short dialogues, in which the participants exchange

words in regular alternation, Bary is primarily concerned with the moral education of young women and not with presenting models of ideal social exchange. Many of Bary's conversations are, in fact, examples of improper social interactions, and feature a man's inappropriate behavior toward a woman. Several other authors also wrote works that served as moral instruction manuals for women, warning women of the seductive powers of men and showing how the cultivated female can defend herself against a male rhetoric of seduction. These works include De Bosc, *L'Honnête femme;* Marquise de Maintenon, *Conversations;* and Saint Gabriel, *Le Merite des Dames.* Many other sources, particularly civility manuals and literary conversations, also advised women to avoid the threat of man's seduction and guard her reputation with care. See Buffet, *Nouvelles Observations;* Courtin, *Nouveau traité; Entretien galans;* Faret, *L'Honneste-Homme;* Méré, *Œuvres posthumes;* and Poulain de La Barre, *De l'Égalité des deux sexes.*

30. For more information on seventeenth-century literary representations of love, see DeJean, *Tender Geographies;* Génetiot, *Les genres;* Harth, *Cartesian Women;* Howard, "Quinault"; Jensen, *Writing Love;* Kritzman, *The Rhetoric;* Lougee, *Les Paradis des Femmes;* Pelous, *Amour précieux;* Timmermans, *L'accès des femmes à la culture;* and *Writing about Sex* (ed. Zanger).

31. Other authors describe this "seduction process," but not as specifically as Bary. See also Scudéry, *Conversations morales,* 871–1017; "La teste à teste," in *Entretiens galans,* 69–95; and Boursault, "Lettres de Babet."

32. "L'esprit de cour qui fait parler le mensonge." Bary, *L'Esprit de cour,* 88.

33. "Beaux yeux, que voulez-vous me dire, / Par vos regards charmans & doux: / Si je me rends, si je cede à vos coups, / Aurez-vous quelque jour pitié de mon martyre?" Ballard, *Livre d'airs de différents autheurs* (1667), f. 25v–26r.

34. Bary, *L'Esprit de cour,* 130–34.

35. Ibid., 133.

36. Ibid., 3. Duty is the subject of several airs published later in the century. See, for example, "Vous estes satisfait," in Ballard, *Livre d'air de différents autheurs* (1684) f. 4v–5r: "Vous estes satisfait, mon severe devoir, / Malgré l'amour, malgré vous-mesme, / Par vos conseils, j'ay quitté ce que j'ayme" ("You are satisfied, my severe duty, / Inspite of love, inspite of yourself, / Because of your advice, I have left the one I love").

37. See in particular Bary, *L'Esprit de cour,* 103–106 and 106–16.

38. "Soyez tendre, soyez fidelle, / Persévérez jusques au bout: / Amant vous toucherez le cœur de vostre belle, / Le temps vient à bout de tout." Brossard, *Livre d'airs sérieux* (1696), 18.

39. Scudéry, *The Story of Sapho,* 58. Scudéry's original title was *Histoire de Sapho,* published as volume 10 of *Artamène, ou, Le grand Cyrus.*

40. "Le sème fondamental de 'galant' (galer=jouer, se divertir) est ainsi le support d'une conception où l'opposition entre savoir et amusement peut être dépassée, où le savoir est transcendé par l'agrément mondain." Viala, introduction to *L'esthétique galante,* 30–34.

41. "Il est de l'esprit même de la galanterie de mêler toujours le sérieux et le plaisant et de n'aborder aucun sujet, si grave soit-il, autrement que sous le couvert d'une 'fiction agréable.'" Pelous, *Amour précieux*, 14.

42. Interpretations of both *Le grand Cyrus* and *Clélie* are given in DeJean, *Tender Geographies*, 44–50, 61–62, 73, 82, 165–66.

43. See Hannon, "Desire and Writing"; and DeJean, *Fictions of Sappho*, 96–110.

44. Ferrand, *A Treatise on Lovesickness*, 225.

45. Ibid., 226–73.

46. "le plus grand plaisir [et délice] du monde," *L'École des filles*, 193.

47. See treatises by d'Angoumois, *La Florence convertie*; de Sales, *Introduction à la Vie Dévote*; and Le Moyne, *La Dévotion aisée*, which instruct women on how to live pious lives.

48. In *La Florence convertie à la vie dévote*, d'Angoumois juxtaposes sin and piety metaphorically as a series of battles between the vanities and love of God. Both are fighting to win over the soul of Florence, who is a wife and mother of noble birth, and both the vanities and love of God present their cases to Florence by describing earthly and heavenly pleasures and rewards, respectively.

49. Bacilly, *Les airs spirituels* (1672), unpaginated preface.

50. Ferrand, *A Treatise on Lovesickness*, 283–84.

51. "nos plus beaux airs étant sur des paroles extrêmement molles et efféminées, capables de faire des impressions dangereuses sur de jeunes esprits." Racine, *Œuvres complètes*, 945–46; in Goulet, *Poésie*, 248.

52. "Un des effets funestes de ces Chansons, est de laisser dans le cœur une tres-grande disposition au crime & au libertinage; en sorte que ceux qui les aiment & qui en font leur divertissement, se laissent facilement engager dans le désordre & dans l'impieté." Lalouette, *Histoire de la Comedie*, 71; cited in Goulet, *Poésie*, 248.

53. "Quel esprit déréglé, quelle aveugle manie, / Veut sans cesse à l'erreur consacrer l'Harmonie? / Idolâtres Chanteurs, entendray-je toûjours / Celebrer dans vos Chants Bacchus & les Amours?" [Bellocq], *La poësie*, 1–2.

54. "C'est le Dieu des Amours, c'est le Dieu des Vendanges, / Dont on entend par tout retentir les loüanges; . . . / Quelle est donc la fureur de ces chansons frivoles? / Faut-il voir, parmi nous, triompher les Idoles? / Et dans l'abisme affreux du culte mensonger, / L'Univers, aujourd'huy, va-t'il se replonger ?" Ibid., 2.

55. All editions of the anonymous *L'École des filles* published in 1655 were seized by government officials and burned. The second edition, in 1688, was published in the Netherlands. Copies of the 1688 edition survived.

56. "les mots qui sont plus doux et plus honnêtes." *L'École des filles*, 236.

57. Ibid., 236–37.

58. "ce sont des choses . . . que l'esprit invente, . . . la longue coutume a fait passer de main en main parmi tous ceux qui ont écrit des choses d'amour. . . . Croyez-moi, ne bannissons point les figures du discours, ne nous brouillons point avec les amants qui font des vers." Sarasin, *S'il faut qu'un jeune*

homme soit amoureux, quoted in in Génetiot, *Poétique du loisir mondain,* 251.

59. Génetiot, *Poétique,* 251. Amorous metaphors were, of course, nothing new to seventeenth-century literature or lyrical poetry, and indeed, many of the same metaphors had been used in literary works since antiquity. For an interesting account of a history of erotic love in medical treatises and its representation in literature, see the introduction to Ferrand, *A Treatise on Lovesickness.*

60. Ferrand, *A Treatise on Lovesickness,* 250. He quotes here from Aristotle.

61. Ibid., 251.

62. *L'École des filles,* 206 and 210.

63. This sort of fluid is referred to in *L'École des filles* as the liqueur of love ("la liqueur d'amour"), first defined on page 197.

64. Ferrand, *A Treatise on Lovesickness,* 233.

65. Ibid., 252.

66. For an explanation of the use of overworked metaphors borrowed from combat to refer to love, see the introduction to Ferrand, *A Treatise on Lovesickness,* 150–51.

67. See, for example, *L'École des filles,* 209, 212 or 259.

68. "Sylvie: Ah! Tyrsis, il est temps, mon Tyrsis. / Tyrsis: Ma Sylvie, / Vas-tu mourir? / Sylvie : Je meurs ! / Tyrsis : Et moy je perds la vie. / Tous Ensemble: Dans ce charmant trépas, / Où l'amour nous assemble, / Ne nous divisons pas, / Mourons tous deux ensemble. / Sylvie: O douceur, ô plaisir, je languis! / Tyrsis : Je me pâme, / Je n'en puis plus, / Sylvie. / Helas! / Et je vays rendre l'ame. / Tous deux. / Dans ce charmant trépas." Perrin, *Œuvres de poésie,* 238–39, in Goulet, *Poésie,* 395.

69. Ferrand acknowledges that sexual intercourse is thought by some to be "the last and only cure to which one must have recourse" (Ferrand, *A Treatise on Lovesickness,* 334). But he goes on to say that this is recommended only in marriage and strongly objects to sexual activity outside of marriage, which is a sin. He then questions this "cure," explaining that if it were so effective, no married man would seek extramarital relations (334–35).

70. Ibid., 350–51.

71. Ibid., 323.

72. Ibid., 226–27.

73. Ibid., 228.

74. Ibid.

75. Bénigne de Bacilly deals at length with ornamentation and its application to second strophes, or *doubles,* of the air in his treatise *Remarques curieuses.*

76. Ferrand, *A Treatise on Lovesickness,* 333–34.

77. "Quand l'amour veut finir les peines d'un amant, / Un seul moment / Paye aisément / Le rude tourment. // O doux moment! O doux fruit des amours, / O doux moment! qui fait les heureux jours, / O doux moment par

quelle injuste loi / N'est-tu pas fait pour moi?" Le Camus, *Airs à deux et trois parties*, 34.

78. Pelous, *Amour précieux*, 14.

79. Two of the most famous female singers of the time, Hilaire Dupuis, Michel Lambert's sister-in-law, and Anne de La Barre, the sister of composer Joseph Chabanceau de La Barre, both performed *airs sérieux* in the most prestigious salons and at court. See Goulet, *Poésie*, 236–37, 249, 382, and 461.

80. The only person referred to is Jesus, but both men and women could address a sacred song to him.

81. In Lambert's collection of twenty airs, there is only one air with a female voice, one dialogue between a male and female, fourteen with a male poetic voice, and four gender-neutral texts. Of the fifty-eight airs that comprise Bacilly's *Les Trois livres d'airs,* there are no song texts with a female poetic voice. In forty-six airs, the poetic voice is male, and in twelve it is gender neutral. Of the sixteen serious airs in La Barre's publication, there are no airs with a female poetic voice, fourteen with a male voice, and two that are gender neutral. There is a slightly different representation in the published edition of airs by Le Camus, which was published after his death by his son Charles in 1678. Of the thirty-two airs, ten have a female poetic voice, fifteen a male voice, and seven are gender neutral. The increased number of airs with a female poetic voice may be due to the date of publication, which is almost twenty years later than the first publications of Lambert's and Bacilly's airs, and almost ten years later than that of La Barre's. Because Le Camus' son determined the choice of his father's airs, he may have had in mind a broader public that preferred a greater variety of poetic voice. These airs are, in fact, different in other ways as well; they were published without second strophes, for example, so there are no musical *doubles*.

82. For a discussion of this phenomenon, see Gordon-Seifert, "Strong Men—Weak Women."

83. Scudéry, *The Story of Sapho*, 87.

84. For an account of female poets and their song texts, see Goulet, *Poésie*, 289–95.

85. "Il est vray je suis rigoureuse, / Mais ma rigueur me fera vivre en paix; // Il n'est rien tel pour estre heureuse, / Que d'estre aymable et de n'aymer jamais." Bacilly, in Ballard, *Livre d'airs de différents autheurs* (1666), 20.

86. The "Avis de consequence" is found in the Part 2 of Bacilly, *Les airs spirituels,* 1688 edition. .

87. "de corriger le mauvais usage que l'on en fait dans les Chansons Françoises (qui pour l'ordinaire ne sont remplies que de Paroles lascives) en y mettant des Paroles de Pieté, & qui n'inspirent des sentimens d'amour que pour Dieu seul." Bacilly, *Les airs spirituels* (1672), unpaginated preface.

88. Bacilly, *Les airs spirituels* (1688), 6.

89. Fumaroli, *La diplomatie*, 307. See also Goulet, *Poésie*, 200–207.

90. Harris, *Hidden Agendas*, 110.

91. Ibid., 110–12.

92. Ferrand, *A Treatise on Lovesickness,* 230.

93. "Quoy qu'elle chante d'une maniere passionnée et qu'on peut effectivement dire qu'elle chante fort bien, elle chante pourtant en personne de condition, c'est à dire sans y mettre son honneur, sans s'en faire prier et sans façon, et elle fait cela si galamment qu'elle en devient encore plus aimable." Scudéry, *Clélie,* 3:1325; quoted in Goulet, *Poésie,* 311, and Gérold, *L'art du chant,* 106.

94. Harris, *Hidden Agendas,* 111.

95. Ibid., 112.

96. Ferrand, *A Treatise on Lovesickness,* 243. Here he is quoting the Roman satirist Juvenal.

97. Ibid.

98. Ibid., 244.

99. "L'Abbé: Ils aiment mieux, . . . une belle voix toute seule. / Le Chevalier: Asseurement, sur tout si cette belle voix sort d'une bouche bien vermeille & passe entre des dents bien blanches, bien nettes & bien rangées." Perrault, *Parallèle des anciens et des modernes,* 217–19, in Goulet, *Poésie,* 250–51.

100. "Elle les chantoit avec plaisir . . . et en les chantant elle faisoit voir les plus belles dents du monde et les mieux rangées. Si l'on applaudissoit à sa voix, on se récrioit sur la beauté de ses dents." *Mercure galant,* March 1697, in Goulet, *Poésie,* 251.

101. "Quand nous contemplons le corail de leurs lèvres, nous ne les voudrions jamais voir ouvertes, mais quand le chant nous découvre l'yvoire de leurs dents qui fait retentir l'air qui en sort, nous ne les voudrions jamais voir fermées." Grenailles, *Le Plaisir des dames,* in Brenet, *Les concerts,* 42.

102. See Dufresny, *Amusemens,* 39; quoted in Timmermans, *L'accès des femmes,* 228.

103. Dupuis was Michel Lambert's sister-in-law; see note 79, above.

104. "Vous sçavez chanter comme Hilaire, / Faire de la Prose & des Vers, / Toucher des Airs / Dessus mille Instrumens divers: / C'est plus qu'il n'est necessaire / Pour charmer; / Mais pourroit-on s'informer / Si vous sçavez aimer?" Sercy, *Suite,* 532.

105. Flamen, *Devises et emblèmes,* 170–73.

106. Ferrand, *A Treatise on Lovesickness,* 233.

107. Ibid., 352.

108. "Dessus la verte fougere, / Tircis avec sa Bergere, / Passent le jour à l'amour: / Ravis d'un plaisir extreme, / Ils soûpirent tour à tour! / Ah qu'il est doux quand on ayme, / De passer ainsi le jour.

A l'ombre prés d'un rivage, / Où dans le fond d'un boccage, / Pendant la chaleur du jour: / Afin d'augmenter leur flame, / Ils se font tous deux la cour: / Qu'il est doux quand on s'enflame, / Et qu'on fait ainsi l'amour." Ballard, *Livre d'air de différents autheurs* (1663), 8.

109. Ferrand, *A Treatise on Lovesickness,* 311–12.

110. See d'Angoumois, *La Florence convertie;* d'Angoumois, *Occupation continuelle;* de Sales, *Introduction à la Vie Dévote;* and Le Moyne, *La Dévotion aisée.*

111. In *L'École des filles*, Fanchon describes her lover's expressions of passion with words that could have been taken from song texts: he complains that she must relieve his pain; he looks at her with dying eyes, tells her of his martyrdom, and indicates that he will die for her. The same cries of sexual pleasure—*Hélas, hé, ah*—also appear in airs as tender sighs or painful cries. See *L'École des filles*, 188, 192–93, and 211.

112. Ferrand notes that Boethius believed music in Phrygian mode, in particular, had "powers for exciting the spirits." Ferrand, *A Treatise on Lovesickness*, 244.

113. [Bellocq], *La poësie*, 1–2.

114. Lalouette, *Histoire de la Comedie*, 71; cited in Goulet, *Poésie*, 248. See note 52, above, for text in French.

8. The Late-Seventeenth-Century Air and the Rhetoric of Distraction

1. Bacilly, *Remarques*, 60–87, and *A Commentary*, 29–40.

2. Bacilly, *Remarques*, 64, and *A Commentary*, 30.

3. From a letter sent to Balzac in 1628. Descartes, *Correspondance*, 1:34; translated in Carr, *Descartes*, 24.

4. Carr, *Descartes*, 66.

5. Ibid., 97.

6. Translated in ibid., 96–97.

7. Ibid., 97.

8. Ibid., 94.

9. Ibid.

10. "Quel esprit déréglé, quelle aveugle manie, / Veut sans cesse à l'erreur consacrer l'Harmonie? / Idolâtres Chanteurs, entendray-je toûjours / Celebrer dans vos Chants Bacchus & les Amours? / Verray-je, à la faveur des concerts & des rimes, / S'etablir, parmi nous, mille impures maximes; / Par l'attrait de la voix surprendre la raison, / Et d'un charme innocent faire un mortel poison? / Le beau Cantique à mettre en la bouche des Dames, / Que le honteux aveu de leurs secrettes flammes; / Qu'un éternel avis de payer à leur tour, / Le tribut prétendu que tout doit à l'amour! / Le merveilleux secret de former la jeunesse, / Que sans cesse en nos Chants décrier la sagesse, / La traiter d'importune; & faire à nos desirs / Une invincible loy de gouster les plaisirs!" [Bellocq], *La poësie*, 1–2.

11. "C'est le Dieu des Amours, c'est le Dieu des Vendanges, / Dont on entend par tout retentir les loüanges ; . . . / Quelle est donc la fureur de ces chansons frivoles? / Faut-il voir, parmi nous, triompher les Idoles? / Et dans l'abisme affreux du culte mensonger, / L'Univers, aujourd'huy, va-t'il se replonger ?" Ibid., 2.

12. Carr, *Descartes*, 66.

13. "Toute leur application est toujours aux manières agréables. . . . Ils ne se servent de leur esprit que pour érudier l'agrément et l'art de plaire, pour les choses qui flattent la concupiscence et les sens." Pierre Nicole, *Essais de morale*, 42:6; translated in Carr, *Descartes*, 66.

14. I mention the works of Berthod and Bacilly to exemplify the trend associated with sacred airs accessible to the singers. I do not intend this account in any way to be thorough. What I refer to here are sacred pieces for solo voice with accompaniment written in the style of the mid-to-late seventeenth-century serious air. See Favier, "Les cantiques spirituels," for a thorough treatment of this repertory.

15. Gordon-Seifert, "From Impurity to Piety."

16. For a fascinating publication history of Bacilly's two books of airs spirituels, see Favier, "Bénigne de Bacilly."

17. Jacques Testu was born near Paris in 1626 and died eighty years later, in 1706. He was born into a well-connected noble family, and in 1662 became *l'abbé commendataire de Belval*. Eventually he obtained the title of *prédicateur du roi* under Louis XIV as well as that of director of the Académie Française. He attended the most prestigious salons of the day and knew many important women quite well, including Madame de Sévigné, la duchesse de Richelieu, Madame de Sablé, and Madame de Maintenon, the king's second wife. Graffin, *Jacques Testu,* 5–7.

18. Bacilly notes that he "found an abundance of material upon which to compose not only this small number of airs, but . . . it seems that this illustrious author had made [his *Stances*] expressively for musical setting. They have all the modulation, all the sweetness, all the expression and *mouvement* necessary to please the most delicate of ears" ("[J]'ay trouvé abondament de la matiere pour faire non seulement ce petit nombre d'Airs, mais autant qu'il y a de Stances, qu'il semble que cet illustre Autheur ait faites expres pour recevoir un Chant qui ait toute la Modulation, toute la Douceur, toute l'Expression & le Mouvement necessaire pour contenter l'oreille des plus delicats"). Bacilly, *Les airs spirituels* (1672), preface.

19. See chapter 1.

20. "[L]orsque la matière que l'on traite est telle qu'elle nous doit raisonnablement toucher, c'est un défaut d'en parler d'une manière sèche, froide, et sans movement, parce que c'est un défaut de n'être pas touché de ce que l'on doit." Arnauld and Nicole, *La Logique,* 97; translated in Carr, *Descartes,* 71.

21. Carr, *Descartes,* 115.

22. "L'Ordre, qui doit nous reformer, est une forme trop abstraite pour server de modèle aux esprits grossiers. . . . Qu'on lui donne donc du corps, qu'on le rende sensible, qu'on le revête en plusieurs manières pour le rendre aimable à des homes charnels: qu'on l'incarne pour ainsi dire." Malebranche, *Œuvres,* 11:33; translated in Carr, *Descartes,* 115.

23. Faret, *L'Honneste-Homme,* 26, 44, 68–69, 79; translated in Seifert, *Manning the Margins.*

24. Faret, *L'Honneste-Homme,* 21. As mentioned in chapter 7, Racine criticized airs as being "set to words that are extremely soft (*des paroles extrêmement molles*) and effeminate (*efféminées*), capable of making harmful impressions on young minds." Racine, *Œuvres completes,* 945–46.

25. "Pour ce qui est des seconds Couplets, comme ce n'est pas d'aujourd'huy qu'on les remplit de Diminutions, aussi est ce une erreur de dire que ce n'est plus la mode d'en faire tant que l'on a fait autrefois. Il est

vray que jadis on eust crù faire un crime de laisser passer une syllabe sans la broder, & que sans consideration aucune de longues ny de brésves ou *fredonner* à tort & à travers, aux despens mesme de la Pronunciation dont on tenoit fort peu de compte." Bacilly, *Remarques*, 225–26, and *A Commentary*, 114.

26. "[I]l ne faut pas dire pour cela que la mode soit le seul fondement de cette reformation, puis qu'il est vray que les Paroles puissent supporter la Diminution, & qu'il n'y ait rien qui s'y oppose." Bacilly, *Remarques*, 225–26, and *A Commentary*, 114.

27. Bacilly, *Remarques*, 103, and *A Commentary*, 47.

28. As mentioned in chapter 1, the Ballard publications do not include notated *doubles*. Christophe Ballard did, however, print *doubles* for many of the airs in the three volumes of *Brunetes ou petits airs tendres* in 1703, 1704, and 1711.

29. Lecerf de la Viéville asserts that "Lully was an enemy of the doubles, passages, *roulements* and all these 'precious' niceties, about which the Italians are infatuated" ("Lully étoit ennemi des doubles, des passages, des roulemens et de toutes ces précieuses gentillesses, dont les Italiens sont infatuez"); quoted in Massip, *L'art de bien chanter*, 94.

30. "[L]es Airs François . . . ne souffrent que des mots doux & coulans & des Expressions familieres." Bacilly, *Remarques*, 93, and *A Commentary*, 43.

31. "[I]l faut qu'il y ait du bon sens, sans pointe & mesme sans équivoque." Bacilly, *Remarques*, 114, and *A Commentary*, 51.

32. "[J]'ay esté sollicité de faire ces sortes d'Airs Spirituels par ma proper inclination, & par des Personnes de la premiere Qualité, qui voyant avec douleur que dans les Maisons de Religion, on instruisoit la jeunesse dans la maniere de chanter avec des Chansons profanes (pour ne pas dire lascives)." Bacilly, *Les airs spirituels* (1672), preface.

33. See Favier, "Plaisir musical," 120.

34. "Si d'amollir le cœurs la musique est coupable, / Le son est innocent, le vers seul est coupable; / Tout concert de lui-même élève mon esprit. / Le poète lui seul m'abaisse & m'attendrit." [Bellocq], *La poësie*, 7.

35. See, for example, *Mercure galant*, November 1679, 213–16, or May 1688, 205.

36. Cited in Massip, *L'art de bien chanter*, 128–29.

37. Cited in ibid., 92–97, 124–27.

38. Ibid., 93.

39. "Ainsi Lambert, qui n'a jamais exprimé dans ses airs des passions très-fortes, n'a pas été obligé de rechercher des expressions si perçantes. Il a pû s'attacher davantage à plaire aux oreilles; et il n'y a rien à dire, que son grand mérite soit de sçavoir leur donner un plaisir délicieux, par de tons aussi heureux qu'ils puissent être." Lecerf de la Viéville, *Comparaison*, 2:162–64; quoted in Massip, *L'art de bien chanter*, 126.

40. Massip, *L'art de bien chanter*, 91–92.

41. Ibid., 99–133.

42. See Lecerf de la Viéville, *Comparaison*, 1:130, 2:79, 2:99.

43. See, in particular, Paris, Bibliothèque nationale de France, Rés. Vma. ms 854.

44. Goulet, *Poésie*, 178–92

45. It is interesting that of the four composers, La Barre or his works are not, to my knowledge, mentioned in sources from the late seventeenth or early eighteenth centuries.

46. *Mercure galant*, May, 1688, 1:205; in Massip, *L'art de chanter*, 88.

47. In Massip, *L'art de chanter*, 111–12.

48. Ibid., 128.

49. See, in particular, Paris, Bibliothèque nationale de France, Rés. ms Vm7 501 and Rés. Vma. ms 854.

50. "[Les expression] qui sont mesme souvent de grand poids & de grande consideration dans la Poësie." Bacilly, *Remarques*, 94, and *A Commentary*, 43.

51. Furetière, *Le Roman bourgeois*, 108–109.

52. See La Barre, "Quand une ame est bien attente," in *Airs à deux parties*, ed. Saint-Arroman, 22v.

53. Massip, *L'art de bien chanter*, 276.

54. Ibid., 271.

55. Ibid., 126–27. This air appears in Ballard's *Recueil d'airs sérieux et à boire* of 1703, labeled "Air sérieux de M. Le Camus."

56. "[Lambert] . . . cherche à traduire la complexité des sentiments exprimés ou sous-jacents." Massip, "Michel Lambert," 1:351.

57. See, for example, Bacilly's "Vous ne pouvez Iris" (Example 4.3). Catherine Massip identifies Bacilly's airs as more "Italianate," in contrast to Lambert's works, which were strongly identified with French musical style. I would suggest that it is the features of Bacilly's style identified above that led Massip to her conclusions. Massip, "Michel Lambert," 1:328.

58. Massip, "Michel Lambert and Jean-Baptiste Lully," 39.

59. Massip, "Michel Lambert," 1:351–52.

60. Ibid.

61. Massip, "Michel Lambert and Jean-Baptiste Lully," 39.

62. Anthony, *French Baroque Music*, 80.

63. Ibid., 56, 58–59, and 69–73.

64. Mersenne, *Correspondance*, 10:236; translated in Walker, "Joan Albert Ban," 253.

65. Lecerf de la Viéville, *Comparaison*, 1:169; translated in Cowart, "Inventing the Arts," 225.

66. Norman, "Ancients and Moderns," 185–86; Dill, "Music, Beauty," 197; and Cowart, "Inventing the Arts," 229–30.

67. Dill, "Music, Beauty," 199.

68. As we have seen in the assessments of the air by church leaders and moralists, when the air was criticized, often only the song text was considered. This phenomenon held true for the Lully-Quinault operas as well. While the music of Lully, when mentioned at all, is generally described with enthusiasm, Quinault's libretti were scrutinized and compared to ancient tragedies and those by Racine, favorably by some (proponents of "modern" works) and unfavorably by others (promoters of literary and artistic standards set by the "ancients"); see Norman, "Ancients and Moderns," 179–82. I should add that religious leaders also criticized Quinault's libretti.

Bibliography

Musical Works Cited

Ambruis, Honoré d.' *Livre d'airs avec les seconds couplet en diminution.* Paris: Ballard, 1685.

Bacilly, Bénigne de. *Les airs spirituels de Mr de Bacilly, sur les stances chres-tiennes de Monsieur l'Abbé Testu, ou fragmens d'icelles, avec la basse continuë, & les seconds couplets en diminution.* Paris: Guillaume de Luyne, 1672.

———. *Les airs spirituels de Mr de Bacilly, sur les stances chrestiennes de Monsieur l'Abbé Testu, ou fragmens d'icelles, avec la basse continuë, & les seconds couplets en diminution.* Paris: Guillaume de Luyne, 1677.

———. *Les airs spirituels de Mr de Bacilly, sur les stances chrestiennes de Monsieur l'Abbé Testu, ou fragmens d'icelles, avec la basse continuë, & les seconds couplets en diminution.* Parts 1 and 2. Paris: Guillaume de Luyne, 1688.

———. *Capilotade bachique à deux parties.* Paris: Ballard, 1667.

———. *III. livre de chansons pour danser et pour boire.* Paris: Ballard, 1665.

———. *IIII. livre de chansons pour danser et pour boire.* Paris: Ballard, 1666.

———. *V. livre de chansons pour danser et pour boire.* Paris: Ballard, 1667.

———. *XXII livre de chansons pour danser et pour boire à deux parties.* Paris: Ballard, 1663.

———. *Meslanges d'airs à deux parties.* Paris: Ballard, 1671.

———. *II. meslanges, de chansons, airs sérieux et à boire.* Paris: Ballard, 1674.

———. *Nouveau livre d'airs.* Paris: Richer, 1661.

———. *Second livre d'airs bachiques.* Paris: Ballard, 1677.

———. *Second livre d'airs. Dedié á son altesse Mademoiselle de Nemours.* Paris: Richer, 1664.

———. *Second livre de chansons pour danser et pour boire à deux parties.* Paris: Ballard, 1664.

———. *Les Trois livres d'airs. Regravez de nouveau en deux volumes. Augmenter de plusieurs Airs nouveaux.* Paris: [Richer], 1668.

———. *Les Trois livres d'airs.* Facsimile edition. Courlay, France: Editions de J. M. Fuzeau, 1996.

Ballard, Christophe, ed. *Brunetes ou Petits airs tendres.* Paris: Ballard, 1703, 1704, and 1711.

———. *Livre[s] d'airs de différents autheurs.* Paris: Ballard, 1673–1694.

———. *Livre[s] d'airs sérieux et à boire.* Paris: Ballard, 1695.

———. *Livre[s] de chansons pour danser et pour boire.* Paris: Ballard, 1673–94.

———. *Meslanges de musique latine, françoise et italienne.* Paris: Ballard, 1725, 1730.

———. *Recueil[s] d'airs sérieux et à boire.* Paris: Ballard, 1695–1721.

———. *Recueil[s] de chansonnettes de différents autheurs.* Paris: Ballard, 1675–86.

Ballard, Robert, ed. *Airs bachiques.* Paris: Ballard, 1672.

———. *I–XVI Livre[s] d'airs de différents autheurs.* Paris: Ballard, 1658–1673.

———. *Livre[s] d'airs pour danser et pour boire.* Paris: Ballard, 1653–73.

Berthod, François. *Livre[s] d'airs de dévotion à deux parties. Ou conversion de quelques-uns des plus beaux de ce temps en Airs Spirituels.* Paris: Robert Ballard, 1656, 1658, 1662.

Brossard, Sébastien de. *Livre d'airs sérieux et à boire.* Paris: Ballard, 1696.

Cambert, Robert. *Airs à boire a deux, et a trois parties. De Monsieur Cambert, Maistre & Compositeur de la Musique de la Reyne Mere, & Organiste de l'Eglise Collegial de Saint-Honoré de Paris.* Paris: Robert Ballard, 1665.

Dandrieu, Jean-François. *Principes de l'Accompagnement du Clavecin.* Paris: Foucaut, 1719.

Fleury, Le Sieur. *Airs spirituels à deux parties avec la basse-continue.* Paris: Ballard, 1678.

Hurel, Charles. *Airs à deux parties avec les seconds couplets en diminution.* Facsimile edition, edited by Jean Saint-Arroman. Courlay, France: Editions J. M. Fuzeau, 1992.

———. *Meslanges d'airs sérieux et à boire à II et III parties.* Paris: Ballard, 1687.

La Barre, Joseph Chabanceau de. *Airs à deux parties avec les seconds couplets en diminution.* Paris: Ballard, 1669.

———. *Airs à deux parties avec les seconds couplete en diminution.* Facsimile edition, edited by Jean Saint-Arroman. Courlay, France: Éditions J. M. Fuzeau, 1992.

Lambert, Michel. *Airs à une, II, III, et IV parties avec la basse-continue composez par Monsieur Lambert, maistre de la Musique de la Chambre du Roy.* Paris: Ballard, 1689.

———. *Les airs de M. Lambert non imprimez, 75 simples, 50 doubles, chez M. Foucault, rue Saint-Honoré.* Facsimile edition of Paris, Bibliothèque nationale, ms 3043, ca. 1692, edited by Jean Saint-Arroman. Courlay, France: Éditions J. M. Fuzeau, 2006.

———. *Les Airs de Monsieur Lambert.* 1st ed. Paris: Richer, 1660.

———. *Les Airs de Monsieur Lambert . . . corrigez de nouveau de plusieurs fautes de gravure.* 2nd ed. Paris: Richer, 1666. Facsimile edition. Geneva: Minkoff Reprints, 1983.

———. *Les Airs de Monsieur Lambert . . . corrigez de nouveau de plusiers fautes de gravure.* 3rd ed. Paris: Richer, 1669.

———. *Airs from* Airs de différents autheurs. Edited by Robert Green. Middleton, Wisc.: A-R Editions, 2005.

Le Camus, Sébastien. *Airs à deux et trois parties. De feu Monsieur Le Camus, Maistre de la Musique de la Reyne.* Paris: Ballard, 1678.

———. *Airs à deux et trois parties. De feu Monsieur Le Camus, Maistre de la Musique de la Reyne.* Edited by Robert Green. Middleton, Wisc.: A-R Editions, Inc., 1998.

Montéclair, Michel Pignolet de. *Brunetes anciènes et modernes.* 1st ed. Paris: Boivin, n.d.

Recueil de chansons choisies. Paris: Simon Bernard, 1694.

Primary Sources

Aristotle. *Poetics.* In *The Rhetoric and The Poetics of Aristotle,* translated and edited by Ingram Bywater, 223–66. New York: Modern Library, 1954.

———. *Rhetoric.* Translated by W. Rhys Roberts. New York: Modern Library, 1954.

Arnauld, Antoine, and Nicole Pierre. *La Logique, ou l'art de penser.* Edited by Pierre Clair and Fr. Girbal. Paris: P.U.F., 1965.

Augustine, Saint. *On Christian Doctrine.* Translated by D. W. Robertson, Jr. New York: Liberal Arts Press, 1958.

Bacilly, Bénigne. *L'Art de bien chanter. Augmenté d'un discourse qui sert de réponse à la critique de ce traité.* Paris: Chez l'autheur ruë Pastourelle, au petit S. Jean, 1679. Reprint, Geneva: Minkoff, 1974.

———. *A Commentary upon the Art of Proper Singing.* 1668. Translated and edited by Austin Caswell. New York: Institute of Mediaeval Music, 1968.

———. *Nouveau recueil des plus beaux airs.* Paris, 1669.

———. *Nouveau recueil des plus beaux airs.* Paris: Chez un Chandelier, 1670.

———. *Nouveau recueil des plus beaux airs.* Paris: G. de Luyne, 1680.

———. *Recueil [et suite de la premier partie] des plus beaux airs.* Paris: Charles de Sercy, 1661.

———. *Recueil [et suite de la troisième partie] des plus beaux airs.* Paris: Ballard, 1667.

———. *Recueil des plus beaux airs.* Paris: Ballard, 1668.

————. *Remarques curieuses sur l'art de bien chanter et particulierement pour ce qui regarde le chant français par le sieur B. D. B.* Paris: Robert Ballard, 1668.

Bary, René. *L'Esprit de cour, ou les conversations galantes divisées en cent dialogues.* Paris: C. de Sercy, 1662.

————. *Méthode pour bien prononcer un Discours.* Paris: Denys Thierry, 1679.

————. *La Rhétorique françoise ou pour principale augmentation l'on trouve les secrets de nostre langue.* Paris: Denys Thierry, 1673.

[Bellocq, Pierre]. *La poësie et la musique. Satire à Monsieur Despreaux.* Paris: Denis Mariette, 1695.

Bérard, Jean Antoine. *L'Art de chant. Dédié à Monsieur de Pompadour.* Paris: Dessaint & Saillant, 1755. Reprint, New York: Broude Brothers, 1967.

Bernhard, Christoph. *Tractatus compositionis augmentatus.* Translated and edited by Walter Hilse. *The Music Forum* 3:31–196. New York: Columbia University Press, 1973.

Boursault, Edme. "Lettres de Babet." In *Lettres portugaises, Lettres d'une Péruvienne, et autres roman d'amour par lettres.* Edited by Bernard Bray and Isabelle Landy-Houillon. Paris: Flammarion, 1983.

Bretteville, Abbé de. *L'Éloquence de la chaire et du barreau selon les principes les plus solide de la Rhétorique, sacre et Profane.* Paris: Denys Theirry, 1689.

Buffet, Marguerite. *Nouvelles Observations sur la Langue Françoise.* Paris: Boubon, 1668.

Cicero. *De inventione.* Translated by H. M. Hubbell. Cambridge, Mass.: Harvard University Press, 1948.

————. *De optimo genere oratorum.* Translated by H. M. Hubbell. Cambridge, Mass.: Harvard University Press, 1948.

————. *De oratore III.* Translated by H. Rackham. Cambridge, Mass.: Harvard University Press, 1948.

————. *Topica.* Translated by H. M. Hubbell. Cambridge, Mass.: Harvard University Press, 1948.

Colletet, G. *L'art de Poetique de Sr. Colletet.* Paris: Antoine de Sommaville, 1658.

Courtin, Antoine de. *Nouveau traité de la civilité.* 2nd ed. Paris: Hellie Josset, 1672.

Cureau de la Chambre, Marin. *Les Charactères des passions.* 5 vols. Paris: Chez Jacques d'Allin, 1662.

D'Anglebert, Jean-Henri. *Principes de l'accompagnement,* printed in his *Pièces de Clavecin.* Paris, 1689.

D'Angoumois, Philippe. *La Florence convertie à la vie dévote*. Paris: Toussaincts du Bray aux Espics meurs et Joseph Cottebray à la Prudence, 1627.

———. *Occupation continuelle en laquelle l'ame devote s'unit tousjours avecque Dieu*. Lyon: Chez Louis Muguet, 1618.

De Bosc, Jacques. *L'Honnête femme*. Paris: Billaine, 1632.

Delair, Denis. *Accompaniment on Theorbo and Harpsichord: Denis Delair's Treatise of 1690*. Translated by Charlotte Mattax. Bloomington: Indiana University Press, 1991.

———. *Traité de l'accompagnement sur le théorbe et le clavecin qui comprend toutes les règles nécessaires pour accompagner sur ces deux instruments*. Paris, 1690. Reprint, Geneva: Minkoff, 1972.

Denis, Jean. *Traité de l'accord de l'espinette avec la comparaison de son clavier avec la musique vocale*. Paris: Ballard and Jean Denis, 1650.

Descartes, René. *Compendium musicae*. [1618]. Translated by Walter Robert. Neuhausen-Stuttgart: American Institute of Musicology, 1961.

———. *Correspondance*. Edited by B. Vélat and Yvonne Champailler. Paris: Gallimard, 1961.

———. *The Passions of the Soul* (1649). Vol. 1 of *The Philosophical Writings of Descartes*, 313–404. Translated and edited by Robert Soothoff. Cambridge: Cambridge University Press, 1985.

Dufresny, Charles. *Amusemens sérieux et comiques*. Paris, 1699, augmented in 1707. Edited by John Dunkley. Exeter University Press, 1976.

L'École des filles ou la philosophie des dames divisée en deux dialoques: agere et pati. . . . Fribourg: Roger Bon Temps, 1668. In *Œuvres érotiques du XVIIe siècle: L'enfer de la Bibliothèque nationale*, edited by Michael Camus, 167–288. Libraire Arthème Fayard, 1988.

Entretien galans, ou, conversations sur la mode, la musique, le jeu, les louanges. Vol. 2. Paris: Jean Ribou, 1681.

Faret, Nicolas. *L'Honneste-Homme*. Paris: Toussaincts du Bray, 1630.

Fénelon, François. *Dialogues on Eloquence*. Translated and edited by Wilbur Samuel Howell. Princeton, N.J.: Princeton University Press, 1951.

Ferrand, Jacques. *A Treatise on Lovesickness*. Translated and edited by Donald A. Beecher and Massimo Ciavolella. Syracuse, N.Y.: Syracuse University Press, 1990.

Flamen, Albert. *Devises et emblèmes d'Amour moralisez*. Paris: Olivier de Varennes, 1653; Paris: Chez Estienne Loyson, 1672.

Fleury, Nicolas. *Méthode pour apprendre facilement à toucher le théorbe sur la basse-continue*. Paris: Ballard, 1660. Reprint, Geneva: Minkoff, 1972.

Furetière, Antoine. *Dictionnaire de musique d'après Furetière*. The Hague and Rotterdam, 1690. Reprint, Societé de Musicologie de Languedoc, 1988.

————. *Le Dictionnaire universel.* The Hague and Rotterdam, 1690. Reprint, Paris: S.N.L.-Le Robert, 1978.

————. *Le Roman bourgeois, ouvrage comique.* Paris: C. Barbin, 1666.

————. *Le Roman bourgeois, ouvrage comique.* Edited by Jacques Prévot. Paris: Éditions Gallimard, 1981.

Gaultier, Denis. *La Rhétorique des dieux.* Edited by David Buch. Madison, Wisc.: A-R Editions, 1990.

Gibert, Balthazar. *Réflexion sur la rhétorique.* Paris: M. David, 1705–1707.

Grenailles, François de Chatounières de. *Le Plaisir des dames.* Paris: Gervais Clousier, 1641.

Grimarest, Jean-Léonor Le Gallois, sieur de. *Traité du récitatif dans la lecture, dans l'action publique, dans la declamation, et dans le chant. Avec un traité des accens, de la quantité, et de la Ponctuation.* Paris: Jacques Le Fevre et Pierre Ribou, 1707.

Hindret, Jean. *L'Art de bien prononcer et de bien parler la langue françoise.* Paris, 1687.

La Borde, Jean-Benjamin de. *Essai sur la musique ancienne et moderne.* Paris: Eugène Onfroy, 1780. Reprint, 1972.

La Croix, Phérotée de. *L'Art de la poësie françoise et latine avec une idée de la musique sous une nouvelle méthode.* Lyon: Thomas Amaulry, 1694. Reprint, Geneva: Slatkine, 1973.

L'Affilard, Michel. *Principes tres-facile pour bien apprendre la musique qui conduiront promptment ceux qui one du naturel pour le chant jusqu'au point de chanter toutes sortes d'airs proprement.* Paris: Ballard, 1694.

Lalouette, Ambroise. *Histoire de la Comedie et de l'opera, où l'on prouve qu'on ne peut y aller sans pecher.* Paris: Louis Josse, 1697.

La Mothe de Vayer, François de. *Considération sur l'éloquence françoise.* Paris: Sébastien Cramoisy, 1638.

Lamy, Bernard. *L'art de parler, avec un Discours dans lequel on donne une idée de l'art de persuader. Troisième edition. Reveuë & amp; augmentée.* Paris: chez André Pralard, 1678.

————. *The Art of Speaking . . . Rendered into English.* London: W. Godbid, 1676.

La Voye Mignot. *Traité de musique pour bien et facilement apprendre à chanter et composer.* 2nd ed. Paris: Ballard, 1666. Reprint, Geneva: Minkoff, 1971.

————. *Traité de musique pour bien et facilement apprendre à composer* (1656). Translated by Albion Gruber. New York: Institute of Mediaeval Music.

Le Brun, Charles. *A Method to Learn to Design the Passions.* Trans. John Williams. London: F. Huggonson, 1734. Reprint, Los Angeles: University of California, 1980.

Lecerf de la Viéville, Jean Laurent. *Comparaison de la musique italienne et de la musique françoise*. 2nd ed. Brussels: François Foppeens, à Saint-Esprit, 1705–1706.

Le Faucheur, Michel. *An Essay upon the Action of an Orator, as to his pronunciation and gesture*. Translated anonymously. London: Nicholas Cox, 1680.

———. *Traité de l'action de l'orateur*. Paris: Augustin Courbé, 1657.

Le Gallois, Jean. *Lettre de Mr le Gallois à Mlle Regnault de Solier touchant la musique*. Paris: Estienne Michallet, 1689. Reprint, Geneva: Minkoff, 1984.

Le Moyne, Pierre. *La Dévotion aisée*. Paris: Antoine de Sommaville, 1652.

Loulié, Etienne. *Elements or Principles of Music*. Translated by Albert Cohen. New York: Institute of Mediaeval Music, 1965.

———. *Eléments ou principes de musique mis un nouvel ordre*. Paris: Ballard, 1696. Reprint, Geneva: Minkoff, 1971.

Maintenon, Marquise de. *Conversations*. Paris: Blaise, 1828.

Malebranche, Nicolas. *Œuvres complètes*. Edited by André Robinet et al. 20 vols. Paris: Vrin, 1958–67.

———. *Le Traité de la nature et de la grace*. Edited by Ginette Dreyfus. Paris: Vrin, 1958.

Masson, Charles. *Nouveau traité des règles pour la composition de la musique* [Paris: Ballard, 1705]. Reprint, Geneva: Minkoff, 1971.

Maugers, Claudius. *French Grammar*. London, 1658.

Ménestrier, Claude. *Des Représentatios en musique anciennes et modernes*. Paris: René Guignard, 1681. Reprint, Geneva: Minkoff, 1971.

Méré, Antoine Gombauld, chevalier de. *Œuvres posthumes*. Paris: Guignard, 1700.

Mersenne, Marin. *Correspondance du P. Marin Mersenne*. 2nd ed. Edited by Cornelis de Waard. Paris: Édition du Centre national de la recherche scientifique, 1969.

———. *Harmonie universelle, Contenant la Théorie et la Pratique de la Musique*. 3 vols. Paris: Sebastian Cramoisy, 1636–37. Reprint, Paris: Éditions du Centre national de la recherche scientifique, 1963.

———. *Questions harmoniques*. Paris: Villery, 1634.

———. *Traité de l'harmonie universelle*. Paris: Baudry, 1627. Reprint, Paris: Fayard, 2003.

Millet, Jean. *La Belle méthode, ou l'Art de bien chanter*. Lyon, 1666.

Nicole, Pierre. *Essais de morale*. Paris, 1733–71; Reprint, Geneva: Slatkine, 1971.

Nivers, Gabriel. *Traité de la composition de la musique*. Paris: Ballard, 1667.

Parran, Antoine. *Traité de la musique théoretique et pratique.* Paris: Ballard, 1639. Reprint, Geneva: Minkoff, 1972.

Pellisson, Paul. *Discours sur les œuvres de Monsieur Sarasin et autres textes,* in *L'Esthétique galante.* Edited by Alain Viala. Toulouse: Université de Toulouse-le-Mirail—Centre "Idées-Formes-Thèmes," 1989.

Perrault, Charles. *Parallèle des anciens et des modernes, en ce qui regarde les arts et les sciences.* Paris: J.-B. Coignard, 1688.

Perrin, Pierre. *Œuvres de poésie de Mr Perrin, contenant les jeux de poésie, diverses poesies galantes, des paroles de musique, airs de cour, airs à boire, chansons, noëls et motets, une comédie en musique, l'Entrée de la reyne, et la Chartreuse . . .* Paris: E. Loyson, 1661.

———. *Recueil de paroles de musique pour le concert de chambre de la Musique de la Reyne.* 1667. Translated and edited by Louis Auld. Vols. 2 and 3. Ottawa: Institute of Mediaeval Music, 1986.

Perrine. *Table pour apprendre à toucher le luth sur la basse continué.* Paris, 1682.

Plato. *The Republic.* In *The Dialogues of Plato,* translated and edited by Lewis Campbell and Benjamin Jowett. New York: Garland, 1987.

Poulain de La Barre, François. *De l'Égalité des deux sexes.* Paris: DuPuis, 1671.

Pure, Michel de. *Idée des spectacles anciens et nouveaux.* Paris: Michel Brunet, 1668. Reprint, Geneva: Minkoff Reprints, 1972.

Quintilian. *Institutio oratoria.* Translated by H. E. Butler. Cambridge, Mass.: Harvard University Press, 1936.

Racine, Jean. *Œuvres complètes de Racine.* Edited by Georges Forestier. Paris: Galimard, 1999.

Rapin, René. *Les Réflexions sur la poétique de ce temps et sur les ouvrages des poètes anciens et modernes.* Paris: F. Muguet, 1674.

Rhetorica ad Herennium. Translated by Harry Caplan. Cambridge, Mass.: Harvard University Press, 1954.

Rousseau, Jean. *Méthode claire, certaine et facile, pour apprendre à chanter la musique.* 5th ed. Amsterdam: Pierre Mortier, 1710. Reprint, Geneva: Minkoff Reprints, 1976.

———. *Traité de la viole.* Paris: Ballard, 1687.

Saint Gabriel. *Le Mérite des Dames.* 3rd ed. Paris: Jacques Le Gras, 1660.

Saint-Lambert, Michel de. *Les principes du clavecin.* 1702. Reprint, Geneva: Minkoff Reprints, 1974.

———. *Principles of the Harpsichord.* Translated and edited by Rebecca Harris-Warwick. Cambridge: Cambridge University Press, 1984.

Sales, François de. *Introduction à la Vie Dévote.* Lyon: Pierre Rigaud, 1609.

Scudéry, Madeleine de. *Clélie, histoire romaine.* A. Courbé, 1655–81.

———. *Conversations morales*. Paris: sur le quay des Augustins, à la descente du Pont-neuf, à l'image Saint-Louis [T. Guillain], 1686.

———. *La Promenade de Versailles*. Paris: Claude Burbin, 1669.

———. *The Story of Sapho*. Translated by Karen Newman. Chicago: University of Chicago Press, 2003. Originally titled *Histoire de Sapho*. Vol. 10 of *Artamène, ou, Le grand Cyrus*. Paris: chez Augustin Courbé, 1653.

Sercy, Charles de. *Suite de la premiere partie du recueil des plus beaux vers Qui ont esté mis en Chant*. Paris, 1661.

Tallemant des Réaux, G. *Historiettes*. Edited by Antoine Adam. 2 vols. Paris: Gallimard, 1961.

Testu, Jacques. *Stances chrestiennes sur divers passages de l'escriture sainte & des Peres*. Paris: Denys Thierry et Claude Barbin, 1669.

Tillet, E. Titon du. *Le Parnasse françois* Paris: J. B. Coignard fils, 1732.

Tosi, Pier Francesco. *Observations on the Florid Song; or Sentiments on the Ancient and Modern Singers*. Translated by J. E. Galliard. 1742, 1743. Reprint, 1969.

———. *Opinioni de' cantori antichi e moderni, o sieno Osservazioni sopra il canto figurato*. Bologna, 1723. Reprint, 1968.

Van Veen, Otto. *Amorum emblemata figures Aencis Incisa*. Antwerp: H. Verdussen, 1608. Facsimile edition. Paris: Aux Amaterus de livres, 1989.

Secondary Sources

A haute voix: Diction et pronunciation aux XVIe et XVIIe siècles. Edited by Olivia Rosenthal. Paris: Klincksieck, 1998.

A Performer's Guide to Seventeenth-Century Music. Edited by Stewart Carter. New York: Schirmer Books, 1997.

Abraham, Claude. "Aperçu de la versification française du 17e siècle." In *La Poésie française du premier 17e siècle: Textes et contextes*, edited by David Lee Rubin, 55–64. Tübingen: Gunter Narr Verlag, 1986.

Adam, Antoine. *L'apogée du siècle*. Vol. 4, *Histoire de la littérature française au XVIIe siècle*. Vol. 4. Paris: Éditions Mondiales, 1968.

———. *La fin de l'école classique, 1680–1715*. Vol. 5, *Histoire de la littérature française au XVIIe siècle*. Paris: Éditions Mondiales, 1968.

Alderman, Pauline. "Antoine Boësset and the *Air de Cour*." Ph.D. diss., University of California, 1946.

Anthony, James. *French Baroque Music from Beaujoyeulx to Rameau*. Revised ed. New York: W. W. Norton, 1978.

———. "Michel Lambert." *The New Grove Dictionary of Music and Musicians*, edited by Stanley Sadie, 10:397–99. London: Macmillan, 1980.

Arnold, F. T. *The Art of Accompaniment from a Thoroughbass, as Practised in the 17th and 18th Centuries*. New York: Dover Publications, 1965.

Ashworth, Jack, and Paul O'Dette. "Basso Continuo." In *A Performer's Guide to Seventeenth-Century Music,* edited by Stewart Carter, 269–96. New York: Schirmer, 1997.

Atcherson, Walter. "Key and Mode in Seventeenth-Century Music Theory." *Journal of Music Theory* 17 (1973): 205–33.

Auld, Louis. "'Dealing with Shepherds': The Pastoral Ploy in Nascent French Opera." In *French Musical Thought, 1600–1800,* edited by Georgia Cowart, 53–79. Ann Arbor, Mich.: UMI Research Press, 1981.

———. *The Lyric Art of Pierre Perrin, Founder of French Opera.* 3 vols. Ottawa: Institute of Mediaeval Music, 1986.

———. "Text as Pre-Text: French Court Airs and Their Ditties." *Continuum* 5 (1993): 15–83.

Beasley, Faith E. *Salons, History, and the Creation of 17th-Century France: Mastering Memory.* Burlington, Vt.: Ashgate, 2006.

Benoit, Marcel. *Versailles et les musiciens du roi, 1661–1733.* Paris: A. et J. Picard, 1971.

Bertrand, E. J. "Michel Lambert: Vie d'un musicien au XVIIe siècle." *Revue et gazette musicale* (1859): 9–156.

Bianconi, Lorenzo. *Music in the Seventeenth Century.* Translated by David Bryant. Cambridge: Cambridge University Press, 1987.

Borrel, Eugène. "L'interprétation de l'ancien recitatif français." *Revue de musicologie* 12 (1931): 13–21.

Bowers, Jane. "La Barre, Chabanceau de." In *Grove Music Online,* edited by Laura Macy. http://www.grovemusic.com, accessed 11 February 2007.

Bray, René. *La formation de la doctrine classique en France.* Paris: Librairie Nizet, 1945.

Brenet, Michel. *Les concerts en France sous l'ancien régime.* Paris, 1900. Reprint, New York: Da Capo Press, 1970.

Brooks, Jeanice. *Courtly Song in Late Sixteenth-Century France.* Chicago: University of Chicago Press, 2000.

Buch, David. "La Rhétorique des Dieux: A Critical Study of Text, Illustrations, and Musical Style." Ph.D. diss., Northwestern University, 1983.

Buelow, George. "The *Loci Topici* and Affect in Late Baroque Music: Heinichen's Practical Demonstration." *Music Review* 27 (1966): 161–76.

———. "Music, Rhetoric, and the Concept of the Affections: A Selective Bibliography." *Notes* 30 (1973–74): 250–59.

———. "Rhetoric and Music." *The New Grove Dictionary of Music and Musicians,* edited by Stanley Sadie, 15:793–803. London: Macmillan, 1980.

———. *Thorough-Bass Accompaniment According to Johann David Heinichen.* Revised ed. Lincoln: University of Nebraska Press, 1986.

Buelow, George, and Hans Joachim, eds. *New Mattheson Studies.* Cambridge: Cambridge University Press, 1983.

Butler, Gregory. "Music and Rhetoric in Early Seventeenth-Century English Sources." *Musical Quarterly* 66 (1980): 53–64.

Cammaert, Gustave. "Les Brunetes." *Revue de la Société belge de musicologie* 11 (1957): 35–51.

Carr, Thomas M., Jr. *Descartes and the Resilience of Rhetoric: Varieties of Cartesian Rhetorical Theory.* Carbondale: Southern Illinois University Press, 1990.

Caswell, Austin. "Bénigne de Bacilly." *The New Grove Dictionary of Music and Musicians,* edited by Stanley Sadie, 2:887. London: Macmillan, 1980.

———. "The Development of the 17th-Century French Vocal Ornamentation and Its Influence upon Late Baroque Ornamentation-Practice: A Comment upon the Art of Singing, and Particularly with Regard to French Vocal Music by Bénigne de Bacilly." 2 vols. Ph.D. diss., University of Minnesota, 1968.

Caswell, Judith. "Rhythmic Inequality and Tempo in French Music between 1650 and 1740." Ph.D. diss., University of Minnesota, 1968.

Chailley, Jacques. "Apport du vocal et du verbal dans l'interprétation de la musique française classique." In *L'interprétation de la musique française aux XVIIème et XVIIIème siècles,* edited by Édith Weber, 451–69. Paris: Centre national de recherches scientifiques, 1969.

Clercx, Susanne. *Le baroque et la musique: Essai d'esthétique musicale.* Brussels: Librarie Encyclopédie, 1948.

Cohen, Albert. *"L'Art de Bien Chanter* (1666) of Jean Millet." *Musical Quarterly* 55 (1969): 170–79.

———. "'La Supposition' and the Changing Concept of Dissonance in Baroque Theory." *Journal of the American Musicological Society* 24 (1971): 63–84.

Cohen, Albert, and Leta E. Miller, compilers. *Music in the Paris Academy of Sciences, 1666–1793.* Detroit: Information Coordinators, 1979.

Combarieu, Jules. *Les rapports de la musique et de la poésie considérés au point de vue de l'expression.* Paris: F. Alcan, 1894.

Corbett, Edward P. J. *Classical Rhetoric for the Modern Scholar.* New York: Oxford University Press, 1965.

Cowart, Georgia. "Inventing the Arts: Critical Language in the Ancien Régime." In *French Musical Thought, 1600–1800,* edited by Georgia Cowart, 211–33. Ann Arbor, Mich.: UMI Research Press, 1989.

———. "Lully *enjoué: Galanterie* in Seventeenth-Century France." In *Actes de Baton Rouge,* edited by Selma A. Zebouini, 35–51. Paris: Papers on French Seventeenth Century Literature, 1986.

————. *The Origins of Modern Musical Criticism: French and Italian Music, 1600–1750.* Ann Arbor, Mich.: UMI Research Press, 1981.

Crampé, Bernard. "De Arte Rhetorica: The Gestation of French Classicism in Renaissance Rhetoric." In *Humanism in Crisis,* edited by Phillipe Desan, 259–77. Ann Arbor: University of Michigan Press, 1991.

Craveri, Benedetta. *The Age of Conversation.* New York: NYREV, 2005.

Culler, Jonathan. *Structualist Poetics: Structuralism, Linguistics, and the Study of Literature.* Ithaca, N.Y.: Cornell University Press, 1975.

Cyr, Mary. *Performing Baroque Music.* Portland, Ore.: Amadeus Press, 1992.

Dainville, François. "L'évolution de l'enseignement de la rhétorique au XVIIème siècle." *Dix-septième siècle* 80–81 (1968): 19–43.

————. *La naissance de l'humanisme moderne.* Paris: Beauchesne et Ses Fils, 1940.

DeJean, Joan. *Fictions of Sappho.* Chicago: Chicago University Press, 1989.

————. *Tender Geographies: Women and the Origin of the Novel in France.* New York: Columbia University Press, 1991.

Denis, Delphine. *La muse galante: Poétique de la conversation dans l'œuvre de Madeleine de Scudéry.* Paris: Honoré Champion, 1997.

Dens, Jean-Pierre. "L'art de la conversation au 17e siècle." *Lettres romanes* 27 (1973): 215–24.

Desan, Philippe. "The Worm in the Apple." In *Humanism in Crisis: The Decline of the French Renaissance,* edited by Philippe Desan, 11–34. Ann Arbor: University of Michigan Press, 1991.

Dill, Charles. "Music, Beauty, and the Paradox of Rationalism." In *French Musical Thought, 1600–1800,* edited by Georgia Cowart, 197–210. Ann Arbor, Mich.: UMI Research Press, 1989.

Ducrot, Oswald, and Tzventan Todorov. *Dictionnaire encyclopédique des sciences du langage.* Paris: Éditions du Seuil, 1972.

Dufourcq, Norbert. "Autour de Sébastien Le Camus." *Recherches sur la musique française classique* 2 (1961–62): 41–53.

Duncan, David Allen. "Persuading the Affections: Rhetorical Theory and Mersenne's Advice to Harmonic Orators." In *French Musical Thought, 1600–1800,* edited by Georgia Cowart, 149–75. Ann Arbor, Mich.: UMI Research Press, 1989.

Durosoir, Georgie. *L'air de cour en France, 1571–1655: Contribution à l'étude de la musique dans le monde français du 17e siècle.* Liège: Mardaga, 1991.

Ecorcheville, Jules. "Lully gentilhomme et sa descendance." *Bulletin français de la Société internationale de musique* 7 (1911): 1–19.

Ehrmann, Jacques. *Un paradis désespéré: L'amour et l'illusion dans l'Astrée.* Paris: P.U.F., 1963.

Elias, Norbert. *The Civilizing Process: The History of Manners and State Formation and Civilization*. Oxford, UK: Blackwell, 1994.

Ellis, Muriel Tilden. "The Sources of Jean-Baptiste Lully's Secular Music." *Recherches sur la musique française classique* 8 (1968): 89–130.

Favier, Thierry. "Bénigne de Bacilly et ses airs spirituels: Pédagogue aigri ou précurseur inspiré?" *Revue de musicologie* 83, no. 1 (1997): 93–103.

———. "Les cantiques spirituels savants (1685–1715)." 2 vols. Doctorat d'État en lettres et sciènces humaines (Ph.D. diss.), Université de Paris IV—Sorbonne, 1996.

———. *Le chant des muses chrétiennes: Cantiques spirituels et dévotion en France (1685–1715)*. Paris: Société Française de Musicologie, 2008.

———. "Chant et apostolat en milieu mondain à la fin XVIIe siècle: Bacilly et ses continuateurs." In *Le Chant, acteur de l'histoire*, edited by Jean Quéniard, 89–99. Rennes: Presses Universitaires de Renne, 1999.

———. "Plaisir musical et parodies spirituelles: Les visages multiples de la reminiscence." In *Le plaisir musical en France au XVIIe siècle*, edited by Thierry Favier and Manuel Couvreur, 115–27. Hayen, Belgium: Éditions Mardaga, 2006.

———. "Les *Stances chrétiennes* de L'Abbé Testu (1669) mises en musique: De la contradiction intérieure au paradoxe artistique." In *Poésie et bible de la Renaissance à l'âge classique 1550–1680*, edited by Pascale Blum and Anne Mantéro, 243–54. Paris: Honoré Champion Éditeur, 1999.

France, Peter. *Rhetoric and Truth in France: Descartes to Diderot*. Oxford: Clarendon Press, 1972.

France, Peter, and Margaret McGowan. "Autour du traité de recitative de Grimarest." *Dix-septième siècle* 132 (1981): 303–17.

Fuller, David. "French Harpsichord Playing in the 17th Century—After Le Gallois." *Early Music* 4 (1976): 22–26.

Fumaroli, Marc. *L'âge de l'éloquence: Rhétorique et "res literaria" au seuil de l'époque classique*. Geneva: Librairie Droz, 1980.

———. *La diplomatie de l'esprit de Montaigne à La Fontaine*. Paris: Hermann, 1994.

Gastoué, Amédée. *Le cantique populaire en France: Ses sources, son histoire, augmentée d'une bibliographie générale des anciens cantiques et noëls*. Lyon: Janin, 1924.

Génetiot, Alain. *Les genres lyriques mondains: 1630–1660: Étude des poésies de Voiture, Vion d'Alibray, Sarasin et Scarron*. Geneva: Libraire Droz, 1990.

———. *Poétique du loisir mondain, de Voiture à La Fontaine*. Paris: Honoré Champion, 1997.

Georgakarakou, Maria. "Marin Mersenne: An Informed Theorist: Discussing Innovations Found in Book VI of *Harmonie Universelle*."

Paper delivered at the International Baroque Music Conference, Warsaw, Poland, July 2006.

Gérold, Théodore. *L'art du chant en France au XVIIe siècle.* Strasbourg: Librairie Istra, 1921.

Gibson, Jonathan. "'A Kind of Eloquence Even in Music': Embracing Different Rhetorics in Late Seventeenth-Century France." *Journal of Musicology* 25, no. 4 (2008): 394–433.

———. "*Le Naturel* and *L'Éloquence:* The Aesthetic of Music and Rhetoric in France, 1650–1715." Ph.D. diss., Duke University, 2003.

Goldsmith, Elizabeth. *Exclusive Conversations: The Art of Interaction in Seventeenth-Century France.* Philadelphia: University of Pennsylvania Press, 1988.

Gordon-Seifert, Catherine. "From Impurity to Piety: Mid 17th-Century French Devotional Airs and the Spiritual Conversion of Women." *Journal of Musicology* 22, no. 2 (2005): 268–91.

———. "The Language of Music in France: Rhetoric as a Basis for Expression in Michel Lambert's *Les Airs de Monsieur Lambert* (1669) and Bénigne de Bacilly's *Les Trois livres d'airs* (1668)." Ph.D. diss., University of Michigan, 1994.

———. "'Precious' Eroticism and Hidden Morality: Salon Culture and the Mid-Seventeenth-Century French Air." In *Eros and Euterpe: Eroticism in Early Modern Music,* edited by Massimo Ossi. Oxford: Oxford University Press, forthcoming.

———. "'La Réplique galante': Sébastien de Brossard's Airs as Conversation." In *Sébastien Brossard, Musicien,* edited by Jean Duron, 181–201. Versailles: Éditions du Centre de Musique Baroque de Versailles (Éditions Klincksieck), 1998.

———. "Strong Men—Weak Women: Gender Representation and the Influence of Lully's 'Operatic Style' on French *Airs Sérieux* (1650–1700)." In *Musical Voices of Early Modern Women: Many-Headed Melodies,* edited by Thomasin LaMay, 135–67. Burlington, Vt.: Ashgate, 2005.

Goulet, Anne-Madeleine. "Les divertissements musicaux du Samedi." In *Madeleine de Scudéry: Une femme de lettres au XVIIe siècle: Actes du Colloque international de Paris, 28–30 juin, 2001,* edited by Delphine Denis and Anne-Elisabeth Spica, 203–16. Arras: Artois Presses Université, 2002.

———. *Paroles de musique (1658–1694): Catalogue des "Livres d'airs de différents autheurs" publiés chez Ballard.* Wavre, Belgium: Éditions Mardaga, 2007.

———. *Poésie, musique et sociabilité au XVIIe siècle: Les Livres d'airs de différents autheurs publiés chez Ballard de 1658–1694.* Paris: Honoré Champion, 2004.

Graffin, Roger. *Jacques Testu Abbé de l'Académie Française (1626–1706)*. Paris: Librarie Alphonse Picard et Fils, 1901.

Grammont, Maurice. *Petit traité de versification française*. 9th ed. Paris: Librairie Armand Colin, 1962.

Green, Eugène. *La parole baroque*. Paris: Desclée de Brouwer, 2001.

Green, Robert. "The Treble Viol in 17th-Century France and the Origins of the *pardessus de viol*." *Chelys* 23 (1986): 64–71.

Guillo, Laurent. "La diffusion des éditions musicales: Le cas de la maison Ballard au XVIIe siècle." *Revue de musicologie* 87 (1998): 280–82.

———. *Pierre I Ballard et Robert III Ballard: Imprimeurs du roy pour la musique (Paris, 1599–1673)*. Versailles: Éditions Mardaga, 2003.

Guinamard, Catherine. "L'art du chant fin XVIIe siècle d'après Bénigne de Bacilly." Mémoire de maîtrise (master's thesis), Lyon II / Sorbonne IV, October 1983.

———. "Les *Remarques curieuses sur l'art de bien chanter* de Bénigne de Bacilly." In *Aspects de la musique baroque et classique à Lyon et en France*, edited by Daniel Paquette, 73–86. Lyon: Presses universitaires de Lyon, 1989.

Guiraud, Pierre. *La versification*. Paris: Presses Universitaires de France, 1970.

Gustafson, Bruce. *French Harpsichord Music of the 17th Century: A Thematic Catalog of the Sources with Commentary*. Ann Arbor, Mich., 1979.

Hallyn, Fernand. *Formes métaphoriques dans la poésie lyrique de l'âge baroque en France*. Geneva: Librairie Droz, 1975.

Hanning, Barbara Russano. *Of Poetry and Music's Power: Humanism and the Creation of Opera*. Ann Arbor, Mich.: UMI Research Press, 1980.

Hannon, Patricia. "Desire and Writing in Scudéry's 'Histoire de Sapho.'" In *L'Esprit créateur* 35, no. 2 (Summer 1995): 27–50.

Hardouin, P. "Notes sur quelques musiciens français du XVIIe siècle, II: Les Chabanceau de la Barre." *Revue de musicologie* 38 (1956): 62–64.

Harris, Ellen T. "Voices." In *Performance Practice: Music after 1600*, edited by Howard Mayer Brown and Stanley Sadie, 97–116. New York: W. W. Norton, 1989.

Harris, Joseph. *Hidden Agendas: Cross-Dressing in 17th-Century France*. Biblio 17. Papers on French Seventeenth-Century Literature. Tübingen: Narr, 2005.

Harth, Erica. *Cartesian Women: Versions and Subversions of Rational Discourse in the Old Regime*. Ithaca, N.Y.: Cornell University Press, 1992.

Harwood, John. *The Rhetorics of Thomas Hobbs and Bernard Lamy*. Carbondale: Southern Illinois University Press, 1986.

Hatten, Robert. *Musical Meaning in Beethoven: Markedness, Correlation, and Interpretation.* Bloomington: Indiana University Press, 1994.

Haydn, Glen. "On the Problem of Expression in Baroque Music." *Journal of the American Musicological Society* 3 (1950): 113–19.

Haynes, Bruce, and Peter R. Cooke. "Pitch." In *Grove Music Online,* edited by Laura Macy. http://www.grovemusic.com, accessed 11 February 2007.

Hazard, Paul. *The European Mind (1680–1715).* Translated by J. Lewis May. New York: Meridian Books, 1963.

Heartz, Daniel. "'Voix de ville,' Between Humanist Ideals and Musical Realities." In *Words and Music: The Scholar's View,* edited by Laurence Berman, 115–35. Cambridge, Mass.: Harvard University Press, 1972.

Houle, George. *Meter in Music, 1600–1800.* Bloomington: Indiana University Press, 1987.

Howard, Patricia. "Quinault, Lully, and the *Précieuses:* Images of Women in Seventeenth-Century France." In *Cecilia Reclaimed: Feminist Perspectives on Gender and Music,* edited by Susan C. Cook and Judy S. Tsou, 70–89. Chicago: University of Illinois Press, 1994.

Isherwood, Robert M. *Music in the Service of the King: France in the Seventeenth Century.* Ithaca, N.Y.: Cornell University Press, 1973.

Jensen, Katharine Ann. *Writing Love: Letters, Women, and the Novel in France, 1605–1776.* Carbondale: Southern Illinois University Press, 1995.

Kearns, Edward John. *Ideas in Seventeenth-Century France.* New York: St. Martin's Press, 1979.

Kennedy, George. *Classical Rhetoric and Its Christian and Secular Tradition from Ancient to Modern Times.* Chapel Hill: University of North Carolina Press, 1980.

Kibédi-Varga, Aron. *Les poétiques du classicisme.* Paris: Aux Amateurs Livres, 1990.

———. "La rhétorique des passions et les genres." *Jahrbuch Rhetorik* 6 (1987): 67–73.

———. *Rhétorique et littérature: Études de structures classiques.* Paris: Didier, 1970.

Kintzler, Catherine. "De la pastorale à la tragédie lyrique: Quelques elements d'un système poétique." *Revue de musicologie* 72 (1986): 67–96.

———. *Parler, dire, chanter: Trois actes pour un meme projet.* Actes du colloque organisé par le Groupe de recherches Rapports musique-texte, GRMT, tenu en Sorbonne-Paris IV, octobre 1995. Paris: Presses de l'Université de Paris-Sorbonne, 2001.

———. *Peinture et musique: Penser la vision, penser l'audition.* Villeneuve d'Ascq: Presses Universitaires du Septentrion, 2002.

———. *Poétique de l'opéra français, de Corneille à Rousseau*. Paris: Minerve, 1991.

———. *Théâtre et opera à l'âge classique: Une familière étrangeté*. Paris: Fayard, 2004.

Kirkendale, Ursula. "The Source for Bach's Musical Offering: The *Institutio oratoria* of Quintilian." *Journal of the American Musicological Society* 33 (1980): 88–141.

Kirkendale, Warren. "Ciceronians versus Aristotelians on the Ricercar as Exordium." *Journal of the American Musicological Society* 32 (1979): 1–44.

———. "Circulatio-Tradition, Maria Lactans, and Josquin as Musical Orator." *Acta Musicologica* 56 (1984): 88–141.

Kritzman, Lawrence D. *The Rhetoric of Sexuality and the Literature of the French Renaissance*. New York: Columbia University Press, 1991.

La Laurencie, Lionel de. *Les créateurs de l'opéra français*. Paris, 1957.

———. *Le goût musical en France*. Paris: A. Joanin, 1905.

Lanham, Richard A. *A Handlist of Rhetorical Terms*. Los Angeles: University of California Press, 1969.

Lasocki, David. "Quantz and the Passions: Theory and Practice." *Early Music* 6 (1978): 556–67.

LeCoat, Gerard. *The Rhetoric of the Arts, 1550–1650*. Frankfurt: Herbert Lang Bern, 1975.

Ledbetter, David. *Harpsichord and Lute Music in Seventeenth-Century France*. London: Macmillan Press, 1987.

Lenneberg, Hans. "Johann Mattheson on Affect and Rhetoric in Music from *Der vollkommene Capellmeister*." *Journal of Music Theory* 2 (1958): 47–84, 193–236.

Lescat, P. *Catalogue des ouvrages de Bénigne de Bacilly: Les trois livres d'airs regravez en deux volumes*. Facsimile edition. Courlay, 1996.

Lévy, Kenneth. "Vaudeville, vers mesurés et airs de cour." In *Musique et poésie au XVIe siècle*, edited by J. Jacquot, 211–23. Paris: Centre national de recherches scientifiques, 1954.

Lilti, Antoine. *Le monde des salons: Sociabilité et mondanité au XVIIIe siècle* Paris: Fayard, 2005.

Lorimer, Elena. "L'Art de Bien Chanter: Singing as Declamation in Bacilly's *Remarques curieuses* (1668)." *The Consort: The Journal of Dolmetsch Foundation* 59 (2003): 3–15.

———."A Critical Study and Translation of Bénigne de Bacilly's Remarques curieuses sur L'art de bien chanter (1668)." Ph.D. thesis, University of London, 2002.

Lougee, Carolyn C. *Les Paradis des Femmes: Women, Salons, and Social Stratification in Seventeenth-Century France*. Princeton, N.J.: Princeton University Press, 1976.

Mace, Dean. "Marin Mersenne on Language and Music." *Journal of Music Theory* 14 (1979): 2–35.

Maître, Miriam. *Les précieuses: Naissance des femmes de lettres en France au XVIIe siècle.* Paris: Champion, 1999.

Maniates, Maris Rika. *Mannerism in Italian Music and Culture, 1530–1630.* Chapel Hill: University of North Carolina, 1979.

Mantéro, Anne. *La muse théologienne: Poésie et théologie en France de 1629 à 1680.* Berlin: Duncker & Humblot, 1995.

Maravall, José Antonio. *Culture of the Baroque: Analysis of a Historical Structure.* Translated by Terry Cohen. Minneapolis: University of Minnesota Press, 1986.

Massip, Catherine. *L'art de bien chanter: Michel Lambert (1610–1696).* Paris: Société Française de Musicologie, 1999.

———. "De l'air sérieux à la tragédie en musique." *Revue de la Bibliothèque nationale de France* 3 (October 1999): 18–74.

———. "French Song around 1700." *Basler Jahrbuch für historische Musikpraxis* 28 (2004): 51–62.

———. "Michel Lambert (1610–1696): Contribution à l'histoire de la monodie en France." 2 vols. Doctorat d'État en lettres et sciènces humaines (Ph.D. diss.), Université de Paris IV, 1985.

———. "Michel Lambert and Jean-Baptiste Lully: The Stakes of a Collaboration." In *Jean-Baptiste Lully and Music of the French Baroque: Essays in Honor of James R. Anthony,* edited by John Hajdu Heyer, 25–40. Cambridge: Cambridge University Press, 1989.

———. "Paris, 1600–1661." In *The Early Baroque Era: From the Late 16th Century to the 1660s,* edited by Curtis Alexander Price, 218–37. Englewood Cliffs, N.J.: Prentice Hall, 1993.

———. *La vie des musiciens de Paris au temps de Mazarin (1643–1661): Essai d'étude sociale.* Paris: A. J. Picard, 1976.

Masson, Paul-Marie. "Les Brunettes." *Sammelbände du Internationalen Musik-Gesellschaft* 11 (1910–11): 347–68.

Mather, Betty Bang. *Dance Rhythms of the French Baroque: A Handbook for Performance.* Bloomington: Indiana University Press, 1987.

Maurice-Castellani, Gisèle. "Les poésies de Malherbe et les musicians de son temps." *Dix-septième siècle* 31 (1956): 296–331.

McClary, Susan. *Feminine Endings: Music, Gender, and Sexuality.* Minneapolis: University of Minnesota Press, 1991.

Millet, E. "Le musicien Michel Lambert (1610–1696) était de Champigny-sur-Veude." *Bulletin des Amis de vieux Chinon* 7 (1968): 186–90.

Monter, E. William. "The Pedestal and the Stake: Courtly Love and Witchcraft." In *Becoming Visible: Women in European History,* edited by Renate Bridenthal and Claudin Koonz, 119–36. Boston: Houghton and Mifflin, 1977.

Morier, Henri. *Dictionnaire de poétique et de rhétorique.* 4th ed. Paris: Presses Universitaires de France, 1989.

Mourgues, Odette de. *Metaphysical, Baroque and Précieux Poetry.* Oxford: Oxford University Press, 1953.

Murata, Margaret. "The Recitative Soliloquy." *Journal of the American Musicological Society* 32 (1979): 45–73.

Nattiez, Jean-Jacques. *De la sémiologie à la musique.* Montréal: Université du Québec à Montréal, 1988.

————. *Fondements d'une sémiologie de la musique.* Paris: Union générale d'éditions, 1975.

————. *Music and Discourse: Toward a Semiology of Music.* Translated by Carolyn Abbate. Princeton, N.J.: Princeton University Press, 1990.

Naudin, Marie. *Évolution parallèle de la poésie et de la musique en France: Rôle unificateur de la chanson.* Paris: A. G. Nizet, 1968.

Newman, Joyce. *Jean-Baptiste Lully and His Tragédies Lyriques.* Ann Arbor, Mich.: UMI Research Press, 1979.

Norman, Buford. "Ancients and Moderns, Tragedy and Opera: The Quarrel over *Alceste.*" In *French Musical Throught, 1600–1800,* edited by Georgia Cowart, 177–96. Ann Arbor, Mich.: UMI Research Press, 1989.

Palisca, Claude. *Humanism in Italian Renaissance Thought.* New Haven, Conn.: Yale University Press, 1985.

————. "The Recitative of Lully's *Alceste:* French Declamation or Italian Melody?" In *Actes de Baton Rouge,* edited by Selma A. Zebouni, 19–34. Paris: Papers on French Seventeenth Century Literature, 1986.

————. "Ut Oratoria Musica: The Rhetorical Basis of Musical Mannerism." In *The Meaning of Mannerism,* edited by Franklin W. Robinson and Stephen G. Nichols, Jr., 37–65. Hanover, N.H.: University of New England, 1972.

————. "Vincenzo Galilei and Some Links between 'Pseudo-Monody' and Monody." *Musical Quarterly* 46 (1960): 344–60.

Paquette, David. "Regard sur l'évolution de l'air de cour." In *Histoire, humanisme et hymnologie: Mélanges offerts au Professeur Edith Weber,* edited by Pierre Guillot and Louis Jambou, 163–77. Paris: Presses de L'Université de Paris-Sorbonne, 1997.

Pelous, Jean-Michel. *Amour précieux, amour galant, 1654–1675.* Paris: Librairie Klincksieck, 1980.

Perella, Lisa. "Bénigne de Bacilly and the *Recueil des plus beaux vers, qui on est mis en chant* of 1661." In *Music and the Cultures of Print,* edited by Kate Van Orden, 239–70. New York: Garland, 2000.

————. "French Song in the 1660s." *Seventeenth-Century French Studies* 20 (1998): 83–94.

———. "Mythologies of Musical Persuasion: The Power and Politics of Song in France 1653–1673." Ph.D. diss., University of Pennsylvania, 2003.

Perelman, Chaïm. *The Realm of Rhetoric.* Notre Dame, Ind.: University of Notre Dame Press, 1969.

Perelman, Chaïm, and L. Olbrechts-Tyteca. *The New Rhetoric: A Treatise on Argumentation.* Translated by John Wilkinson and Purcell Weaver. Notre Dame, Ind.: University of Notre Dame Press, 1982.

Performance Practice: Music after 1600. Edited by Howard Mayer Brown and Stanley Sadie. New York: W. W. Norton, 1989.

Pessel, André. "De la conversation chez les précieuses." *Communications* 30 (1979): 15–35

Picard, Roger. *Les salons littéraires et la société française, 1610–1789.* New York: Brentano's, 1943.

Pineau, Joseph. *Le mouvement rythmique en français: Principes et méthode d'analyse.* Paris: Librairie Klincksieck, 1979.

Pinson, Joseph. "L'expression dans la musique de chambre pour instruments à vents en France, 1680–1760: Essai de rhétorique musicale." Ph.D. diss., University of Montréal, 1987.

Pirro, André. *Descartes et la musique.* Paris: Librairie Fischbacher, 1907. Reprint, Geneva: Minkoff, 1973.

Poole, Elissa. "The *Brunetes* and Their Sources: A Study of the Transition from Modality to Tonality in France." *Recherches sur la musique française classique* 25 (1987): 187–206.

———. "The Sources for Christophe Ballard's *Brunetes ou petits airs tendres* and the Tradition of Seventeenth-Century French Song." Ph.D. diss., University of Victoria, 1984.

Powell, Newman. "Rhythmic Interpretation in the Performance of French Music from 1650–1735." Ph.D. diss., Stanford University, 1959.

Prunières, Henri. "Un maître de chant au XVIIe siècle: Bénigne de Bacilly." *Revue de musicologie* 8 (1923): 156–60.

Quittard, Henri. "L'air à voix seule: Ses origines." *Revue musicale* (1905): 443–45.

Ranum, Patricia. "Audible Rhetoric and Mute Rhetoric: The Seventeenth-Century French Sarabande." *Early Music* 24 (1986): 22–39.

———. "Les 'caractères' des danses françaises." *Recherches sur la musique française classique* 23 (1985): 45–70.

———. *The Harmonic Orator: The Phrasing and Rhetoric of the Melody in French Baroque Airs.* Hillsdale, N.Y.: Pendragon Press, 2001.

Rasmussen, Mary. "Viols, Violists and Venus in Grunewald's Isenheim Altar." Paper given at the AMS New England Chapter Meeting, Harvard University, 13 February 1992.

Reilly, Allyn Dixon. "Georg Andreas Sorge's *Vorgemach der musicalischen Composition:* A Translation and Commentary." Ph.D. diss., Northwestern University, 1980.

Riffaterre, Michael. *Semiotics of Poetry.* Bloomington: Indiana University Press, 1984.s

Rivera, Benito. "The Seventeenth-Century Theory of Triadic Generation and Invertibility and Its Application in Contemporaneous Rules of Composition." *Music Theory Spectrum* 6 (1984): 63–78.

Robinson, Lucy. "Le Camus, Sébastien." In *Grove Music Online,* edited by Laura Macy. http://www. grovemusic.com, accessed 9 January 2007.

Rohrer, Katherine Tinley. "'The Energy of English Words': A Linguistic Approach to Henry Purcell's Methods of Setting Texts." Ph.D. diss., Princeton University, 1980.

Rosand, Ellen. "The Descending Tetrachord: An Emblem of Lament." *Musical Quarterly* 65 (1979): 346–59.

———. "Lamento." In *The New Grove Dictionary of Music and Musicians,* edited by Stanley Sadie, 10:412–14 . London: Macmillan, 1980.

Rosow, Lois. "French Baroque Recitative as an Expression of Tragic Declamation." *Early Music* 11 (1983): 468–79.

Royster, Don Lee. "Pierre Guédron and the Air de Cour, 1600–1620." Ph.D. diss., Yale University, 1973.

Rubin, David Lee, and Mary B. McKinley, eds. *Convergences—Rhetoric and Poetic in Seventeenth-Century France.* Columbus: Ohio State University Press, 1989.

Ryhming, Gudrun. "L'art du chant français au XVIIe siècle selon Bénigne de Bacilly." *Revue musicale de Suisse Romande* 35, no. 1 (1982): 10–25.

Sadowsky, Rosalie D. L. "Jean-Baptiste 'Abbé' Dubos: The Influence of Cartesian and Neo-Aristotelian Ideas on Music Theory and Practice." Ph.D. diss., Yale University, 1960.

Salazar, Philippe-Joseph. *Le culte de la voix au XVIIe siècle: Formes esthétiques de la parole à l'âge de l'imprimé.* Paris: Honoré Champion, 1995.

Sanford, Sally. "Solo Singing I." In *A Performer's Guide to Seventeenth-Century Music,* edited by Stewart Carter, 3–29. New York: Schirmer, 1997.

Schulenberg, David. "Composition before Rameau: Harmony, Figured Bass, and Style in the Baroque." *College Music Symposium* 24 (1984): 130–48.

Seifert, Lewis. *Manning the Margins: Masculinity and Writing in Seventeenth-Century France.* Ann Arbor: University of Michigan Press, 2009.

Sexuality and Gender in Early Modern Europe: Institutions, Texts, and Images. Edited by James Grantham Turner. Cambridge: Cambridge University Press, 1993.

Silin, Charles. "L'influence des poètes de cour sur la formation de jeune Louis XIV." *Cahiers de l'Association internationale d'études françaises* 9 (1957): 77–99.

Singing Early Music: Pronunciation of European Languages in the Late Middle Ages and Renaissance. Edited by Timothy McGee, with A. G. Riggs and David N. Klausner. Bloomington: Indiana University Press, 1996.

Snyders, Georges. *Le Goût musical en France aux XVIIe et XVIIIe siècles.* Paris: J. Vrin, 1968.

Spink, J. S. *French Free-Thought from Gassendi to Voltaire.* London: Athlone Press, 1960.

Stanton, Domna. *The Aristocrat as Art: A Study of the Honnête Homme and the Dandy in Seventeenth- and Nineteenth-Century French Literature.* New York: Columbia University Press, 1980.

Stark, James. *Bel Canto: A History of Vocal Pedagogy.* Toronto: University of Toronto Press, 2003.

Strosetzki, Christoph. *Rhétorique de la conversation: Sa dimension littéraire et linguistique dans la société française du dix-septième siècle.* Paris: Papers on Seventeenth Century French Literature, 1984.

Strunk, Oliver. *Source Readings in Music History.* New York: W. W. Norton, 1950.

Tolkoff, Lyn. "French Modal Theory before Rameau." *Journal of Music Theory* 17 (1973): 151–63.

Tomlinson, Gary. "Madrigal, Monody, and Monteverdi's 'Via Naturale alla Imitatione.'" *Journal of the American Musicological Society* 34 (1981): 61–108.

———. *Music in Renaissance Magic: Toward a Historiography of Others.* Chicago: University of Chicago Press, 1993.

Tiersot, Julien. "Une famille de musiciens français au XVIIe siècle: Les De La Barre." *Revue de musicologie* 8 (1927): 185–202; 9 (1928): 1–11, 68–74.

Timmermans, Linda. *L'accès des femmes à la culture (1578–1715).* Paris: Éditions Champion, 1993.

Tunley, David. "The Union of Words and Music in Seventeenth-Century France—The Long and the Short of It." *Australian Journal of French Studies* 21 (1984): 281–307.

Unger, Hans-Heinrich. *Die Beziehungen zwischen Musik und Rhetorik im 16.–18. Jahrhundert.* Berlin: Würzburg, 1941. Reprint, Hildesheim: Olms, 1969.

Van Wymeersch, Brigitte. *Descartes et l'évolution de l'esthétique musicale.* Sprimont, Belgium: Mardaga, 1999.

Verchaly, André. "La métrique et le rhythme musical au temps de l'humanisme." In *Report of the Eighth Congress of the International*

Musicological Society, edited by Jan LaRue, 66–74. New York: Bärenreiter, 1961.

Viala, Alain, ed. *L'esthétique galante: Paul Pellisson, Discours sur les œuvres de Monsieur Sarasin et autres textes.* Toulouse: Société de Littératures Classiques, 1989.

Vignes, Jean. "*L'Harmonie universelle* de Marin Mersenne et la théorie du vers mesuré." In *A haute voix: Diction et pronunciation aux XVIe et XVIIe siècles,* edited by Olivia Rosenthal, 65–85. Paris: Klincksieck, 1998.

Wack, Mary Frances. *Lovesickness in the Middle Ages: The* Viaticum *and Its Commentaries.* Philadelphia: University of Pennsylvania Press, 1990.

Waite, William. "Bernard Lamy, Rhetorician of the Passions." In *Studies in Eighteenth-Century Music: A Tribute to Karl Geiringer on His Seventieth Birthday,* edited by H. C. Robbins Landon and Roger E. Chapman, 388–96. New York: Oxford University Press, 1970.

Walker, D. P. "The Aims of Baïf's Académie de Poésie et de Musique." In *Music, Spirit and Language in the Renaissance,* edited by Penelope Gouk, 91–100. London: Variorum Reprints, 1985.

———. "The Influence of *Musique mesurée à l'antique,* Particularly on the *Air de Cour* of the Early Seventeenth Century." In *Music, Spirit and Language in the Renaissance,* edited by Penelope Gouk, 141–63. London: Variorum Reprints, 1985.

———. "Joan Albert Ban and Mersenne's Musical Competition of 1640." *Music and Letters* 57 (1976): 233–55.

———. "Musical Humanism in the 16th and 17th Centuries." In *Music, Spirit and Language in the Renaissance,* edited by Penelope Gouk, 1–72; 55–72. London: Variorum Reprints, 1985.

Walter, Eric. "Les auteurs et le champ littéraire." In *Histoire de l'édition française,* 2:499–518. Paris: Fayard, 1990.

Wessel, Frederick T. "The *Affektenlehre* in the Eighteenth Century." Ph.D. diss., Indiana University, 1985.

Williams, Peter. *Figured Bass Accompaniment.* Edinburgh University Press, 1970.

Winegarten, René. *French Lyric Poetry in the Age of Malherbe.* Manchester: Manchester University Press, 1954.

Wolf, Peter. "Metrical Relationships in French Recitative of the Seventeenth and Eighteenth Centuries." *Recherches sur la musique française classique* 18 (1978): 29–49.

Writing about Sex: The Discourses of Eroticism in Seventeenth-Century France. Edited by Abby E. Zanger. Special issue, *L'esprit créateur* 25 (1995).

Yates, Frances. *The French Academies of the Sixteenth Century.* London: Warburg Institute, 1947.

Index

general, 12, 16; performance of airs in, 18–19; on transcription of, xiii, 303n61. *See also* La Barre, Joseph Chabanceau de

airs de cour, 4, 11, 299n2

Airs de Monsieur Lambert (Lambert): description of, 17–22; general, 12, 15; performance of airs in, 18–19, 20–22; on transcription of, xiii, 303n61. *See also* Lambert

airs de mouvement, 12, 217, 298n8

airs sérieux. See airs, serious

alexandrine. *See* song texts

Alibray, Vion d,' 23, 24

Ambruis, Honoré d,' 13, 17

amitié: in airs, 246; in the *Carte de Tendre,* 183, 248; in emblems, 245, 292, 293; and Flamen, 245; as type of love, 245. *See also* Ferrand; Scudéry

antansgoge. See Bacilly, *antithesis* in airs by; Bretteville, on *antithesis;* elocution, *antithesis;* Grimarest, on *antithesis;* Lambert, *antithesis* in airs by; rhetoric, *antithesis*

Anthony, James, 4

aporia. See Bacilly, doubt in airs by; elocution, doubt; Lambert, doubt in airs by; Lamy, on doubt; rhetoric, doubt

Aristotle, 138

Arnauld, Antoine: on accessory meaning, 312n75; on the manipulation of eloquence, 275, 277; on passions, 275, 277; on pleasure, 275, 277; on rhetoric, 42; on the rhetoric of distraction, 271

Arnold, F. T. A., 227

art of conversation. *See* conversation, the art of; salons, Parisian; Scudéry, on the art of conversation

Ashworth, Jack, 221, 222, 228

aspiration. See Bacilly, on *accent;* La Barre, Joseph Chabanceau de, *accent;* ornamentation, *accents*

Bacilly, Bénigne de: "A l'ombre de ce bocage," 32; on *accent* (*aspiration* or *plainte*), 53, 185, 199, 201, 202, 208, 211, 215, 218; airs (general), 13; on airs, 103, 269; *airs spirituels* by, 16, 260, 262, 274–277, 279, 280, 342n16; on *airs spirituels,* 260, 262, 279; *anacephalaiosis* in airs by, 175; *anamnesis* in airs by, 146, 181; anger, musical representation of, 118, 119, 120, 121, 122–123, 144, 154, 157, 177, 178, 180, 181, 242; on *animer,* 195, 199; *antithesis* (antansgoge) in airs by, 142, 145; "Apres milles rigueurs," 193–194; "Au milieu des plaisirs," 85–86; "Au secours ma raison," 80, 81, 117–120, 135, 154, 167, 175, 181, 195, 220, 255, 289–290; "Auprez des beaux yeux," 82; Ballard, airs in the collections of, 13, 20, 281; and Ballard collections, 19; bass line, texted, 17–18, 227; basso continuo accompaniment in airs by, 223–226; on basso continuo accompaniment, 220–221; biography, 13, 15–16; bittersweet love, airs about, 126, 128–129, 135–136, 163; boldness (courage or *le pouvoir*), musical representation of, 69, 72–75, 91, 106, 107, 118, 119, 120, 121, 122–123, 129–130, 142, 151, 177, 181, 182, 238; on breath support, 187–188; *Brunetes ou petits airs tendres* and airs by, 281; *cadence* as harmonic progression, 327n16; *cadence* as vibrato, 189; *cadence* (trill or *tremblement*) in airs by, 43, 185, 189, 190, 195–197, 198, 199, 201, 211, 218; Caswell on Bacilly, 5; conventions of expression in airs by, 275, 280; conversation in song, 235; dance airs, 15, 131–133,

211, 216, 282; on dance airs, 216–217; death, musical representation of, 106, 107, 182; death in airs by, 182; on *demi-port de voix*, 193–194, 213; despair, musical representation of, 65, 67, 90, 106, 107, 126–128, 142, 144, 145, 146, 147, 154, 178, 181, 282; on *diminutions* (*passages*) and in airs by, 19, 155, 185, 199–202, 209; "D'où vient cette sombre tristesse," 275–277, 295; "D'ou vient que de ce Bocage," 54; *double cadence*, 197, 198; *doublement du gosier*, 199; on *doubles* and in airs by, 13, 19, 140–144, 146–148, 199, 200, 338n75; doubt (or *aporia*) in airs by, 172; "Dûssay j'avoir mille rivaux," 126–129, 163, 174, 178, 283, 290; editions of airs, 298n11; "En vain j'ay consulté l'amour et le respect," 172, 173–174, 183, 291; enticing love, airs about, 129–130, 131, 136–137; *epimone* in airs by, 175; on eroticism in airs by, 248; exclamations in airs by, 36, 144, 161, 170; figured bass in airs by, 223–226; *flexion de voix*, 197, 198; on *galant*, 29; *galant* in airs by, 9; gavottes, 131–132; on gavottes, 211, 217; general, 1, 4, 6; *gradation* (climax) in airs by, 148, 167, 182; happiness, musical representation of, 88, 95, 131, 132–133, 275; "Il est vray je suis rigoureuse," 261; "Il faut parler," 73, 75, 151–153, 182, 290; "Il n'est parlé," 220; images of war in airs by, 117; *inegalité* in airs by, 201; influence, 9; irony in "Au secours ma raison," 119; "Je fais ce que je puis," 201, 233; "Je suis bien las d'entendre," 30; "Je tasche en vain," 178; "Je voy des amans

chaque jour," 32–33, 34, 35, 178; joyous love, airs about, 32, 132–133, 137; on languor, 54; languor, musical representation of, 81, 82–83, 93–94, 117, 118, 120, 122, 163, 177, 241; Lecerf de la Viéville on, 281; legacy of, 9, 280, 281, 282; *Livres d'airs de différents autheurs* and airs by, 281; *Livres de chansons pour danser et pour boire* and airs by, 15, 281; love, the burning fires of (*le feux de l'amour*), musical representation of, 92, 107, 275; maxims in airs by, 122, 177, 178, 273; on meaning in music, 280; *Mercure galant* and airs by, 281; metaphor in airs by, 31, 182, 251; on meter, 216, 320n14; meter changes in airs by, 125, 129; minuets, 132–133; on minuets, 216; "Mon sort est digne de Pitié," 25–26, 36, 67, 68, 144–150, 154, 167, 175, 181, 182, 215, 220, 282, 283, 303; on *mouvement*, 29, 217–218; *Nouveau livre d'airs*, 12, 16; "On est heureux," 88, 178; *onedismus* in airs by, 180; organization of expressions in airs by, 139–140; on ornamentation, 8, 46, 103, 185, 188, 189, 278–279; ornamentation in airs by, 142, 144, 147, 148; painful love, airs about, 106–108, 124, 134–135; passions, on the musical representation of (general), 53, 54, 56; passions in airs by, 62, 64, 89–95, 97–98; passions juxtaposed in airs by, 107, 119, 120, 126–128, 129; passions mixed in airs by, 107; pastoral references in airs by, 27, 30, 37; performance of airs (general), 19; "Petit abeille mesnagere," 27, 31, 37, 132–133, 238, 242, 269, 290; "Petits aigneaux," 139–144, 167, 170;

as poet, 24–25; poetic style, 38; poetic voice (gender) in airs by, 260; on *port de voix*, 192–195; on *port de voix glissé*, 194; *port de voix* in airs by, 192–195; on *port de voix ordinaire*, 192–193; on *port de voix perdu*, 194; "Pour donner à mon coeur," 162–164, 170, 174, 183, 241, 291; "Pour la bergere Lisette," 131–132, 154, 290; praise for, 281, 282; "Le Printemps est de retour," 33, 34, 35, 50–51; on pronunciation, 8, 46, 103, 185, 188, 202–210, 278; publications (general), 6, 12, 13, 19, 20; "Puisque Philis est infidelle," 73, 74, 82–83, 120–123, 135, 154, 169, 175, 177, 178, 179, 180, 181, 197, 206, 242, 290; "Qu'il couste cher de voir Silvie," 160–161, 215, 220, 290; *Recueil[s] des plus beaux airs*, 24, 232–233; regret, musical representation of, 117, 121, 144, 146, 147, 181; *Remarques curieuses sur l'art de bien chanter*, xiii, 5, 8, 15–16, 46, 189, 198, 278; repeats in airs by, 218, 220; revenge in "Puisque Philis est infidelle," 120, 135; and rhetoric, 2, 7, 46, 53; and salon culture, 231; sarabande, 106, 282; on the sarabande, 211, 216; *Second livre d'airs*, 12; seductions (musical) in airs by, 238, 241, 242; "Si je vous dis," 106–107, 282, 289; on singing (general), 229; on singing in salons, 187–188; on song texts, 23, 25, 38, 56, 248, 279, 282, 305n77; sorrow, musical representation of, 78–79, 80, 93, 106, 107, 119, 120, 121, 163, 170, 172, 181, 182, 275, 282; spiritual airs (*airs spirituels*), 9, 16, 260, 262, 279, 280, 342n16; style of airs, 6, 11, 13, 18, 282–283, 284, 285, 286; on syllabic quantity (syllable

stress), 103, 185, 188, 200, 210–216, 309n41; "Tantost je suis sous l'Empire," 169; tenderness (tender love), musical representation of, 74, 84, 85–86, 94–95, 106, 107, 117, 119, 121, 126–128, 129, 130, 131, 132, 144, 151, 163, 178, 183, 217, 238, 275, 282; on *tendre*, 29; transcriptions of airs, xiii, 303n61; translation of song texts, xiii, 303n61; *tremblement étouffé*, 53, 197; on vocabulary, 279; on vocal quality, 8, 188; on vocal registers, 191; on voice types, 189, 191; "Vous ne pouvez Iris," 106–108, 135, 182, 223–226, 227, 228, 241, 289; "Vous sçavez donner de l'amour," 72–74, 129–130, 183, 251, 290; on women singing airs, 262; word-painting, 117, 275. *See also* conventions of expression, in *airs spirituels*; *Les Trois livres d'airs*

Ballard family: *Airs bachiques*, 299n7; "Beaux yeux, que voulez-vous me dire," 241; *brunetes*, 200n19, 279, 343n28; *Brunetes ou petits airs tendres*, 5, 281, 298n8; "C'est aux amans que la saison," 269–270, 295; Christophe, 5, 12, 18, 281, 298n8, 300n19, 343n28; description of publications, 18–22; *doubles* in the publications of, 269, 279, 343n28; general, 13, 278; *Livres d'airs de differents autheurs*, 3, 5, 12, 15, 22, 235, 261, 265, 268, 281; *Livres d'airs pour danser et pour boire*, 299n7; *Livres d'airs sérieux et à boire*, 268, 299n7; *Livres de chansons à danser et à boire*, 15, 281; *Meslanges de musique latine, françoise et Italienne*, 281; performance of airs in, 20–22; poetic voice (gender), in collections by, 261; printing practices, 300n27;

Index

321nn28,36; on rhetoric, 42,
271; on sorrow (sadness), 62, 78,
92, 94, 318n62; on tender love,
62, 84, 94; on tenderness, 84
désespoir. See Bacilly, despair, musical representation of; Bretteville,
on despair; Descartes, on despair;
Grimarest, on despair; La Barre,
Joseph Chabanceau de, despair,
musical representation of;
Lambert, despair, musical
representation of; Le Camus,
Sébastien, despair, musical representation of; passions, despair
Desmarest, André Cardinal, 6
Desmarest, Henri, 6
despair. *See* désespoir
Diderot, Denis, 6
discours harmonieux. See rhetoric
disposition (*dispositio*), 7, 24, 44,
138, 139, 187, 256; conclusion
(*peroratio* or *epilogus*), 138, 139,
140, 142, 143, 145, 151, 152,
153, 157–158, 160, 162, 170,
256, 257; confirmation (*confirmation* or *amplificatio*), 138,
139, 140, 144–148, 151, 152,
153, 154–156, 157, 160, 162,
170, 256, 257; *divisio* (or *partitio*), 138; introduction (*exordium*), 138, 139, 140, 145, 151,
152, 153–154, 157, 160, 162,
322n13; narration (*narration* or
praecognitio), 138, 139, 140,
144, 151, 153, 154, 160, 162,
322nn7,13; parts of, 138–140;
proposition (*proposition, definitio* or *explicatio*), 16, 138, 139,
140, 142, 145, 151, 153, 154,
157, 160, 162, 163, 170,
322nn7,16; refutation (*refutation*
or *reprehension*), 138, 139, 140,
142, 145, 153
doubles (second strophe), 7, 13, 19,
140–144, 146, 148, 154–155,
159, 199, 200, 211, 256–259,
269, 278–279, 281, 284, 319n11,

338n75, 343nn28,29. *See also*
Bacilly, on *doubles* and in airs by;
La Barre, Joseph Chabanceau de,
doubles; Lambert, *doubles;* Le
Camus, Sébastien, *doubles;* Lully,
doubles; ornamentation, *doubles*
douleur. See Bacilly, sorrow, musical
representation of; Bretteville, on
sorrow; Descartes, on sorrow;
Grimarest, on sorrow; La Barre,
sorrow, musical representation
of; Lambert, sorrow, musical representation of; Le Camus, sorrow,
musical representation of; Le
Faucheur, on sorrow; passions,
sorrow
drinking songs, 5, 11, 19, 24, 30
Duncan, David, 159
Dupuis, Hilaire, 24, 264, 339n79,
340n103
Durosoir, Georgie, 4

L'École des filles, 250, 337n55; on
combat, 253; on erotic vocabulary, 250, 253, 341n111; on fire
and sexual desire, 250–251
elocution (*elocutio*), 7–8, 24, 35–40,
44–45, 158, 187; *abruptio*, 167,
322n8, 324n44; *anacephalaiosis*,
175; *anadiplosis*, 166; *anamnesis*,
145, 146, 181; *anaphora*, 166,
168; *antansgoge*, 36, 172; *antistasis*, 175; *antithesis* (or *antansgoge*), 36, 142, 146, 167, 172,
174; *antitheton*, 321n41; *antonomasis*, 181; *circulatio*, 172; doubt
(or *aporia*), 48, 171–172,
324n56; *epanorthosis* (or *correction*), 166; *epimone*, 175; *epistrophe*, 321n39; exclamation, 36,
48, 167–168, 169–171, 324n51;
figurae dictionis (word-figures),
165–166; *figurae sententiae*
(phrase-figures), 165–166; figures
(general), 7, 8, 28, 36, 37, 38, 44,
47, 48, 52, 61, 146, 154, 158,
159, 165–169, 310n52; figures

(musical), 159, 165–166, 176, 168–169, 278, 282, 324n49; *gradation* (or climax), 102, 148, 167, 182, 325n72; interrogation (or *erotesis*), 180, 324n56, 325n68; maxims (or *sententiae*), 121, 122, 177–179; metaphors, 31, 32, 36, 37, 38, 75, 159, 166, 167, 169, 182–183, 243, 250, 251, 253, 261, 279, 338n59; musical-rhetorical figures or language, 165–167, 168, 169; *onedismus*, 180, 181; paradox, 172, 174; *paronomasia*, 167, 325n64; personification, 179, 286; *polyptoton*, 104, 167, 324n43; punctuation, 44, 45, 47, 53, 64, 159, 164, 312n80; repetition, 36, 48, 104, 166, 174–175, 321n39, 324n43; *synonymia*, 104, 167, 324n43; syntax, 7, 8, 24, 35, 38, 158–159, 160–165
emblematic treatises, 245, 251; erotic images and language in, 251. *See also* Flamen; Van Veen
enticing love. *See* Bacilly, enticing love, airs about; La Barre, Joseph Chabanceau de, enticing love, airs about; Lambert, enticing love, airs about; love, enticing; song texts, enticing love
Entretiens galans, 234
erotesis. See Bretteville, on interrogation; elocution, interrogation; Grimarest, on interrogation; La Barre, Joseph Chabanceau de, interrogation in airs by; Lambert, interrogation in airs by; rhetoric, interrogation
erotic melancholia. See lovesickness
eroticism: in airs, 248–250, 255; and death, 254; in "D'un feu secret," 256–259; in novels, 3; in song texts, 2, 8, 243; vocabulary in erotic novels, 250, 251. *See also L'École des filles;* emblematic treatises, erotic images and language in; Flamen; Van Veen

false eloquence. *See* rhetoric of distraction
falsetto. *See* performance practices
Faret, Nicolas, 278
Fénelon, François, 138–139
Ferrand, Jacques, 297n5; on battling lovesickness, 255; on the classification of love, 245; on the cure for lovesickness, 255, 259, 338n69; on fantasized sex, 259; on lovesick women turning into men, 262; on lovesickness (general), 31, 245, 250, 251; on the role of the eyes in spreading lovesickness, 251; on seduction and the eyes, 264–265; on seduction and the voice, 263; sexual climax as a cure for lovesickness, 255, 259; on solitude and lovesickness, 264; on the symptoms of lovesickness, 250, 256, 306n100; *A Treatise on Lovesickness,* 31. *See also* lovesickness
figured bass. *See* basso continuo accompaniment
figures of speech. *See* elocution, figures (general); rhetoric, figures and figurative language (general); Flamen, Albert: on *amitié,* 245–246, 247; "Combat Maintains It," 253, 254, 255, 294; *Devises et emblèmes d'Amour moralisez,* 245; emblems, 245, 246, 247, 252, 253, 254; "He Cannot Safeguard Himself from All the Heat," 264, 265, 295; "Love Joins Them Together," 246, 291–292; on male arousal, 251; "More Inside Than Outside," 251, 252, 293; "They Love Without Touching Each Other," 247, 292–293
French song. *See* airs, dance; airs, serious; drinking songs
La Fronde, 244
Furetière, Antoine: on *accent,* 311n67; on Lambert, 281; on Le Camus, 281; on the passions,

297n4; *Le Roman bourgeois,*
281, 282; on song texts, 22, 281,
282, 287

galant: aesthetic, 6, 7, 8, 23, 242–
244, 260, 266, 334n9; eroticism,
244; *galant* conversations, 237–
242; love, 24, 28, 125, 303nn58,
59,62; in the *Stances* of Testu,
274–275, 298n8; style, 9, 29
gavotte. *See* airs, dance
Génetiot, Alain: classification of
song texts, 28, 303n58, 304n62;
on metaphors, 183, 326n74;
Poétique du loisir mondain, 22;
on the relationship of rhetoric
and poetry, 40; on salons,
Parisian, 333n2; on song texts,
23, 183, 304n72
Georgakaradou, Maria, 190
Gérold, Théodore, 4
Gibson, Jonathan, 165, 309n37,
310n49
gigue. *See* airs, dance
Goulet, Anne-Madeleine: on
Conversations morales, 231–232;
*Poésie, musique et sociabilité au
XVIIe siècle: Les Livres d'airs de
différent autheurs publiés chez
Ballard de 1658–1694,* 5,
332n99; on *Promenade de
Versailles,* 231; on Scudéry, 231;
on song texts, 22
Green, Eugene, 207
grief. *See* Bacilly, sorrow, musical
representation of; Bretteville, on
sorrow; Descartes, on sorrow;
Grimarest, on sorrow; La Barre,
sorrow, musical representation
of; Lambert, sorrow, musical representation of; Le Camus, sorrow,
musical representation of; Le
Faucheur, on sorrow; passions,
sorrow
Grimarest, Jean-Léonor Le Gallois
de: on anger, 120; on *antithesis*
(or *antansgoge*), 174; on boldness
(courage or *le pouvoir*), 69, 91;
on the classification of passions,
64; definitions of vocal music,
43–44; on despair, 65, 89; on
exclamations, 170; on the figures,
48; on *gradation* (climax), 182;
on happiness, 87, 95; on interrogation (*erotesis*), 180; on love,
the burning fires of (*les feux de
l'amour*), 75; on moving (persuading) the passions, 51, 52; on
the passions, 48, 61, 62, 89–95;
on recitation, 61, 64; on rhetoric
applied to music, 43–44; on rhetoric applied to texts, 2; setting
song texts to music, 313n84,
315n11; on sorrow, 78, 92, 94;
on tenderness (tender love), 84,
94; *Traité du récitatif dans la lecture, dans l'action publique, dans
la declamation, et dans le chant,*
6, 43, 61; on word-painting,
313n84
Guarini, Giovanni Battista, 23
Guinamard, Catherine, 198, 199,
329n46

Harris, Ellen, 191, 192
Harris, Joseph, 262, 263
Heinichen, David: *Der General-Bass
in der Composition,* 59; on inven-
tion, 59; passions, representation
in song texts, 59
Hermite, François Tristan L,' 24
Hotman, Nicolas, 15
Huygens, Constantine, 55

invention (*inventio*). *See* rhetoric
Italian music, 286; influence of, 9,
11; Lecerf de la Viéville on, 9,
281

Jansenism. *See* Arnauld; Lamy, and
Jansenism; Nicole
joie de vivre, 243, 266–267
joy. *See* Bacilly, happiness, musical
representation of; Bary, on
happiness; Bretteville, on happiness; Descartes, on happiness;

Grimarest, on happiness; La Barre, happiness, musical representation of; Lambert, happiness, musical representation of; Le Camus, happiness, musical representation of; passions, happiness

joyous love. *See* Bacilly, joyous love, airs about; La Barre, Joseph Chabanceau de, joyous love, airs about; love, joyous; song texts, joyous love

La Barre, Anne de, 16, 339n79

La Barre, Joseph Chabanceau de: *accent* (*aspiration* or *plainte*) in airs by, 198–199; "Ah! je sens que mon Coeur," 123–124, 125, 203, 242, 283, 290; *anacephalaiosis* in airs by, 175; anger, musical representation of, 123, 242; and Ballard collections, 19; bass line, texted, 17–18, 221, 227; basso continuo accompaniment in airs by, 221, 226; biography, 16–17; bittersweet love, airs about, 135–136; boldness (courage or *le pouvoir*), musical representation of, 69, 75, 91; conventions of expression in airs by, 57, 280; conversation in song, 235; death, musical representation of, 182; death in airs by, 182; "Depuis quinze, jusqu'à trente," 305n85; despair, musical representation of, 65, 67, 90, 107, 123; *doubles,* 19; editions of airs, 298n11; enticing love, airs about, 136–137; exclamations in airs by, 170; "Forests, solitaires et sombres," 30–31, 59, 179; general, 1, 4, 6; happiness, musical representation of, 95; influence of, 9; interrogation (*erotesis*) in airs by, 180; "J'avois juré de n'aymer plus," 67–68; joyous love, airs about, 137; languor, musical representation of, 83, 93–94, 109;

on Le Camus, 16; legacy of, 9, 280, 281, 344n45; love, the burning fires of (*le feux de l'amour*), musical representation of, 76, 92, 123, 178–179; maxims in airs by, 178; metaphors in airs by, 182; meter changes in airs by, 123, 125, 283; musical seductions in airs by, 237, 242; painful love, airs about, 124–126, 134–135; passions in airs by, 62, 64, 89–95, 97–98; performance of airs (general), 19; personification in airs by, 179; "Petit ruisseau," 182, 183; poetic voice in airs by, 260, 339n81; pronunciation in airs by, 203; publications (general), 6, 12, 13, 17, 19, 20, 298n11, 301n27; "Quand on vous dit que l'on vous ayme," 75, 178–179; "Quand une ame est bien atteinte," 178, 283, 284; range in airs by, 191; recording of airs by, 229; regret, musical representation of, 107; repeats in airs by, 218; revenge in "Ah! je sens que mon Coeur," 123; and rhetoric, 2, 7; rhetoric in airs by, 6; and salon culture, 231, 339n79; "Si c'est un bien que l'esperance," 175, 176–177, 283, 291; song texts, 28, 38; sorrow, musical representation of, 78–79, 80, 81, 93, 107, 109, 182, 283; style, poetic, 38; style of airs, 6, 11, 13, 18, 282, 283, 284, 285, 286; tempo markings in airs by, 123; tenderness (tender love), musical representation of, 84, 85, 94–95, 107, 109, 178, 179, 180, 283; transcriptions of airs by, xiii, 303n61; translation of song texts, xiii, 303n61; "Tristes enfans de mes desirs," 80, 81, 107–108, 109, 180, 191, 218, 289; "Un feu naissant," 83; "Vous demandez pour qui mon coeur soupire," 17,

218; writings about, 4. *See also*
Airs à deux parties avec les sec-
onds couplets en diminution

La Barre, Pierre de, 16

La Croix, Phérotée de: *L'Art de la*
poësie françoise, 43; *chanson* (the
definition of), 58; on discourse
(passionate), 98; figures of speech
(use of), 36; on *harmonie univer-*
selle, 43; on love, *tendre* and *gal-*
ant, 303n59; on moving the passions, 66; on *nombre,* 49, 50, 66;
rhetoric applied to music, 43,
49–52; rhetoric applied to texts,
2; on rhymes, 32, 34; on song
texts, 23–24, 25, 26; on song
texts, types of, 24, 25, 26; on
style, literary or poetic, 37; on
syllable count, 34. *See also* rhetoric, *nombre*

La Suze, Henriette de Coligny,
Comtesse de, 24, 25, 231

La Ville Lacépède, Bernard de, 6

La Voye Mignot, 45, 159, 312n80

Lalouette, Ambroise, 248

Lambert, Michel: airs (general), 13;
Airs à une, II, III, et IV parties,
13; *Airs de Monsieur Lambert*
non imprimez, 260–261; airs in
the Ballard collections, 281;
anger, musical representation of,
115, 125, 134, 181; *antistasis* in
airs by, 175; *antithesis* in airs by,
26, 36, 174; *antonomasis* in airs
by, 181; attributions to, 16; and
the Ballard publications, 19–22;
bar line, the placement of, 102,
103; bass line, texted, 17–18,
221, 227; basso continuo accompaniment in airs by, 221, 226–
227; biography, 14–15; bittersweet love, airs about, 26, 36, 65,
126, 128–129, 135–136, 187;
boldness (*le pouvoir*), musical
representation of, 69–72, 91, 98,
99, 100, 102, 104, 105, 106,
110, 112, 115, 116, 154, 155,

156, 157, 178, 284; *Brunetes ou*
petits airs tenders and airs by,
281; *cadence* (trill or *tremble-*
ment) in airs by, 195, 196, 198;
conventions of expression in airs
by, 280; conversation in song, 57,
235, 236; death, musical representation of, 98, 99, 101, 103–
104, 105, 106, 113, 114, 154,
180, 182, 227, 250, 256, 259,
284; death in airs by, 182; declaration of love, musical setting of,
98–106; "Depuis que j'ay veu vos
beaux yeux," 273–274; despair,
musical representation of, 65,
66–67, 90, 99, 103–104, 105,
106, 110, 112, 113, 115, 116,
154, 158, 180, 182, 284; disposition in airs by, 153–158; *double-*
ment du gosier in airs by, 199;
doubles, 19, 154–158, 200;
doubt (or *aporia*) in airs by, 172;
"D'un feu secret," 76, 77, 126,
174, 183, 204, 250, 256–259,
289; and Dupuis, Hilaire,
339n79, 340n103; editions of
airs by, 298n11; enticing love,
airs about, 27; eroticism in airs
by, 256–259; exclamations in airs
by, 36, 170, 171; on figured bass,
192, 301n28; Furetière on, 281;
general, 1, 4, 6; happiness, musical representation of, 87, 95; "Il
faut aimer," 178; *inegalité* in airs
by, 201; influence, 9; interrogation (or *erotesis*) in airs by, 180;
"Inutiles pensers," 65–66, 67, 79;
"J'ay juré mille fois," 201, 218,
219–220, 236–237, 261, 291;
"J'ay si bien publié vos attraits,"
232–233; "J'aymerois mieux
souffrir la mort," 26–27, 87–88,
196–197, 198, 202; "Je vous voy
tous les jours," 15; "Jugez si ma
peine est extreme," 33–34, 35,
36, 49–51, 66–67; lament, musical representation of, 100–101,

102; languor, musical representation of, 81–82, 93–94, 109, 110, 112, 113, 116, 242; on Le Camus, 17; Lecerf de la Viéville on, 15, 280, 281, 285–286; legacy of, 9, 280–281, 282; *Livres de chansons, pour danser et pour boire* and airs by, 281; love, the burning fires of (*le feux de l'amour*), musical representation of, 76, 92, 99, 102, 106, 126, 155, 157–158, 284; maxims in airs by, 178; *Mémoire de Trévoux,* and airs by, 281; *Meslanges de musique latine, françoise et italienne* and airs by, 281; metaphor in airs by, 182–183, 250, 251–252, 261; meter changes in, 102–103, 116, 125; "Mon ame faisons un effort," 14, 76, 77, 98–106, 114, 125, 153–158, 167, 175, 182, 193, 207, 218, 226–227, 228, 250, 284, 289; "Mon coeur qui se rend à vos coups," 65–66, 110–114, 116, 125, 182, 192, 195, 214–215, 218, 227, 242, 289; musical seductions in airs by, 237, 241, 242; *nombre* in airs by, 49; "Non n'aprehendez point," 69–72; "O Dieux comment se peut il faire," 84–85, 172; painful love, airs about, 98–106, 124–126, 134–135; parody of "Depuis que j'ay veu vos beaux yeux," 273–274; passions in airs by, 62, 64, 89–95, 97–98, 107, 117; performance of airs, 19; "Philis j'arreste en fin," 218; poetic voice in airs by, 260–261, 303n57, 339n81; poets of song texts, 25; *port de voix* in airs by, 193; "Pourquoy faut-il belle Inhumaine," 180, 181, 205; "Pourquoy vous offencer," 20–22, 175, 180, 181, 241; praise for, 281, 282; pronunciation in airs by, 203, 204, 205,

207; publications (general), 6, 12, 13, 17, 19, 20, 298n11, 301n27; "Puisque cette Ingrate Beauté," 199, 200; "Puisque chacun doit aymer à son tour," 27, 236–237; "Que me sert-il," 36, 39, 64, 66, 81–82, 117, 161–162, 171, 213; recitation (declamation), 102, 103, 104; *Recueils d'airs sérieux et à boire* and airs by, 281; *Recueils de chansonnettes de différents autheurs* and airs by, 281; regret, musical representation of, 110, 112, 116, 182; repeats in airs by, 218; repetition in airs by, 167; and rhetoric, 2, 7; rhetoric, the applications of, 6, 7; rhyme in airs by, 33; rondeau, 283–284; and salon culture, 24, 231; "Si l'ingrate ne m'aime pas," 205; on song texts, 28; song texts for airs by, 28, 38; sorrow, musical representation of, 50, 66, 78–80, 93, 99, 100, 102, 104, 105, 106, 113, 115, 116, 117, 153, 154, 157, 167, 179, 180, 181, 182, 242, 284; style, poetic, 38; style of airs, 6, 11, 13, 18, 282, 283, 284–285, 286, 344n57; "Superbes ennemis du repos de mon ame," 79–80, 81, 114–116, 251–252, 261, 289; syllabic quantity in airs by, 213, 214; syntax in airs by, 39, 161–162; tenderness (tender love), musical representation of, 74, 84–85, 94–95, 99, 100, 104, 105, 106, 109, 110, 111, 112, 113, 115, 116, 154, 157, 158, 181, 242, 284; throat accent in airs by, 202; transcriptions of airs, xiii, 303n61; translation of song texts, xiii, 303n61; on transposition, 191–192; vocal range in airs by, 191–192; writings about, 4, 5. *See also Airs de Monsieur Lambert* lament, 100–101, 102, 168, 178. *See also* Lambert, lament, musical representation of

Lamy, Bernard: on accessory meaning, 52–53, 55–56, 277; biography, 310n53; on *circulatio*, 172; on conclusion, 157; on confirmation, 154; Descartes, the influence of, 48, 49, 301n53; on disposition, 138, 322n7; on doubt, 172; on eloquence, 48; on exclamations, 169; on figures, 48; on introductions, 153; and Jansenism, 310n53; *L'art de parler, avec un Discours dans lequel on donne une idée de l'art de persuader,* 48; on moving the passions, 48, 52–53, 55–56, 61, 66, 98; on *nombre,* 49, 50, 66; on persuasion, 48, 52; on rhetoric, 48–53; on style, literary or poetic, 37; on syntax, 38

langueur. See Bacilly, languor, musical representation of; Descartes, languor; La Barre, Joseph Chabanceau de, languor, musical representation of; Lambert, languor, musical representation of; Le Camus, Sébastien, languor, musical representation of; passions, languor

Le Camus, Charles, 13, 300n13, 339n81

Le Camus, Sébastien: "A quoy pensier-vous Climène," 233–234, 334n21; "Ah! fuyons ce dengereux sejour," 235–236, 335n26; "Amour, cruel Amour," 171; anger, musical representation of, 120; Ballard collections, 19; Ballard publications and airs by, 281–282; bass lines in airs by, 18; basso continuo accompaniment in airs by, 226; biography of, 16–17; boldness (courage or *le pouvoir*), musical representation of, 69, 75, 91, 179; *chanson-*

nettes, 284; conventions of expression in airs by, 57, 280; conversation in song, 234, 235–236; "Delices des Estez," 31; despair, musical representation of, 65, 67, 68, 90, 178; *doubles,* 19, 284; editions of airs by, 298n11; eroticism in airs by, 259; exclamations in airs by, 170, 171; "Forests, lieux écartés," 179; "Forests solitaires et sombres," 179; Furetière on, 281; general, 1, 4, 6; happiness, musical representation of, 87, 95; "Il n'est rien dans la vie," 178; influence of, 9; "J'ay si bien publié vos attraits," 232–233; "Je fais ce que je puis," 201, 233, 334n18; "Je passais de tranquilles jours," 284; "Je veux me plaindre," 284; "Laissez durer la nuit," 235; languor, musical representation of, 80–81, 83, 93–94, 109; Lecerf de la Viéville on, 281; legacy of, 9, 280, 281, 282; love, the burning fires of (*le feux de l'amour*), 76, 92; maxims in airs by, 178; *Mémoire de Trévoux,* airs by, 281; musical figures in airs by, 282; musical seductions in airs by, 238–239; "Non, il n'est pas en mon pouvoir," 83; "On n'aime plus dans ces boccages," 178, 238–240, 284, 291; painful love, airs about, 124–126, 134–135; passions in airs by, 62, 64, 65, 89–95, 97–98, 107, 280, 284; pastoral references in airs by, 31; performance of airs, 19; personification in airs by, 179; praise for, 281, 282; pronunciation in airs by, 203; publications (general), 6, 12–13, 17, 19, 20, 301n27, 339n8; "Quand l'amour veut finir les peines d'un amant," 259; "Que les jaloux transports," 76, 77; "Que vous flattez mes resveries," 167, 168, 170, 171, 235, 335n24; repeats in airs by, 218; and rhetoric, 2, 7; rhetoric applied to airs by, 6; and salon culture, 231; song texts, 28, 38; sorrow, musical representation of, 78–79, 80, 93, 94–95, 109, 178, 241; style of airs, 6, 11, 13, 18, 284, 285, 286; style of poetry, 38; syntax in airs by, 303n61; tenderness (tender love), musical representation of, 84, 85, 94–95, 109, 178, 241; transcriptions of works, xiii, 303n61; translation of song texts, xiii, 303n61; "Vous serez les témoins," 68. *See also Airs à deux et trois parties*

Le Faucheur, Michel: on boldness (*le pouvoir*), 68, 91; classification of passions, 64; on the figures, 48; on happiness, 87, 95; on love, the burning fires of (*les feux de l'amour*), 75; on moving the passions, 52; on the passions, 48, 61, 62, 89–95; on recitation, 61, 64; on sorrow, 78, 93; on tenderness (tender love), 84, 91; *Traité de l'action de l'orateur*, 61

Lecerf de la Viéville, Jean Laurent: on Bacilly, 281; on French airs, 9; on Italian music, 9; on Lambert, 15, 280, 281, 284, 285–286; on Le Camus, 281, 284; on Lully, 343n29; on musical aesthetics, 45

Lenneberg, Hans, 165

Livres d'airs sérieux et à boire. See Ballard family

Longueville, Duchesse de, 244

Louis XIII, 14, 16, 230

Louis XIV, 14–16, 187, 230, 342n17

Loulié, Etienne, 47

love: bittersweet, 25, 26, 28, 36, 61, 65, 94, 126–129, 135–136, 169, 182, 183; definition of, 25; enticing, 25, 27, 28, 97, 129–132, 136–137, 304n62; eroticism, 2, 3, 8, 29, 243, 244, 245, 248, 250, 251, 252, 254, 255, 260, 261, 263, 266, 268, 279, 338n59; *galant*, 24, 28, 32, 97, 132–133, 137, 169, 303nn58–59, 304n62; as a game, 2, 28, 231, 241, 242, 243, 262; joyous, 25, 28, 32, 97, 132–133, 137, 169, 304n62; metaphors of, 32, 36, 182, 243, 250–251, 261, 279, 338nn59,66; obsession with, 3, 243, 245; painful, 25, 26, 28, 59, 60, 61, 65, 97–126, 134–135, 169, 182, 255, 303n58, 304n62

love, the burning fires of (*les feux de l'amour*). *See* Bacilly, love, the burning fires of, musical representation of; Bary, on love, the burning fires of; Bretteville, on love, the burning fires of; Descartes, on love, the burning fires of; Grimarest, on love, the burning fires of; La Barre, Joseph Chabanceau de, love, the burning fires of, musical representation of; Lambert, love, the burning fires of, musical representation of; Le Camus, Sébastien, love, the burning fires of; Le Faucheur, on love, the burning fires of; passions, love, the burning fires of

love songs. *See* airs, condemnation of; airs, dance; airs, serious; love; lovesickness, in airs

lovesickness: in airs, 246, 250; causes, 250; cures, 255, 259, 264, 338n69; death by, 36, 59, 182, 183, 245, 250, 253, 254, 255, 256, 259, 306n100, 326n74; descriptions of, 30–31, 245; discourse, the affect on, 256; disease (*une maladie*), 30, 31, 36, 59, 75, 91, 182–183, 295; and the eyes, 36–37, 246, 251; history of, 297n5; and intercourse, 259, 338n69; lovesick women turning into men, 262; and medical treatises, 3, 8; passions associated with, 256; sexual desire, 183,

250; and solitude, 59, 264; symptoms of, 59, 250, 306n100;
women as most susceptible to,
266. *See also* Ferrand
Lully, Jean-Baptiste: airs by, 11, 283;
Cadmus et Hermione, 5; *doubles,*
279, 281, 343n29; musical style
of, 283, 284, 285, 286; recitatives
by, 103, 285, 321n40; rondeau,
283–284; and salons, 231; *tragédie en musique,* 5, 285, 286,
299n12, 307n15, 344n68; writings about, 4, 6
lyric poetry. *See* song texts

Maintenon, Madame de, 336n29,
342n17
Malebranche, Nicolas: on the
manipulation of eloquence, 275,
277; on passions, 271, 275, 277;
on pleasure, 275, 277; on rhetoric, 42, 271, 277; on rhetoric of
distraction (false eloquence),
271, 272
Malherbe, François de, 23
Marais, Marin, 6
Massip, Catherine: on Lambert,
Michel, 5, 285; *L'art de bien
chanter: Michel Lambert (1610–
1696),* 5; on Le Camus, 284; on
Lecerf de la Viéville, 281; on
Lully, 285; "Michel Lambert and
Jean-Baptiste Lully," 285
Masson, Charles, 45; on dissonance,
53–54, 321n42; on musical composition and imitation, 57; on
musical representation of passions, 53–54, 58; on musical
style, 159; *Nouveau traité des
regles pour la composition de la
musique,* 58; rhetoric and its
applications to music, 53
Masson, Paul-Marie, 5
Mattheson, Johann, 159, 165–166,
167, 324n56, 324n56
medicine, 3, 235. *See also* Ferrand;
lovesickness
Mémoires de Trévoux, 280

memory (*memoria*). *See* rhetoric,
memory
Mercure galant, 12, 268, 280, 281,
307n19
Mersenne, Marin: on *accens,* 63, 65,
67, 98; on anger, 123; on breath
support, 188–189; on *cadences*
(trills and *tremblements*),
328n38; on *diminutions (passages),* 169, 278, 325n64; on disposition, 44, 138; on elocution,
44–45, 159; on figures, 159, 165,
169, 324n49; *Harmonie universelle,* 6, 44; on the musical competition of 1640, 54–55, 286–
287, 315n11; on musical composition, 53, 57, 96; on musical
meaning, 70, 287, 314n97; on
the musical representation of passions, 51, 53, 56, 65, 67, 315n10,
316n35, 319n77, 320n26,
321n37; *musique accentuelle,* 44,
50; on ornamentation, 45, 155,
278, 325n64; rhetoric applied to
music, 44–45, 51, 53; rhetoric
applied to song texts, 2; on setting song texts to music, 315n11;
on singing, 229; on throat articulation, 189–190; *Traité de
l'harmonie universelle,* 169; on
vibrato, 189–190
metaphors: in airs, 250–259; burning, 250; combat, 37, 251, 253,
254, 255, 261, 294, 338n66;
death, 36, 75, 166, 167, 250,
253–255, 259, 261, 182–183,
243, 326n74; empire of love, 6,
169, 183; eyes, 183, 251–252,
261; fire, 75, 250–251, 256, 261;
heat, 250; pastoral references, 37.
See also rhetoric, metaphor
meter, 135, 136, 137; Bacilly,
according to, 216; *le binaire,* 216;
changing meters, 11, 55, 72, 74,
102–103, 116, 123, 125, 135,
136, 137, 269, 282, 283,
313n84, 313n90, 320n14; cut
time, 216; *la majeur,* 216;

mesure, 217; *la mineur,* 216;
Rousseau, according to, 216; *le
trinaire,* 216; *le trinaire double,*
216; *le trinaire simple,* 216. *See
also composer entries for specific
references to meter in serious airs*
Millet, Jean, 278
minuet. *See* airs, dance
mode, 54, 55, 114, 117, 120, 123,
125, 126, 131, 132, 135, 136,
137, 242, 317nn37,39, 319n77,
320n26, 321n34, 341n112
Molière, Jean-Baptiste, 231
Monteverdi, Claudio, 168, 328n25
Montpensier, Duchesse de (la
Grande Mademoiselle), 244
Morier, Henri, 6
mouvement. See Bacilly, on *mouvement;* passions, *mouvement;* performance practices, *mouvement;*
Rousseau, on *mouvement*
the musical competition of 1640. *See*
Descartes, on the musical competition of 1640; Mersenne, on the
musical competition of 1640
musique mesurée, 41

Neoplatonic academies, 41–43,
44, 45
Nicole, Pierre: on accessory meaning, 277; on education, 273; on
the manipulation of eloquence,
275, 277; on passions, 275, 277;
on pleasure, 273, 275, 277; on
rhetoric, 42, 271; on rhetoric of
distraction, 271, 272
nombre. See La Croix, on *nombre;*
Lambert, *nombre* in airs by;
Lamy, on *nombre;* rhetoric,
nombre
Nouveau livre d'airs, 12, 16
novel: erotic, 245. *See also titles
under authors' names and titles
listed separately*
numerosa oratio. See rhetoric
Nyert, Pierre, 11, 299n3

O'Dette, Paul, 221, 222, 228
orality, 184, 186–188, 210
Orléans, Gaston d,' 14, 16
ornamentation: *accents (aspiration
or plainte),* 185, 198, 209, 211;
animer, 195, 199; arpeggiation,
222; *battement du gosier,* 195,
197; *cadence* (trills or *tremblements*), 53, 141, 185, 189, 190,
195–198, 199, 201, 202, 211,
213, 218, 328nn37,38; *chute,*
329n46; controversy surrounding, 278–279; *coulé,* 193, 222,
313n84, 329n46; *coulé de tierce,*
329n46; *coulements,* 201; *coup
de gosier,* 193, 194; *demi-port de
voix,* 193, 213, 218; *diminutions
(passages),* 19, 142, 148, 155,
159, 169, 185, 186, 199–202,
209, 211, 216, 278, 343n29; dotted notes, 201; *doublement de
gosier,* 53, 193, 199, 200, 218;
doubles, 7, 13, 19, 140–144, 146,
148, 154–155, 159, 199, 200,
211, 256–259, 269, 278–279,
281, 284, 319n11, 343nn28,29;
and expression, 217–218, 229;
inegalité, 201; *liaison,* 195, 196–
197, 198, 201, 202; and
Mersenne, 155, 278; and Millet,
278; *pincé* (mordent), 193, 199;
port de voix, 192–193, 199, 222;
port de voix glissé, 194; *port de
voix ordinaire* or *plein,* 193; *port
de voix perdu,* 194; *roulements,*
201; *tremblements étouffé,* 218.
*See also each ornament listed sep-
arately under Bacilly;* pronunciation, *gronder*
Ovid: *Metamorphosis,* 23, 306n100;
Remedies of Love, 255

pain. *See* Bacilly, sorrow, musical
representation of; Bretteville, on
sorrow; Descartes, on sorrow;
Grimarest, on sorrow; La Barre,
sorrow, musical representation

of; Lambert, sorrow, musical representation of; Le Camus, sorrow, musical representation of; Le Faucheur, on sorrow; passions, sorrow

painful love. *See* Bacilly, painful love, airs about; La Barre, painful love, airs about; Lambert, painful love, airs about; Le Camus, Sébastien, painful love, airs about; love, painful; song texts, painful love

paradox. *See* Bacilly, *antithesis* in airs by; Bretteville, on *antithesis;* elocution, *antithesis;* Grimarest, on *antithesis;* Lambert, *antithesis* in airs by; rhetoric, *antithesis*

parody, 275; of airs, 9; by Berthod, 260, 273

Parville, 16

passacaglia, 34, 283, 284, 297n1

passages. See Bacilly, on *diminutions* and in airs by; Mersenne, on *diminutions;* ornamentation, *diminutions*

passions, 297n4; accessory meaning, 52–53, 277; and accompaniment, 222, 225–226; agitated, 64–78, 96; anger, 18, 48, 54, 55, 69, 90, 98, 115, 118, 119, 120, 121, 122, 123, 125, 134, 144, 154, 155, 157, 177, 178, 180, 181, 242, 321n37; boldness (courage or *le pouvoir*), 60, 61, 68–75, 90–91, 98, 99, 100, 102, 104, 105, 106, 107, 110, 112, 115, 116, 118, 119, 120, 121, 122–123, 129–130, 134, 135, 136, 137, 142, 151, 154, 155, 156, 157, 165, 166, 177, 178, 179, 181, 182, 238, 241, 284; descriptions of, 47–48; despair (*le désespoir*), 60, 61, 64–68, 89–90, 99, 103–104, 106, 107, 110, 112, 113, 115, 116, 123, 126–128, 134, 135, 142, 144, 145, 146, 147, 154, 158, 178, 180, 181, 182, 192, 222, 241, 282, 284; expression of, 1–4, 217; happiness (*le contentement,* joy, or satisfaction), 60, 61, 87–88, 95, 96, 131, 132–133, 136, 218, 275; juxtaposition of, 99–101, 134, 136; languor (*la langueur*), 60, 61, 64, 80–83, 93–94, 96, 109, 110, 112, 113, 116, 117, 118, 120, 122, 134, 163, 177, 183, 218, 241, 242; love, the burning fires of (*les feux de l'amour*), 60, 61, 75–78, 91–92, 99, 102, 106, 107, 123, 126, 155, 157–158, 178–179, 241, 275, 284; mixture of, 99–101, 134, 136; modest, 64, 78–86, 93–95, 96; *mouvement,* 29, 47, 117, 216, 217–218, 277, 283, 312n78, 342n18; moving the, 47, 49, 51, 52–57, 58, 63, 154, 286; musical representation of (general), 53–57, 59, 60, 64; *musique accentuelle,* 44, 50; neutral, 64, 87–88, 95; and ornamentation, 217–218; primary, 7, 60, 61, 62, 64, 89, 134; psychophysiology of the passions, 61, 271–272; regret, 107, 109–110, 112, 116, 117, 121, 136, 144, 146, 147, 181, 182, 183; rhetorical function, 47–53; sorrow (*la douleur,* grief, or pain), 55, 60, 61, 64, 66, 78–80, 81, 92–93, 94–95, 96, 99, 100, 102, 104, 105, 106, 107, 109, 113, 115, 116, 117, 119, 120, 121, 134, 153, 154, 157, 163, 167, 168, 170, 172, 178, 179, 180, 181, 182, 183, 217–218, 222, 226, 241, 242, 275, 282, 283, 284; tempo, 53, 103, 123, 125, 216, 283, 315n35; tenderness (*la douceur,* tender love, or sweetness), 60, 61, 64, 67, 72, 74, 80, 84–86, 94–95, 96, 99, 100, 104, 105, 106, 107, 109, 110, 111, 112, 113, 115, 116, 117, 119,

Racine, Jean, 248, 321n40, 344n68
Rambouillet, Marquise de, 333n2
Rameau, Jean-Philippe, 286
Ranum, Patricia, 4, 6
recitative, 103, 188, 217, 221, 238, 283, 285, 320n14, 321n40
Recueil de chansons choisies, 187
Recueil[s] des plus beaux airs. See Bacilly
religion (religious leaders/theologians): condemnation of airs, 3, 267, 268, 269, 271, 272–273; divine love, 3; education, 248, 273, 279. *See also* Arnauld; Malebranche; Nicole; rhetoric, Jesuits and rhetoric; rhetoric of distraction
rhetoric: *abruptio,* 167, 322n8; *amplificatio,* 32; *anacephalaiosis,* 175; *anadiplosis,* 166; and analysis, 2, 3, 5–9; *anamnesis,* 146, 181; *anaphora,* 166; *antistasis,* 175; *antithesis* (or *antansgoge*), 36, 142, 146, 167, 172, 174; *antonomasis,* 181; *circulatio,* 172; *discours harmonieux,* 49; doubt (*aporia*), 48, 171–172, 324n56; *ellipsis,* 48; eloquence, 3, 40, 42, 47, 48, 52, 268, 277, 278; *epanorthosis* (*correction*), 166; *epimone,* 175; *epistrophe,* 321n39; exclamation, 36, 48, 65, 90, 144, 161, 167–168, 169–171, 213, 214, 324n51; false eloquence, 271–272; *figurae dictionis* (word-figures), 165–166; *figurae sententiae* (phrase-figures), 165–166; figures and figurative language (general), 3, 6–8, 36–37, 47, 48, 158, 159, 165–169, 279; in French music, 4, 287; in French songs, 6–8, 267, 286, 287; *gradation* (climax), 102, 148, 167, 182, 325n72; *hypozeuxis,* 38; interjections, 214; interrogation (*erotesis*), 170, 214; invention (*inventio*), 7, 24, 44, 58, 59; irony, 117, 119;

Jesuits and rhetoric, 271; *loci topici,* 59; maxims (*sententiae*), 121, 122, 177–179; memory (*memoria*), 47, 299n14; metaphor, 31, 32, 36, 37, 38, 75, 159, 166, 167, 169, 182–183, 243, 250, 251, 253–255, 259, 261, 279, 326n74, 338nn59,66; *nombre,* 49–52, 66; *numerosa oratio,* 49; *onedismus,* 180, 181; paradox, 172, 174; *paronomasia,* 119, 167, 325n64; *peristasis,* 144, 145; personification, 179, 286; persuasion, the art of, 43, 57, 48, 49, 51, 52; in poetry, 40, 53; *polyptoton,* 104, 167, 324n43; pronunciation, 7; repetition, 36, 48, 104, 159, 166, 167, 174–175; schemes, 36, 166; sixteenth-century, and music, 41–43, 44; *synonymia,* 104, 167. *See also* disposition; elocution; performance practices, *actio;* rhetoric of distraction
rhetoric of distraction (false eloquence), 8, 271–280; in airs, 272, 277; Arnauld on, 271; Bellocq on, 249, 271–272; Descartes on, 271; Faret on, 278; function of (psychophysiology, social dimension, expression of), 272; Malebranche on, 271, 272; Nicole on, 271, 272; parodies as remedy for, 260, 273–274; psychophysiology of the passions, 271–272. *See also* airs, devotional; airs, spiritual
Richelieu, la Duchesse de, 342n17
rondeau, 32, 175, 283, 284, 297n1
Ronsard, Pierre de, 23
Rousseau, Jean: on Le Camus, 16; on *mesure,* 217; *Methode claire, certaine et facile, pour apprendre à chanter la musique,* 216, 217; on *mouvement,* 217; on repeats, 218; on tempo, 216; *Traité de la Viole,* 221
ruelle. See salons, Parisian

sadness. *See* Bacilly, sorrow, musical representation of; Bretteville, on sorrow; Descartes, on sorrow; Grimarest, on sorrow; La Barre, sorrow, musical representation of; Lambert, sorrow, musical representation of; Le Camus, sorrow, musical representation of; Le Faucheur, on sorrow; passions, sorrow

Saint Augustine, 50, 315n14

Saint-Lambert, Michel de: *Les principes du clavecin,* 45; rhetoric and its application to musical compositions, 2, 45–46, 309n37; on style, 159

Salazar, Philippe-Joseph, 186–187

salons, Parisian: airs composed and performed in, 1, 2, 6, 8, 11, 24–25, 184, 187, 230, 234, 260, 268; *amitié* (general), 246; art of conversation, 2, 8, 25, 184, 187, 231, 232, 237, 243; conversation in song, 57, 234–235, 236; *conversations galantes,* 237–242, 246; *le culte de la voix,* 187–188; description of (general), 230, 297n2, 333nn1,2; hidden meaning in airs by, 244–245, 262; influence on literature and poetry, 230–231; *jeu littéraire, un grand* (a grand literary game), 231, 243, 262; *jeux d'esprit* (games of wit), 231, 243, 260; and orality, 184, 187–188; on proper behavior, 243; seduction of salon members, 243; singing style associated with, 188; song texts, 22, 24–25, 231–232; women singing airs in, 262–263. *See also* Ferrand; *galant,* aesthetic; Scudéry; seductions, musical

sarabande. *See* airs, dance

Sarasin, Jean François, 23, 24, 250

satisfaction. *See* Bacilly, happiness, musical representation of; Bary, on happiness; Bretteville, on happiness; Descartes, on happiness; Grimarest, on happiness; La Barre, happiness, musical representation of; Lambert, happiness, musical representation of; Le Camus, happiness, musical representation of; passions, happiness

Scarron, Paul, 23, 24

Scheibe, Adolphe, 167

Scudéry, Madeleine de: "A quoy pensiez-vous, Climène," 233–234; on *amitié,* 245; on the art of conversation, 243; *Artamène, ou, Le grand Cyrus,* 244; on battling lovesickness, 255; *Carte de Tendre,* 36, 183, 246–248, 249, 266–267; *Clélie, histoire romaine,* 36, 231, 244–245, 255, 262; conversation in prose, 232; conversation in song, 233, 234; conversation in verse, 232; hidden meaning in airs by, 244–245, 262; *Histoire de Sapho* (The Story of Sapho), 243, 245, 261; on improper love, 244–245, 246–248, 250, 260; *joie de vivre,* 243; as poet, 24, 231, 233; as salon participant, 8, 24; on Sarasin, 250; song texts in the literary works of, 231–232; on women singing airs, 261, 262–263

Second livre d'airs, 12

seductions, musical: improper advance, 238–241; *L'Esprit de cour, ou les conversations galantes divisées en cent dialogues,* 237, 238; maintaining respect, 241–242; perseverance, 241–242; as a process, 237–243; reaction to her rejection, 241–242; revenge, 242; role of the voice in, 263–264; shared love, 242; unfaithful lover, 242; women and, 262–262, 266–267; women singing as men, 260–262, 266–267

Sévigné, Madame de, 16, 342n17

song texts: *alexandrine,* 35, 38; bittersweet love, 25, 26, 28, 36, 61, 65, 94, 126–129, 135–136, 169, 172, 182, 183; caesura, 35, 49–50, 51, 214; classification of, 24, 28, 304n52; criticism of, 282, 287, 344n68; *commun,* 35; complaints of rejection, 117–119; death, 36, 75, 98, 99, 101, 103–104, 105, 106, 113, 114, 166, 167, 182–183, 243, 250, 253–255, 259, 261, 326n74; declaration of love, 98–108; description (general), 23–24, 25, 302n40, 304n64; enticing love, 129–132, 136–137; hemistich, 35, 38, 160, 207; influence on, 23, 304n72; joyous love, 132–133, 137; love as an appropriate topic in, 286; measure, 38, 160; member, 38–40, 160; on musical settings (general), 96–98; painful love, 97–126, 134–135, 136; passions in, 24, 47, 58–60; pastoral references in, 5, 11, 23, 24, 25, 27, 29–32, 37, 38, 243, 264–266, 269, 286, 298n8; periods, 38–40, 160, 164; poetic voice (gender), 260–264, 269, 303n57, 339n81; poets of, 23–25, 231; rhymes, 32–35, 329n39; strophe, 32, 38–40; structure, 32–35; style (elocution), 35–40, 47, 158–159; subject types, 25–28, 58–59, 97–98; suffering in silence, 108–116; syllable count, 34–35; syntax in, 38; threats of revenge, 120–124; on translations of, xiii, 303n61; vocabulary, 25, 279; writings on, 22–24. See also *galant;* metaphors; rhetoric, figures and figurative language; rhetoric, in poetry
songs. *See* airs, serious; love songs
Sorge, George Andreas, 84
Stark, James, 188, 192
Stubbs, Stephen, 229

supposition (substitution), 70, 79, 80
sweetness. *See* Bacilly, tenderness, musical representation of; Bretteville, on tenderness; Descartes, on tenderness; Grimarest, on tenderness; La Barre, Joseph Chabanceau de, tenderness, musical representation of; Lambert, tenderness, musical representation of; Le Camus, Sébastien, tenderness, musical representation of; Le Faucheur, on tenderness; passions, tenderness
syllabic quantity, 8, 16, 46, 103, 185, 186, 188, 190, 200, 210–216, 222, 229; and accompaniment, 222; long, 212, 213, 214, 215, 216, 218, 222, 320n17; monosyllables, long, 214–215; monosyllables, semi-long, 215; monosyllables, short, 215; semi-long, 212, 213, 214; semi-short, 212, 214; short, 212, 213, 214, 215, 216, 222; symmetry, 212–213, 214, 215, 320n18

Tallemant des Réaux, Gédéon, 15
Tasso, Torquato, 23
tender love. *See* Bacilly, tenderness, musical representation of; Bretteville, on tenderness; Descartes, on tenderness; Grimarest, on tenderness; La Barre, Joseph Chabanceau de, tenderness, musical representation of; Lambert, tenderness, musical representation of; Le Camus, Sébastien, tenderness, musical representation of; Le Faucheur, on tenderness; passions, tenderness
tendre, 28–29, 229
Testu, Jacques, 274, 279, 342n17
Theocrates, 23
theologians on divine love, 3

Tosi, Pier Francesco, 191
tragédie en musique, 5, 285, 286
tremblements. See Bacilly, *cadence* in airs by; Lambert, *cadence* in airs by; Mersenne, on *cadence;* ornamentation, *cadence*
trill. *See* Bacilly, *cadence* on airs by; Lambert, *cadence* in airs by; Mersenne, on *cadences;* ornamentation, *cadence*
Les Trois livres d'airs (Bacilly, Bénigne), 12, 17–19, 25

Urfé, Honoré de, 23, 29

Van Dyck, Stephan, 229
Van Veen, Otto: *Amorum emblemata,* 251; emblems, 251, 253; erotic images and language in emblems, 251; "The Shock Enflames," 251, 253, 293–294
vaudeville, 12
Venus, 74, 84, 318n53
Viala, Alain, 244
Virgil, 23
Voiture, Vincent, 23, 24

Williams, Peter, 227
Women singing airs, 2, 4, 8, 260–264, 268; Bellocq, Pierre, on, 249, 272–273; as cross-dressing, 260; games of love, 260, 262; poetic voice (gender) in song texts, 260–264, 269, 303n57, 339n81; seduction through singing, 262–266; singing in salons, 262
word-painting, 117, 168

CATHERINE GORDON-SEIFERT is Professor of Music and Chair of the Music Department at Providence College.

www.ingramcontent.com/pod-product-compliance
Lightning Source LLC
Chambersburg PA
CBHW060323100426
42812CB00003B/868